Date Due	ASHCROFT	
JUL - - 1985		
AUG 2 1 1985		
AUG - 7 1987		
AUG 2 8 1987		
OCT - 8 1987		
DEC 1 2 1988		
MAY 2 1 1991		
JUL 1 4 1993		

May I present . . .

Books by Dilys Winn

MURDER INK
MURDERESS INK

MURDERESS INK

THE BETTER HALF OF THE MYSTERY
PERPETRATED BY DILYS WINN

BELL PUBLISHING COMPANY
NEW YORK

This edition is published by Bell Publishing Company,
distributed by Crown Publishers, Inc.,
by arrangement with Workman Publishing Company, Inc.
h g f e d c b a
1981 EDITION

Manufactured in the United States of America

Library of Congress Cataloging in Publication Data

Winn, Dilys.
   Murderess ink.

   Reprint. Originally published: New York:
Workman Pub., c1979.
   Includes index.
   1. Detective and mystery stories, English—
History and criticism—Addresses, essays,
lectures.   2. Detective and mystery stories,
American—History and criticism—Addresses,
essays, lectures.   3. Women in literature—
Addresses, essays, lectures.   I. Title.
PR830.D4W5 1981   823'.0872'09   81-12264
ISBN 0-517-36057-8   AACR2

Cover photograph: Jerry Darvin
Designer: Paul Hanson
Hair and make-up: Steve Lowe
Stylist: David James

Super Sleuth

Out in California, there's a willowy redhead who enters a crime scene every day. She drives up to it in a long, sleek, black van (license plate: ARSENIC), steals in the back way, switches on a hotline (dial: 981-CLUE), then riffles pages with long, blood-red fingernails.

Her name is Ruth Windfeldt and she has been behaving this mysteriously since October, 1975, when she opened Scene of the Crime, a bookshop with a resident bat (embedded in crystal), a tea table, a trick fireplace and a stock of reading matter to set a mystery heart palpitating.

From the Scene of the Crime, Ruth plans forays to foreign and domestic crime capitals, reviews the literature and handles murderous requests, provided they're legal.

I'm delighted I don't live in a ruthless world, and it is with great pleasure I dedicate *Murderess Ink* to her at the Scene of the Crime.

Secret Service

Murderess Ink would like to thank the little English lady in bifocals (Robin Leeds), the blackmailer (Carol Brener), the bureau snoop (Sarah Newell), the other woman (Ann-Victoria Phillips), the concocter of vial schemes (Jennifer Rogers), the grieving widow (Arleen Keifetz), the Burberry stalker (Caroline Rowntree), the fleeing damsel (Carole Gilmore), the dowager and her daughter (Rachel O. Smiley and Rachel Matteson), the man with the pitchfork (Christopher Day), the rotten kid (Connie Brooks), the clue-dropper (Lynda Serrecchio), the mysterious footnote (Carolyn Fiske), the ghost (Ben Matteson) and the stateliest hotel in the East (Mohonk Mountain House, New Paltz, New York), for letting their mug shots be snapped.

Murderess Ink would also like to thank the following bodies in the following libraries: Howard Gotlieb, Twentieth Century Archives, Boston University; Mike Sutherland, Special Collections, Occidental College; Brooke Whiting, Department of Special Collections, Research Library, University of California, Los Angeles.

And, the wily detectives who researched every crime in this book: Robert Aucott, Carol Brener, Donna Dennis (photography), Peg Dickerman, Ben Kane, Betsy Lang, Marjorie Mortensen, Mike Nevins, Jim Olander, Tina Serlin, Charles Shibuk and Carol Wallace.

Most especially, *Murderess Ink* would like to thank Lynn Strong for her fine penmanship and Sally Kovalchick for her master mind.

CONTENTS

The eavesdropper

MARTY NORMAN

Dame Agatha

Sally the sleuth

4. SIDEKICKS

Wives

Stalking the Private Eyes

Interrogating the Cops

Mysterious footnote

5.
SKULLDUGGERY

This May Strike You as Crazy But . . .

Last Seen Wearing

Advice from the Experts

Nanny

EDWARD GOREY

Proven Effective

6. SUSPECTS

Book'Em

7. STAKEOUT

Crime Wave

MARTY NORMAN

8. THE SYSTEM

Signed Confession

I confess.

This is my second crime of passion. And I may commit another someday.

It all began innocently enough: a murder a day, savored in the privacy of my reading chair. Then I became insatiable. I craved jewel thefts, bank heists, political intrigues, clever little traps for the police.

After years of plotting, I hand-picked my accomplices; each had quite a reputation as a criminal mastermind. Together, we pulled off the biggest caper of the year. You may remember it; it made all the papers. Murder Ink.

Now I sense it's time to strike again.

Same M.O., different partners in crime. We call ourselves Murderess Ink, and plead guilty to proving the female of the species is not only deadlier than the male, but wackier.

Over fifty of us settle the questions that have been haunting the crime field: What was the plot to immortalize Christie? Who was the hard-boiled dame that landed Marlowe? How do you knit a noose, clothe a corpse, dress to kill? Are there 10 fun things to do with arsenic, 13 ways to trick up a bed-sitter, 20 reasons not to trust an Englishwoman? Is the nanny shadier than the dowager?

Murderess Ink nabs Hitchcock's heroines, the Belles of St. Trinian's, Lady Macbeth and the damsel-in-distress who spent a weekend with a rotter. It tracks the woman of mystery from the attic to the tea lounge to the family plot. It shadows her husband, her boyfriend, her murderer, her victim. It builds a case against the Brothers Grimm, reveals the secrets of the privet hedge, takes the time to chat up the neighbors.

I confess.

I did it and I'm proud of it.

Won't you join me in my second crime of passion?

Chapter 1
SURVEILLANCE

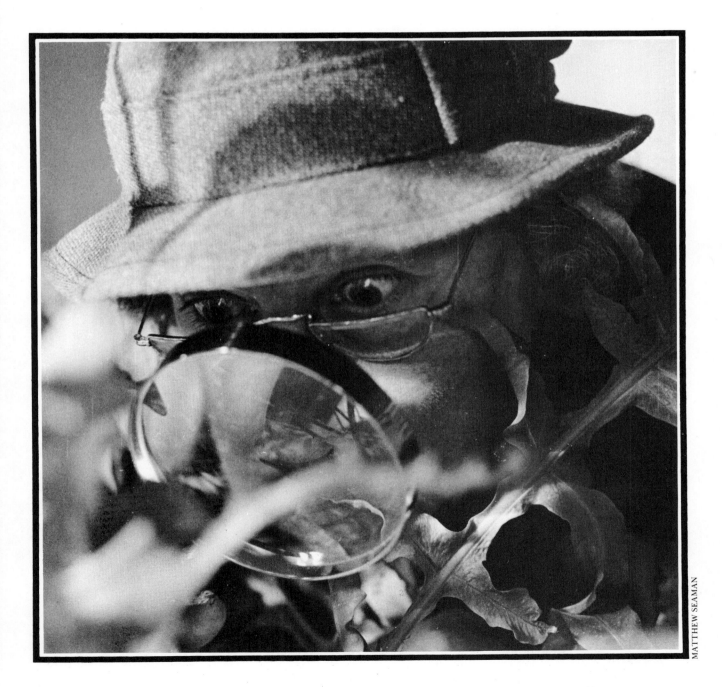

A WOMAN OF MYSTERY
Dilys Winn

I used to be a thief. At age eight, I wanted a lipstick so badly I cased the five-and-ten-cent store for an hour, and when no one was looking, lunged across the counter for a tube of Purple Passion, grabbed it and ran like hell. I got away with it, too, until my brother caught me admiring myself in my swag and blurted out to Mother that her daughter was throwing stolen kisses at the bathroom mirror. My bottom still throbs when I think about my punishment.

Years after this episode, a crook with a hankering for a hi-fi dropped by my apartment and fire-escaped away with his heart's desire, which finally balanced out my crime career. I have now been both perpetrator and victim, and that's probably as good a definition of this "woman of mystery" as you're likely to get.

Still, something nags at me: my experiences seem curiously flat when I compare them with those of fictional mystery women. Do I have to wait until I'm as old as Miss Marple for the really exciting things to happen? Or, being well past Nancy Drew's age, have I already blown it?

I must know because I ache to play detective, to scramble into a taxi and gasp, "Follow that car." My not-so-secret fantasy is to usher all the suspects into the library and dazzle them with my conclusions. Before I call this life quits, I want to solve just one baffler.

But nobody ever asks me to.

Where did I go wrong?

I thought I'd mastered all the moves. I can knock back a double martini as readily as Nora Charles, wise-crack my way through a tense situation, too. I knit. I own a trench coat and keep my plimsolls in good repair. I have, on permanent loan from my uncle, high-powered binoculars, and I've even named my dog Watson.

A quiet place to read.

FPG

Surely that speaks well of my qualifications.

Granted, my Latin is a little rusty, but then I'm not really counting on a proposal from Lord Peter, and though my steno is feeble, Perry Mason is way out there in California and I'm angling for an East Coast job.

But where is it? My case eludes me.

I'm dying to go for a walk and bump into a distraught woman in white. I have an extra nightie in my drawer for her. After I prove who she is and secure her homestead, I plan on borrowing her laudanum eyedrops. Maybe then I, too, will see ghosts and be able to find my way to the crypt at the bottom of the rose garden.

I've been boning up on these inheritance cases, and I think I've got them licked. The first thing I have to do is establish a curfew: no one will be allowed out after sunset. Next, if I can't convince my client to move to the city, I'll insist on her property being leveled. That will eliminate the snagging-twig, villain-behind-every-tree problem. Finally, I'll hunt for the long-lost relative. I haven't quite figured out a polite way to ask people to strip and show me their birthmark (or lack of same), but I'm working on it.

I ask you: Could Miss Cayley do any better? Could Clarice Dyke? Could Dorcas Dene?

But where is my case?

Why can't I have a husband unjustly imprisoned so I can devote my life to procuring his release? Frankly, I think it would take me only half the time it took Lady Molly.

I wouldn't even mind if I were incarcerated. I'd have all that time to review the customs of Gypsies. Who knows — with a little luck, I might deduce a real murderer. There is a precedent: Helen Mathers' *As He Comes up the Stairs*.

I'm jealous of those detectives who were invited to a stately home, who had the thrill of interrogating a Lord, a Lady, a Dame. Really, it's a pity nobody throws house parties anymore. I'd be willing to walk Lady Alleyn's Alsatian. And if I were given a few days' notice, I'd arrive with enough knowledge of Egyptian canopic jars to join in the small talk. I shall always consider it one of God's little cruelties that I wasn't born in time to protect the 1930's gentry. My small comfort is knowing that I don't have to diet to fit some secret panel.

Actually, I'm not sure I would have been given my own case back then. I haven't cracked the Why weren't there any women detectives in the twenties and thirties question yet. But I'm mulling it over.

I would gladly interrupt my mulling, however, if a little sister knocked on my door. Boy, would I lace into her. Split personality or no, she wears too much make-up.

I'd be tough with her; but maybe not quite as harsh as Ms. Beale would be. At least not till my brown belt changes to black. I can see myself now: ramrod fingers jabbing at midriffs.

But where is my case?

I'm tired of sitting through matinées uninterrupted by the sandbagged indisposition of the heroine.

I'm bored with faculty meetings run by scholars who refuse to plagiarize.

I demand to know: Where is my case? I'm frustrated by the wholesome monotony of my existence.

How many times must I plead with Sue Carstairs to take me for a joy ride in her prowl car? When will Solange Fontaine introduce me to her père at the Sûreté? I've worn myself out waiting for Hilda Wade to intuit I want to be her co-consultant.

I'm getting desperate.

Why is it everybody gets a case but me? Could it be I keep my nose in a book and they keep theirs in the air, sniffing for clues?

THE TEN MOST WANTED LIST

Case Pending
(Dell Shannon)

The Daughter of Time
(Josephine Tey)

Gaudy Night
(Dorothy L. Sayers)

Green for Danger
(Christianna Brand)

The James Joyce Murders
(Amanda Cross)

Murder Against the Grain
(Emma Lathen)

The Pale Horse
(Agatha Christie)

The Talented Mr. Ripley
(Patricia Highsmith)

Tiger in the Smoke
(Margery Allingham)

Unsuitable Job for a Woman
(P. D. James)

MEN WHO KNOW HOW TO HANDLE WOMEN

Some of the best women characters to appear in mysteries were put there by men.

In *11 Harrowhouse,* Gerald A. Browne created an extremely wry lady who was in on a diamond heist.

In *The Lively Dead,* Peter Dickinson depicted a sensible, solid, sound-thinking landlady.

In *Stealing Lillian,* Tony Kendrick featured a street-wise kid who was so tough she practically smoked cigars.

In *The Secret Lovers,* Charles McCarry presented an elegant double agent who protected her husband like a mother hen.

In *Tomorrow's Ghost,* Anthony Price offered a fantasy-riddled woman who could no longer distinguish between life and make-believe.

Most women writers have not done as well. And anyone who wants to learn a little more about feminine psychology (are you listening, Freud?) would do well to pay attention to Messrs. Browne, Dickinson, Kendrick, McCarry and Price.

Mrs. Kipling ogles her husband Rudyard, though he swore the female was deadlier than the male. Obviously, she forgives him for the slur.

MURDERESS INK OPINION POLL

In order of popularity, the readers listed their favorite authors as Dorothy L. Sayers, Ruth Rendell, Emma Lathen, P. D. James, Josephine Tey and Ngaio Marsh (whose name they consistently misspelled).

Mystery writers, on the other hand, ranked Christie first, had Sayers and Lathen neck-and-neck in second place, then filled out their top ten with Charlotte Armstrong, Christianna Brand, Margery Allingham, Jacqueline Wilson, P. D. James, Tey and Marsh.

Both readers and writers concurred on the best mystery writing couples: Richard and Frances Lockridge, and Maj Sjöwall and Per Wahlöö.

Everybody also agreed that the best mystery characters were the old standbys: Miss Marple, Nancy Drew, Nora Charles, Lady Macbeth.

Given the opportunity to entertain five authors at dinner, the readers issued the most invitations to Margaret Millar, Muriel Spark, Ruth Rendell and Emma Lathen (for whom savvy readers saved two places). The writers tended to expect the dead to arise for the occasion, particularly Edgar Allan Poe and Wilkie Collins.

Regarding the contents of Miss Marple's larder, the groups deduced that it contained: her knitting, a plate of little grey cells, an antidote cruet, some elderberry wine donated by two sisters, a dismembered joint.

It was suggested that Troy Alleyn painted in the style of (a) Constable, (b) Turner, (c) Bonnard, (d) Motherwell. Only a handful remembered that she was a portrait painter.

Without exception, they concluded that Irene Adler was having an affair with the Hound of the Baskervilles.

The groups decided that Mme. Maigret should clean Jules' raincoat with a mixture of Dijon mustard, Perrier water, Calvados and carbolic acid.

They were unsure what Harriet Vane wore to her wedding, but many excused their ignorance on the grounds that they hadn't been invited.

They imagined the typical Gothic house to have: stairs that creak, a century's worth of cobwebs, a dense ghost population, no electricity, a sliding panel behind the bookcase.

They swore women made rotten spies because they simply cannot keep a secret.

They feared that the highest-ranking woman at Scotland Yard was a char and were firmly convinced that the role a woman most often plays in a mystery is that of corpse (before dying, she was most likely to have been a governess, a disgarded mistress, a kidnapee).

According to the poll, all private eyes' secretaries are blond, stacked, smart, in love with the boss, and use a cologne that smells a lot like bourbon.

When a woman turned out to be the murderer, her method usually was: not messy, with kindness, vicarious, a variety of poisons (ranging from whatever was handy in the cabinet under the sink to whatever was plentiful in the garden to whatever the chemist would sell her — arsenic, more than likely).

The most common adjective mystery readers used to describe crime fiction was "escapist."

The most common adjective mystery writers used to describe their work was "underrated."

ORIGIN OF THE DETECTIVE BUSINESS

Newton Newkirk

Adam was the first detective who ever happened. One day he woke up with a pain in his side.

"Gee-whizz," he exclaimed, "somebody has swiped one of my ribs." (*the first theft*)

"Here it is," said a sweet voice behind him. (*the first clue*)

Adam turned swiftly and beheld a beautiful woman. (*the first woman in the case*)

"Yuh-yuh-yes," gasped Adam, "there it is, but whatizzit?" (*the first mystery*)

"Why, I am your missing rib," replied the woman. (*the first confession*)

"Absurd," retorted Adam. "What is your name?" (*the first instance of cross-examination*)

"I am Eve," said the woman.

"Huh," snorted Adam, "you look more like 'September Morn.' " (*the first case of mistaken identity*)

Thereupon Eve blushed and excused herself. A few minutes later she returned wearing a modern fig-leaf costume — the waist had a plunging neckline and the skirt was slashed. (*the first disguise*)

Later Eve handed Adam what she called an apple. (*the first trap*)

After Adam bit into it he found it to be a *LEMON*. (*the first doublecross*)

Right there is where the Serpent concealed in the tree overhead broke forth in a suppressed chuckle of mirth. (*the first detectaphone*)

One evening Adam came home from his daily toil, hungry and tired. He had been plowing on a steep hillside all day behind a refractory dinosaur and was hungrier than a couple of goats.

"I have a surprise for you, Adam," gushed Eve, as she kissed him on the front piazza. "Guess what?"

"Corned megatherium beef and cabbage," exclaimed Adam. (*the first theory*)

"Oh, pshaw, Adam, it isn't anything to eat — it is something the stork left on the front doorstep."

"Ah-ha," hissed Adam. "A girl?"

"No, not a girl," Eve replied; "guess again."

"Aw, shucks," sighed Adam; "I never was any good at guessing."

"Adam, you are the most stupid man I ever saw. Now, think hard — if it isn't a girl, what *must* it be?"

Adam pondered deeply a moment and then in a flash of almost human intelligence he exclaimed, "Ah, I know now — a BOY!" (*the first deduction by elimination*)

After supper Adam loaded his old shotgun and took his place on the doorstep. (*the first gunman*)

"What are you waiting for?" asked Eve.

"I'm waiting for that stork to come back," snapped Adam. (*the first threat*)

And so it was in the beginning . . .

Newton Newkirk has disappeared without a trace. Reprinted by permission of Ellery Queen's Mystery Magazine.

IN PURSUIT OF AN ENDING

Gregory Mcdonald

"**I** don't like the word *murderess*," she said. "It bothers me."

"It bothers many," I said. "Especially those confronted by a murderess. Most of all, I expect, does it agitate those confronted by someone they suspect is about to become a murderess."

"I don't think you should do something for *Murderess Ink*," she said.

"Why is that?" I asked.

We were having drinks in the Palm Court, which struck me as a distinctly proper place to talk about women who commit murder, although I hadn't known that was what we were going to do. We were surrounded by widows trading secrets over expensive cucumber sandwiches.

Over the years, my friend had helped me become more sensitive to all matters concerning women. Her point always was that I was much too casual regarding the small matters, the details, the semantics of women in their struggle for equality.

Equality? Empirically, I knew there were differences between men and women. Growing up, I discovered women had greater physical stamina than I, over duration, wrote neater papers, got more attention from teachers, had electrical skin and a remarkable propensity to say no to me before I'd asked them anything.

My friend had taught me there was always a touch of the charlatan in anyone who argued empirically.

She tested her vodka gimlet. "You remember that series of columns you did for the newspapers answering that age-old question as to why, historically, such a very small percentage of artists — composers, writers, painters, etcetera — are women?"

"Of course."

"Certain pips had squeaked that these figures prove women, generally, categorically, have much less creative ability than men. Some had even drawn graphs and things to show creativity was an adjunct solely to male sexuality."

"Yes, yes." Why had I thought we were going to talk about where we were having dinner? I like looking forward to dinner, but not forever.

"And then you came along and did these columns, back straight on your white horse, lance out, all your armor clanking."

"Haven't I thanked you for helping me with all that? That was a million years ago."

"You wrote that historically there were fewer women artists because historically so very few women had been educated, exposed to the world, given the opportunities to be artists. And that the world had suffered, badly, as a result. Your statement was that all human experience had been looked at through only one eye. Devastating."

I said, "Ah, shucks."

"The columns caused a sensation, for those early days, and, for a moment there, I really think you were feeling good about yourself."

"I had struck a blow."

"And then there was that dinner party I took you to."

"Oh, yes."

"You didn't enjoy that dinner party."

IN CONCLUSION

Charles Scribner, Jr.

One of the most frightening publishing mistakes that I can remember happened about thirty-five years ago. By some concatenation of errors, the final chapter of Margerie Bonner's *The Last Twist of the Knife* was left off. It was later found in the bottom drawer of the editor's desk. We tried to make amends by printing the chapter in a special pamphlet and offering it at no cost to every reader who felt the denouement of the book was unsatisfactory. In point of fact, I don't believe we got any requests for it, which raises all kinds of speculation as to how carefully one reads a detective story.

Charles Scribner, Jr., is chairman of Charles Scribner's Sons.

"Boiled fish," I said. "Anyone who serves boiled fish and tomato . . ."

"All the women there complained because in your columns, consistently, relentlessly, you had referred to people as actresses, sculptresses and authoresses."

"I remember the room grew warm. I thought it was the steam from the boiled fish."

"A sculptor," my friend said, "is a sculptor is a sculptor."

"That has a nice ring to it. Pity the topic of the moment isn't horticulture."

"And your argument was . . .?"

"Entirely correct. I do believe: that a sculptor is a sculptor — which is a high estate; that a sculptress is a woman who has had to overcome far greater obstacles than a man in attaining education, experience, opportunities, to become a sculptress — which is a higher estate."

"Is art created by women greater than art created by men?"

"No. But it is a greater attainment."

"You referred to George Sand as an authoress."

"Yes." I remembered my argument hadn't done me much good at that dinner. I had had to backstroke to the kitchen wall.

"So the word *murderess*," my friend said. "What does it mean?"

"A woman who has committed murder," I said. "Possibly a woman who commits murder. You know, as a regular thing. Tuesdays and Fridays. Or, possibly, just a woman who slays the soul of her dinner companion."

"Is a *murderess* more or less than a *murderer*?"

"People end up just as dead," I observed.

"According to your theories, is murder a greater attainment for a woman than it is for a man?"

Thinking of the most typical female murder — that of a woman who does in a brutalizing male, seldom soon enough — I said, "Yes, I think so."

"Is murder a greater crime for a woman, or less?"

"Ah — "

"Should a woman receive greater punishment for the act of murder, or less?"

"Traditionally, the courts have been more tolerant, more understanding toward those who needn't shave."

"A murderer," said my friend, "is a murderer is a murderer."

"Equality in all things," I agreed.

"It's these attitudes we must do in," said my friend. "I don't think you should contribute to a volume called *Murderess Ink*."

"All right," I said. "I won't."

"Now," she said with finality, having disposed of the volume and an idea I'd had for it with her vodka gimlet. "What are we thinking about dinner?"

"I thought we might really treat ourselves."

"Oh?"

"Yes," I said. "To a lobstress."

Gregory Mcdonald is a regional vice president (for New England) of the Mystery Writers of America. He has received two Edgar awards: one for Fletch, *the other for* Confess, Fletch.

The Cucumber Six: (Clockwise) H. R. F. Keating, Avon Curry, Dilys Winn, Peter Dickinson, Julian Symons, Celia Fremlin.

VIGIL IN MAYFAIR

A Tale Unfolds over Cucumber Sandwiches

SCENE I

RENDEZVOUS AT CLARIDGE'S

(Partially concealed by a potted palm, a suspicious character waits. A second conspirator enters the lobby, glances furtively round; crosses to palm.)

"Is that . . . ?"

"No. Not yet."

"We were told three o'clock. When . . . ?"

"Have patience. Admire the fronds."

(Botanical interlude terminates with agitated stage whisper.)

"They've come."

"Good."

"Not good. You chose unwisely."

"We thought it secure."

"Bah. Follow me."

"But what of Julian?"

"Shh. No names."

"Never mind. He's here."

(Exeunt.)

SCENE II

TEA LOUNGE OF THE EUROPA

"China or India?"

"India."

"India."

"India."

"India."

SCENE III

CHIEF'S OFFICE

"Well, Winn?"

"Suspects positively identified, sir. Tape running at Europa. Claridge's aborted."

"Commendable, Winn. Proceed."

"Worse than we thought, sir. Incorrigibles. All of them."

(Pulls out notebook, rifles pages; retrieves palm frond from floor.)

"Symons, Julian. Committed *Bloody Murder* in '72. Carries dagger: honorary award, he claims. Hangs out with Eric the Skull. Prizes small statue: Edgar somebody, probably famous criminal mastermind. Left country for a year, consorted with well-known American trouble-makers.

"Fremlin, Celia. Specialty: *The Hours Before Dawn.* Ships records of her crimes to Boston gent: for posterity, she says. Scares folks half to death. Considered extremely dangerous. Owns statue matching Symons': private club?

"Keating, H. R. F. Also carries dagger, gold-plated. Explanation: token of esteem from cohorts — a likely story. Known associate: an Indian named Ghote. Last seen on BBC pro-gramme, explaining his M.O.

"Dickinson, Peter. Carries *two* daggers. Al-ibi: they were giving them away! Rarely seen with evil-minded element; possibly first offence.

"Curry, Avon. Pseudonym; uses several. Period commencing spring '75, ending spring '76, known as 'Madame Chairman': reference to heading up nasty band of Britons."

(Snaps notebook shut; smirks.)

"Awaiting new developments, sir."

SCENE IV

CUCUMBER SANDWICH TO RIGHT OF ECLAIR

FREMLIN: Women make very good victims.

SYMONS: I should agree with you if you said murderers, not victims.

FREMLIN: Nonsense. Someone once asked me how I'd like to die and I said I'd like to be murdered. It would be sudden; it would have some point to it, the man would be gaining from my death; it would be exciting; it would get me into the news. A woman should definitely be the murderee.

CURRY: I notice you're absolutely certain a *man* will murder you.

DICKINSON: And a dying message perhaps?

FREMLIN: Yes, I should like to say a thing or two before I died. The method should be such that I have thirty seconds or so before I collapse to the floor. It ought to be painless, though. Perhaps a tea-soluble poison . . .

KEATING: However, Celia, traditionally in a mystery, when you're given those thirty seconds you manage to wriggle out of it. This is the mistake made by every murderer in every book. He answers all your questions, then the Inspector walks in, arrests him and rushes you to hospital.

SYMONS: I still maintain it's more interesting to have a woman be the murderer. It's so nicely unexpected of her, since she's commonly thought of as the tenderer sex.

DICKINSON: I believe that is contrary to fact, your woman murderer. In life, six times as many men do murder.

CURRY: Indeed. Indeed.

SYMONS: True, if you're talking about serious crime — although in Britain the statistics are so low, one hates to draw conclusions. But one can spot the murderer in three out of every four Christie books because in three out of four the murderer is a woman. Look for someone rather attractive. If, in addition, she's been very much persecuted in the story — several narrow escapes from death and so forth — one can be absolutely sure she's the murderer.

KEATING: I have a fat male villain in every book. Someone once pointed it out to me, and I was furious until I looked and he was right. In my early books, I had difficulty getting *any* woman into them. I used to stop and say there's no reason why he can't be a woman, and go back and change it. I don't think anyone noticed but me. I've since improved.

SYMONS: I've never actually attempted to write about a woman from the inside — by which I mean her thoughts and views of the world. My women are peripheral in the sense that I dare not do more with them. I know too little.

DICKINSON: I used a woman character once. Lydia Timm. And I'm delighted to say, after reading it a reviewer announced that Peter Dickinson must be a pseudonym for a woman.

CURRY: They used to take it for granted that I was a man, and I liked that very much.

DICKINSON: Lydia was a competent woman who thought she could cope with more than she could. There's a point toward the end, a fight in the kitchen, when she picks up a knife and finds she can't use it. That struck me as right.

FREMLIN: I switched to a male character once. It was an extremely liberating experience, a tremendous feeling of adventure, of exploring new continents. For the first time, I realized how much a writer makes a character herself. I've always felt that men were terribly boring about their cars, but in this new role I became obsessed with one — possessed by it, really. It's something I've never felt about cars before or since. You might find, Julian, that you understand far more than you think you do.

SYMONS: At my age, you know your limitations.

CURRY: I remember reading a novel by a woman writer that was shown through a man's eyes. She'd gone through several days with him and he'd never shaved once. Finally, he went home, showered, changed his clothes and complained about his feet — that's a particularly woman's thing to do, anyway — and I thought, his *feet*! What about his *chin*! As crime writers, we must notice not only that men are bigger, and heavier when they walk, but that their daily regime is different.

SYMONS: The best novelists are bisexual in the sense that their make-up contains, if they're male, female components. They are then able to create male and female characters.

KEATING: Peter has a good deal of the feminine in him.

CURRY: Yes, he's fortunate.

SYMONS: There are stories written by women that are nonspecifically from a woman's point of view. Elizabeth Ferrars, for example. One wouldn't know whether her books had been written by a woman. In Celia's case, and in Daphne du Maurier's, the opposite is true. One has no doubt by page ten that the book was written by a woman.

KEATING: Yet men like to read Celia's stories. It's the Damsels-in-Distress that irritate me. They seem to emphasize what people have to eat and what clothes they have on. The surface of life. I may use food to make a scene more vivid, but I don't dwell on it.

CURRY: Regardless of what people say, there is such a thing as femininity in writing, and there is a charm in writing from it.

FREMLIN: It may turn out that men and women are not the same after all.

KEATING: If there is something to this liberation business, then surely by now women ought to be able to create a character who did the same aggressive things as a private eye.

FREMLIN: If men were truly liberated, as is supposed, they would write of domestic problems and teen-age life and children. And I cannot think of a good book by a man on those subjects.

SYMONS: So far as I know, there are no women spy writers. MacInnes is not really a thriller writer; she's more romantic suspense.

KEATING: Yet Francis Clifford is very capable of doing women. On the other hand, Le Carré is not very good with them.

CURRY: Spying is foreign to women. They would have to do a lot of research about the intelligence service. The technology of spies is beyond women these days. It's all about in-tercontinental ballistic missiles. So tedious. If one could deal in human terms with the pain of being a spy . . .

FREMLIN: Yes, I do think women tend to read books with more of a feeling of identifying with someone in them. A woman's book is one with a lot of interpersonal relationships in it, and a setting a woman is familiar with.

KEATING: I was affronted when Freeling killed Van der Valk. One must not betray the reader halfway.

DICKINSON: Don't you think the reader, in a way he can't quite put his finger on, is upset with a book that badly disrupts the form? I think detective-novel readers are very ordinary people, conservative in their outlook.

SYMONS: Yes, but the mystery boundaries have enlarged. When I think of a Golden Age crime story, it's about a very nasty man who gave a house party and gathered round all the people who detested him: his discarded mistress, the man he recently cheated in business, and so on. One used to be able to say there must be a detective. That's no longer true. Or there has to be a crime and a happy ending, but Celia disproves those.

FREMLIN: In one of my books, everyone thought there was a crime but there wasn't. And I once made one of my nicest characters die on the next-to-last page. It was just logical for her to do so.

SYMONS: I think there's a sort of amorphous center now that four out of five writers cling to. Emma Lathen carries on the traditional detective story in a superb way.

KEATING: And P. D. James took the classical form and made it come alive as a contemporary novel. I like her Cordelia Gray.

DICKINSON: I thought rather well of Pamela Branch.

CURRY: How about that old battleaxe who runs the typing service for Lord Peter? A great girl. And Polly Burton was endearing. And that Charlotte Armstrong Texan who yelled at everyone to stop shooting at her because she was one of the good guys. I liked her enormously.

FREMLIN: I think one is inspired to write a book.

ALL: You have thirty seconds in which to do it, Celia.

GOTHIC, HAD-I-BUT-KNOWN, DAMSEL-IN-DISTRESS

Stalking the Elusive Distinction

Ann B. Tracy

MATTHEW SEAMAN

My friends keep asking me embarrassing questions, right out loud, in public — thinking I can answer them because I teach English 321: Gothic Lit.

"What's the difference between Gothic and detective fiction?"

"But didn't the Gothic novel really stop after Ann Radcliffe?"

"Don't heroines ever wear anything but nightgowns?"

Alas, even in the eighteenth century, when "Gothic" was first applied to "novel," the word didn't mean anything very useful. Clara Reeve, for instance, explained that she called *The Old English Baron* (1777) a Gothic story because it was "a picture of Gothic times and manners," by which explanation she presumably meant to counteract the alternative definitions of "uncouth" and "in bad taste." Now, two hundred years later, descendants of the first Gothic novels are legion, if mostly collateral, which makes "Gothic" as a critical term spectacularly unmanageable. A number of obviously dissimilar novels have elements in common — beleaguered heroines, murders, mysteries, secret passages, and so on. And yet Victoria Holt is not quite Ann Radcliffe (though she sometimes very nearly is), and neither one is Mary Roberts Rinehart.

The original Gothic heroines were never dowdy governesses, nor (a fact now too little known) were they accustomed to be seen abroad in their nightgowns; they were aristocratic knockouts, orphans or semi-orphans, brought into hostile environments by kidnapping or flight, typically, rather than by employment or marriage. Their nocturnal adventures usually found them fully clothed, they having earlier dropped upon their moldy beds from shock and exhaustion. The environment, however, not the heroine, distinguishes Classic Gothic; as well as the traditional clutter of castles, bones, monks, owls and tapestries, the novels conjure up a psychic environment that stresses delusion, mistaken identity, lunacy, unexpected cataclysm, pursuit, suspense, pitfalls and the brevity of human happiness.

The Gothic world in the novels of Ann Radcliffe and others (e.g., T. J. Horsley Curties, Eliza Parsons, Eleanor Sleath, Mary Julia Young) is depraved and unstable, a place theologians would identify as fallen, where heroines are ill-advised to trust their own perceptions or even the evidence of their senses, let alone any human relationship or institution. Physical circumstances contribute to a feeling of moral decay: ruined castles, grass growing in broken crenelations, tapestries hanging in tatters; gardens instead of forests, darkness instead of daylight. Ancestral sins are visited upon the innocent. Heroines are without the support of their families: generally, mothers are dead; frequently fathers are, too. Uncles are notoriously unreliable, often villainous, intent upon rape or murder but deterred in the nick of time by recognition of their nieces. Lovers, if any, are otherwise occupied in armies or dungeons. As for Mother Church, girls who flee to her bosom are likely to find themselves in the hands of corrupt and bad-tempered abbesses or pursued by lecherous monks. Further, they are subject to futile prophetic dreams in which trusted faces unmask to reveal malevolent grins or sometimes shred away in a phenomenon best described as the instant molder. Eaton Stannard Barrett, in his witty burlesque of the Gothic (*The Heroine*, 1813), has his kidnapped heroine, Cherubina Wilkinson, cry out in upper case: "O DIRE EXTREMITY! O STATE OF LIVING DEATH!

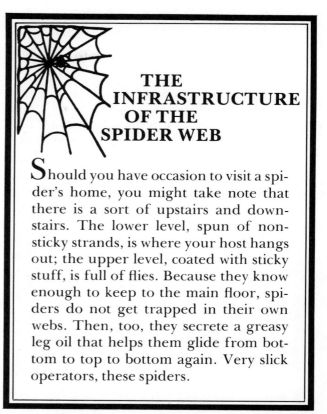

THE INFRASTRUCTURE OF THE SPIDER WEB

Should you have occasion to visit a spider's home, you might take note that there is a sort of upstairs and downstairs. The lower level, spun of non-sticky strands, is where your host hangs out; the upper level, coated with sticky stuff, is full of flies. Because they know enough to keep to the main floor, spiders do not get trapped in their own webs. Then, too, they secrete a greasy leg oil that helps them glide from bottom to top to bottom again. Very slick operators, these spiders.

IS THIS A VISION? ARE THESE THINGS REAL? ALAS, I AM BEWILDERED." Cherubina is a fool, but she knows what Gothic is all about.

The closest modern descendant of Classic Gothic, the Damsel-in-Distress romance, whether it be fancy-dress or a struggle to get a modern heroine into some reasonable facsimile of a castle, is noticeably less concerned with philosophy. That is its most important difference from Classic Gothic, but there are some interesting changes in the heroine as well. The modern damsel is not always conspicuously attractive. She may consider herself plain and shy, or be plain and slightly crippled, or suffer from some peculiarity of upbringing. For such heroines, *Jane Eyre* (1847) is almost certainly the germinal work. (These are girls of whom people sometimes kindly say, "She only wants bringing out." When the hero releases her from her shell, is he performing a modern analogue to freeing the earlier Gothic heroine from a dungeon?) The new heroines are as isolated as the old — caught up in new jobs, perhaps, or hasty marriages — but they are rather less helpless. They

MY WEEKEND WITH A ROTTER
Anne Maybury

"Oh, it was ghastly.

"One May, many years ago, I went down to Bournemouth for a little holiday. I stayed at this charming hotel, right on the cliffs, in a beautiful top-floor suite with French windows and a lovely balcony that extended across the adjoining suite. A friend had the room connecting with mine, and a couple we knew were in the suite just past ours, with the common balcony.

"Well, we had hideous weather, constant rain, and since most of the people at the hotel were rather stuffy, a group of us — oh, say, six or eight — stayed together the whole time. We'd commandeer one of the lounges and dance all night, and at twelve the porter would bring round sandwiches and coffee. It was lovely.

"Into this crowd came a young man, an officer in the Royal Air Force. He was brought in because he knew a wing commander who was part of our group.

"One morning, I left them all to have drinks with friends who were staying at another hotel, and when I returned I found everyone, including the newcomer, having a drink before lunch in the lounge. They were all quite tiddly, and when I sat down someone leaned over and said, 'Anne, can you tell fortunes by reading palms?' and since I'd had a few drinks myself I said, 'Yes, certainly,' and reached for the nearest hand and made something up. Then this Neville, the new pilot, thrust his hand at me and said, 'Tell me what you see.' So I looked at it and jokingly said, 'Neville, I can't tell you, it's too awful — no, no, I'll say no more,' and dropped his hand very quickly. At this point, we all got up to enter the dining room and he drew me aside and said, 'Anne, what did you see?' Still kidding, I told him, 'I don't want anything to do with you. I can't say more, never ask me again.' And, of course, I thought no more about it.

"The couple in the adjoining suite checked out the next day, and Neville went straight to the front desk and demanded their room. The clerk was very polite but told him no, the room was reserved. Well, Neville got very upset and insisted he must have it, he must, and then he tried a bribe. It didn't work, and he didn't get the room.

"The next morning, as I was leaving, I saw him in the foyer and he grabbed my hand and said, 'Anne, we'll get together in London, won't we? I'll see you there?' And I said, 'Yes, yes, goodbye,' and that was that.

"About a week later, the friend who'd shared the suite with me rang up and said, 'Have the police been round to see you?' and I said, 'No, whatever for?'

" 'Well,' she said, 'you know who Neville was, don't you? *Heath the murderer!*'

"After I'd left the hotel, he'd met a young woman, taken her out to dinner and, on the way home, killed her. And it turned out he'd killed two women before her!

"Apparently, he was panic-stricken when he thought I knew about him because of my crazy palm-reading. And he'd wanted that adjoining suite so badly because he'd planned on using that connecting balcony to come to my room, enter the French windows, and. . .

"I would never use this experience in a book. It makes me shudder."

Anne Maybury has written numerous romantic suspense novels, the latest of which is Radiance.

do not, on the whole, suffer from the overwilling suspension of disbelief that characterized their eighteenth-century counterparts. When the heroine of Victoria Holt's *Kirkland Revels* (1962) sees a spectral monk at the foot of her bed, she assumes that someone is trying to frighten her into miscarrying; the heroine of Daoma Winston's *Sinister Stone* (1966) sees a light on the rock where her predecessor died and goes out to investigate. Further, the happy-ending rewards of modern heroines seem rather more substantial than those of their great-great literary grandmothers. Abby Adams Westlake calls this kind of novel "Girl Gets House," an unromantic but not unjustified view of the business. If these novels are less chilling than the earlier ones, there is a compensating pleasure in our confidence that we may sit back and watch how, not whether, things turn out happily.

Neither the Classic Gothic heroine nor the modern damsel should be confused with the sometime victim, sometime investigator of the Had I But Known's (HIBK's, Ogden Nash called them) by Mary Roberts Rinehart, Leslie Ford et al., whose lineal ancestor is probably Wilkie Collins' Marian Halcombe (*The Woman in White*, 1860). HIBK's are a peculiar business, for while the heroine/narrators are explaining what happened, they are no longer distressed by anything except remorse that they did not know earlier what they knew later. The reader presumably is not in much suspense about the survival of the heroines, who are obviously alive to tell the story. The narrators' ability to present an ironic overview of prior events gives the novels a cerebral tone not available to Classic Gothic or Damsel-in-Distress stories. HIBK's do not philosophize, however. Although the heroines wonder at their own blindness in not having said or done such-and-such, which in the light of later knowledge would have been useful, they do not reflect upon the inadequacy of human knowledge in general.

Philosophical considerations aside, there is a last-ditch test for genre: ask yourself what the heroine will find behind the black curtain (in the secret passage/in the trunk/in the attic). A waxwork body in a state of waxwork putrefaction, with waxwork worms? This is a Gothic find,

QUICK, PASS THE SMELLING SALTS

Gothic ladies keel over at the slightest provocation, such as being left out of the will. What's fascinating is that they never swoon in private; they seem to do it only in front of an audience.

To revive them, give them a stiff whiff of sal volatile (spirits of ammonia). If you've none at hand, don't fret — just loosen their bodices, and wait. They'll come to when they hit the floor. In other words, a prone position will cure them.

Usually, a faint is preceded by pallor, cold sweat and nausea. Then the pulse slows. Next, *whoosh* — out like a light. This is the vasco-vagal syncope (the common faint), in which the blood pressure falls (hypotension) and the heart rate slows (bradycardia) precipitously. In rare instances, atropine is needed to bring the subjects round.

While they're lying there, you might consider the possibility of concussion. Particularly if the floor is bare. Or you might muse upon why they were left out of the will in the first place.

manufactured in days of yore as a reminder of human mortality and doing its job once again. A costume worn earlier by a pseudo-phantom? The damsel has confirmed her own sensible conclusions and can move three squares nearer the happy ending. A yellowing snapshot of the villain as butler? O God, Had She But Known!

Ann B. Tracy, an associate professor of English at State University of New York, Plattsburgh, consistently avoids attics, cellars and secret passages.

THE HOBGOBLIN PRINCIPLE
A Batty Look at the Supernatural

Do you believe in ghosts? Rap once for yes, twice for no.

The reason I ask is, I think something's trying to materialize over there in the corner, but my candle's gone out and I can't be sure.

Does it seem a little chilly to you all of a sudden?

If those wisps of ectoplasm unfurl into Harold, I'm leaving. My conscience is clear, of course. I had no idea I'd the strength to dislodge the boulder, but you know Harold — always had to pin the blame on somebody.

They tell me ghosts come from nerves. Like hives. When you're fidgety, your system manufactures them; when you're calm, it makes them go away.

HAROLD, IF YOU CAN HEAR ME, I'M CALM. I'M REMARRIED AND I'M CALM.

What was that? Sounded like someone was banging the shutters.

You wouldn't happen to have a clove of garlic on you, would you? A rabbit's foot might do. I get so confused with these things: the horsehoe protects your house and the crucifix

> *"Do I believe in ghosts?"* I have seen too many to believe in them.
>
> SAMUEL TAYLOR COLERIDGE

guards your soul and if your nose itches you're going to kiss a fool, is that right?

Forget about the garlic. I just remembered that's for those things who drink blood. Harold liked milk.

Do you smell something burning?

Just yesterday, I told Francis — you've met my Franny, haven't you? Harold's business partner? We eloped the morning after the inquest. I told Franny we'd have to do something about the fireplace. It hasn't worked right since the accident. No, not that one. The other time, when the poker fell from the mantel and concussed poor Harold. I think he must have jarred the flue when he crashed. Have you ever seen such a dent? He practically demolished the fender.

I'm sure I smell something burning. What could burn in all this mist? Funny how the weather turned. One minute balmy, the next howling like a banshee.

Not that I believe in them.

Agnes? Is that you at the piano? She'll drive me mad with that tune — hasn't stopped playing it since she heard about her son. Won't admit she's doing it, either. You should have seen her at the cemetery. I thought she'd hop right in the coffin with him. And when the will was read out, she went dead white. Well, naturally, Harold was going to leave Cambric Hall to me, why was it such a surprise? Lord knows, she heard us arguing about it often enough.

The table just moved. There it goes again. Probably the floor settling. These old homes do moan and groan. This morning, there was a

THE MIDNIGHT FLIER

Bats — *Chiroptera,* to the Greeks — evolved from a primitive branch of placental animals called *Insectivora.* The only mammals that can fly, they have brown eyes and fur to match, though some of them look like they've been at the henna bottle.

The largest bat weighs 900 grams (2 lbs.), hardly enough to collapse the attic floor. His wing span is 1.5 meters (5 ft.).

The smallest bat is almost invisible; if he were a clue, you'd overlook him. He weighs 1.5 grams.

The most common North American bat, *Myotis lucifugus,* is a little brown furry thing that will gladly stay out of your hair, if you'll stay out of his. He tips the scales, just barely, at 5 grams. His biggest Western Hemisphere brother, *Vampyrum spectrum,* hails from the semitropical regions of Latin America, and is a chubby 190 grams.

Both sometimes feed on insects, small rodents, fish, fruit or flower nectar. Then, of course, sometimes, some of them slurp blood.

Vampire bats, known to scientists as *Desmodontidae,* neatly slit the skin with their sharp-chiseled incisors, then curl their tongues to form an open-topped tube, which they contract with a peristalsis-like motion.

They walk stealthily, propelling themselves along with their forearms as well as their feet. When they've picked out a victim, they vigorously lick her skin before biting into her. This serves two purposes: to see how deeply asleep she is and to spread an anticoagulant enzyme (from their saliva) on her epidermal surface. This ensures that dinner will not dry up before they're finished with it. Vampires can usually be found hanging around herds of domestic animals. They might want a snack.

Vampires weigh 30 grams, have rich auburn fur, and a fondness for warm climates; they favor the tropical zones. Europe has never had a vampire bat population.

Vampires almost never attack humans. Unless they're taunted with the cruel appellation "Dracula."

BOO

The Great Houdini swore he was coming back, but thus far no one's seen him.

And Arthur Conan Doyle regularly attended séances in hopes of catching a glimpse of his departed son.

Ghosts have been sighted, however, in R. C. Ashby's *He Arrived at Dusk* and *Out Went the Taper,* in John Dickson Carr's *Scandal at High Chimneys,* in Shirley Jackson's "The Haunting of Hill House," in Henry James' "The Turn of the Screw," in Dorothy Macardle's *The Uninvited,* in Hake Talbot's *Rim of the Pit.*

God-awful thump coming from the stairs, as if someone were climbing up and down them. Scared me half to death. Harold used to walk like that — b-o-o-m, b-o-o-m, b-o-o-m. His Big Ben feet, I used to say.

I wonder where the twins are. They're moving, you know. Franny and I had a long talk with them and explained that after all, we were honeymooners and we needed our privacy. I suppose we could have asked them to stay, but those long faces depressed us. We *all* felt simply terrible about Harold, but they seemed — bitter, somehow. Besides, it's not that we owed them anything. Harold's sister's children could hardly be called our responsibility.

True, Carla did nurse her uncle through that dreadful period when everything he ate upset his stomach and Carl did discover that someone was diddling with the company checkbook, but Franny and I feel we have a new life ahead of us and needn't be confronted daily with these trying reminders of our past.

That man is such a consolation to me.

He should have phoned by now, but I suspect the lines are haywire again. We've been having problems with the exchange lately. Last Wednesday, I answered seven calls and no one was there. When I said hullo, all I heard was silence. Quite peculiar. Perhaps a child was playing tricks. Harold used to do that as a boy.

Phew. Do you smell that? Absolutely rank, like the algae on the underside of Harold's boulder. It seems to be coming from that corner, from that pulsating green mass.

I'll have to ask Druthers to see this room is thoroughly gone over. But he's been so difficult recently. I know Harold had promised him a small increment, but I just don't see how he can expect one with all the expenses I've had to bear: first, the hospital charges and Dr. Wycherley's bill (that one was truly unreasonable; Harold slipped away before he even had time to connect the oxygen), then the resodding of the plot, not to mention Hiram's fee for validating the will I found in the night table that superseded the one sequestered in the vault.

Ah, the lights have come on.

No. False alarm. It's that corner of the room. Glowing. It seems to be spreading. My God, it's coming toward me.

HAROLD, GO 'WAY. GO 'WAY.

My hair's turned white, and my skin, what's happening to my skin? It's covered with mold.

HAROLD, DON'T DO THIS TO ME. WHAT IS IT, HAROLD. PLEASE, please, please, no . . .

Harold rapped on the table once.

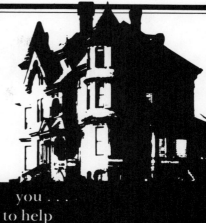

FPG

you . . . .
to help
no one
there was
remembered
you suddenly
to scream
and you wanted
your soul
ooze into
you felt dampness
the latch and
and bolted
yanked you inside
and a sinewy arm
to the ancestral home
Welcome my dear
thundering voice say
and heard a
you stumbled
you became and when
the more apprehensive
and the closer you got
alone
a night there
you had to spend
of the will
but to qualify for your share
haunted and wouldn't go near it
The villagers swore the place was

CLIFF HANGER

GOLDEN AGE LEGACY: THE HOUSE PARTY

Between 1918 and 1935, English authors considered it impolite to murder anyone below the rank of Earl. And even he had to be handled with white kid gloves — the butler's. First, the gentleman had to be entertained. Since he was not the sort of bloke who worked for a living, inviting him to an office bash was out. Instead, he was packed off to a weekend house party, where he found a decent game of whist, an amiable hock, warmed bed linens, and a shoot arranged in his honor.

There are worse ways to die.

Today, it's chic (and sometimes profitable) to spoof these Between-Wars mysteries. Think of the films *Murder by Death* and *Death on the Nile*. Pick up a copy of James Anderson's *The Affair of the Blood-Stained Egg Cosy*. Their perpetrators tweaked the prose of the Twenties. Unfortunately, what got lost in the process was the era's very real upper-class elegance.

Raymond Chandler once railed that nobody *he* knew could relate to books with titles such as *The Corpse with the Freckled Teeth* and with plots that involved a matriarch, a Lord, an Aubusson and an exceedingly rare poison, holed up in a Georgian inkwell. Partisans of the genre flared back that nobody *they* knew could find much kinship with back-alley bodies run through with a meat cleaver. Neither was being particularly fair to the other, but currently the author charged with elitism is in more disfavor than the one labeled hard-boiled.

True, Sayers and Christie and Allingham and Marsh (still) have a definite Upstairs-Downstairs mentality. And certainly their characters are fashioned out of the most snobbish cardboard. But their books can also boast a real gentility, and why shouldn't we enjoy that, at least for a reading span of two hours or so?

Who wouldn't appreciate a weekend in a venerable old home, described in terms that would make the National Trust covet it, where mornings were spent polishing silver for guests to use that night? How could we be so churlish as to refuse just one cup of literary tea or a walk through a mystery garden at dusk? In fact, if we could afford a private library with 10,000 volumes bound in Moroccan calf and embossed in gold, identical to the house party host's, wouldn't we, too, rush to set it up, then invite friends over to sit there by the fire grate, sherry in hand, to read?

Listen, don't knock a dream.

Besides, some of our mothers never taught us manners, and we're relying on these stylish authors and their modern-day descendants — Marilyn Erskine, Elizabeth Lemarchand, Catherine Aird, maybe even Christianna Brand — to teach us a lesson.

The first thing we have to get straight is that every mystery house party occurs in a house with a name rather than a street address. Over the rim of his bourbon glass, Chandler would probably call one "The Cutes." Christie preferred End House, Styles, Littlegreen House and Gorston Hall. Marsh developed Nunspardon Manor, Frantock, Danes Lodge and Quintern Place. And Sayers sent Peter and Harriet to honeymoon at Talboys.

If the house appellation ends in "ing" (e.g., Beckoning), the "g" is dropped when the word is verbalized. This is fondly referred to as the Wimsey pronunciation, after the aristocratic sleuth who popularized it.

Next, we must understand that a weekend at Merroway Court (Christie) or Riddlesdale Lodge (Sayers) demands more in the way of wardrobe than jeans and clogs. Ladies are re-

Lord and Lady Guest exchange confidences at the porte cochère.

ROYAL PROTOCOL

The house party is shaping up nicely. Lady Sarah has accepted with pleasure, Lady Richard has accepted with pleasure, Lady Littleworth has accepted with pleasure, Her Grace, the Duchess of Bedlam, has accepted with pleasure, and Mary, Duchess of Bedlam, has accepted with pleasure.

This means the full house will include the daughter of a peer (Sarah), the wife of the younger son of a peer (Richard), the wife of a peer or a peeress in her own right (Littleworth), the wife of the highest-ranking peer (Her Grace), and the mother of the highest-ranking peer (Mary).

Now, if you only knew what a peer was, you'd know who'd been invited.

After the King, the Queen, and all the Princes and Princesses, the next royal rung belongs to the Duke. He is married to the Duchess. She is addressed as "my lady" or "Your Grace" but is referred to as "Her Grace" or "the Duchess of Bedlam." Since the Duke wed, his mum is called "Mary, Duchess of Bedlam" or "the Dowager Duchess." When he dies, his eldest son will become the new Duke and inherit all his titles (a Duke can also be, in order of importance, a Marquess, an Earl, a Viscount, or all of them, or some of them, depending on how generous the King and Queen have been to him). Until that day, sonny will adopt pater's highest-ranking subsidiary title and become either "the Marquess of Chaos" or "the Earl of Ruin" or "the Viscount of Wimbledon." Second sons are known forevermore as Lord Terence Twaddle (the family last name); similarly, third and fourth sons, and on down the line. Daughters will be known as "Lady Jane Twaddle," "Lady Violet Twaddle," and

so on, even if they marry someone beneath their station, in which case they will be known as Mr. Ian & Lady Alexandria Smythe. Lady Alexandria always retains her title, which finds its roots in the Anglo-Saxon *hlafdige,* meaning "loaf-kneader," which does not conjure up a particularly royal image.

When the Marquess marries, his wife becomes the Marchioness of Chaos. Collectively, they are referred to as Lord & Lady Chaos. Their first son will become the Earl of Ruin (highest-ranking subsidiary title of the Marquess), and should he marry, his wife will be the Countess of Ruin. Their other children will have to make do with a simple Lord Alan So-and-So and Lady Prudence So-and-So.

Upon marriage to the younger son of a Duke or a Marquess, a woman will assume her husband's first name. Ergo, Lady Richard.

The Earl and Countess's first son will take the highest-ranking title available to him, e.g., Viscount of Wimbledon. Their second son will be the Honourable Clarence Mandrake and his sister will be Lady Claire Mandrake.

When Lord and Lady Inclement (anyone other than a first son and his bride) have children, they become the Honourable Rupert Dimple and the Honourable Elspeth Dimple.

There are two hereditary titles belonging to non-peers: Baronet (Sir Adam Epping, Bart. & Lady Epping) and Knight (Sir Matthew Shallow, KCB & Lady Shallow). In addition, there are eleven orders of knighthood that are bestowed, not inherited. The initials following the name indicate the nature and rank of the title.

quested to bring hats for the garden party and several long dresses for dinner, which on Friday is followed with port in the billiards room for the men, gossip in the drawing room for the women, and on Saturday with a violin quartet in the conservatory attended by all. The fine points of the house party wardrobe have recently been articulated by Douglas Sutherland in two wry volumes, *The English Gentleman/Lady.* Of particular interest to the lazy: a guest does not do her own unpacking; that is the responsibility of the maid. Of note to the finicky: the breakfast tray arrives with the *Times* neatly folded on it, and boots left outside the bedroom will be smartly polished by morning.

The house party should include no more than ten, no less than six. At least three of the participants should be related, though one may be disinherited during the weekend. A hostess will not inflict people "in trade" on her guests, even though their shops bear the seal By Appointment to His Majesty the King. Nor will she invite a graduate of one of the "red-brick" universities to drop by; it's the Eton-Harrow/Cambridge-Oxford school tie or nothing. A retired colonel is welcome, as is a newly-returned-from-the-heathens missionary, a dowager keen on birds and aspidistras, and a charming ward — provided she has a small talent for watercolor scenes and a new fiancé, who will be meeting all but two of the other guests for the first time.

Appropriate conversation for a house party guest consists of inquiring after the Duke's toe (the man suffers gout), admiring the host's setter ("Fine dog, that Brandy. Good blood line."), commenting on the weather ("A bit damp, wot?"), verifying the train schedule to town (only if the guest is an amateur detective).

Since house party activities can be quite exhausting, people may be excused from the hunt to take a little nap. Before retiring, however, they must compose a small note, which they then tuck under the finger bowl or door of the highest title present.

The house party is not deemed a success unless several rounds of croquet are played, strawberries and fresh meringues are served on the lawn, a discussion of Etruscan burial rites is held and the Reynolds portrait of the original builder of the house is identified as a fake.

A house party is considered at an end when the murderer is brought to justice. Confrontation scenes may be held in the library, now that someone has figured out how to unlock it from the outside.

Some of us will be reluctant to leave.

But not Chandler. He'd say good riddance.

EXECUTING A CURTSEY

There are three basic styles of mystery curtseying: the Servant Girl, the Social Climber, the Grand Dame.

The Servant Girl begins with a blush and a furious bobbing of the head. A dozen bobs are sufficient. Then the apron hem is lifted slightly and kneaded into a pleat with both hands. When the pleat is damp from excitement, the knees are (a) knocked twice and (b) flexed just deep enough to bring the eyes level with the honoree's belt. This position is maintained until one has memorized the coat of arms on the buckle. While rising, one repleats and rebobs to the accompaniment of a titter.

The Social Climber starts with a snub (nose in the air), quickly followed by a double take (neck in a swivel). Then a false smile is affixed to the lips, the right knee is lowered to the ground and the arms are extended with pinkies raised. When one is positive the pinkies have been noticed by the honoree, drop forehead to left knee and hold it there until the Queen's birthday list is announced. If not mentioned, slink out of the room in shame; if cited, immediately assume the Grande Dame.

The Grande Dame commences with a slight pursing of the lips and tilting of the head so the jaw seems more prominent. Then one blinks — the signal for Jennings to step forward and do your curtseying for you.

TRANSATLANTIC DOUBLE TALK

Sarah Newell

Are you thrown into a frenzy of confusion when tarts order marrows, when pandas prowl lay-bys, when toffs mount their penny-farthings?

If so, you have doubtless been the victim of The Great British Mystery, which poses a linguistic obstacle course for Americans.

Herewith, the mystery reader's glossary, for a more complete understanding of foul deeds in fair Albion.

British	American
The charred corpse wrapped in a *petrol*-soaked tarpaulin in the *boot* of the Daimler was difficult to identify as the vicar's wife.	*gasoline* *trunk*
Constable Postlethwaite discovered several strands of blonde hair stuck to the *mud-guard* of the suspect *estate car*.	*fender* *station wagon*
With a cry of exasperation, Amanda spun the stolen Bentley into the *lay-by* and flung up the steaming *bonnet*.	*highway rest area* *hood*
The blowzy *tart* complained that no *toffs* ventured forth in a *pea-souper*.	*hooker* *gentlemen* *fog*
They found the Duchess strung up by her own *suspenders*, with her hose full of *ladders* bunched round her ample calves.	*garter belt* *runs*
Her usually well-coiffed hair was a sight: the force of the axe had crushed the *slide* against her temple, and her *fringe* was matted with blood.	*barrette* *bangs*
The plucky spinster donned an old pair of *wellies* and an outsize *mac*, and took up position with the only weapon at hand — a furled *brolly*.	*rubber boots* *raincoat* *umbrella*
The *char* never lived to regret pilfering the arsenic-laden *sweet* from the silver dish on the sideboard; by nightfall, she had *dropped off the perch*.	*cleaning lady* *candy* "*kicked the bucket*"
Little did Nanny know, as she pushed Algernon's *pram* around the Serpentine, that the microfilm was taped to the inside of his *nappy*.	*baby carriage* *diaper*

British	American
The crooked *turf accountant* spent his ill-gotten gains on *bangers and mash* for himself and *toad-in-the-hole* for the pert young filly he met at the *pub*.	*bookie* *sausage & potatoes* *sausage in batter* *bar*
She acquired the fatal dose from a disreputable *chemist* in a seedy *bed-sitter* above an *ironmongery* on the Edgware Road.	*druggist* *studio apartment* *hardware store*
Reconnoitring the *greengrocer's*, Bertha eyed two *marrows* that would fit very nicely under her *jumper*.	*vegetable stand* *squash* *sweater*
While the *panda* gave chase round Piccadilly *Circus*, she leapt from the *lorry* and ran toward the *tube*.	*squad car* *traffic circle* *truck* *subway*
Felicity never got to use her *return* to Harrogate; instead, she spent a *fortnight* in the *nick* for wandering through the V & A in nothing more than her red lace *smalls*.	*round-trip ticket* *two weeks* *jail* *undies*
When the *peeler* wasn't looking, naughty Alicia let the air out of his *pennyfarthing's* tyres and fled across the *herbaceous border* into the *coppice*.	*cop* *high-wheeler bicycle* *flower bed* *thicket*
As the decoy approached the *off-licence*, the *spiv* loitering by the *pillar box* with a *fag* in his mouth sidled over, intent on doing her bodily harm.	*liquor store; crook* *mailbox; cigarette*
Eliza did not rise for refreshment during the *interval;* she'd been neatly skewered to the back of her three-*quid* seat.	*intermission* *$2*

Sarah Newell is a fugitive hackette from the British Isles, masquerading as a writer in New York City.

THE KITCHEN SINK SCHOOL OF WRITING

Someone's in the kitchen with Dinah and he doesn't look like the repairman from Sears no matter what his uniform says, because with it he's wearing a ski mask, surgical gloves and a very dapper silk scarf. Now he's taken off the scarf and is playfully wrapping it round Dinah's neck. Oh, stop it, you two. At this rate, the breakfast dishes will never get done.

In kitchen encounters logged by authors, Dinahs rarely voice the usual homemaker's complaint: "I'm stuck in the house alone all day." Their time is killed with postmen, plumbers, roofers, claim adjusters, power-line checkers, gas-meter readers, trash collectors, telephone representatives, delivery boys, moving men and ticket sellers to the policemen's ball — none of whom actually works for the organization mentioned on his I.D. card.

Still, Dinahs dutifully invite them in. Quite candidly, somewhere between their second cup of coffee and their morning soap opera, Dinahs seem to have mislaid the thing that gets most of us through life: an instinct for self-preservation.

The early sixties were especially trying for them. During those years, insurance statistics listed their primary cause of death as "House-

A woman will always sacrifice herself if you give her the opportunity. It is her favourite form of self-indulgence.

The Circle
W. SOMERSET MAUGHAM

hold Accident," but fictionally that second noun is worth a quibble. In the Sink School of Writing, when a woman exits (permanently) the kitchen, it's anything but unintentional; the procedure has been as rigidly organized as the Stillman Diet:

7:15	Wake Nathan
7:30	Wake kids
7:50	Feed everybody
8:05	Kiss Nathan off
8:07	Chase after Nathan with briefcase
8:10	Forget to bolt back door
8:20	Wave Jenny & Chris bye-bye
8:27	Change Courtnay
9:16	Call pediatrician about C's rash
9:19	Soothe C's tears
9:20	Forget to replace receiver
9:45	Second cup of coffee
9:51	Answer doorbell
9:52	Repairman (or whatever) enters
10:00	Struggle with repairman
10:18	Lose struggle
10:20	Repairman leaves by back door (alternate route: kitchen window)

Though the outcome is always the same — death to Dinah — there is some variation allowed in method. One homemaker attracted a rubbish burner who was so enthralled by her staring at him from inside the Thermopane, he stopped what he was doing (incinerating Edith), walked over and stuck his rake through the glass to make contact.

Once, a Dinah got lucky. The coffeepot was handy. If she hadn't scalded her visitor, who knows to what excesses his ardor might have driven him? He did return another day, with a change of costume (mechanic's overalls replaced diaper-service jumpsuit). This time, Dinah had had it.

Most Sinks like Dinahs to be mothers in their twenties, with husbands who travel a lot. The phone, then, becomes an important Sink prop. The assailant must discontinue service well before the regular call-in from the traveling man. Ergo, the routine Sink kits out its intruder with wire cutters in his back pocket. If he daren't use them before he enters (Mama is watching the kids in the sandbox from the kitchen window and would see), he must remember to inactivate the machine once he's inside. Crafty authors (see timetable) make their Dinahs his accomplice in this.

For the utmost in slyness, some Sink writers appropriate a leaf from the psychological terrorist's book: they have their bounder phone ahead and whisper dirty words at the housewife, who becomes so distraught (and possibly frustrated; her husband's been gone a long time) that she herself lifts the receiver off the hook.

Dinah's authors don't give her much to fight back with. There's the ubiquitous diaper pin, of course, but Dinah usually forgets it's right there on her blouse. And anyway, lately manufacturers have made the catch impossible to open ("Don't pinch the baby bottom, that's our slogan"); even if she did remember, she'd undoubtedly be dead by the time she unfastened it. True, the kitchen has numerous artifacts that could be considered dangerous, but in Sink novels they tend to backfire on Dinah. Her iron, for example. When she heaves it, the appliance lands on her toe.

Moreover, current Dinahs don't even have a sugar bowl to reach for. Being weight-conscious, they've switched to saccharin packets. In the fifties, they would have tossed the crockery at the attacker, missed him by a mile, but when he came after them, he would have tripped on the crystals scattered on the floor. How can you make someone skid under a one-inch envelope?

The bread-knife-wielding Dinah is apt, in a Sink, to grab the blade wrong side first. That smarts.

As with any good mystery, the Kitchen Sinker emphasizes motive. Turns out, Dinah's kitchen faces three sticky areas: her neighbor's garage, her other neighbor's garden and (just barely) the letter box on the corner. Dinah's murderer knows she's witnessed his (a) torrid liaison with the Avon lady on the kitchen table, (b) burial rites for his business partner or (c) the posting of the blackmail note. He might forgive her for this if she had a job that left her no time for putting two and two together, but since she doesn't, she's on his hit list.

Surprisingly, these little tales of domestic malice are seldom read by men — not even confirmed misogynists, who ought to have an affinity for their philosophy. For men, the Sink's fatal flaw is its insistence on presenting matters from the housewife's point of view. The authors demand an empathy for the victim, not a licking of the chops for the handiwork of the villain.

But clearly there's a message here for all of us: Never linger over a second cup of coffee. Never allow anyone to track across the kitchen floor. Never be tied to an apron string.

That Sinking feeling: aprons are no protection.

THE CARVERY: THE HOUSEWIFE FIGHTS BACK

In de-boning William, is it more efficient to use the 9″ bread knife or the 8″ all-purpose knife?

As any morgue attendant will tell you, women no longer reach for a vial of poison when they've had just about enough of that so-and-so's behavior. They pluck a knife from the drawer and go straight for the heart. More often than not, they detour through the kidneys and liver, but in the heat of anger who could expect them to remember anatomical geography?

Why have housewives adopted the slice-and-chop system? For one thing, it's easy. For another, it's handy. They don't have to run to the store to pick up a weapon — it's sitting right there in their kitchens, waiting for them.

At present, women do more damage with knives than anything else. Mysteries, however, have not caught up with this real-life fact. They still favor more picaresque methods: a firm cosh with the bookend, a splash with the lye, a lucky shot with the blunderpuss. But any day now you may expect to read about a neat twist with the fillet knife.

Hacker

Carver

Ripper

Cleaver

Slicer

THE G-RATED MYSTERY

In an ordinary novel, if two characters share a single bed and one of them starts in with the heavy breathing, we know what's coming next: the sexy stuff. Big, fulsome paragraphs about intriguingly situated dimples and erotically entwined knees (we can get a charley horse just reading about them).

The same setup in a mystery book, however, leads to something quite different: lights out on the chapter. We never do discover if Reginald, so recently returned from India, has perfected exercise 9 in the *Kama Sutra,* or if Melissa is a real blonde. Instead, we turn the page and learn that one of them has expired during the night, the other is missing, and the Inspector is on the way.

Not exactly titillating, is it?

Crime writers are abysmally discreet. We can rest assured that if Nora Charles pats the fourposter, it's for Asta to join her, not Nick. The rule of thumb seems to be: Never describe in detail any act too intimate to conduct over a cup of tea at the vicar's.

Boudoir shenanigans are out, obviously, but also shrouded in mystery are even less blatant maneuvers. When was the last time you read about a marriage proposal that was sealed with a kiss, for instance? In *Gaudy Night*, the author was so ashamed of the whole subject that she forced her hero to render the offer in Latin. That's hardly playing the scene for passion. Now, if she'd let Wimsey huskily voice the suggestion in French and developed things from there, we might have had a section worth dog-earing.

This sexual timidity has caused the mystery writer to invent a new literary technique, the BBP (Between Books Phenomenon). With the BBP, anything even mildly prurient is relegated to the nether region "between" volumes. Wedding ceremonies, for example. Dame Ngaio did not invite readers to watch Troy marry Rory. She simply presented her fans with a *fait accompli*: single today, hitched tomorrow, and with no prying eyes to witness the changeover. Well, who could blame her? Weddings, with their implications of lace-edged underwear and midnight romps on the percale, are awfully spicy.

The most famous BBP involves Conan Doyle's Dr. Watson. Actually, according to the Canon, there was a BBP[1], a BBP[2], and a BBP[3]. Our man John was married three times, and not one of the ceremonies made it into print. Ah, those Victorians. So modest. What's more, the first and third occasions were deemed sufficiently naughty that even the names of the wives have been obscured, as if the mere mention would make our hearts burn with longing. This "no-name wife" convention has been carefully

> *"Who told you she was a housekeeper?"* Blackstone asked curiously.
>
> *"She did — no — that is, she said you might call it that,"* Moran answered him.
>
> *"I prefer to call her his mistress."*
>
> *"What!"* Moran jumped up, astounded. *"Do you mean to say . . . well!"* He sat himself down again. *"Now you have told me something."*
>
> Cat's Paw
> ROGER SCARLETT

If I only knew how to begin.–

upheld by modern writers, who know all too well where our fantasies might lead us if we had a name to put to them.

Nor is this the extent of the mysterious inhibition. Pregnancies are definitely a *verboten* topic, a BBP. Mrs. Chan, Charlie's wife, has eleven children. Can you remember any discussion of how she got them? But there's a peculiar double standard in action here. While a continuing character is never depicted mid-pant, a one-booker might be. Of course, she will die for her pleasure and that probably appeases the crime writer's conscience.

The novice mystery reader, not understanding the BBP process, often spends hours searching for a title that doesn't exist. It's not uncommon to find this poor soul balefully inquiring of the bookseller, "But haven't you got the one where they get married?" This is the danger in weaning a child on straight novels; she grows up to expect more from the mystery than it has any intention of producing.

Still, there are some deliciously revealing episodes if we understand that crime writers use alcohol the way movie directors use water — as a symbol for passion. Clearly, these literati feel no one would indulge in this sort of thing unless under the influence. For every cinematic dissolve to a crashing wave, a cascading waterfall, a cleansing rainstorm, there is a fictional cut to Charles as he reaches for the wine glasses, Gerald as he pops the champagne cork, Phillip as he steers Stephanie toward the Café Noir. Although sex is imminent, it will not be consummated in print. No matter. With a little imagination, you can fill in the gap yourself. You, after all, have no reason to behave as if Walt Disney were your editor, John Calvin your proofreader.

Numerous scholars have tried to explain why mysteries are so wholesome. The most sensible conclusion seems to be that the majority of mystery writers were severely traumatized by a too-explicit nursery school game of show-and-tell. One crank felt that women were the root of all good. Since more women write mysteries and more women read mysteries, he reasoned, and since they do not have a wealth of locker-room dialogue to draw on, it's small wonder that they keep things sanitized. That may be so, but re-

"In a way, we're a ménage à trois: you, me, and Agatha Christie."

gardless, the argument is flawed. One must consider that in our culture it is the men who are the idealists, the women the pragmatists; the men the abstractionists, the women the concrete pin-it-downers. If anything, women would be *more* likely to embellish their stories with details.

We're talking exclusively hard-cover situations, of course. Matters change radically when we survey the paperback original and pulp markets. *The Girl from H.A.R.D.* borders on the pornographic, and there has never been a really tasteful detective magazine — they all lavish great care in such exact descriptions as how the rope felt when it dug into Mabel's jutting breasts while the Fenimore Gang was having its way with her. Back in the thirties, a Canadian publisher (he must have been new to the job) censored some of the illustrations in the American stories he reprinted. He kept an art staff working day and night adding ruffles to scandalously low V-necks and deeper hems to skirts that barely covered lasciviously ample rumps. But he was the exception. Everyone else was, and is, immersed in the tawdry. It would be interesting to see what would happen if a subscriber filed a "Do Not Deliver Sexually Oriented Material" voucher with the post office. The U.S. Mails would probably have to get a Supreme Court ruling on the matter.

One final thought about the G-rated mystery. If we define it as escape literature, what are we escaping?

CLEAVAGE AND WHAT IT MEANS

IN A GOTHIC

Orphans are notoriously flat-chested, a fact they try to hide beneath four thicknesses of black bombazine. The minute a bat screeches, however, or a twig snaps, or a hand turns a knob with an ominous creak, they shuck their mourning clothes for cobweb-sheer nighties, which reveal every *thump, thump* of their agitated hearts. Once that heaving bosom is exposed, its owner is in for a tough few chapters. There'll be a barrage of direly worded letters, a corridor rush-hour of ghosts, a banquet of arsenic-laden delectables. The instant the bosom subsides and is again decorously swathed in chin-high pleats, the happy ending is in sight.

IN A STATELY HOME

Dowagers are ample-bosomed. Being addicted to surpluses, they also feature hyphen-heavy names, e.g., Alicia-Bedelia Wentworth-Rohr. The vaster their thoracic expanse, the closer they are in age to the Georgian teaspoons set out on the trolley. And the more likely they are to indulge in the time-honored hobby of switching principal beneficiaries. Milady's breast is the focal point of the country weekend, as on it reposes the heirloom brooch — which will be hocked by an impatient legatee, swiped by an insolent chit of a serving girl or have its pin dowsed with poison by Sunday noon. The English well-endowed are always victims.

IN A HARD-BOILED

Clients are invariably sweater girls, Lana Turner look-alikes with Lizabeth Scott voices (that's why they hang out in California — they're waiting to be discovered). They're a perfect 34C, and anytime one's thrust into a case you can bet your trench coat she's as crooked as stocking seams. She uses her cleavage to stash the wad of hundreds from the Terwilliger job, to distract the shamus from coherent thought, to billet a bullet meant for Sam the Weasel, who was standing behind her (lucky him). Sometimes it happens that a client is underdeveloped mammary-wise: she's a kid sister, and honest.

IN A SPY THRILLER

Double agents are voluptuous, the better to worm secrets out of a James Bond mentality. The more obvious they get, say, in black lacy half-cups, the more frequently they confront cigarette butts (lighted) in the hands of sadistic inquisitioners. Spies loyal to Our Side never appear in lingerie. The single exception is when one strips to conceal the microdot on the freckle just below her left breast. This act will be observed by the good guy (hiding in the closet) and the bad guy (lurking behind the drapes), who will burst out — guns ablaze — and kill the female agent in their cross fire.

IN A SWEDISH PROCEDURAL

Scandinvaian career girls do not have breasts.They do, however, have prominent nipples, with a deep brown tint that contrasts smartly with their lank blond hair — worn long to disguise their concavity. Once per book, the Northerner will undress and hop into bed with her married policeman boyfriend. This means it's going to rain. He will contemplate her nipples for the duration, an activity which makes him wax philosophical about contemporary society and the melancholia basic to all cold climates.

THE WHYDUNIT
Novels à la Freud

Imagine, please, that someone has just handed you a piece of paper. On it is a drawing of a quite ordinary urn. The figure is white and seems to be resting against a black background. But then something odd happens. The urn disappears, and in its place, facing each other across a narrow gully of white, are two black profiles. You look at them awhile and they vanish, as the urn pops up again. And on and on it goes: now the urn, now the profiles.

This phenomenon, familiar to any perceptual psychologist, is called the figure ground reversal. The elements on the page don't change; what you see depends on what you choose to focus on.

In the classic mystery, the emphasis is on the urn — the "thing," be it a will, a jewel, a map, a clue or a murder weapon. In the psychological crime novel, the attention is riveted to the profiles — the "characters," and what makes them tick.

Conceivably, two writers could take the same basic situation, and one could produce an intellectual puzzle mystery while the other developed a novel à la Freud.

The hallmark of the psychological thriller is the relationships between its major characters. Don't get confused. In a classic mystery, everyone is a relative — the vicar is uncle of the schoolteacher who is ward of the laird who is father-in-law of the villain who is illegitimate son of the colonel — but no one actually relates to anyone else. Teacup confidences are not to be equated with deep, personal involvements. To paraphrase a line from an old Nichols and May routine: There is proximity, but no closeness.

The crux of the psychological story is the intense interacting of its principals. In fact, their behavior is more important than the crime itself, which is used only as background against which their characters unfold.

Typically, the psychological tale is presented in an underplayed prose style. The emotions are jarring enough; you don't need an hysteric shouting in your ear at the same time. Visually, the stories are bleak. Nobody ever walked away from a psychological novel wanting to buy the protagonist's house or move to his town. The author's concern is the interior rather than the physical landscape. But if he suddenly describes a rainstorm, it's not just to fill in time; it's an amplification of something, some feeling, that's important to his characters and your understanding of them.

Curiously, the author most often credited with being the paterfamilias of the psychological novel doesn't really write them. Simenon is a brighter Christie, that's all. When Maigret puffs away on his pipe, trying to deduce how so-and-so could have done whatever, he uses a process that countless little old ladies, Miss Marple included, rely on: intuition. A character can be intuitive and insightful, can talk about motive until you're sick to death of it, and still not exist in a psychological novel. What Maigret proves is that Marple would have made a pretty fine French police officer, once she got the hang of the language.

Similarly, a raft of books have been written about psychologist, psychoanalyst, psychotherapist and psychiatrist sleuths that don't meet three-dimensional requirements, either. These variations on the cerebral detective theme contain nothing more than newfangled stock characters, who are too busy analyzing to feel. You can't make a psychological novel out of that — though you can create a decent classic mystery.

The psychological thriller is not restful. In-

GUIDE FOR THE TENSION-PRONE

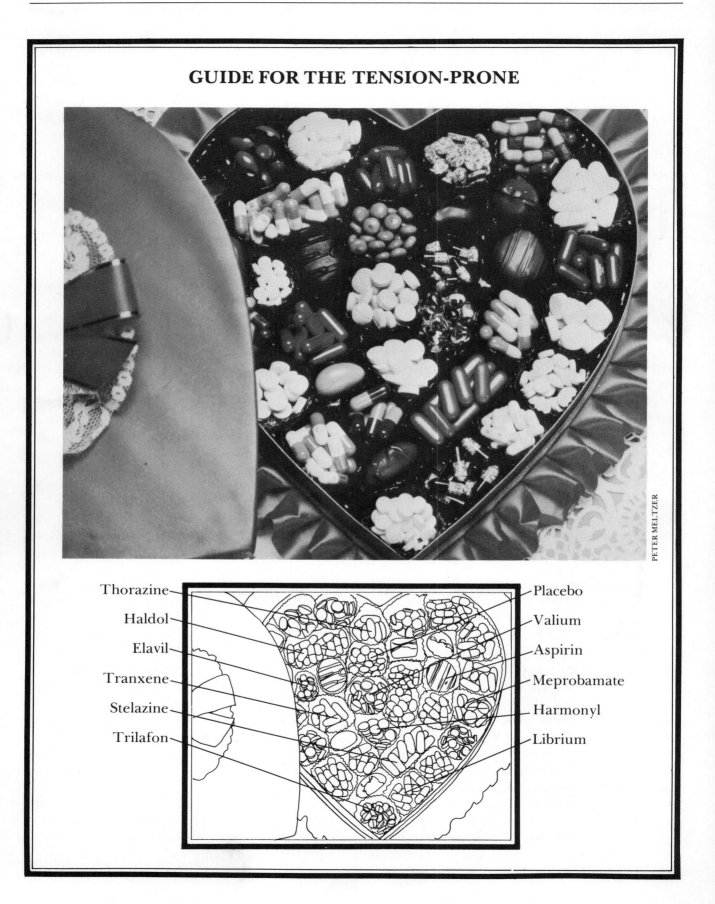

PETER MELTZER

Thorazine

Haldol

Elavil

Tranxene

Stelazine

Trilafon

Placebo

Valium

Aspirin

Meprobamate

Harmonyl

Librium

deed, it evokes such tension that the books should be offered with a free Librium prescription. It's lacerating living in the mind of the obsessed, even if only for an hour or two. And you don't come away feeling all's right with the world and truth, beauty and justice triumph.

Still, if you can stand it, the experience is enlarging. Try Jennie Savage's *The Nemesis Club,* Jacqueline Wilson's *Truth or Dare,* any of Ruth Rendell's non-Wexford novels, any by Celia Fremlin.

After all, you can't spend your whole life contemplating urns.

THE CAT COMPLEX

Patricia Highsmith

Cats provide something for writers that humans cannot: companionship that makes no demands or intrusions, that is as restful and ever-changing as a tranquil sea that barely moves. Writers' minds, I think, are active or disturbed enough to need the soothing aura of a cat in the house. A writer is not alone with a cat, yet is enough alone to work. Semyon, my younger Siamese, interrupts me only when he is hungry. Since he is neither fat nor greedy, I always oblige him by going to the kitchen and getting something for him.

Cats as Watsons? Coming by accident onto the facts? I should think they would be worse than dogs at detecting. Both depend on their noses more than on their eyes, but would a cat *care*? Out of curiosity, it might lead the way to a corpse, might also register hostility to a person by an astonishingly deep growl or by leaving the room. I have seen both my Siamese, however, seek out the lap of a visitor who detested them.

A writer could "use" a cat to sniff at a floorboard at exactly the right time, but this is one of those possibilities that ring true in life and false in fiction. I've never used such a trick in my writing, but I recently made use of a cat's predatory habit by having it drag a pair of

COURTESY PATRICIA MOYES

Catty women include Miss Highsmith, Patricia Moyes (whose Siamese this is), Pauline Glen Winslow, Dell Shannon, Christianna Brand and Mary Stewart.

human fingers, attached to their shattered metacarpals, through the cat door while a game of Scrabble was going on in the living room.

Patricia Highsmith received the Silver Dagger award from the Crime Writers' Association for The Two Faces of January.

WHAT EVER HAPPENED TO HARI?

Pssst. Allen Dulles, who knows a thing or two about deep cover work, claims Elizabeth van Lew was "the single most valuable spy the North ever had" during the Civil War. Pass it on.

Pssst. Kim Philby, British Intelligence's pet operative (and, unfortunately for them, Russia's too), refers to Jane Archer as one of the two best agents in the employ of MI5. Pass it on.

Pssst. Julia Child admits she spent the bulk of World War II in Chunking, under the auspices of the OSS. Pass it on.

Pssst. By 1976, El Kamas Enterprises of Anaheim, supplier of mercenaries, recruited as many women as men for surveillance missions and demolition work. Pass it on.

Pssst. Mata Hari was not executed by the French for her lousy dancing. Pass it on.

Imperative: Get these "secrets" to mystery novelists — and fast. They've been writing as if the intelligence community were a private men's club. Untrue. History clearly disagrees. From the time Elizabeth van Lew planted an agent in Jefferson Davis' household, collected the information and funneled it from Richmond to Washington, women have functioned admirably in the espionage world. They've done everything the men have except hide the microfilm in a tube of shaving cream; they inserted it in a container of bath talc instead. (Scotland Yard's Black Museum has a couple of souvenirs, including the very powder bottle that Ethel Rosenberg tinkered with.)

Still, despite their real-life roles, women spies rarely make it to the fictional printed page. And when they do, they're usually given minor assignments (tidying up the safe house, purchasing batteries for the wireless) or sexual ones (pillow-talking with Bond). The housekeeper/errand-runner spies are all named Marie. They

Mlle. Hari. The microdot is in her navel behind pearl.

joined the Maquis at seventeen and spit in the face of the Gestapo when hauled in for questioning at twenty-four. The bedmate spies have curves like the Amalfi Drive, a mane of hair that would strike envy in the heart of Trigger and a habit of converting to whichever side happened to kiss them last; typical of the breed are Philip Atlee's Miss Nan-Cho from *The Last Domino Contract* and John Luckless' Chalice from *The Death Freak.* Neither group seems as efficient at their respective jobs as van Lew, Archer or Child. But they often wind up dead, just like Miss Hari.

Three who fare somewhat better are Peter O'Donnell's Modesty Blaise, Anne Bridge's Julia Probyn and Dorothy Gilman's Mrs. Pollifax. At least they're not relegated to walk-on roles; they take center stage.

Modesty made her debut in the funny papers (where she yet appears) but has also found time to romp through eight novels and one short-story collection. Of course, if Somerset Maugham were alive to read about her, he'd scan one chapter and swoon.

When Mr. Maugham, a retired Secret Service man himself, introduced Ashenden in 1928, he double-crossed the spy fraternity. His agent was not heroic in the manner of John Buchan's Richard Hannay, not zealously patriotic à la Sapper's Bulldog Drummond, and certainly not invincible like the chaps in the Sexton Blake and William LeQueux yarns. If we can believe the word of those privy to the stuff cloaked behind the Official Secrets Act, Ashenden was realistic. He didn't traffic with exotic blondes, expensive gadgetry or plots to blow the world to smithereens. He relied on his wits to combat political intrigues.

That's much too tame for Miss Modesty. Why should she reason with a defector when she can get the same result by karate-chopping his sternum? Why should she feel alienated and alone when a bed with a gentleman in it is right over there? O'Donnell spawned Modesty from 007's glamorous rib. Maugham and Ashenden might have been more sympathetic if he'd lifted her from one of George Smiley's.

Surely, Maugham would have sent Ashenden to wrest the spy business from the clutches of Julia Probyn and Mrs. Pollifax, too. Julia does most of her spying at embassy soirées and often

WHY WOMEN DON'T WRITE SPY NOVELS
Ken Follett

A spy story is about a man who appears to lead a fairly ordinary life but in fact goes about secretly doing enormously important things like toppling governments, stealing folders, killing people and saving the world. It's a fantasy many men — writers and readers — can share. (I used to know a man who liked to step into a doorway, hold a ballpoint pen to his lips and mutter: "Open channel D.") We have this fantasy because we're trained to seek power: through promotion at work and through money; over a wife and children, and ultimately, in international politics, over other nations.

When women write spy stories or general thrillers, the plot is often just a channel through which a love story can flow. What is interesting about the story developments is the way they affect the relationship between the heroine and the man — is he true or false, is he as brutal as he seems, and why is he lying to her? Women have different fantasies because they're trained to seek not power but a powerful man.

Thank heaven, women are no longer being trained quite so effectively for the housewife-mother role, and those who are sometimes fight it. Radical feminists want to see women develop new motivations, but it seems more likely that they will simply acquire existing male motivations (and fantasies). In that case, we might see some good women spy writers emerging.

There are some of us who think that would be small consolation.

Ken Follett received an Edgar award from the Mystery Writers of America for his spy novel Eye of the Needle.

ADVICE FOR WOULD-BE SPY WRITERS

Ross Thomas

First read the good ones, and read a lot of them: Eric Ambler; John Le Carré; Gavin Lyall; all of the Mac-Donalds, no matter how they're spelled; Graham Greene, particularly *This Gun for Hire;* Maugham and his secret agent, *Ashenden.* Then go off someplace and write your book. Do it to entertain yourself. (I only write what interests me.)

I don't know why more women haven't taken a crack at the big thriller. The only two authors of any prominence I can think of are Helen Mac-Innes and Mary Stewart.

I would welcome a good woman spy writer. I'd read her. And the field's wide open.

Ross Thomas received an Edgar award from the Mystery Writers of America for his spy novel The Cold War Swap.

guised as Rosalind Russell, she turned up on movie screens.

Readers weaned on the works of Ambler, Greene and Le Carré will marvel at the lack of political ideology in these gals' books. If their authors have any insight into how the Iron Curtain was lowered, why the Cold War came to pass, they keep it firmly to themselves. To date, there are no feminine counterparts to Smiley or even Harry Palmer. The excuse usually offered is that women do not stalk real spy corridors; that you could spend a lifetime with MI5 (or MI6, DI5, DI6, KGB, GRU, OGPU, S.D.E.C.E. and Langley) and not bump into a woman with top-level clearance. Nonsense. What do they think Jane Archer had?

Women spy writers are about as rare as women spy characters. Baroness Orczy with her Pimpernel stories would probably qualify, but then you'd have to jump several decades to reach Margery Allingham and *Traitor's Purse,* and skip a few more to arrive at Joyce Porter and her hilarious Edmund Brown, who in *Sour Cream with Everything* and *Chinks in the Curtain* acted like an Anglo Inspector Clousseau set loose amongst the moles. Last year, Marilyn Sharpe, wife of a U.S. Congressman, brought us *Sunflower,* and this year Mary McCarthy has given us *Cannibals and Missionaries.*

Pssst. There's room for more. Pass it on.

seems more concerned with the state of the pâté than with the state of nations. She behaves like a Helen MacInnes heroine who's suddenly come into a lot of money and been asked to join the diplomatic circle.

Like Modesty and Mrs. Pollifax, Julia is a series character. She's surfaced on eight occasions, always in time for the holiday ball — at which agents slowly wend their way through the receiving line, bussing their enemies on both cheeks before selling them off to the highest bidder.

The intrepid Mrs. Pollifax has to skimp along on a far tauter budget, but then she only works part-time for the CIA: her real vocation is being a suburban widow. Extraordinarily resourceful, she leaps over problems in logistics that would stump an Einstein.

Thus far, Mrs. P. and the company have been in cahoots on five cases, and once, dis-

CALL CONTROL IMMEDIATELY

The CIA public information number is (703) 351-7676. Memorize and burn this page.

Chapter 2
SCHEMERS

FOUNDING MOTHERS

Even for readers of supreme endurance, the first full-length detective novel written by a woman presents an awesome challenge. The several hundred pages of Seeley Regester's *The Dead Letter* (1867) offer up a murder, a robbery, an illegitimacy, a wild-goose chase from Brooklyn to Mexico, a rejected suitor (orphaned, to boot), a second rejected suitor, a child clairvoyant, an amoral chemist, a seamstress with a secret love, two sisters with the same beau, their despotic papa, and an independently wealthy police detective who declines a salary but takes two years to wrap up the case and assemble everyone in the parlor for the denouement.

Tedious though it may be, *The Dead Letter* is the first attempt by a woman to crack the world of Poe, and we're stuck with it until the day when a fastidious scholar unearths an even earlier (and hopefully superior) effort.

Miss Regester grew up in Erie, Pennsylvania, published her first novel at fifteen, tendered her mystery mishmash at thirty-six and cranked out perfectly dreadful books until her death in 1886. Her real name was Metta Victoria Fuller Victor, and the only clue to why she used a pseudonym is the quality of her work: who would willingly sign her own name to such drivel?

Until *The Dead Letter*'s recent disinterment, historians labeled Anna Katharine Green the winner of the Who Was First sweepstakes. Her first novel, *The Leavenworth Case* (1878), introduced all the elements of the cozy read: a body in the library mysteriously dispatched while rewording the will; a diagram of the scene of the crime; a facsimile of a handwritten letter (with sinister implications); enough wainscotting to keep the entire carpenters' guild employed for life; a stealthy butler; a passel of greedy relatives; a deeply concerned narrator (the deceased's lawyer); and Mr. Ebenezer Gryce, a portly detective so beneath the suspects in station that the question is why he never used the servants' entrance. *Leavenworth* (named in honor of the Dear Departed, not the prison) also featured one of the first literary instances of ballistics testimony, a coroner's inquest and much legal mumbo jumbo, apparently picked up by the author at her attorney father's knee and used to bolster the novel's subtitle, *A Lawyer's Story*.

WHAT'S THE LITTLE WOMAN BEEN UP TO?

Louisa May Alcott, best known for Amy, Beth, Meg, Jo and Marmie, supplemented her income by churning out characters with less pacific natures for Frank Leslie's steamy weekly newspapers. They appeared under the by-line A. M. Barnard, and the curious can find them in two recent collections: *Behind a Mask: The Unknown Thrillers of Louisa May Alcott* and *Plots and Counterplots: More Unknown Thrillers of Louisa May Alcott*.

In fact, the tale holds up rather well. Gryce may seem a tad colorless, a bit stodgy these days, but probably no more so than the characters he was patterned after: Wilkie Collins' Sergeant Cuff and Charles Dickens' Inspector Bucket. In *The Affair Next Door* (1897) and again in *Lost Man's Lane* (1898), Gryce was assisted by the mystery's first spinster sleuth, Amelia Butterworth. An incorrigible snoop, Miss Amelia adored prying into other people's business and quite happily admitted she'd been badly bitten by the detecting bug and had no wish to recover.

In *The Golden Slipper* (1915), Miss Green presented another nosy female, Violet Strange, whose success in large part rested on her owning an acutely clue-sensitive bloodhound. Like her predecessor Amelia, though several generations younger, Violet was highborn and pesky, unmarried, and unrecompensed for labor.

Born in Brooklyn and educated in Vermont (Ripley Female College), Miss Green married furniture tycoon Charles Rohlfs and settled in Buffalo, New York, where she died in 1935. She had originally planned on being a poet but was sidetracked by the success of *Leavenworth*.

Meanwhile, over in England, L. T. Meade (Elizabeth Thomasina Meade Smith) was busy penning approximately 250 stories for small children and sentimental young ladies. Eventually tiring of this (and who wouldn't), she and the pseudonymous Dr. Clifford Halifax collaborated on a series of tales involving a country doctor. These appeared in *The Strand* magazine (1894) and were hailed as Britain's first medical mysteries.

Miss Meade joined forces in 1898 with another pseudonym, Robert Eustace, to create the first female master crimimal, Madame Koluchy. The *Strand* short stories were published in book form the following year as *The Brotherhood of the Seven Kings*. Definitely the brains of her outfit, Madame Koluchy concocted schemes which she then ordered her gang of Italian thugs to carry out. Her nemesis was the taciturn Norman Head, a peculiarly reclusive detective with the philosophical bent of Charlie Chan.

In 1903, Meade and Eustace decided that as nasty as Madame Koluchy was, they could do worse; so they supplanted her with Madame Sara, an out-an-out murderess who killed her way through *The Sorceress of the Strand*. Between these two villainesses, Meade took time to write about a woman on the other side of the law, sleuth Florence Cusack. Appearing in *Harms-*

THE FIRST BUTLER

Who taught him to behave with the decorum of a red herring? No one's really sure, but we have our suspicions: Anna Katharine Green, back in 1878. The gentleman she employed to butle *The Leavenworth Case* was extremely fond of tiptoeing down corridors with a furtive air, serving port with a sinister flourish and answering the door with disquieting aplomb. And ever since his first appearance, the butler has been as indispensable to the stately home mystery as the body in the library.

Everett attends Anna Katharine Green.

worth magazine (1899–1900), the four Cusack stories wasted many paragraphs rhapsodizing over the heroine's dark blue eyes and raven black hair.

The founding mother with the fanciest pedigree was undoubtedly Emmuska, Baroness Orczy, of the Hungarian nobility. Though all her books were written in English, she spoke not a word of the language before fleeing to London in her early teens.

In "The Case for Miss Elliot" (1901), the Baroness originated what has since become a staple of detective fiction: the armchair sleuth. Her Old Man in the Corner rarely left the back booth of a London tearoom, which he used more as an office than as a restaurant. While waiting for Polly Burton, his Watson, to bring him clues, he tied complicated knots in a length of string, then meticulously untied them and began all over again. Contemporary armchair detectives such as Nero Wolfe behave in a very similar manner: minimal movement, maximum conjecturing.

In a sense, 1905 could be called a banner year for the Baroness. In addition to *The Old Man in the Corner,* she had both a play and a novel version of *The Scarlet Pimpernel* produced. The Pimpernel, Sir Percy Blakeney, was a seemingly fainthearted Englishman who almost single-handedly flummoxed the Continentals during the French Revolution.

In 1910, the Baroness created *Lady Molly of Scotland Yard.* The title character headed up the Yard's "Female Department," accepting the position for the sole purpose of proving (by covering every contingency) that her husband had been unjustly imprisoned. It took her twenty years to do it.

The most famous of the founding mothers, Mary Roberts Rinehart, is also the most often maligned — usually for the sins of her imitators. Typical complaints mention a preponderance of childish heroines, an inexplicable enthrallment with nightgowns, a plethora of midnight raids on the attic (or the crypt) and an overreliance on supernatural gobbledygook. True, it is difficult to find a Rinehart novel without these elements, but a formula is a formula and Mrs. Rinehart's spearheaded a whole new movement.

Cartoon substantiation of the Murderess Ink *poll, which ascertained that mystery writers learned to write before they were ten.*

Beginning with *The Circular Staircase* (1909), readers had a choice: they could opt for one of the dazzlingly eccentric sleuths who were present at this time (Sherlock Holmes, for example) or they could read about a woman of average intelligence who fussed her way through an awful predicament — sometimes of her own making. Enough mystery fans favored the latter to get Mrs. Rinehart out of debt and into a Park Avenue apartment.

Every Rinehart story has two things in common: multiple murders and a slew of "Had-I-But-Knowns." Open a Rinehart book at random and ten-to-one someone will be aiming a gun, thrusting a knife or ruefully mumbling, "Had I But Known then what I know now . . ." It is this grammatical construction that devils Mrs. Rinehart's reputation. Granted, she is guilty of overuse, but other members of what has come to be tagged the Had-I-But-Known school are even worse offenders.

Trained as a nurse, Mrs. Rinehart picked a member of that profession as her first series sleuth, introduced in *Miss Pinkerton* (1932). Nurse Adams (dubbed "Pinkerton" by the police because of her investigative abilities) appeared in two novels, several novellas. Letitia (Tish) Carberry, continuing lead in another series, was seen even less frequently.

Poor Carolyn Wells is the founding mother most of us have forgotten about. Now and then, a reader dipping into the Haycraft-Queen mystery-milestone list will notice an entry for 1909 called *The Clue*. A short line just beneath it identifies it as "the first Fleming Stone book," and the usual response to that is "What's a Fleming Stone?" He was Miss Wells' continuing character, who unraveled sixty-one puzzle-type mysteries. Only Simenon's Maigret and Gardner's Perry Mason have appeared in more cases. (Nick Carter doesn't count; he was written by a veritable regiment.)

How could such a persistent busybody be overlooked? Blame it on Well's sluggish prose. Still, John Dickson Carr fans might consider rallying to her defense; she did try for the truly baffling plot complexity (grade her A for effort, C— for execution).

With *The Technique of the Mystery Story* (1913), Miss Wells demonstrated than an only so-so novelist could be a gifted teacher. This was the first of the how-to-write-a-mystery manuals and included not only a list of don'ts for the would-be writer — even then, cigarette ash as a clue was a cliché — but verbal mug shots of famous crime authors and their creations. Now out of print and, unfortunately, out of libraries, *Technique* contains such solid information that it deserves to be reissued.

Finally, a word or two should be said about the founding mothers who preferred to remain anonymous. Back in the 1800's, a woman's place was at the pianoforte, the embroidery hoop, the tea trolley. If she could manage a few bars of Mozart, a neatly tatted hankie edge, a sweet "one lump or two?" she was considered a woman of some accomplishment. Nothing more was required of her; in fact, anything more was frowned upon. Living under such claustrophobic conditions, most women didn't dare write more than a shopping list. Surely, they reasoned, they'd be relegated to the old maid heap if they published a mystery under their own byline. Ergo, "By Anonymous." We may never know how often that phrase cloaks a feminine hand at the quill. But if we learn of a woman who couldn't play a note, who sewed a crooked seam, who was usually absent at teatime, we ought to conclude she was in cohoots with Anonymous. How else would she have been whiling away all those hours? To her, the unknown founding mother, we say thank you.

THE BLACK THUMB

Peter V. Tytell

In 1904, assistant editor Mary E. Holland traveled to St. Louis to oversee *The Detective* magazine's police display at the Louisiana Purchase Exposition. Also at the fair was Detective Sergeant John Kenneth Ferrier, security supervisor for the British crown jewels and promoter of the fingerprint system invented three years earlier at New Scotland Yard by Edward R. Henry. Quick to recognize the significance of Ferrier's doctrine, Mrs. Holland enlisted as his student and by the close of the fair had become a full-fledged expert in this new means of detection.

After further studies in Europe, during which she spent weeks in Paris with the legendary Alphonse Bertillon, Mrs. Holland passed the Yard's severest tests in fingerprinting. She then returned to the States, where she was soon a familiar figure at police gatherings. Her students were the chiefs of many identification bureaus, including the National Bureau for Criminal Information and Identification in Washington, D.C., and the identification section of the Departments of the Army and Navy.

Her pioneering activities won her the appellation "Mother of American Fingerprint Identification."

Peter V. Tytell is a questioned document examiner working in New York City.

MURDER IN GRANDMA'S ATTIC

Kathleen L. Maio

1861 ***East Lynne*** by Mrs. Henry (Ellen Price) Wood

Within twenty-five years, this novel sold over a million copies in the U.S. alone—for which Mrs. Wood received not a penny. Its standard "sensation" fare of seduction and betrayal is nicely supplemented by a murder.

1862 ***Lady Audley's Secret*** by Mary Elizabeth Braddon (Maxwell)

Perhaps the most famous of sensation thrillers. The wicked Lady A. will stop at nothing, including murder, to hide her ugly secret. Several of Braddon's later novels feature women as amateur sleuths/Eumenides.

1863 ***The Mad Hunter*** by M(ary) A(ndrews) Denison

In this early American dime novel, by the wife of a Baptist preacher, fraud and attempted murder are uncovered by the title character. Crude detecting at best: if he can't find legal proof, the Mad Hunter extorts confessions with a little help from God . . . and a gun.

1866 ***The Dead Letter*** by Seeley Regester (Mrs. Metta V. F. Victor)

First known appearance in nine issues of *Beadle's Monthly*, followed by a 50¢ novel edition in September, 1866. Still very readable. When gentleman sleuth Mr. Burton is stumped, he exploits the psychic powers of his daughter, Lenore.

1867 ***The Four Fifteen Express*** by Amelia B. Edwards

This novella's first book publication was in *Mixed Sweets from Routledge's Annual.* Good for train aficionados. William Langford investigates the disappearance of a railroad official carrying £ 75,000.

1875 ***A Woman in the Case*** by Miss Bessie A. Turner

John Hardy is a very likable detective—so likable that he gets the fortune as well as the girl. The author claims that her novel is "founded in fact."

1878 ***The Leavenworth Case*** by Anna Katharine Green (Rohlfs)

The appearance of this classic body-in-the-library mystery created a brouhaha involving the identity of the author: many found the book "manifestly beyond a woman's powers." At one time labeled "the first American detective novel," it remains the first American detection best seller.

1879 *Shadowed by Three* by Lawrence L. Lynch, Ex-Detective (Emma Murdoch Van Deventer)

Not one, but three professional detectives track down a female desperado skillful at stiletto murders. Lynch's books are notable for their epic proportions (they often run over 600 pages) and their hard-boiled sensibilities.

1884 *The House on the Marsh* by Florence Warden (Florence A. Price James)

This early Warden effort is a prototype for the modern Gothic — a first-person narrative by a young governess with a pathetically unsuspecting nature.

1887 *The Upland Mystery: A Tragedy of New England* by Mary R. P. Hatch

The first mystery novel by one of Anna Katharine Green's closest friends is based on the Bugbee murders of Lancaster, New Hampshire. True crime and psychical phenomena formed the basis for most of Hatch's fanciful mysteries of northern New England.

1894 *The Experiences of Loveday Brooke, Lady Detective* by C(atharine) L(ouisa) Pirkis

Seven stories that illustrate the superior talents of one of the most effective early women sleuths. The "first" of this collection is now scarce and extremely valuable. Pirkis' earlier thrillers, though not detective novels, often feature amateur sleuthing by women.

1895 *The Long Arm* by Mary E. Wilkins (Freeman)

Wilkins is known primarily as a New England "local colorist," but this fascinating novella exhibits her decided talent in mystery writing. More noteworthy than the detecting is the confession of the murderer.

1889 *The Eye of Fate* by Alice Maud Meadows

A detective novel without being a whodunit. Inspector McNab is a professional policeman whose hobby, photography, saves an innocent young woman from the gallows.

1902 *The House Opposite* by Elizabeth Kent (Caroline K. Everett)

Mr. Merritt may be a famous detective, but he may never unravel this New York City hatpin murder. Kent, an essayist and portrait painter, was an invalid. She produced only one other mystery novel.

1902 *Beyond the Law* by Gertrude Warden (Jones)

The mysterious death of a brilliant forensic scientist, on the eve of his testimony in a notorious murder case, leads his brother to investigate. Used with frequent success, the murder weapon is a nicely constructed lethal chamber.

1903 *The Sorceress of the Strand* by L. T. Meade (Elizabeth T. Meade Smith)

Written with the scientific collaboration of Robert Eustace (pseud.), whose name for some reason was omitted in the 1903 and 1904 collections. First published in *The Strand Magazine*, the stories feature the villainous Madame Sara, "one of the greatest criminals of her day." Meade (and Eustace) also created the female sleuth Miss Cusack.

1908 *The Hemlock Avenue Mystery* by Roman Doubleday (Lily Augusta Long)

Miss Long was a poet, novelist, critic and active clubwoman. As Roman Doubleday, she published four highly diverting mysteries with amateur detectives and a good deal of romance and humor. This was her first and by far the most popular.

1908 *The Circular Staircase* by Mary Roberts Rinehart

Elitism (and racism) aside, this Had-I-But-Known is a brilliant blend of detection and comic terror in which Miss Rachel Innes, "a D.A.R.; a Colonial Dame," lays down her knitting and gets "mixed up with a vulgar and revolting crime."

1909 *The Clue* by Carolyn Wells (Houghton)
Since Wells' *A Chain of Evidence*

(first serialized in 1907) was not published in book form until 1912, *The Clue* holds the honors as her first detective novel. The author once admitted that reading an Anna Katharine Green mystery convinced her that this genre was her "happy hunting ground."

1910 *Lady Molly of Scotland Yard* by Baroness (Emmuska) Orczy

Lady Molly and her Watson, Mary Granard of the Yard's "Female Department," solve several challenging mysteries — including the crime that sent Lady M.'s new husband to prison. The Baroness also, of course, created the "Old Man in the Corner" stories.

1911 *The Bride of Dutton Market* by Marie C(onnor) Leighton

Perhaps best known for two novels written in conjunction with her husband, *Michael Dred, Detective* and *Convict 99*, Leighton herself produced a large body of mystery fiction. This title features both a female narrator and a female detective, Ida Lee.

1912 *The Trevor Case* by Natalie Sumner Lincoln

A burglar gets a disheartening surprise when he opens a safe and finds the dead Mrs. Trevor. Blackmail, the Mafia and a courtly Russian count all play a part against the political backdrop of Washington, D.C.

1913 *The Lodger* by Marie Belloc Lowndes

Lowndes' most celebrated example of her gift for the terror mystery. The suspense of this Jack-the-Ripper story is heightened by its psychological insight and unlikely atmosphere of genteel poverty.

1915 *At One-Thirty* by Isabel (Egenton) Ostrander

Early work in Ostrander's prolific if regrettably short career (under her own name as well as the pseudonyms Robert Orr Chipperfield, Douglas Grant and David Fox). The novel brings a murder

Eek!

investigation by a blind detective to a highly satisfying but hardly legal solution.

1916 *The Black Eagle Mystery* by Geraldine Bonner

A charming mystery by an author who also wrote Westerns. Two narrators relate a suitably twisty tale of murder among tycoons. One, a recurring Bonner character, is Molly Morgenthau Babbitts, a former "hello girl" (switchboard operator) turned part-time sleuth for the firm of Whitney & Whitney.

Kathleen L. Maio is currently researching a book on women's early contributions to the mystery genre. She finds most of her material in attics.

THE PLOT TO IMMORTALIZE CHRISTIE

Mme. Tussaud, founder of the world's most famous waxworks, was born in Strasbourg in 1761. She spent her childhood in Paris, then moved to Versailles to tutor the King's sister in wax modeling. She whiled away the Revolution molding heads of the victims (former acquaintances). In 1794, her uncle died, bequeathing her his collection of life-size wax portraits. Eight years later, she shipped them to England and opened a museum. Before her death in 1850, she had been parodied by Dickens and caricatured by Cruikshank. Today, Mme. Tussaud's includes five real-life murderesses in the Chamber of Horrors, and Dame Agatha in the Conservatory. Says one staff member: "No one recognizes her. Everyone knows the name, but not the face."

Sir Arthur Conan Doyle, the only other mystery writer to be honored by Mme. Tussaud's, was on display from 1929 to 1934. His head is currently at rest behind the blood-red storeroom doors in Wookey Hole, about 125 miles from London.

Dame Agatha (right) confronted her doppelgänger (left) for the first time in 1972, at a specially arranged private meeting in the museum's Grand Hall. Visitors will discover Alfred Hitchcock's look-alike surveying Mrs. Christie's from behind potted ferns.

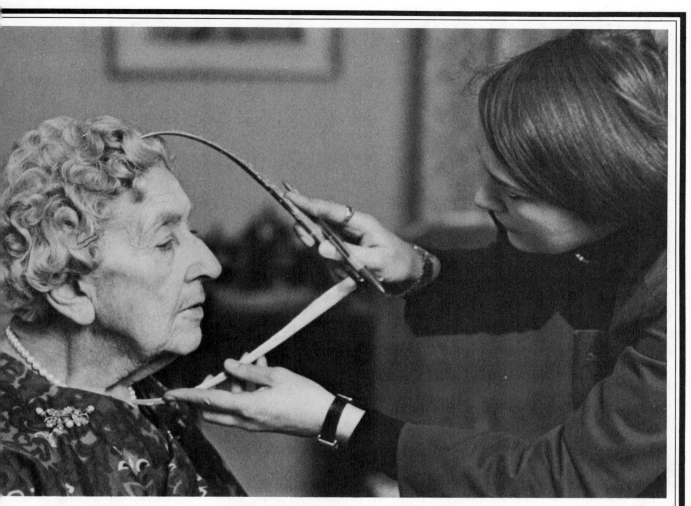

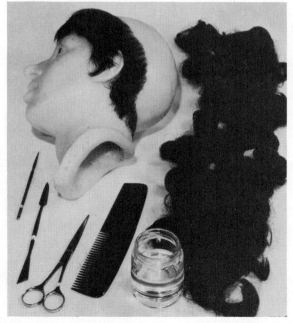

Sculptor Lyn Kramer measures Dame Agatha from the tip of her little grey cells to the top of her beads. Mrs. Christie sat for two caliper appraisals and approximately a dozen mug shots.

Mme. Tussaud's was founded in Paris in 1770, moved to England in 1802 and settled in the Marylebone Road, London, in 1835. It receives 2.5 million tourists each year.

It takes three months to complete a figure. The head is constructed from twelve separate pieces. The wax mixture consists of three parts of bleached beeswax to one part vegetable tallow. Human hair (not from the subject) is implanted in the wax scalp, then styled. All replicas wear clothing donated from the wardrobes of their real-life counterparts.

THE GRAND MASTERS OF CRIME

Dorothy B. Hughes

In the year 1954, the Mystery Writers of America presented a new and most prestigious award, the Grand Master. The need for it was apparent. Some of the greatest names in mystery had never received the Edgar (Allen Poe) award for best mystery of the year, yet they were as important to the genre as those of their peer group who had. The new honor would recognize the value not of a single title but of the entire body of an author's works.

As to the writer selected to receive the first Grand Master, the decision must have been unanimous. Agatha Christie *was* a Grand Master, over all and sundry. (Had there been prescience, she might have been dubbed a Grand Dame, but that was left to her queen, Elizabeth II.) There can be no denying that she was the most distinguished woman mystery writer of her time. Her Belgian detective, Hercule Poirot, is one of the immortals. Miss Marple, the village spinster who solves crimes, is no less important to Christie devotees. Dame Agatha wrote eighty-eight books in her eighty-six years, sixty-eight of them novels. Some of her finest included non-mysteries, character studies that were strongly autobiographical, written under the pen name Mary Westmacott. By the seventies, more than 400 million copies of Christie books, printed in 103 different languages, had been sold.

She was also the leading mystery playwright of her time. Her greatest success, *The Mousetrap*, opened in London in 1952 and even now, more than a quarter-century later, is playing to packed houses in the West End. Most noteworthy of her plays must be *Witness for the Prosecution*, an adaptation from one of her short stories, which garnered all possible dramatic awards and later became one of her spectacularly successful motion pictures.

Like many writers, Agatha Christie experimented in poetry and the short story (she won prizes in both fields) before attempting a novel. Her first manuscript, *The Mysterious Affair at Styles* (1920), introducing Poirot, went from publisher pillar to post before it was accepted. Her seventh novel, *The Murder of Roger Ackroyd* (1925), made her a cause célèbre, and from then on she never left the heights. Most admired of her books were *Ackroyd* and *Ten Little Niggers*

The manuscript title page of Ngaio Marsh's autobiography, showing her alternate title suggestions. The manuscript is now part of the Twentieth Century Archives Collection, Boston University.

PHOTOGRAPH TED MURPHY

MISS DU MAURIER'S DISCLAIMER

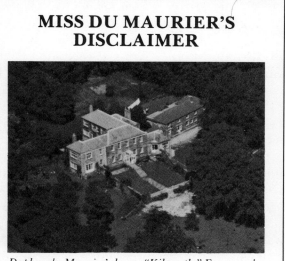

Daphne du Maurier's home, "Kilmarth." For more detail, consult The House on the Strand.

Do remember, though, that I am *not* a crime writer in the true sense of the word and therefore do not really qualify to be included in your mystery list. True, Maxim de Winter shot his wife in *Rebecca*, and the narrator in *My Cousin Rachel* was never sure of his cousin in connection with the death of Ambrose Manaton, but I have always insisted that these two novels, written many years ago now, were studies in jealousy and not in crime.

I was amazed to receive the Grand Master Award. The "trophy," which reposes outside the room where the grandchildren stay when they visit, banishes sleep!

(1939), the latter changing title to *Ten Little Indians* and *And Then There Were None*. Her own favorites — "The two which satisfy me best" — were *Crooked House* and *Ordeal by Innocence*. She also confessed that on rereading *The Moving Finger*, more than seventeen years after it was written, she found herself "really pleased" with it. The book she liked least, no matter how often she studied it, was *The Mystery of the Blue Train* — "commonplace, full of clichés, with an uninteresting plot." Of it she also wrote, "Many people, I am sorry to say, like it," and added, "Authors are always said to be no judge of their own books."

For all her honors and splendors, Dame Agatha revealed in her autobiography: "I still have that overlag of feeling that I am *pretending* to be an author." And she quotes what she said to herself before appearing at the Savoy gala, celebrating the tenth birthday of *The Mousetrap*: "This is Agatha, pretending to be a successful author, going to her own large party, having to look as though she is someone."

Fifteen years elapsed before, in 1970, the MWA again named a woman to the Grand Master. She was Mignon G. Eberhart. And the choice could only have been unanimous, for there was at the time and still is no more eminent American woman in mystery. Eberhart has written more than sixty novels, all highly successful, from her early Nurse Keate stories to her most recent work. Of this record, one critic has noted: a Mignon G. Eberhart novel, without need of a mystery plot, would stand on its own, a mirror of the modes and manners of the twentieth century.

Even in her first book, *The Patient in Room 18* (1929), Eberhart had the hallmark of a professional. The $5,000 Scotland Yard prize went to her second, *While the Patient Slept* (1930). In the heyday of magazines, her name on the cover of such as *The Saturday Evening Post* and *The Ladies' Home Journal* ensured a sellout.

While in her early thirties, Eberhart was honored for her literary value with a D.Litt. degree from Nebraska Wesleyan University. It is difficult to keep in mind that she was born in the Midwest (Nebraska, near Lincoln), as she is the definitive stylist of New York City and its commuting suburbs. After fifty years of creative mystery writing, Eberhart still composes at least two books a year — books of which a *New Yorker* critic wrote: "The ingredients are tested and the cook's hand is sure."

After Eberhart's award, seven years passed before another woman received the high honor. Then, in 1978, not one but three women writers were named Grand Master.

Two were Dames of the British Empire. Daphne du Maurier had never actually been defined as a member of the mystery scene, though

HOMAGE TO MRS. HUGHES

Mignon G. Eberhart

Whenever I wish to feel the authentic shiver down the spine, the true frisson of terror, I reread *The So Blue Marble*. While in real life I would take the most strenuous measures to avoid the terrible twins and their cohort, Wobblefoot, I chill happily when I meet them within the covers of Mrs. Hughes' novel.

For me, one of her strongest appeals is that she does not repeat *ad infinitum* the same set of characters in each work. (If she does, I must have missed a book or two — and I can't have done that!) I must grant that the Sherlockian formula of the brilliant detective and his not-so-brilliant friend who reconnoiter in case after case has proved entertaining, but I incline toward a new and different detecting element each time. I appreciate the fact that Mrs. Hughes introduces characters who spring from the framework of a specific story, ones who act intentionally or even unintentionally to discover and prove the guilt of the murderer (and this is very important; we don't just assume guilt — we have been presented with enough evidence to sway a jury).

Mrs. Hughes also excels at mystery criticism. She is careful, knowledgeable, completely objective, and there is never anything in her reviews that sounds smart-alecky. In 1950, she received an Edgar for this talent.

When she was named a Grand Master, those of us who were already members of this small circle were pleased and flattered by the choice. I can think of no one who would add more stature to the honor.

Mignon G. Eberhart is a past president of the Mystery Writers of America.

she had written some of the major suspense books in the genre — *Frenchman's Creek, Jamaica Inn, My Cousin Rachel* and, of course, the classic *Rebecca*. Today, she would be called a Gothic novelist, a misnomer from its inception. Better would be the label Brontëist, for *Rebecca* followed the *Jane Eyre* pattern, not without a flavor of *Wuthering Heights*.

More important for Dame Daphne's mystery identity were her short-story collections, in particular *The Apple Tree*, published in the United States as *Kiss Me Again, Stranger*. Later, this collection received from Penguin a more pertinent title, *The Birds and Other Stories*. Both the title story and its cinema version can reawake terror long years after the first reading or viewing.

The second Grand Master of 1978 was Dame Ngaio Marsh. Of all the great women mystery authors who come to mind, Ngaio Marsh is the only one whose writing can be said to be an avocation rather than a vocation. Primarily, she is of the theater, in both Australia and New Zealand, and in Great Britain.

The detective created by Ngaio Marsh for her mystery cases is Inspector Roderick Alleyn, one of the most intelligent of his ilk, and one without the quirks that were popular when he debuted in the thirties. On one occasion, the august critic of the New York *Times* said of Dame Ngaio: "She writes better than Christie."

What she writes is urbane, knowledgeable, enchanting, whether the locale is a sheep farm in the back country of the colonies or high society in London. She is a writer's writer; we admire her so tremendously that it is easy to fall into adjectival overpraise. Yet all one needs is to remember that she wrote one of the great mystery classics, *Death of a Fool*, for which she created a folk legend. If this appears something simple, consider what a sense of anthropological and mythological intuitiveness as well as how much study must go into such a coup. To borrow the word as used by T. S. Eliot, *Death of a Fool* is an Epiphany.

And the third Grand Master of 1978 was I.

Dorothy B. Hughes is the author of the biographical study Erle Stanley Gardner: The Case of the Real Perry Mason.

A FACE-TO-FACE ENCOUNTER WITH SAYERS

Josephine Bell

Godolphin School
1726

I first met Dorothy in 1910, when at the age of twelve and eight months I went to Godolphin School, Salisbury, as a boarder at School House.

Godolphin was founded in 1726 by Elizabeth Godolphin, sister-in-law of the first earl of that name, as a charitable institution for the instruction of eight girls, orphaned or semi-orphaned, of the Church of England. In the expansion of women's secondary and higher education in latter Victorian times, the little school was enlarged into a girls' public school, with five "houses" of boarders and a large contingent, as well, of day-girls from the town. It still flourishes on these lines.

Dorothy in 1910 was about eighteen and in her last year at school, preparing and hoping to continue her studies at Oxford University. She was tall, slim and dark, with a large mouth and a snub nose and very bright black eyes. Not at all a pretty girl, according to school-girl standards of the time, but strikingly different from the other seniors in the house. She wore her hair "up," as seniors were expected to do, but instead of the usual side combs and "bun" at the back, she swathed the long end of her black hair round her head and fastened it in place with a black ribbon attached to a buckle. Naturally, this distinguished her altogether from her fellows.

She was more lively, too, and talked more fluently, more often. Returning from my bath at the start of house bedtime (I was the youngest there that year), I'd find her on the landing, reciting long speeches from Shakespeare, loudly, with much animation and gesture — in spite of Matron's protests, who wanted to get the juniors into their beds and out of the way before the main body of the house came thronging up from evening prayers.

Yet Dorothy made little stir in the school. She did write for the school magazine: notably a piece about a skeleton found not far away in some digging at Old Sarum, once a Roman military camp and later a Saxon town. A favourite walk from the school across the downs outside Salisbury, in my day it was just a number of grassy mounds on a hill beside the road. The archaeologists had explored some of the mounds and so found the skeleton, which gave Dorothy

THE D.L.S. FAN CLUB

Ralph Clarke, the president of the Dorothy L. Sayers Society, knows more about Lord Peter's creator than you ever dreamed of asking: to wit, the colour of her pet parrot's feathers (pink and grey), the name of the aunt who lived with her (Maud), the condition of her attic (mouldering, with a pungent aroma of cat), the titles of her husband's two major works *(The Gourmet's Book of Food and Drink, The Craft of the Short Story),* and the number of quotations she impishly insinuated into *Busman's Honeymoon* (200).

To Mr. Clarke, Miss Sayers is practically one of the family. He semi-adopted her about five years ago, when he became involved with the Witham Preservation Society. One of the first things on the agenda was to restore the two adjoining houses Miss Sayers had owned from the early 1920's until her death in 1957. They were a mere ten paces down the street from Mr. Clarke's own house, and he took an active interest in their refurbishing. When this was completed in 1975, a sizable crowd gathered to hear Ian Carmichael make a short speech and to oversee the placement of a discreet sign on No. 22/24 Newland Street: "Dorothy L. Sayers 1893–1957 novelist, theologian and Dante scholar lived here." Dorothy's former digs proved such a tourist draw that it was decided to start a D.L.S. society, with Mr. Clarke, a retired army officer, late of the Royal Engineers, as presiding officer.

Membership in the society costs just under $5 a year, and the benefits include: a bimonthly newsletter prepared by Mr. Clarke; access to the D.L.S. archives, maintained in the Clarke home; an invitation to the an-

Miss Sayers' front door. The brick Georgian front is false; the house actually dates from the 1750's.

COURTESY RALPH CLARKE

nual general meeting each November (Mrs. Clarke serves a light tea and a buffet supper). The society also makes available to its members, at a minimal charge, copies of Sayers' correspondence, ephemera and book lists. Perhaps the most delightful society offering is three D.L.S. outings, carefully plotted by Mr. Clarke and comprising a tour of the Fens, another of Oxford and a third of London; the well-organized trips not only pinpoint the scenes of the D.L.S. crimes, but cite the book reference so that Dorothy herself can act as your guide.

For further information regarding the society, contact Mr. Clarke, Roslyn House, Witham, Essex CM8 2AQ, England.

the basis for her horror tale of an abandoned prisoner.

I did not see her again, though I read and admired her books, until 1938, when Freeman Wills Crofts took me to the annual dinner of the Detection Club in London. On that occasion, C. Day Lewis was being admitted as a new member. The club was founded in 1932 by G. K. Chesterton, who was also the first president. When I went to that dinner, E. C. Bentley was president and Dorothy L. Sayers was secretary. She was no longer slim, but her hair was still black and straight, and cut in a severe page-boy bob with a fringe. She wore a floor-length red velvet gown and long dangling gold earrings. Reluctant to recognise me when I addressed her as Dorothy and mentioned the Godolphin, she just said coldly, "Oh yes, Miss Bell?" She had not forgotten.

I had already written two books when I was invited to join the Detective Club, but I refused with regret. I was then a widow with four small children, living in Guildford, a country town thirty miles from London; above all, I was very poor and could not afford the expenses involved — though dinner at the Dorchester was not a tenth of what it would be now. It was not until after the war that I was asked again, when Julian Symons proposed me for membership. This time, I accepted with much pleasure.

Dorothy was by then president of the Detection Club. She was a little stouter than before, her hair now quite white, pleasantly waved, and her dress, of the afternoon or cocktail type, unremarkable. The club's meetings (this was 1955) were held monthly during the winter, in one room of a house in a narrow lane behind Regent's Street. The room really belonged to a firm whose offices occupied the rest of that floor of the house. Here I was accepted into the club, and this time Dorothy had no difficulty in recognising me as a member of her old school.

She had given up writing detective stories by then and was wholly occupied in religious works and interests. She was an excellent talker, a very clever woman, and could be kind — though more often was inclined to offend, perhaps unknowingly, though sometimes, I think, "with malice aforethought."

But in spite of all this we did continue to admire her crime books, though we laughed over her infatuation with Peter Wimsey. And we were all sad when she died, quite alone in the hall of her house, her Christmas shopping parcels beside her.

Josephine Bell is one of the founding members of the Crime Writers' Association. She served as its chairman in 1959–60.

COURTESY GODOLPHIN SCHOOL

Godolphin School, Salisbury, attended by D.L.S. and Josephine Bell.

MARGERY ALLINGHAM AND "THAT SILLY ASS"

If you're going to credit your leading man with a Cambridge education, surely you must see to it that he learns more there than knotting the old school tie. Yet when Margery Allingham first strolled Albert Campion through the Suffolk countryside in *The Crime at Black Dudley* (1929), she made him so dim-witted one could only assume he got his degree through "pull."

Campion seemed the perfect upper-class buffoon. He had too many teeth (most of them buck), a receding chin, the coloring of an albino bunny (obviously the result of wanton inbreeding), the most languid posture this side of a noodle — and a tendency to chirp, in an effete falsetto, such phrases as "Who would dream of the cunning criminal brain that lurks beneath my inoffensive exterior?"

Granted, such gentlemen are not uncommon at mystery house parties where guests scramble through trapdoors, pierce each other with fifteenth-century daggers and seek out lost documents by candlelight, but usually they ful-

Margery Allingham and her two border collies — Belle, a bitch, and Brock, a working trial champion — in the garden at D'Arcy House.

COURTESY JOYCE ALLINGHAM

fill the role of victim, not Great Detective.

What could Miss Allingham have been thinking of? Peter Wimsey, perhaps? Bertie Wooster?

Regardless, four books later she came to her senses and began the process of toning down. Where Campion had been fatuous, she made him urbane; where he had been eccentric, she made him avuncular. And the revisions worked: soon everyone, Miss Allingham included, stopped referring to the character as "that silly ass."

According to Miss Allingham's younger sister, Joyce, the smoother side of Campion was based at least in part on Philip ("Pip") Youngman Carter, Margery's husband. "I think she took Pip's sophistication for him. Marge had a terrific simple streak — not worldly at all. That was pure Pip."

Whether this is true or not, Pip did feel comfortable enough with the character to finish *Cargo of Eagles*, the book left half-completed at his wife's death in 1966, and after that to create his own adventures for the man, *Mr. Campion's Farthing* and *Mr. Campion's Quarry*.

Unlike Campion, Pip was not a Cambridge graduate. He attended the London Polyclinic, where at seventeen he made the acquaintance of Margery, a classmate who was awfully keen on Shakespeare. At the time, she wanted nothing more than to conquer her stutter and attempt the stage, preferably in one of the Bard's plays. On their first date, the young couple went to the Old Vic.

In many ways, Campion's love life paralleled Pip and Margery's. He, too, met his future wife when she was in her late teens, and he, too, had to wait six years for the wedding. His bride, Lady Amanda Fitton, had one sister and one brother, some money problems, a lovely old home, an artistic bent and a rather staggering beauty — all of which could be said about Margery herself.

Most pictures of Miss Allingham show her as an exceedingly fat, fiftyish matron. But in her youth she was the spit and image of her mother, a delicate Edwardian beauty who hired a tutor to teach her daughter how to enter a room with grace, how to sit at a piano, how to pour tea. Joyce Allingham refers to this as "Margery's un-

ALLINGHAM TRIVIA

EX LIBRIS

PHILIP & MARGERY YOUNGMAN CARTER

The bookplate (pictured) was designed by "Pip" Carter, Margery Allingham's husband. Each title in their library contained one, including *Blackerchief Dick* (the first Allingham novel and not a mystery), *The White Cottage Mystery* (the second Allingham and one she was not fond of), *The Crime at Black Dudley* (introducing Albert Campion), *Mystery Mile* (presenting Lugg and Inspector Oates), and *Sweet Danger* (featuring Lady Amanda for the first time).

fortunate early education," but the fact remains, it gave her a certain presence. And like her mother and the Lady Amanda, Margery was a knockout.

No blood, of course, was bluer than Campion's. He didn't dare breathe his real name when involved in a case lest he taint it with scandal. This led to his choosing several aliases

COURTESY JOYCE ALLINGHAM

Margery, age ten, with her mother, whom she called "Em," short for Emily.

(Campion for one, but also Mornington Dodd, Tootles Ash — from Allingham and Campion's "silly ass" period — and Hewes). Eventually, the clue is dropped that the first initial of his last name is K, but the letters that follow remain a mystery. "Kent," as in "the Duke of," might not be a bad guess, though Allingham insinuates it has even closer connections to the throne.

Neither Margery nor Pip could claim anywhere near so exalted a pedigree. Campion, however, would probably have found D'Arcy House, the Allinghams' Queen Anne residence, quite up to his standards. In a small Essex village about fifteen minutes' drive from Dorothy L. Sayers' home in Witham, D'Arcy House is the equal of any Allingham mystery manor — minus only the sliding panels and the maze. The gardens are elaborate, and Margery liked planning the flower beds. "She never actually worked in them herself," says Joyce. "She just enjoyed designing them, then letting the gardener do it."

Off to one side of the property is a large stable, built in 1816, which Margery and Pip had remodeled into a studio for themselves. Her work area was the balcony; his, the ground floor. She could peek over the oak-paneled balustrade and watch him sketch jacket designs for her books. A bell alerted them to what was transpiring in the main house: one dong meant mealtime; two, you're wanted on the telephone; three, please come say hello to the visitor; and four, stay away at all cost — pandemonium.

Even though Margery strengthened her characterization of Campion through the years, she clearly grew less interested in him. He began to appear farther and farther back in her novels, until in *Black Plumes* he disappeared entirely. In *Tiger in the Smoke,* which many consider her masterpiece, he plays such an insignificant part that when the film was made the scriptwriter left him out and the story didn't suffer.

Pip, on the other hand, never took a back seat. Without him, Joyce maintains, Margery probably would not have kept on working; he was the one who nudged her to get on with it. Joyce remembers that her sister needed constant reassurance, and that it was Pip's task to supply it. "Tis my best, isn't it?" she'd ask plaintively each time she finished a project — a rather strange bit of insecurity for her, considering she'd been writing since childhood. "The whole family scribbled," says Joyce. "Marge found it terribly dull at home until Mother presented her with a big bottle of Stephen's blue ink, a handful of paper and a nib, and Father outlined a plot for her. She rewrote it three hundred times, until she was satisfied."

From this perfectionist's hand would come Campion, hero of twenty-four cases (add two more to include Pip's stores); the spectacular redhead Amanda Fitton; Campion's thug factotum, Magersfontein Lugg; and Yard Inspectors Oates and Corkran. Ellery Queen, impressed with the cast of characters and Miss Allingham's treatment of them, included her short story "The Question Mark" in the first issue of *Ellery Queen's Mystery Magazine.*

Margery's own favorite novels were *Sweet Danger,* which introduced Amanda, and *Tiger in the Smoke,* which featured her first truly evil man. Yes, Margery, they were indeed your best.

THE IRREPROACHABLE MISS TEY

Catherine Aird

The life of Josephine Tey is as free from high drama as was that of Jane Austen.

Born in 1896, she was a member of that sad age group of young women who would almost certainly have been married but for the high death toll of the First World War. She was educated at the Anstey Physical Training College in Birmingham, England — by no means a common precursor of a literary career, though she later turned it to excellent account in her detective story *Miss Pym Disposes*. She had not been teaching long when her mother died and she relinquished her job, returning to Inverness to look after her father. Here she stayed uneventfully until her last illness and death on 13 February 1952, at the early age of fifty-five.

She began her writing with some verse, then turned to short stories and to the small literary competitions in the distinguished weeklies that were a prominent feature of the publishing scene in the twenties and thirties. Finally she entered a larger competition run by the English publisher Methuen. Her winning entry — *The Man in the Queue*, written, it is said, in a fortnight — was published in 1929 under the first of her two pseudonyms: Gordon Daviot. (The other was, of course, Josephine Tey. Her real name was Elizabeth Mackintosh.)

Despite this success, she abandoned the detective genre to write two straight novels, *Kif — An Unvarnished History* and *The Expensive Halo*, and to script three plays: *Richard of Bordeaux, Queen of Scots, The Laughing Woman*.

Seven years after her first detective story, she published another, *A Shilling for Candles*, using the pseudonym Josephine Tey for the first

time but bringing back Detective Alan Grant, who had made his debut in her initial effort. Having returned to the form, she again moved away and demonstrated remarkable versatility by writing *Claverhouse*, a scholarly biography of the Scottish leader, and a three-act play based on the Old Testament character Joseph.

It was not until after the Second World War that detective stories came once more from her pen. Probably the best known (it was filmed)

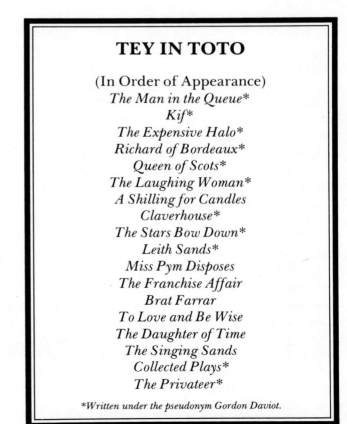

TEY IN TOTO

(In Order of Appearance)
*The Man in the Queue**
*Kif**
*The Expensive Halo**
*Richard of Bordeaux**
*Queen of Scots**
*The Laughing Woman**
A Shilling for Candles
*Claverhouse**
*The Stars Bow Down**
*Leith Sands**
Miss Pym Disposes
The Franchise Affair
Brat Farrar
To Love and Be Wise
The Daughter of Time
The Singing Sands
*Collected Plays**
*The Privateer**

Written under the pseudonym Gordon Daviot.

The National Gallery portrait of Richard III (1452–85) that so intrigued Inspector Grant in The Daughter of Time. *The artist is unknown.*

NATIONAL PORTRAIT GALLERY

is *The Franchise Affair,* a fictional presentation of the famous Canning case. Elizabeth Canning was a young woman who in 1753 vanished from her home and reappeared some four weeks later, declaring she had been kidnapped and held prisoner against her will. She said she had been ill-used by an old woman and compelled to live an immoral life by being starved in an upper room. All England was divided on whether Elizabeth Canning was innocent; it was a *cause cé-lebre,* and her trial for perjury lasted eight days.

Aficionados will find the immediate link with *Franchise* and be left in little confusion about what Tey believed. Betty Kane (and it seems to me the reader was meant quite early on to align Kane not only with Canning but with Cain) was evil.

Brat Farrar is, I think, my own favourite Tey, and a real tour de force. Here there is no Alan Grant as detective. The centre of interest is shared between Brat Farrar himself and Beatrice Ashby, to whose house he comes. The author in this work epitomizes all that is good in detective fiction: excellent writing, the strictest fair play with the reader, sound plotting, characters that are well-drawn without being exaggerated, and a complete absence of tub-thump-

ing for any class, creed or cause. (She also shows a wide knowledge of horses and racing.)

Understatement is the keynote to Josephine Tey's writing. There is great delicacy about *To Love and Be Wise,* which is on the surface a detective story but is also a careful study of the faces of love. Though revenge via transvestism constitutes the plot, that nutshell does not convey the sensitive overtones: the clues are very neat indeed.

The Daughter of Time, published in 1951, is responsible for much of the widespread and continuing interest in the Murder of the Two Little Princes in the Tower. The novel was a stone thrown into a pool whose ripples, nearly thirty years later, are still lapping their way through the library shelves marked "History." Looking back, it becomes easier to see how this important detective story came to be written. Its author was a practised writer of detective fiction as well as a skilled and knowledgeable student of history. It is fitting that this consummation of the two arts should have been the last of her books published in her lifetime.

Tey's detective novels were few both in number and in relation to her total output as a writer. The first, *The Man in the Queue,* was in many ways the least skilled. It did, though, feature the theatrical background that obviously intrigued her. Detective Alan Grant's entree to the rather rarefied world of theatrical stars was his friendship with Miss Marta Hallard. It would be fair to describe Grant, a policeman, and Hallard, an actress, as "just good friends." No hint of anything so definite as entanglement appears in their relationship, nothing even so positive as the time-honoured phrase "old flame." In fact, on several occasions — one with the charming Viscountess Kentallen in *The Singing Sands* — Grant is full of sound reasons for not marrying. It could be a case of "Methinks he doth protest too much," but I rather doubt it.

Josephine Tey gave us a very real world, a world in which the reader can believe. Her death leaves those who cherish her works still lamenting its untimeliness and wondering what else might have come from her pen had she lived.

Catherine Aird is the author of eight mysteries; the most recent is Some Died Eloquent.

THE DEVIOUS MIND OF RUTH RENDELL

Ruth Rendell gets away with committing the most heinous crimes by couching them in deceptively mild prose. If any other writer cracked up a minister's car, invited wasps to a birthday party, inflicted an eye hemorrhage on a chief inspector, strangled one young woman in an open field, bludgeoned another in a forest and let a third come to a dismal end at a rock concert, critics would insist she'd taken instruction at James Hadley Chase's knee. With Rendell, they draw analogies to Christie.

She is a master of the final twist and the last-page surprise. Yet she says, "It bothers me when people compare me to Christie. I think she was superficial." She's a bit more taciturn when aligned with Tey, but really yearns to be mentioned in the same breath with Patricia Highsmith and Julian Symons. And, in fact, half the time she deserves to be. The other half? Well, indeed she can be a Christie write-alike.

It all depends on which Rendell you happen to pick up. Her Wexford series falls into the classic English mold, what with the Chief Inspector and Burden mulling over clues and motives while downing a pint at the Olive and the Dove, Wexford quoting from books with the erudition of a Cambridge Lit. major, and both of them maneuvering through the stately elms of the Sussex countryside.

Her non-Wexfords, however, are more complex, with enough pathology to interest Freud. She refers to them as having "a rich texture," implying they are character studies of obsessed personalities. To read them is to delve into Krafft-Ebing territory. They're a bit on the kinky side, and guaranteed to disturb anybody who had planned on settling down with a Poirot figure for an hour or two.

Though these suspense chillers now predominate, Miss Rendell is not yet ready to dunk

Wexford in the Reichenbach. She says she has one regret about him: "Had I given it any thought when I introduced him in *From Doon with Death,* I wouldn't have made him so old. I would have started him out at about fifteen, so he could've gone on forever. My son once told me he thought Wexford was my father. I told him he might be right; I could see the similarities."

If that's true, it follows that Miss Rendell's dad was a highly moral man, bookish — a bit of an intellectual — and unfortunately rather humorless. He also favored gray double-breasted suits that needed a good pressing, gained weight as he grew older and lost his hair as he added pounds. He was not an attractive man (his wrinkled gray skin would look right at home on an elephant), but his daughter — Sheila, in Wexford's case — bore him a strong resemblance, and she was considered the local beauty. And if Wexford and Rendell *père* are, in fact, interchangeable, then the latter was so reserved hardly anyone dared call him by his first name — if, indeed, they even knew it.

Miss Rendell admits to being a devoted Simenon fan (she taught herself French by reading the Maigret novels in the original), and she, too, has made her inspector a keen student of human nature. Like Maigret, Wexford tries to arrive at a psychological portrait of his prey; he builds up his case, little foible by little revealing foible. Mostly, he seems to come into contact with domestic squabbles carried to the nth degree — murder.

Burden, his assistant, turns out to be just that. When his wife dies, he virtually goes round the bend, indulging in an extended orgy of self-pity. Even the tolerant Wexford snappishly concludes the wrong person may have been taken. He also gets himself involved with the mother of a missing child *(No More Dying Then),* a situation that Wexford deals with via the ostrich-and-sand method. The Chief Inspector has firm rules about mingling with suspects: One simply doesn't, and if one can't help oneself, then one resigns. By pretending he knew nothing of the affair, he was able to keep Burden on staff — a funny kind of duplicity for Wexford to engage in, given the illogic of it, but apparently the only way he knew to handle it.

Wexford's marriage is more placid than his clients', for sure, but surprisingly it's the one area in which he plays it close to the chest. His wife never hears of his cases; he never brings his work problems home. Perhaps that's why Dr. Crocker has to write him out prescriptions for hypertension.

The Rendell suspense *oeuvre,* on the other hand, zeroes in on family relationships. The plot of *One Down, Two Across* hinges on a mother-in-law's distaste for her son-in-law, the son-in-law's envy of her bank balance, and the daughter-wife's acting as drudge for both. In *The Secret House of Death,* a divorcée whose husband left her for another woman becomes enmeshed in the lives of an equally dissatisfied couple, which culminates in her discovering the body of the wife and her lover.

In a Rendell novel, a couple is not a happy thing to be.

In her private life, it's had some bad moments, too. Says she: "I married the same man twice. We were separated four or five years inbetween." Now, however, it is he who reads her books before they go to her editor and offers comments on them. "My husband's view is generally the one my editor will take. It's remarkable, really."

With several exceptions, Miss Rendell is very proud of her output. "In my twenties, I wrote some very bad short stories which were rejected. I still have some of them, but I shall leave instructions to my son to burn them after I'm gone. And I hate my third novel, *In Sickness and in Health.* I think it's a silly book and that the protagonist is a stupid woman. She's thirty-eight years old, and pregnant, and doesn't know it, and thinks her husband is trying to poison her. I would never write that now. I'm ashamed of it."

Only one disaster in nineteen attempts is a pretty clean record, and it's offset by a recent Gold Dagger award for her documentation of a psychopath, *A Demon in My View.* If you haven't yet read it, be warned: Just as there are some movies too scary to see alone, there are some books that should not be read if no one else is in the house. Miss Rendell confesses, "I'm a very intense person." Would you expect her characters to be otherwise?

MUST-READS

Not so long ago, the mystery reader's version of a pilgrimage to Mecca was a stopover at London's Charing Cross Road. The fan journeyed there hoping to find bookstore upon bookstore upon bookstore teeming with mystery titles by authors who used S's instead of Z's, periods outside the parens, character names such as Hermione and Olive, and civilized plots incorporating a barrister, a nanny, a don, an inclement Royal. These books would all have been written between the Great War and the Battle of Britain, would be mustily attired in a yellow Gollancz dust wrapper or a green-and-white Penguin Stripe, and would rarely cost more than 25p. The assumption, of couse, was that if one poked long enough around a Charing Cross secondhand shop, one would spy a Sayers, an Allingham or a Tey that had never been published in the States.

Alas — and you may need a bracing cup of tea before you hear this — things have come to such a sorry state that with the exception of the behemoth Foyles and the bedraggled Pooles, it's virtually impossible to find a bookstore (let alone a book) at the former readers' paradise.

The hunt is on: Where *do* readers go to find new titles by old favorites? Since 1972, when Murder Ink first opened its garage door, approximately fifteen mystery bookstores have sprung up — in such non-English locations as Paris, Toronto, Milwaukee, Philadelphia, Chicago, Boston, Providence, Seattle, and Sherman Oaks, California. The Grande Dame, indisputably, is the East Coast's Murder Ink®; the Heiress Apparent, the West Coast's Scene of the Crime™. Still, even Carol Brener and Ruth Windfeldt, respective owners of the two shops, cannot stock what is nonexistent. They warn that you must make your peace with the fact that dead authors, no matter how inventive they were in life, have yet to discover a method of publishing new works in the Hereafter. You

Mrs. Newgate Callendar, having read a sensational novel, grows hysterical and tears her hair after the manner of first-class heroines.

simply must resign yourself to this. Or make a career out of rereading your old standbys.

Can anyone replace the old standbys? Well, it's possible you may have overlooked a talent or two. Herewith, a list of underappreciated must-reads for the devout Anglophile.

Have you ever heard of Mary Kelly? Miss Kelly is the antithesis of the crank-em-out-one-a-month school. Her slim output, under a dozen titles, includes the impeccable *Spoilt Kill,* which won a Crime Writers' award in 1961. Miss Kelly created Inspector Nightingale, married him to a singer, set him loose among misbehaving students at the University of Edinburgh. She can jangle your nerves with the best of them.

Staying up north for the moment, we bump into Janet Caird, another trouble-in-the-

TWENTY REASONS NOT TO TRUST AN ENGLISHWOMAN

1. She'll escort you down the tube.
2. She'll drown you in tea.
3. She'll knit you an ascot with a bloodstain on it.
4. She'll bludgeon you with a frozen leg of lamb, then overcook the evidence.
5. She'll serve you porridge with the bitter aftertaste of almonds.
6. She'll transform you into mulch.
7. She'll hire Mrs. Danvers to look after you.
8. She'll ask you to redeem the family jewels — from the Tower.
9. She'll invite you for a quiet country weekend, then surround you with ten of your dearest enemies.
10. She'll tell you to mind your head when the real imperative is to watch your step.
11. She'll insist you take a constitutional in the fog.
12. She'll demand that you drive on the wrong side of the road.
13. She'll auction you off at Christie's.
14. She'll turn on your gas fire but neglect to light the jet.
15. She'll push you off the white cliffs of Dover.
16. She'll book you a one-way ticket on the 4.50 to Paddington.
17. She'll stiffen your upper lip with her brolly tip.
18. She'll swear to you she's a duchess — but in a Cockney accent.
19. She'll defame you in the Agony Column.
20. She'll abandon you at Left Luggage.

quadrangle writer, also familiar with the dark underside to heather. Small border towns with a preponderance of rocks are her specialty, and she makes them so treacherous you'll yearn for the comparative tranquillity of Times Square.

E. C. R. Lorac, who has enough initials to invite H. R. F. Keating over for a bowl of alphabet soup, sometimes dogs the footsteps of Scottish Chief Inspector Robert Macdonald, sometimes frequents London town houses and sometimes scampers about pastoral Devon with murder on her mind. Detective fiction purists will find Miss Lorac's classic style amenable to their taste. She doesn't loiter in the Freudian murk.

If you've not yet opened a Georgette

Heyer, a treat is in store. No one furnishes a statelier home, or sneaks in more of that ultra-dry British humor. Her refinements include scandalously bad sportsmanship at the bridge table (*Duplicate Death*), a locked-room puzzle for Christmas (*Envious Casca*) and mysterious comings-and-goings at an abandoned priory (*Footsteps in the Dark*). She throws a terrific house party, probably as good as Allingham's.

Mary Fitt is equally at home in the Manor House. She crowds it with suspects and landscapes in fog, and you better be careful — isn't that a maze over there? Of course. Inspector Mallett handles her confrontation scenes, coming to them armed with Dr. Fitzbrown's scientific evidence. The two are invincible. A little dull maybe, but isn't that the English way?

Ellis Peters, with *Death and the Joyful Woman* (1961), provided the perfect answer to the frequently asked: Has anything good been written since the thirties? Kid sleuth Dominic Felse is so appealing that you'll want to adopt him. Even while holidaying on the Subcontinent (*Death to the Landlords!*), he makes time for whodunit work. Other cases are handled by his dad, a C.I.D. man, and in one instance (*The Grass Widow's Tale*) his mum.

Mostly, Sara Woods stays within the well-appointed confines of the Queen's courts. Her barrister, Antony Maitland, appears in all her Shakespearean-titled tales. No lip is stiffer than his, no continuing character better connected: his uncle, Sir Nicholas, is a baronet, which doesn't stop him from perambulating the moors for clues in Tony's company. Mrs. Woods is as inventive at trial situations as Erle Stanley Gardner — but a bit more formal.

Gwendoline Butler has investigated Oxford (circa late 1800's), Malta and other outposts dear to the Anglophile's heart. She has wandered Upstairs, Downstairs, and in the M.P.'s chambers. She is particularly fond of girls — though her series sleuth is a male, Inspector Coffin — and giggles them through the schoolyard, the drawing room and mayhem. Butler at her best: *A Coffin for Pandora*.

Dorothy Dunnett (two N's, two T's, please) is partial to aesthetic plots. Artists and opera stars exchange bon mots while the bodies pile up on the floor. Once, she ventured to Canada to pull a nanny caper, but it's more usual for her to hang out among the explosively creative types on mysterydom's most bloodied isle. Nonpretentiously literate, that's Dunnett. A Dorothy L. Sayers without the airs. Witty, too.

Margaret Yorke, more power to her, has managed to squeeze one more tutoring sleuth into the congestion called Oxford. Dr. Patrick Grant is well-suited to Academia, fitting right in with his late grading, his floor-to-ceiling books, his vaguely preoccupied gaze. If only he could get his sister to stop fussing. Regardless, one hopes he never takes a sabbatical.

Joyce Porter may claim the distinction of having created a sleuth with the brains of Watson, the belly of Gideon Fell and the teeth of Mortimer Snerd. Inspector Wilfred Dover, Scotland Yard's poorest, excels at free-loading, overeating and fumbling the case. Strangely, he's wonderfully funny, and brings new meaning to the term anti-hero. Miss Porter has also concocted his female equivalent, the eminently likable — though no less obnoxious — Constance Ethel Morrison-Burke. The "Hon. Con." speaks illy of the lower classes. Both a snob and a bully, she proves humor in the mystery is not dead.

If only Pamela Branch had written more! The woman was a genius at skewing English foibles. She made tea sandwiches unsafe to eat, held intimate little gatherings unhealthy to attend. And she did it all with an insouciant touch, a bit of devilment. Not many authors can combine elegance with a poke in the ribs and make you sit still for it. Pamela Branch could.

Unfortunately, several of these must-reads have passed out of print (E. C. R. Lorac, Mary Fitt, Pamela Branch), some are not in paperback (Mary Kelly, Sara Woods, Joyce Porter) and some are just now making the transatlantic crossing (Margaret Yorke, Dorothy Dunnett). That's where the mystery specialty shops come in. Most of them offer a "search service": you leave your request, name and address, and when the book turns up they notify you. It happens more often than you might think. Meanwhile, try the library. But skip the trip to Charing Cross Road — unless you're planning on going there to open a mystery bookstore, in which case we'll be right over.

THE BEST AMERICA HAS TO OFFER

If authors were always as talented as their dust-jacket blurbs claim, they'd all have a letter from the Pulitzer committee framed on their wall, a ticket to Stockholm in their pocket, a scroll from the National Book Awards people hanging over their typewriter, a small bust of Edgar Allan Poe (from the Mystery Writers of America) decorating their mantel, and a gold dagger (from the English Crime Writers' Association) paperweighting their blotter. They'd also surely have a series under development with a major TV network, a script about to be filmed for *Masterpiece Theatre* and Alfred Hitchcock bidding for the rights to their complete output.

THE INDEFATIGABLE CHARACTER

Dame Adela Beatrice Lestrange Bradley has appeared in 50 Gladys Mitchell books.

Daphne Wrayne crops up in 46 Mark Cross titles.

Maud Silver sleuths through 32 Patricia Wentworth novels.

Not quite so tireless are Stuart Palmer's Hildegarde Withers (17 titles), Ben Sarto's Miss Otis (18) and Leslie Ford's Grace Latham (15).

They all have a way to go, however, before they catch up with Carolyn Wells' Fleming Stone. He's shown up 61 times (frankly, once would have been enough).

Clearly, this is not the case. What, then, are we to make of the book cover quote that heralds Miss So-and-So as the most innovative crime writer since 1841? If we're wise, we remember this is only the opinion of the person quoted. We're allowed to be skeptical: after all, it did not come down the mountain with Moses.

Cynics insist that endorsements can be "bought," that is, coaxed from a famous friend who owes a favor to the author or publisher. Sometimes, the cynics are right. There are three or four caper writers who routinely admire each other's work, and for a long time they shared the same agent and the same poker table.

On the other hand, accolades can be bona fide and still gull the reader. One West Coast novelist of the hard-boiled school produces a quote only if he's genuinely liked the book. The problem is, he has yet to compliment a work similar to his own. When browsers spot his name championing an author they've never heard of, however, they leap to the conclusion the two share common themes and styles. Wrong.

But what about the enthusiastic hosanna from a book reviewer? Well, it's only fair to say that the Podunk *Weekly* and the Metropolitan *Daily* have different standards. It may well be that Podunk's coincides with yours, whereas the more prestigious paper's does not. This is the "critic's darling" vs. "reader's pet" controversy.

A few years back, a fat spy novel was garnering all the positive adjectives in the *Thesaurus.* Not only did the book receive flamboyantly loving reviews, but the author merited lengthy interviews in which reporters concluded if he'd been born sooner, the wheel and sliced bread would have been invented much earlier. Readers flocked to bookstores and the magnum opus landed on the best-seller lists, where it stayed for months. Sound like this was one instance in which the critics and public concurred? Then what do you make of the shopkeeper who was taking an inventory and happened to notice that her remaining copies (all from the same printing) were misbound, and that approximately thirty-five pages had been omitted? Since not one purchaser came by for a refund or a new copy, her conclusion was: They never got that far; they bought the book, but didn't finish it. The "critic's darling" is often for the coffee table, sad to say, not the night table.

This same shopkeeper, by the way, was also flabbergasted when readers would pop in for "that book mentioned in the *Daily* last week," after the paper had slaughtered it. From this she deduced that people forget the content of a review — whether it was pro or con — and only recall that a certain title was discussed.

"Reader's pets" rarely get idolatrous reviews; usually they're brushed off in a sentence or two, with a "nice job," "typical handling" or "neat twist at the end." This does not deter the "pet's" fans who'd search out their manuscripts if they were reduced to printing and mailing them from their basement.

The "pets" who come in for the most abuse are those specializing in damsels with perpetual distress. Even their fans are cruel to them in public. If they're caught reading Rae Foley or Barbara Michaels, they swear they found the book on the subway or their godmother left it at their house. What's happened is, the newsboys have made them ashamed to admit what they like. That's silly. If you can walk around with Spillane in your back pocket, you ought to be able to carry Phyllis Whitney in your purse — without a blush.

One of the book clubs has an unwritten law concerning a specific "pet": Anything she submits, they take, even if they've skimmed it and don't much care for it. She has established her audience — who'll clamor for the new title, second-rate though it may be.

Does a "reader's pet" ever overlap a "critic's darling"? Yes and no. Emma Lathen comes to mind. The Misses Lathen appeal to both, as does P. D. James. But if we discount them, who else is there? It's difficult to find writers intellectual enough to please the reviewers and interesting

THE DOUBLE NOMINEE

In 1967, the Mystery Writers of America nominated six books for best mystery of the year. Two of them, *The Gift Shop* and *Lemon in the Basket,* were by Charlotte Armstrong. Nobody before or since has duplicated her feat. She did not, however, win. The Edgar went to Donald E. Westlake for *God Save the Mark.* The other candidates were Dick Francis' *Flying Finish*, George Baxt's *A Parade of Cockeyed Creatures* and Ira Levin's *Rosemary's Baby.*

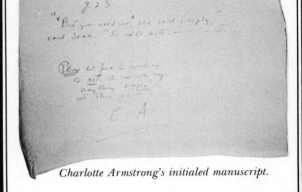

Charlotte Armstrong's initialed manuscript.

enough to satisfy the public.

Bearing in mind that any attempt to list the best America has to offer boils down to the purely subjective (and, in this case, wishful thinking), the editor of *Murderess Ink* commends to you the following.

The Bellamy Trial by Frances Noyes Hart, published in 1927 and based on the Hall-Mills murder, in which a woman and her married lover were accused of killing his wife, who thoughtlessly objected to their affair when she found out about it. This is the courtroom drama to end all courtroom dramas, as documented by a pair of reporters (male and female). And frankly, when the defendants take the stand, they prove so ingratiating you'd consider having a bit of a romance with one of them yourself.

WHO IS LANGE LEWIS?

Jacques Barzun and Wendell H. Taylor, coauthors of *Catalogue of Crime*, were asked to name their favorite women writers. They jointly cited Ngaio Marsh, Ruth Rendell, Dorothy L. Sayers and — Lange Lewis, about whom you probably know absolutely nothing.

Lewis penned five books: *Murder Among Friends; Meat for Murder; Juliet Dies Twice; The Birthday Murder; The Passionate Victims.* Series character Richard Tuck appears in all of them.

When asked to justify his choice of Lewis, Barzun replied, "She writes compactly — that's a great point. She has a fine sense of drama. Her characters (after her first effort) are well conceived, not out of the common stock. Her plots are simple and strong, clues fair and sufficient for Lt. Tuck to work with. And she does not go in for the props of domesticity and 'woman's world' to furnish out her novels. Her excellent women types are the equals of men and often their superiors. Will that do?"

Other Barzun favorites were M. V. Heberden and Patricia McGerr. Taylor, in a listing he preferred we keep alphabetical, also admired Margery Allingham, Christianna Brand, Agatha Christie, Elizabeth Daly, Emma Lathen and Josephine Tey.

Death of a Doll by Hilda Lawrence, published in 1947 and featuring Mark East, a personable New Yorker who also appears in two other superb Lawrence works, *Blood Upon the Snow* and *A Time to Die*. This time his task is to unravel who murdered whom and why at a staid woman's residence, which is similar in many respects to the Barbizon Hotel, where gentlemen are not allowed above the main floor and boarders all hail from out of town and have more than a fair share of naïveté. Miss Lawrence only wrote four books, then stopped. If you haven't read at least two of them, consider yourself deprived.

In the Last Analysis by Amanda Cross, published in 1964 and introducing English professor Kate Fansler to the crime field. (Kate has surfaced four times since.) There is enough of the "literary" about *Analysis* to make one think Dorothy L. Sayers has come back to life, this time with a sense of humor. Cross, blessedly, leavens her quotations with wit. This particular plot hinges on Kate's absolving a chum of a murder charge, and fans of the academic mystery (as well as patients on the analytic couch) will delight in the author's slyness.

Beginning with a Bash by Alice Tilton, published in 1937 and from the same mind (Phoebe Atwood Taylor's) that brought you the Asey Mayo Cape Cod stories. *Bash* pits schoolteacher Witherall, "Bill Shakespeare," against the bludgeoner of Professor North, and if ever an author could make you die laughing, it's Tilton. She's one of the few writers, male or female, English or American, who can romp through a murder without slighting it.

If there is a leitmotif running through these four books, it's humor, from the subtle (*Bellamy* and *Doll*) to the dry (*Analysis*) to the outrageous (*Bash*). Readers who prefer their mysteries "straight," without a chuckle or two, should turn to the pages of Charlotte Armstrong (particularly that little gem, *Mischief*) and to any of Margaret Scherf's Martin Buell tales (solid sleuthwork by a clergyman). If you're the type who prefers torment and anguish (both your own and the characters'), Elizabeth Sanxay-Holding will prove suitably devious, and if you'd rather a case of the Had-I-But-Known regrets, there is nothing even vaguely comparable to Mabel Seeley's *The Listening House*, her first effort in the genre. And lest we forget, there's Constance and Gwenyth Little for charm, Holly Roth for the housewife's dilemma and Patricia McGerr for the lady spy.

And that ought to keep you in trouble for a while.

THE MYSTERY FUNNYBONE: CRAIG RICE

How many authors can claim a President of the United States as a fan? In the thick of World War II, Craig Rice received a letter on official White House stationery. "Thank you for taking my mind off my troubles for an evening," it said, and was signed Franklin Delano Roosevelt. Typical of Craig, she bragged about it for days, then lost it.

She was the first woman mystery writer to earn a *Time* magazine cover story, the first to have her own mystery magazine produced (*Crime Digest*) and the only one to ghost a dedication to herself (George Sanders' *Crime on My Hands,* which she wrote for him, includes the tribute: "For Craig Rice, without whom this book would not have been possible").

Under the Rice by-line she penned one Gothic (*Telefair*), one true crime book (*45 Murderers*) and eighteen wacky mysteries. In *The Right Murder,* she invented the characters Michael Venning and Daphne Sanders and later appropriated their names as pseudonyms, using Venning three times and Sanders once. She wrote two crime novels for her good friend Gypsy Rose Lee (*The G-String Murders; Mother Finds a Body*), moonlighted by churning out soaps while she covered the crime beat for a Chicago newspaper, scripted two *Falcon* films, created reams of serious poetry and took copious notes on the Wisconsin pioneers for a novel she never found time to write.

She also tried her hand at one children's serial. "It appeared on the pillow, a page a night," says Iris Follows Metcalf, the middle child of Craig's three. "It was perfectly delightful, about three kids who happened to have our names, Nancy, Iris and David, and who went to purchase a purple jackrabbit for their mum, accompanied by a cross-eyed bear called Gladly. It was full of her outrageous puns, but it was also a lesson for us. My sister was then going through a phase when she'd take everything too seriously, too precisely. So, in one part of the story, we reached the Land of Literal-Mindedness, where if someone said, 'I'll be with you in a minute,' everybody else timed her on the clock. It was Craig's way of telling Nancy to ease up. I don't remember how the thing ended, and unknowing twits that we were, we'd read it every night and just throw it away."

Home Sweet Homicide, Craig's tenth mystery, was loosely based on her family. The character Dinah is Nancy, April is Iris and Archie is David. (The movie version gave the role of lady novelist to Lynn Barry.) "We knew she was writing about us and made suggestions as she went along," says Iris. "Some, she even used."

Craig and her first grandchild.

COURTESY IRIS FOLLOWS METCALF

EDITORIAL APPROVAL

Lee Wright

I accepted the manuscript of *Eight Faces at Three,* Craig Rice's first book, on the basis of fifty pages and found out later that it had been turned down by some twelve publishers. What foolish people there are in the world! The word for Craig's work — and no other word so exactly fits its overwhelming character — is "lovable." Her people were so appealing that even Craig had the devil's own time selecting the murderer. I remember one particular case that prompted me to write indignantly, "You can't have X as a murderer. He's a darling. Unfortunately, I can't think of any character in the book who isn't." And Craig proved her versatility by inserting a brand-new character into the manuscript, which she managed with consummate ease and which made me and everybody else very happy.

After four, or five, or six books starring her famous trio (Helene and Jake Justus, and Malone, an extraordinarily gifted lawyer who does his best work "under the influence," which is most of the time), she invented a new pair who were just as beguiling and amusing: Bingo and Handsome. Bingo was one of those street photographers who take your picture as you walk down the avenue, then run after you, saying, "Give me twenty-five cents and your address, and I'll mail you the picture." Handsome was a perfectly beautiful young man, unfortunately with an IQ in numbers so low they had not been invented yet. He had one tremendous gift in addition to his beauty: a prodigious memory that was entirely visual. Handsome could remember the page of the New York *Times* on which a given story had appeared and could summon it at will by closing his eyes and projecting his mind (what there was of it) to that page and quote precisely what the reviewer or reporter had written. This gift, together with Bingo's street-smart wit, made the two a great detective team, and Craig involved them in hilariously funny murders. That was *her* gift. She could manage humor without damaging suspense. And that is a unique trick.

She had no one way of attacking her books. They sprang from someone she'd met, or an object she'd seen. Once, at a nightclub, she saw the bass fiddler's instrument case and said to her companion, "Wouldn't that be a great way to carry a dead body out of a nightclub?" When he pointed out that it was too small, she said wistfully, "A child, perhaps?" And when he answered, "You know you can't kill a child, the readers won't stand for it," she thought for a moment. Then she said hopefully, "A small adult?" And thus was born *The Big Midget Murders,* one of her most successful books.

The work of Craig Rice can be summed up in this paragraph of the Detroit *News*: "Like Caesar, Craig Rice is able to do three things all at the same time: write very well, be tremendously funny, and still guide her plot to a logical conclusion."

We shall not see her like again.

Lee Wright is currently an editorial consultant to Harlequin Books.

THE LUCKY STIFF

E. T. Guymon, Jr.

Craig Rice, the one and only Craig Rice. I wrote to her in 1939, when her first book came out, and we became instant friends. We did not actually meet, however, until 1941, when she moved to Santa Monica from Chicago. She was living then with her third husband, Lawrence Lipton, and her three children, Nancy, Iris and David.

In 1948, about a year after her divorce from Lipton, she met and began going with Henry (Hank) DeMott, a good-looking personable young man somewhat her junior. They would drop by our San Diego home for a drink on their frequent trips to and from Tijuana, and during one of these visits Craig announced she was going to marry Hank. At the same time, she asked me what I was going to give her for a wedding present. Somewhat taken aback, I replied, "What do you want, Craig?" She said, "I want to be married in your library," and I said, "Sold!"

What a wedding it was! When she told me she had previously been married by a Protestant minister, a Catholic priest and a Jewish rabbi, I immediately suggested a judge. My good friend Gordon Thompson, presiding judge of the Superior Court, was delighted to perform the ceremony. Craig wanted me to give her away, and Hank wanted me to act as best man. Judge Thompson said he saw no reason why I should not perform both functions.

Came the day of the wedding, April 30, 1948, scheduled for 8:30 P.M. Hank and his parents had stayed at a hotel. Craig was our house guest. How she loved publicity and how she got it!

For twenty-four hours, the telephone had rung, telegrams had poured in and the press clamored to attend. Only a small group, about a dozen people, were present at the actual ceremony.

At that time, I was walking with the help of a cane because of a knee injury, but I managed to hobble along and deliver Craig to Hank. Then I stepped around, became best man and was able to hand Hank the ring without fumbling. Throughout the ceremony, Craig carried a black book that everyone assumed was a prayer book. Actually, it was a copy of her own *The Lucky Stiff* without its dust jacket. At the conclusion of the ceremony, Craig autographed copies of *Stiff* for the guests and we adjourned to the dining room. There the cake was cut, champagne flowed, the couple was toasted and flash bulbs popped. The layer cake, by the way, was crowned with a dove, but around the base was a solid row of little ivory skulls.

COURTESY E. T. GUYMON, JR.

Craig Rice. So brilliant, so unpredictable, so much fun, so warm-hearted and, finally, so tragic. I loved her very much.

E. T. Guymon, Jr., is a member of the Editorial Board of the Mystery Library.

Craig's typewriter and a few cookie crumbs shared the kitchen table. While she was thinking, she tatted and chain-smoked Kools. During the war, when cigarettes were hard to get, people sent her packs of Luckies and Camels, which she put in a box with menthol crystals so they'd taste more like her brand.

According to her daughter, Craig "could write almost as fast as she could type." All she needed for inspiration was a low bank balance. Since at various times she supported three children and *their* children, a brother and several husbands (past, present and future), she was always working on a novel or a new short story. Most of her correspondence to her agent began: "Can you get me an advance and how soon?" Only in the year or so before her death (caused by a degenerative muscle disease and compounded by alcoholism) did she slow down. Left unfinished when she died in 1957 was *The April Robin Murders,* which her agent funneled to another of his clients, Ed McBain; since Craig kept no outlines, McBain's major problem was figuring out whodunit.

Craig's work has been described as detective farce, screwball mystery, nutty caper. She herself has been called witty, daffy, corny and hard-boiled. Actually, her books — not to mention her life style — belong to the Elliot Paul (*Hugger-Mugger in the Louvre*) and the Hecht-McArthur (*The Front Page*) school.

Her best-known novel repertory company was stocked with John J. Malone, a criminal lawyer who thought nothing of tampering with a jury if the occasion arose (and it did); Jake Justus, a freewheeling job-hopper who started out as a reporter, became a press agent, wound up as owner of the Casino nightclub and on the sly tried a little mystery writing (Craig had her editor, Lee Wright, declare that his *Mongoose Murders* was unpublishable); Helene Justus, a truly rotten driver who, thank God, was rich enough to have a chauffeur (Butch, who, thank God, rarely let her at the wheel); Daniel von Flanagan, an Irish cop who added the *von* to his name because he hated stereotypes; Max Hood, a Chicago gangster who changed the décor in his apartment from pink froufrou to Mexican serape to Louis XII through XVI; and Joseph Di Angelo, a.k.a. Joe the Angel, who was part

AUTHOR CRAIG RICE
Successful murder still requires imagination.
(*Books*)

Craig was the first mystery writer to make the cover of Time, *in 1946. Two of her novels,* Trial by Fury *(1941) and* Home Sweet Homicide *(1944), form part of the Haycraft-Queen Cornerstones of Detective Fiction list.*

pimp, part psychiatrist, part bookie, part gossip columnist (i.e., saloonkeeper, at the City Hall Bar).

J.J., Jake and Helene formed a hilarious triumvirate, always getting their man, though often by the pub crawler's route — the three of them drank more than anyone on record, except maybe Craig Rice.

In *The People vs. Withers and Malone,* J.J. had a new partner: tropical fish enthusiast Hildegarde Withers. Spinster Withers, of course, was the creation of Stuart Palmer, one of Craig's closest friends. Apparently, the two authors collaborated by sitting down and plotting out the stories, then sending Palmer off to write them.

The most fun Craig had, confides her daughter, was in thinking up her titles. Some of the best are *The Corpse Steps Out, Having Wonderful Crime, My Kingdom for a Hearse* and *Trial by Fury.* We suggest you read them all. And have a good belly laugh.

ELIZABETH DALY: AGATHA CHRISTIE'S FAVORITE WRITER

Lenore Glen Offord

When Agatha Christie sat down to read a mystery, whose pages was she turning? Elizabeth Daly's. Not one of us Daly enthusiasts would quarrel with the choice, but we have to guess at the dear Dame's reasons.

Both she and Miss Daly were gentlewomen, writing about the social stratum they knew best; both had chief characters combating evil in nonviolent ways; both were excellent plotters and surprisers.

The same, however, could be said of a number of other writers, so there must have been something extra that tipped the balance in Miss Daly's favor. Something besides the period ambience, the intellectual sleuth, the intricate caseload. In a word, this extra quality was charm. Miss Daly virtually preempted it as a mystery commodity.

Come. Let us ring the Gamadges' doorbell and rediscover it.

We are somewhere in Manhattan's East Sixties, on a quiet street with trees that cast rather dangerous shadows if one is walking alone at night in the middle of a murder investigation. We are facing an attractive old house, three-storied, built of brick but painted gray, with white trim. Miniature dry fountains now used as planters flank the front door (once, one provided a foothold for a criminal breaking into

Gamadge's office). The house has a settled aspect, an inviting one, as though generations of a single family had enjoyed it for years — which, in fact, they have. It belonged to Henry Gamadge's grandfather, and Gamadge himself was born here about 1907. In the room that was once Grandfather's library, at the rear of the house, are tall windows that overlook a small garden adjoining the premises of Gamadge's favorite club — and provide a good way to get safely into the house if a suspect is lurking out front.

Though we've had no news of the Gamadges since 1951, surely they exist to this day, at least in the minds of devoted readers. In this group are Clara Gamadge, two small sons, Athalie the cook, Theodore the houseman, the invaluable Harold Bantz (the morose, secretly romantic lab assistant), one or two yellow cats and a magnificent chow dog.

To arrange a meeting with Gamadge himself, we must navigate past old Theodore, who disapproves of those of us who come to call on his employer for his services as amateur criminologist (for which he accepts no fee). More than likely, Theodore will announce us to Gamadge only as "a person," leaving us standing downstairs in the hall. We might then catch a glimpse of the first-floor laboratory, where Henry carries on his number one profession, expert in disputed documents.

As Gamadge approaches us with a long, lurching stride, we are struck by his amiable expression and easy manner — something he keeps with everyone, from a family of Gypsies to a broken-down doctor to an ancient aristocrat. We could pick him out handily from a crowd: tallish, thinnish, with a bit of a stoop from poring over questionable papers. He is rather blunt-featured, one might almost say colorless, but we soon learn his appearance is deceptive. His bland expression has gulled several dozen murderers, conspirators and impostors whose mistake it was not to see beyond to the mind that seizes on discrepancies in their stories, their little character foibles. Our great fascination with Gamadge comes from being equally unable to read his mind, to find anything except good manners in his noncommittal conversation.

He is not one of those detectives who announce they know who's guilty but won't tell us because our too-open faces will give away the secret. He simply doesn't announce, and we have to wait for the full denouement, just like his nearest and dearest. When there's a real necessity, he can spring into action fast enough, but he prefers to do his detecting by watching and listening. This may, on the surface, seem so urbane as to be almost dull; and yet in every situation Gamadge deals with there is a sense of evil

The Gamadge town house. A framed photograph of Henry rests on the small table just in front of the antique screen. From this perspective, Henry gets a good view of his leather-bound books and a hint of garden greenery. On clear days, he can practically see into his club.

THE DALY OUTPUT

(In Order of Appearance)

Deadly Nightshade

Unexpected Night

Murders in Volume II

The House Without the Door

Evidence of Things Seen

Nothing Can Rescue Me

Arrow Pointing Nowhere
(Murder Listens In)

The Book of the Dead

Any Shape or Form

Somewhere in the House

The Wrong Way Down
(Shroud for a Lady)

Night Walk

The Book of the Lion

And Dangerous to Know

Death and Letters

The Book of the Crime

at work, like a small icy stream running underground, of whose existence we're just barely, uneasily aware. He, however, not only recognizes it, but pinpoints it.

When we encounter Gamadge with the police, we discover that he never withholds facts from them. But without proof, he won't give them his conjectures. His friend Nordhall of the NYPD is often bewildered, but gallantly goes along with this man who can "do anything with handwriting" and can find anything in a book, from a gun to a hint from William Shakespeare. In *The Book of the Crime,* Gamadge even ferrets out a clue from a pair of thin volumes that he never lays eyes on. In another case, an onlooker remarks that he has "seen a man walk a tightrope before, but not with three people hanging on each side of him." Well put. We rely on Gamadge knowing that he has all the answers and that by following his lead, we should be able to guess them. We *should* be, but . . .

Somehow, it just seems natural to trust Gamadge. All of us do it, including an obscure art teacher who doesn't even know his name but let's him spirit her out of a dangerous spot nonetheless. It's a feat at which he excels.

One sure way of involving his attention is to come round armed with a problem that is decidedly queer. Consider the situation reported in *Murders in Volume II,* where a governess who disappeared a hundred years before ostensibly returns, bringing the volume of Byron that went with her into the fourth dimension. Think of the cryptic notes crumpled into balls and thrown out the window in *Arrow Pointing Nowhere,* and the cry for rescue written like a crossword puzzle in *Death and Letters.* Gamadge couldn't resist any of these, nor the chance, in *Somewhere in the House,* to see a grisly wax image in a bricked-up music room. This kind of oddity invariably catches his interest, but what makes him plunge wholeheartedly into a case is simply anger.

The problem that, naturally enough, rouses Gamadge's worst inner fury is one that puts Clara in danger. In *Evidence of Things Seen,* the appearance of an unnerving figure that might be a ghost sets her up for a murder indictment. When Gamadge learns of these goings-on at the summer cottage, he is incensed — and never mind the ghost, this alone can give any reader a chill.

From all but a few of his sixteen recorded cases, Gamadge retains a good friend, an employee, a consultant; from one, he acquired a perfect wife. Most of us welcome this character continuity. We cozy into it. We become attached to Clara, to those marmalade cats who like Henry the best, to Schenck and Harold and J. Hall, Bookseller. We know they are real.

What do you mean, they're not? Agatha Christie undoubtedly was convinced of it. Do you think anyone could pull the wool over *her* eyes?

Lenore Glen Offord has written eight mystery novels and received an Edgar award for her mystery reviews in the San Francisco Chronicle.

MARGARET MILLAR AND THE GREATEST OPENING LINES SINCE "IN THE BEGINNING..."

In sentence one, she states that the old man is rich; in two, that he has extra time on his hands; in three, that he's sitting at the country club composing an anonymous letter.

That's *The Murder of Miranda.*

In another sentence one, a young woman is tapping along with the aid of a white cane. By the start of the next paragraph, she's wondering if her seeing-eye dog realizes she isn't blind.

That's *Wall of Eyes.*

Mrs. Millar has pulled off this kind of zinger twenty-three times, beginning in 1942 with *The Devil Loves Me.* Little wonder, then, that she was elected to head up the Mystery Writers of America, that her *Beast in View* won the organization's Edgar, that Alfred Hitchcock chose to film the title for television, that Mary Astor opted to star in the movie version of *Rose's Last Summer,* and that there are mystery readers who swear Mrs. Millar is more talented than, or at least as talented as, her husband Ross Macdonald (Kenneth Millar).

Mrs. Millar doesn't attract fans; she creates addicts. When her new hardcover comes out, they rush home to devour it. Dinner can wait. The dog can wait. They tell friends they'll call them back. That book gets finished in one sitting. And quoted from for months after.

Inevitably, a mind so trenchant arouses talk. And fantasies:

What do you think she's really like? Can you imagine the two of them in the same house? She's plotting to kill him, of course. And slowly, methodi-

cally, he's working toward a confrontation. Oh God, is it evil.

Would you forgive them for being amiable and well-behaved?

Actually, Mr. and Mrs. Millar are shy people. He spaces each thought with a Pinteresque pause. She speaks a little too loud, a little too fast, in the manner of someone very timid who's trying to hide it.

He has been in analysis; she has not. Yet she admits there is something about her writing style that tempts psychiatric journals to review her, that her first three mysteries featured psychiatrist sleuth Paul Prye (make of the name what you will), that her early ambition was to be an analyst.

Undoubtedly, the Millars are the two most famous former residents of Kitchener, Ontario, where they grew up. Their surname is the Canadian version of "Miller." Same pronunciation, different spelling. Though she concedes: "I've given up correcting people. Ken still does, all the time, but I'll let a 'mil-*lar*' pass."

Her father was town mayor, and she remembers him coming home from Council meetings absolutely frustrated by Mabel Dunham, the local librarian. "He'd say to us, 'That Mabel! We weren't going to give her any money for books, we didn't want to do it, but she started to cry and wouldn't stop until we gave in.'"

To Ken Millar, on the other hand, a schoolboy just Margaret's age, Mabel Dunham and her library were wonderful. "Ken's ambition was to

HAL BOUCHER

Margaret Millar and her husband, Ross Macdonald. The Millars were childhood sweethearts. Her interest in mysteries piqued his.

read every book in the library," says Margaret. "It was remarkable what she had there," acknowledges Ken. "We were fortunate to have her." Besides, he hid his pipe — forbidden by his parents — on top of one of the Dunham stacks.

Both Millars believe the Canadian educational system a superior one. They stress it gave them enormous advantages. (Mrs. Millar puckishly notes that her classical background — Greek and Latin — has made it easy for her to decipher medical terminology.)

Their life together, they insist, is quiet. "We have a lot of work to get through," says Ken. The Millars write about three hours a day, six days a week. She works in the morning, he in the afternoon, but he admits they've slowed down a bit; a few years ago, they could concentrate for longer periods. Both prefer the longhand method. "I have a very short temper when it comes to mistakes," concedes Mrs. Millar. "I once threw a typewriter out a second-story window."

She started writing when she was eight. Her first story concerned four sisters who were three months apart in age. "I was sixteen before I found out why everyone thought this was hilarious."

Her interest in mysteries piqued Ken's, though he preceded her in creating a private-eye sleuth: Lew Archer first appeared in '49; her Steve Pinata did not debut until 1960 (*A Stranger in My Grave*). Recently, in *Ask for Me Tomorrow* and *Miranda,* she's featured Tom Aragon, a young lawyer protagonist.

Between the two books came a serious illness, in which Mrs. Millar underwent surgery for lung cancer. Though recovered, Mrs. Millar says: "Don't let anyone tell you you're not always looking over your shoulder after it. Because you are."

Miranda was finished during a violent attack of shingles. "It was a real test for her," says her husband. She says, "I wanted to see if I could do it. I remember sweating out that last page. I don't think anyone could tell from reading the book, though, what I was going through." True. Contrary to what you might expect, it happens to be very funny, with its maniacal poison-pen writer who cribs country club stationery for his efforts, its two meddlesome schoolgirls and its carefully preserved widow who views herself as if through a soft-focus lens. Says Margaret, "I used to write light books, then I got serious. I don't know why I'm funny again."

Actually, there has always been a bite to her work, an ability to nail a character so deftly, you think: Boy, I'm glad she's not *my* enemy. Her husband refers to this as "Margaret's somewhat sarcastic style." Her incisiveness is the result of hard work. "Some days, I'll write a sentence ten times. If I knew a lot of mystery writers who did that, then I think I'd read more of them. I can't stand sloppy writing and sloppy structure. I miss some of the older writers: Elizabeth Saxony-Holding, Helen McCloy, Charlotte Armstrong. I consider Christie an excellent plotter. When I read *Witness for the Prosecution,* I knew she really had a twisted little mind. I wished I had thought of it."

When the Millars aren't writing, they're apt to be hiking three miles down the beach with their dogs, doing laps in their beach club pool or attending a local trial.

They own four pets: two shepherds, one

HAL BOUCHER

The Santa Barbara beach club Margaret Millar used as the setting for Miranda.

Newfoundland and one mystery breed, Misty, who adopted Mr. Millar on one of the walks.

"One of our best friends is a Supreme Court Judge out here," says Mrs. Millar. "He helps me with all the Grand Jury things in my books. His secretary will call and say, 'We have a beauty in courtroom five; get on over.' I remember a really vicious case when the jury was impossible. They brought in goodies to eat in little brown bags, and they sent the bailiff in to ask the judge which was worse, the death penalty or life imprisonment—they didn't know."

Their beach club (which served as a model for the one in *Miranda*) is where they do all their entertaining. Mrs. Millar admits, "I don't do any cooking anymore. I put in my dues. There are wonderful restaurants in the area, and the club, and we eat all our meals out." One Christmas, a club lifeguard gave her a subscription to *Verbatim,* a quarterly for people who love words. "It has an absolutely unsolvable puzzle," she claims, after years of trying. She and Ken used to be double-crostic fans; on one vacation, they each brought along a book of them and had a contest to see who'd do better. He won. "Ken is terribly mathematical, a bloody genius."

In the Millar household, who picks up after whom? The chores are divided. "When we can't stand it anymore, we get out the vacuum. Sometimes Ken will do it without being asked." Still, she is regarded as the family organizer, he as the pack rat.

Ken: From time to time, I need to be rescued from the swamp.

Margaret: I am the picker-upper, thrower-outer. You haven't missed anything yet, have you?

Ken: Not seriously, no.

Oddly, it is he who answers all his mail, she who lets hers pile up. "My system is to heap it by the side of my chair, then six months later say, Well, it's certainly too late to answer *that,* and throw it out."

At a recent party they attended, a friend went round the room asking guests what expression they used the most. If they couldn't answer, the other partygoers pointed it out. Ken's favorite phrase was carefully measured: Do not become alarmed. Margaret's, flung at anyone who got in her way, was: Watch it, you old goat.

Her fans' would be: Write faster, Mrs. Millar. And tell your husband to get cracking, too.

THE MILLAR BOOKSHELF

The Devil Loves Me
The Weak-Eyed Bat
The Invisible Worm
Wall of Eyes
Fire Will Freeze
The Iron Gates
Experiment in Springtime
It's All in the Family
The Cannibal Heart
Do Evil in Return
Vanish in an Instant
Rose's Last Summer
Wives and Lovers
Beast in View
An Air That Kills
The Listening Walls
A Stranger in My Grave
How Like an Angel
The Fiend
The Birds and the Beasts Were There
Beyond This Point Are Monsters
Ask for Me Tomorrow
The Murder of Miranda

HELEN MᴬᶜINNES: THE FEMALE LUDLUM

578. PORNIC (Loire-Inf.) — Vue générale

The Brittany coast.

Helen MacInnes has ruined more vacations than bad weather. Those of us who've read a number of her seventeen books have come to expect our travels to include an encounter with an attaché in the Wagon-Lit corridor, a soul-searing tryst with a spy whose escape depends on our alibi or, at the very least, a special request from the State Department to rendezvous with a courier on a hillside of edelweiss. When none of this transpires, our journey is a flop. We feel cheated sitting next to a dentist from Schenectady on our no-frills tour bus.

To read a MacInnes is to be stricken with wanderlust. Often, the next book we reach for is a dictionary of foreign phrases. And then it's straight to the passport office, and on to the airline counter. Herself a peripatetic, MacInnes moved from Glasgow to London, then to Oxford, New York and La Jolla. From these bases, she's made excursions to every country (except Poland) mentioned in her novels. Given the ac-

curacy of the background detail in her books, either she has total recall or she takes the best snapshots this side of the Kodak board room and uses them for reference. She seems to know every historical cobblestone in the Plaka, every weeping gargoyle on Notre Dame. Undoubtedly, she is one of the world's most conscientious guides. Even Kate Simon, doyenne of travel writers, would have to concede that MacInnes is picture-postcard perfect at describing Paris, Rome, London, Salzburg, Athens, Venice, Warsaw, Málaga.

The typical MacInnes plot hinges on an idealistic young couple defending the rights of the Free World. *Above Suspicion,* for example, pits an Oxford don and his wife against the Nazi apparatus. *Assignment in Britanny* features a British officer and a French farmgirl who sabotage a Gestapo coastal garrison. *The Salzburg Connection* drops an American lawyer and a troubled Continental into a neo-Nazi hotbed.

The Roman Forum, where Caesar was stabbed and MacInnes heroes orated on the terrors of totalitarianism.

Hitler is her quintessential villain, but she also has several thousand nasty words to say about fascists and communists. Detractors would have us believe that her principal method of punishing these totalitarians is a lengthy tongue-lashing, and truthfully she is not an imaginative torturer. In fact, her preference for evoking rather than depicting blood makes her unique among thriller writers, who as a group have a high tolerance for gore.

Her protagonists will remind us of ourselves on our best behavior. They proceed the way we like to think we would if we were trapped in similar circumstances. The heroes and heroines are brave, intelligent, quick-witted and good. And besides, they can recognize a Bernini fountain when they see one.

Usually, a MacInnes character finds the time to fall in love, and only once, in *The Venetian Affair,* does it turn out badly. MacInnes integrates romance with derring-do, never emphasizing one at the expense of the other.

The Capitol Building, Washington, D.C., whose corridors seethe with good intentions (and bad) in a MacInnes novel.

Interestingly, critical reviews of MacInnes will begin by labeling her a spy writer, then before the end of the paragraph will tag her "romantic suspense." Why this fate does not also befall Robert Ludlum is inexplicable. They are both old-fashioned "storytellers," producing

The Málaga streets, where MacInnes agents elude each other while donkeys bray at their antics.

"page-turners," "good-reads," "I-can't-wait-to-see-the-movie" books. They both ignore the technical folderol, the doomsday devices, and turn their efforts instead to researching locales. They both think men and women belong together, that a little romance won't flag the pace. And they both have a hammerlock on the bestseller list. But he gets to be one of the boys — a spy thriller writer — and she gets to be the little woman — a romantic suspense writer. Maybe it's because he uses shorter sentences.

Never mind. The next time you take a vacation to Paris, Rome, London, Salzburg, Athens, Venice, Warsaw, Málaga, stow a MacInnes in your suitcase. You won't be disappointed. And you'll be able to find your way around town.

THE GOTHIC LADY WEARS A BEARD

It sometimes seems that the greatest mystery mystery is not whodunit, but whowroteit. All too often, the name on the title page turns out to be the book's first red herring. Is the author really who he says he is? Or does a secretive feminine hand push the typing keys for him?

A musty prowl through ancient stacks leads us to deduce that, in fact, he is likely to be a she. Peter Curtis is actually Norah Lofts; Stephen Hockaby is Gladys Mitchell; Anthony Gilbert, Lucy Malleson; Michael Venning, Craig Rice; Tobias Wells, DeLoris Forbes; David Frome, Mrs. Zenith Jones Brown.

Just when we're convinced there are no male writers left, another suspicion sidles in: perhaps a woman's by-line is a cover-up, too. Maybe *she* is a *he*.

Feeling like masquerade guests who can hardly wait till midnight, we visited the home of Gothic specialist Rose Brock. Her door was answered by a gentleman with a Burl Ives beard and a Budweiser gut. His name, he informed us, was Rose Brock. It was also (*gasp*) Joseph Hansen.

Hansen, as any reputable critic will tell you, belongs in the Chandler-Hammett ball park. His David Brandstetter novels are lean, spare and tough — hardly the sort of things that wind up with plantation belles on their dust jackets (not to mention graveyards, wrought-iron balconies and the hint of a clinging vine).

"Uh, Rose . . ." We stumbled, then tried again. "Er, Joe . . . what's going on?"

"Back in '67," he said, "when I was writing the first Brandstetter, *Fadeout*, I became uncertain. I faltered and thought I couldn't go on. This was the time when Gothics were covering every rack, and I felt maybe I should find out what they're all about and do one of them in-

stead. I bought a half-dozen, read them and made a bet with myself I could do better. Of course, you always think that. I had great fun with it and finished in two months. Then I sent it round and round, and round and round, and nobody wanted it. I finally took it to an agent, and he placed it right away — with a publisher who had turned me down flat. Don't tell me an agent isn't needed in this business. The book was called *Tarn House*, and readers who come to it knowing my Dave stuff will find the style somewhat different. Lots plummier."

Hansen was perfectly willing to make Rose a one-shot author, but his agent was not. To quiet the man, he dug deep in his files, pulled out an extraordinarily complicated outline (the synopsis took up seven typed pages, single-spaced) and mailed it off. Unfortunately for Hansen, the agent loved it, Harper & Row loved it, Bantam loved it. He found himself committed to a book he detested.

"To do it, I, who loathe research, had to spend eighteen months in the library checking out volumes on the Reconstruction period, on woman's place in the South, on Louisiana geography, on voodoo practices. Every day, I hated my life. I still don't like *Longleaf*, but it's sold more copies than anything I've ever done. I get wonderful letters about it, telling me I really know New Orleans inside and out. And the irony is, I've never been near the place."

Hansen insists that, despite her triumphs, he's retired Miss Brock. The masculine Damsel-in-Distress field, including such stalwarts as Morris Hershman (hiding behind the skirt of Evelyn Bond), W. E. D. Ross (Clarissa Ross, Marilyn Ross), Brett Halliday (Sylvia Carson, Kathryn Culver) and all-time champ Michael Avallone (Priscilla Dalton, Jean-Anne de Pré, Dora

Highland, Dorothea Nile, Edwina Noone) will

THE ANDROGYNOUS NAME

Hillary Waugh

I'm the only person I know who, upon introducing himself, has to spell *both* his names. If the misspelling of one's name is bad for one's identity, consider the additional fact that "Hillary," with whatever number of L's you want, is given as often to girls as to boys.

It was in the latter part of 1946 that I submitted, with the customary trepidation, my first mystery novel to a publisher. Six weeks went by without a word — surely, I thought, this meant serious consideration — and then I received a letter of rejection. They were returning the manuscript, but because of the railroad strike I would have to send them more money for postage. I shouldered the extra cost and back it came, accompanied by a form rejection slip, the package addressed to "*Miss Hillary Waugh.*"

When publication ultimately followed, and I had a shelfful of books to my credit, I let myself think I'd achieved a certain renown in the field. But such is the stuff of dreams. Not long ago, I made reservations to attend the First International Congress of Crime Writers in London, saying I'd like to share a room with author John Ball. A shocked Congress Committee wanted to know who this *female* was, who had the effrontery to sign up for a male roommate.

It certainly keeps one humble.

Hillary Waugh is the executive vice-president of the Mystery Writers of America. His nom de Gothic is Elissa Grandower.

hear not another word from her.

Also on the discard heap, though for entirely different reasons, is the Hansen pseudonym James Colton. In 1967-68, Joe wrote a book that no major publisher would touch. Called *Known Homosexual*, it finally found a home with a small Los Angeles press. As Hansen recalls it, an editor took him to lunch, praised the manuscript and then, with much embarrassment, requested revisions. "I don't know how to tell you this, Joe," she said, "but you're going to have to stop closing the door every time they go to bed." Hansen agreed to the rewrite but put the Colton name on the spine. In 1977, the company wanted to reissue the book without the elaborations. Delighted, Hansen said yes and reverted back to being himself on the credit line.

Regarding the five completed Brandstetter novels, Hansen says: "My preference is for the old-fashioned puzzle in the Hammett-Chandler-Macdonald tradition. I write about homosexuals, and as a consequence I've written about lesbians. I love to write about women, and I think I do it with some success. I'm not trying to convert anybody, but to show that homosexuals are real people, and to handle them in a straightforward, intelligent, articulate manner. I have no plans to kill off Dave. Remember Cecil Harris? Cecil may come back. I'm thinking about that. Much as I admire it, I do not enjoy rereading my own work. I know I repeat phrases from book to book, and I shouldn't. I'd like to do a mainstream novel next. I've finished part of one on a National Endowment grant, but I need another to complete it."

Meanwhile, Hansen is teaching a course in how to write detective fiction at UCLA. This is his third semester at it, and he's been so impressed with eight of his students that he's put them in touch with his agent. He's particularly proud of Anne Marie Breton's *To Fly from Eagles*, an historical romance, Cynthia Applewhite's *Sundays*, a hilarious and terrifying novel about a ten-year-old girl, William Harry Harving's *Rainbow*, about a con artist, and Hershey Eisenberg's *The Rinehart Action*, a thriller. He dubs them "my prizes."

Hansen teaches on a one-to-one basis. He corrects every comma in the manuscript, giving a detailed written critique as well. He also pre-

BEARDING THE PSEUDONYM
James H. Olander

In private life, the author wore lipstick; on her dust jacket, she sported a beard (or at least the potential for growing one). Can you match the mysterious females on the left with their masculine alter egos on the right?

1.	Morna Doris Brown	a. Joseph Shearing
2.	Zenith Jones Brown	b. E. X. Ferrars
3.	Dolores Hitchens	c. Gordon Daviot
4.	Emma Redington Lee	d. Lawrence L. Lynch
5.	Gabrielle Long	e. D. B. Olson
6.	Elizabeth MacIntosh	f. John Stephen Strange
7.	Lucy Malleson	g. E. C. R. Lorac
8.	Isabel Ostrander	h. David Frome
9.	Georgiana Ann Randolph	i. Michael Venning
10.	Edith Caroline Rivett	j. Anthony Gilbert
11.	Holly Roth	k. Lee Thayer
12.	Dora Shattuck	l. Francis Bonnamy
13.	Dorothy Tillet	m. K. G. Ballard
14.	Audrey Walz	n. Richard Shattuck
15.	Emma Murdoch Van Deventer	o. Robert Orr Chipperfield

Answers

1-b; 2-h; 3-e; 4-k; 5-a; 6-c; 7-j; 8-o; 9-i; 10-g; 11-m; 12-n; 13-f; 14-l; 15-d

Dr. James H. Olander is associate professor of English at the New York Institute of Technology.

pares a reading list for his students ("Since they're going to be picking up styles anyway, they should be reading the best"), hands out S. S. Van Dine's "Twenty Rules for Writing Detective Stories" and strongly advises that his pupils buy Symons' *Mortal Consequences* and Strunk & White's *Elements of Style*.

Concludes Hansen: "I like talking about the mystery. It's endlessly fascinating to me. I take it very seriously."

Now, if Rose Brock could just stop being frivolous, perhaps he'd admit her to his class.

MISOGYNIST REX

John McAleer

In "Blood Will Tell," Archie Goodwin watches Nero Wolfe devour the title page of a new book "with the same kind of look a man I know has for a pretty girl he has just met." Add to this the disclosure that Wolfe's "orchids were his concubines: insipid, expensive, parasitic and temperamental," and we perceive, in ample outline, a man bent not merely on excluding women from his life but on thinking of them as avoidable nuisances. Evidence strengthening this supposition is readily mustered. Clara Fox, in *The Rubber Band,* after inspecting Wolfe's brownstone on West Thirty-fifth Street, pronounces it "the most insolent denial of female rights the mind of man has ever conceived." Why? "No woman in it from top to bottom, and the routine is faultless." Chance does not account for that. Archie tells us "it would suit Wolfe fine, if one never crossed the doorsill."

Additional, well-placed cudgel blows would seem to establish, beyond cavil or stricture, Wolfe's stance as an unyielding misogynist. Wolfe says: "You can depend on a woman for anything except constancy." And: "When they stick to the vocations for which they are best adapted, such as chicanery, sophistry, self-advertisement, cajolery, mystification, and incubation, they are sometimes superb creatures."

Rex Stout himself seems to block Wolfe's every avenue of escape from this slough of bias. I asked him if Wolfe agreed with Geoffrey Chaucer that the three things women most excel at are "weeping, weaving, and lies." He replied: "Not quite. Nero Wolfe doesn't think women are good liars."

Since Rex Stout is the source of Wolfe's ex-

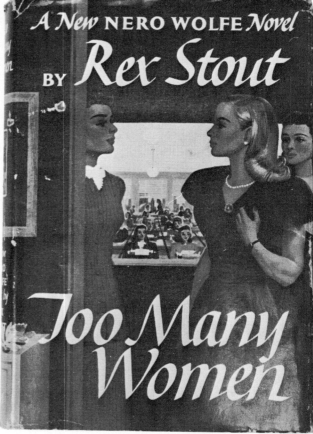

Published in 1947, Too Many Women *involves Nero and Archie with a Wall Street firm that has 500 female employees — and one dead male stockbroker.*

istence, how responsible is he for Wolfe's alleged misogyny? Of the 103 authors Rex says Wolfe read, in the course of the Wolfe saga, only seven are women. Five of these — Dorothy Osborne, Edith Hamilton, Rachel Carson, Laura Z. Hobson and Miriam Schneir — get no more than cursory mention. Another, Mary McCarthy, actually is "ditched" by Wolfe after a two-chapter trial. Although Wolfe is hardly gracious about it, the seventh, Jane Austen, receives her due homage — "Wolfe held it against Jane Austen for forcing him to concede that a woman could write a good novel."

Possibly Rex's intention, in making Wolfe's reading habits one-sided, was to make the characterization consistent, but there is ample reason for doubting that. Eighteen of the writers Wolfe read were friends of Rex Stout. Only one, Laura Hobson, was a woman. Yet Rex was on solid footing with many other women writers — Edna Millay, Rebecca West, Margaret Pulitzer, Kay Boyle, Pearl Buck, Dorothy Fields, Elizabeth Janeway, to mention some. None is on Wolfe's bookshelves. Their exclusion from the saga amounts to an intentional snub.

"Women are the caretakers of the earth but a biological trap." Thus does Jack Kerouac damn womankind with faint praise. Dostoevsky, Conrad and Verne held like opinions. Rex Stout (who once said that, as a boy, he dreamed repeatedly of being held captive in the marsupial pouch of a possessive kangaroo) knew Conrad personally and read "every word he ever wrote." He also admitted, in a phrase that appears to replicate Wolfe's grudging recantation, "I used to think that men did everything better than women, but that was before I read Jane Austen. I don't think any man ever wrote better than Jane Austen."

We could be wrong about Rex's misogyny. Authentic misogynists, including the androgynous Agatha Abbey in "The Zero Clue," see women as inferior. Rex, quite otherwise, delighted in intelligent women. His mother was just such a person, as was her mother, a collateral descendant of Benjamin Franklin. (Indeed, Rex assigned to Nero Wolfe many of his grandmother's characteristics.) Moreover, Rex's immediate family consisted of his brilliant wife and two daughters as sharp-witted as their parents.

When Margaret Pulitzer died, Rex spoke of her "quick and sharp mind, good judgment, wide information, accurate and effective use of words." He admired the novels of Josephine Tey and was dismayed that she had not received

PLAYING SECOND FIDDLE TO NERO

When Stout's publishers asked him, in 1936, to create a detective to switch off with Nero Wolfe, Rex filled the order with Theodolinda ("Dol to a few") Bonner, a lady sleuth whose behavior patterns overlap those of Wolfe. Dol is "immune" to men. She dislikes being touched. She is informed, quick-witted, decisive and competent, though once, when thwarted, she labels herself "a damned female quidnunc." Dol has the further attribute of being beautiful, though we hear perhaps too much about her caramel-colored eyes and curling canopy of long, black lashes.

After Dol first appeared, in September 1937, Rex's New York editor wrote to her London counterpart: "*The Hand in the Glove* is doing almost as well as Nero, but whether or not there will be another Dol Bonner mystery we can't be sure." In fact, Dol's agency prospered; however, we don't encounter her again till twenty years later, when, mink-clad, she turns up as Wolfe's operative in "Too Many Detectives" (1956), then in *If Death Ever Slept* (1957) and *Plot It Yourself* (1959). While Dol is Archie Goodwin's age, it is Wolfe, as Anthony Boucher noted, who makes "sheep's eyes" at her. He even invites her to breakfast and dinner, and seats her at his right. Archie is nonplussed, of course, but enough intrigued by Dol and her lovely assistant, Sally Colt, to wonder if "there might be some flaw in my attitude toward female dicks." With predictable brio, he concludes: "If she hooks him and Sally hooks me we can all solve cases together and dominate the field." *J.McA.*

the acclaim due her. Rex's foremost female characters — Lily Rowan ("I would tackle a tiger bare-handed to save her from harm"), Lucy Valdon, Hattie Annis, Julie Jaquette, Clara Fox, Rachel Bruner, Cora Ballard, Mrs. Jasper Pine, Mrs. Barry Rackham — all are women of intel-

lect. "Dad could never stand a dumb woman," says Rex's daughter, Barbara. "If she was beautiful it helped for a little while, but not for long."

And there is the matter of murderers. Doyle and Chesterton were reluctant to let women commit murder in their detective stories. In nearly a third of the Nero Wolfe stories (twenty-two out of seventy-two), the murderer is a woman. Did Rex see himself as ungallant? His retort: "I bow, uncover, stand, and open doors. GKC and Doyle overdid it."

"Am I wrong in contending that Wolfe is not a bona fide misogynist?" I asked Rex.

"No," he replied.

The evidence is there to support him. Archie says: "If woman as woman grated on him you would suppose that the most womanly details would be the worst for him, but time and again I have known him to have a chair placed for a female so that his desk would not obstruct his view of her legs . . . . the older and dumpier she is the less he cares where she sits." But Wolfe can and does speak for himself: "Not like women? They are astonishing and successful animals. For reasons of convenience, I merely preserve an appearance of immunity which I developed some years ago under pressure of necessity." What was that pressure? Could it be the bonding instinct — primitive man's urge to segregate himself for the hunt? A detective is a continuator of that tradition. In that role a woman could be, to him, an incumbrance. Emotional involvement with her could cloud his judgment. Seen from that vantage point, Wolfe's wariness of women actually is complimentary.

To consider one last point. Archie says Wolfe once was married and his wife tried to kill him with compresses steeped in a penetrating poison.

"What became of Mrs. Wolfe?" I asked Rex.

"Archie doesn't record her fate," he told me, "but I have reason to believe Wolfe murdered her."

Now, I ask you, is this any man on whom to pin the petty label of misogynist?

WATSON WAS A WOMAN

When, on the last Friday of January, 1941, Rex Stout declined to toast "Dr. Watson's Second Wife" at the annual meeting of the Baker Street Irregulars, the 25 members present knew something was amiss. And so it was. Rex had astonishing news for them. Watson was really Irene Watson (Irene Adler, if you like), and Holmes was her spouse. With such phrases from Watson as "I am one of the most long-suffering of mortals," Rex gave awesome credibility to his thesis. The Irregulars were staggered. Spitefully, Frederic Dorr Steele, the renowned illustrator, told the others that, should occasion offer, he would depict Charles Augustus Milverton (whom Holmes called "the worst man in London") with a Stoutian beard. Later, Dr. Julian Wolff, mounting a formal rebuttal to Stout, recalled that Inspector Lestrade had said Watson was a "strongly built man — square jaw, thick neck, mustache," an argument which regrettably carries little weight in the present day, when women have infiltrated the docks as stevedores. A graver peril to the Stout thesis is "A Scandal in Baker Street," the work of Britain's Colin Davies, who says Holmes himself was — a woman! Watson speaks of Holmes' "high voice," "smooth chin" and long white fingers with "their extraordinary delicacy of touch." Moreover, he is unfamiliar with rugger jargon, the birthright of any Victorian lad. But why labor the obvious? *J. McA.*

John McAleer received the Mystery Writers of America Edgar award for Rex Stout: A Biographical Study.

Chapter 3
SNOOPS

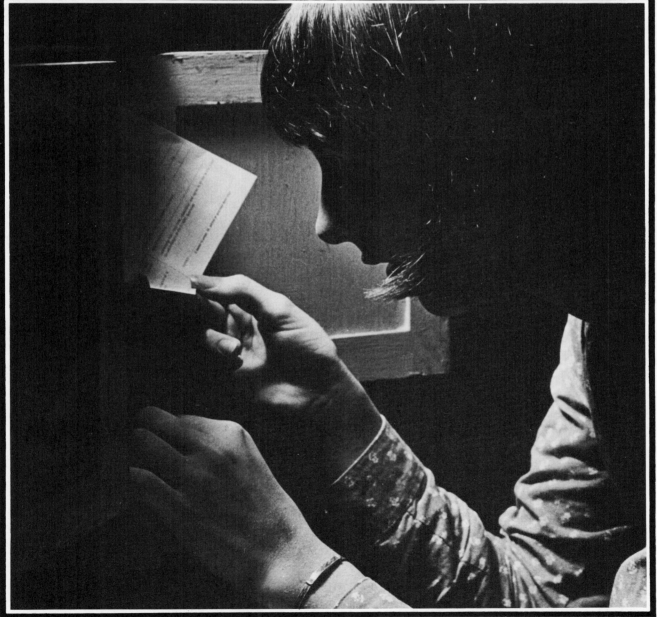

THE KNITTING BRIGADE

While the murderer loads his pistol, and the soon-to-be murderee cackles over his will, dear Miss Biddy debates which to knit next — the pram cover or the balaclava. The moment the shot is fired, however, and the offending document hurled into the fire, she jams the knitting into the pocket of her mac (she's chosen the balaclava pattern) and intuitively heads for the back fence. Quicker than you can say Madame Defarge, she tries to climb over it but drops her needles in the process. Stooping to retrieve them, she chances upon two hairs of the dog (strange breed, the mystery dog, never barks), a garnet ear-bob, a bit of ash (probably nothing, just part of the rose mulch) and a plimsole tread. With a chortled "Aha!" she backs away, minding her step, and trundles off in the direction of the constabulary — leaving a trail of yarn behind her.

Oh, you read that one, did you? Then you'll remember that dear Miss Biddy, in the course of the investigation, finished both the helmet and the pram cover, and was two-thirds through an Angora tea cosy (about par for the course for the knitting busybody).

As you've undoubtedly surmised by now, no self-respecting English village mystery would be complete without its needle-clicker. She is as indispensable as the corpse, and a whole lot noisier. As a matter of fact, it's rather astonishing, considering the row she's making, that she can hear the sotto voce threat, the mumbled telephone conversation, the alibi hatched at the other end of the room. Our more sensitive authors deal with this by having their Miss Biddys put down their knitting and pour tea at crucial moments in the plot.

There are three distinct mystery knitting personality structures. Scholars have labeled type I the *Maud Marple*. *Maud* refers to Maud Silver, Patricia Wentworth's engaging snoop,

who surfaced in 1928 *(Grey Mask)*, then vanished until 1937 *(The Case Is Closed)*, then appeared once, sometimes twice a year, until 1961 *(The Girl in the Cellar)*. *Marple*, of course, alludes to Jane Marple, Agatha Christie's indomitable sleuth, who popped up in 1930 *(Murder at the Vicarage)* and concluded her seventeen visits in 1976 *(Sleeping Murder)*.

The *Maud Marple* (a.k.a. *M&M;* a.k.a. *Miss Biddy*) suffers through later life on a fixed income and the occasional handout from a niece or nephew. Her only extravagance is morality. She interviews clients or calls on suspects at the drop of a stitch and lulls them into confidences with the hypnotic drone of her needling. She is thin, wispy and covered with lint, which complicates her detective work; often the lint is mistaken for a clue. Though unmarried, she is the archetypal Granny, and one soon discovers that the families she attracts seem to have an inordinate number of black sheep. Her accomplishments include an ecclesiastic turn of phrase, an intuitive sense of when to head for the back fence and a woolly train of thought (too much lint), which inexpicably results in the right person's comeuppance.

The *Maud Marple* purchases all her yarns and needlecraft supplies from the venerable old firm of Patons & Baldwins Limited, founded in 1920 when the company begun by John Paton in Alloa in 1805 merged with the James and John Baldwin concern, which had been a Halifax landmark since 1785.

Patons & Baldwins offer, still, a minimum of six egg cosy designs, at least a dozen varieties of tea cosies and even something suitable for the toast rack. In addition, they feature everything a baby could possibly want except mother's milk: booties, bonnets, mittens, bloomers, vests, sweaters, jackets, coats, scarves, crib blankets, pram covers, stroller rugs, pillow throws and

HOW TO KNIT A NOOSE

Purl two,
drop one.

MARTY NORMAN   CONCEPT: JACQUES BARZUN

cuddle toys. Also, for when *Maud Marple* wishes to outfit herself, it presents the fluffiest collection of shawls this side of St. Mary Mead (and where did you think those came from, anyway?).

The second mystery knitting persona has never actually been caught casting on. She has been termed the *Maud Marple Metaphor* (a.k.a. *M&M&M;* a.k.a. *Mrs. Biddy*) and is a widow who has no time to knit — she's too busy being eccentric. Gladys Mitchell's Dame Beatrice Adela Lestrange Bradley is a choice example, as is Dorothy Gilman's Mrs. Pollifax. The *M&M&M* has forsaken the manor house for the Home Office and the back entrance to Langley. She dotes on spooks, be they the sort who boo at midnight or defect at dawn. No matter what age she admits to (and it's usually post-menopausal), she comes across as a senior citizen with good wind and only mildly arthritic legs. Her detective work is more strenuous than the *Maud Marple*'s, and mystery readers are inclined to, metaphorically, provide her with knitting needles for her own protection.

The *M&M&M* cannot abide the cold (a symptom of advancing years). She is always dressed for a January foray into the upper reaches of the Himalayas, though it may be an uncommonly warm June and she has no intention of walking further than the post office. She wears twin sweater sets — the cardigan buttoned as haphazardly as a stoolie's lip — and knee-high cable-knit socks so bulky that it's impossible to determine the true silhouette of her legs. Her knitwear wardrobe is intended as compensation for her lack of skill with the Patons & Baldwins products.

The third mystery knitting personality type has been called the *American Maud Marple* (a.k.a. *A&M&M;* a.k.a. the *Shopping Bag Lady*). There are many *A&M&M* practitioners, including, in order of appearance: Leslie Ford's Grace Latham; Cortland Fitzsimmons' Ethel Thomas; D. B. Olsen's Miss Rachel and Miss Jennifer, the Murdock sisters; Torrey Chanslor's Amanda and Lutie Beagle, another sister duo; Louisa Revell's Julia Tyler; Phyllis Bentley's Marion Phipps. The *A&M&M* likes to speak in a Southern accent (the closest thing to English intonation heard on this side of the Atlantic), has manners that could rival the Queen's, and a tendency toward tacking heirloom lace on any and

WARMING  THE POT

Cold tea is an abomination. To keep the brew from getting chilled, Patons & Baldwins Limited, Alloa, Scotland, suggest you knit a coat (a tea cosy) for the pot. This design was first presented in the 1930's.

THE COSY.

MATERIALS: — 6 ozs. BEEHIVE Double Knitting — the original was worked with 3 ozs. each Light Blue (shade 1586) and Dark Blue (shade 1405). Two No. 7 "BEEHIVE" Knitting Needles. A China Head.

ABBREVIATIONS: — K. = Knit plain; L. = Light Blue; D. = Dark Blue.

¶ **Work at a tension to produce 5 stitches to the inch — the correct size will only be obtained by exactly following this instruction!**

The pleats are formed by each colour being drawn across the back of the colour just used and keeping all the strands to the wrong side of the work throughout.

Using the Light Blue Wool, cast on 98 stitches. Work 6 rows in plain knitting. Proceed as follows: —

1st row. — K. 1L., join in the Dark Blue, 6D., *7L., 7D., repeat from * to the last 7 stitches, 6L., 1D.

2nd row. — K. 1D., 6L., * 7D., 7L., repeat from * to the last 7 stitches, 6D., 1L.

3rd row. — K. 1L., 6D., *7L., 7D., repeat from * to the last 7 stitches, 6L., 1D. Repeat the 2nd and 3rd rows once, then the 2nd row once.

7th row. — K. 1D., 6L., * 7D., 7L., repeat from * to the last 7 stitches, 6D., 1L.

8th row. — K. 1L., 6D., * 7L., 7D., repeat from * to the last 7 stitches, 6L., 1D.

Repeat the 7th and 8th rows twice.

13th row. — K. 1L., 6D., * 7L., 7D., repeat from * to the last 7 stitches, 6L., 1D.

14th row. — K. 1D., 6L., * 7D., 7L., repeat from * to the last 7 stitches, 6D., 1L.

Repeat the 13th and 14th rows until the work measures 7½ inches from the commencement, ending with the 14th row. Proceed as follows: —

1st row. — K. 2 tog.L., K. 3D., K. 2 tog.D., * K. 2 tog.L., K. 3L. K. 2 tog.L., K. 2 tog.D., K. 3D., K. 2 tog.D., repeat from * to the last 7 stitches, K. 2 tog.L., K. 3L., K. 2 tog. D.

2nd row. — K. 1D., 4L., * 5D., 5L., repeat from * to the last 5 stitches, 4D., 1L.

3rd row. — K. 2 tog.L., K. 1D., K. 2 tog.D., * K. 2 tog.L., K. 1L., K. 2 tog.L., K. 2 tog.D., K. 1D., K. 2 tog.D., repeat from * to the last 5 stitches, K. 2 tog.L., K. 1L., K. 2 tog.D.

4th row. — K. 1D., 2L., * 3D., 3L., repeat from * to the last 3 stitches, 2D., 1L.

5th row. — K. 2 tog.L., K. 1D., * K. 2 tog.L., K. 1L., K. 2 to g.D., K. 1D., repeat from * to the last 3 stitches, K. 2 tog.L., 1D.

6th row. — K. 1D., 1L., * 2D., 2L., repeat from * to the last 2 stitches, 1D., 1L.

7th row. — (K. 2 tog.L.) twice, * K. 2 tog.D., K. 2 tog.L., repeat from * to the last 4 stitches, (K. 2 tog.D.) twice. Break off wool and run end through remaining stitches, draw up and fasten off securely. Work another piece in same manner.

TO MAKEUP THE TEA COSY. —

Sew up the side seams, leaving each seam open for 3¼ inches and commencing the opening 2 inches from the lower edge. Make 2 plaits of three strands of L., and 6 strands of D. Drape over shoulders of China Head, cross each at back and front and attach to waist. Run a thread round the top of Cosy and attach to the China Head.

everything — be it a high-backed chair or a high-necked silk afternoon dress.

Like the *M&M* and the *M&M&M*, the *A&M&M* is creepily intuitive, often finding herself at the scene of a crime just when she's wondering where her next case is coming from. It has been suggested that the *A&M&M* uses her knitting needles as a divining rod, and that they unfailingly point to mystery shenanigans.

The *A&M&M* usually relies on a sidekick: human in the case of Grace Latham (Colonel John Primrose); animal in the Murdock situation (Samantha the cat). But her greatest ally is the parcel of knitting paraphernalia imported from Patons & Baldwins Limited that links her forevermore with *Maud Marple*.

CHATTING UP

Audrey and Lionel had a dreadful row in the cinema queue and Marcia's been strutting about in a fancy new coat and you must

THE NEIGHBORS

IMOGEN CUNNINGHAM   BURK UZZLE/MAGNUM

at this but David's business is failing and he's taken to drink and Lydia's been awfully weepy lately and the doctor's medicine just see

SPINSTER DETECTIVES

Amanda Cross

Spinster detectives, whether they have been left on the shelf or have climbed upon it voluntarily, turn their solitude into power and their superfluity into freedom. The spinster detective has managed, with enormous cunning and one or two talents, to translate her virginity into autonomy. Her brains, too, are intact.

The "elderly busybody female sleuth," as Michele Slung has called her, arose in the late

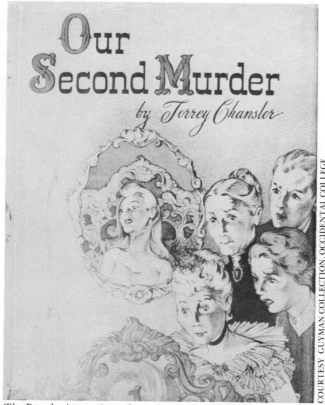

The Beagle sisters, Amanda and Lutie, owe their crime careers to their brother, Ezekiel. When he died, he willed them his detective agency. The two plucky spinsters enjoyed their first murder in 1940; their second, in 1941.

COURTESY GUYMAN COLLECTION, OCCIDENTAL COLLEGE

Victorian age, a maiden aunt washed up from the seas of boredom. It was, however, in the years between the wars in England, when the enormous shortage of marriageable males became palpable, that the spinster detective hit her stride. Her first incarnation was not, as is widely believed, Agatha Christie's Miss Marple, but Dorothy L. Sayers' Miss Climpson, who in *Unnatural Death* (1927) beat out Miss Marple by three years. Sayers, unlike Christie, did not segregate her male and female detectives into discrete narratives. Rather, Lord Peter created, supported and employed Miss Climpson and her unmarried, perhaps unmarriageable colleagues. In fact, he established a bureau of otherwise superfluous and bored females to whom life had no purpose and provided them with one. They chased criminals, asked questions no policeman could ask, unearthed secrets no policeman could guess. Miss Climpson and her consoeurs, in *Strong Poison*, save Harriet Vane from hanging only to free her for the alternative dangers of Lord Peter's passion. It is worth recording that Miss Murchison, a thirty-eight-year-old spinster "with a strong, ugly, rather masculine face," who helps save Harriet, has, by *Gaudy Night*, left Miss Climpson's service for marriage. Only Miss Climpson remains invincibly virginal, ineluctably herself.

Miss Marple's self is less constant. Introduced in *The Murder at the Vicarage*, where she explains her endless curiosity as a hobby, Miss Marple is a somewhat sinister, not altogether lovable maiden lady. As the vicar himself says, "If I were at any time to set out on a career of deceit, it would be of Miss Marple that I should be afraid." Confined within the small town of St.

Testing for virgins. If a unicorn rests its head in the subject's lap, she is one.

Mary Mead, Jane Marple is described by Colonel Malchett as "that wizened-up old maid"; of fragile appearance, she misses nothing and is quite disinterested in her observations. The later Miss Marple, as we all know, while she never achieved the sympathetic absurdities of Margaret Rutherford, became much more worldly, generous and roving.

Marple's original style was, after she had deserted it, repeatedly embodied in the person of Miss Maud Silver, Patricia Wentworth's spinster. A "little middle-aged person with small, neat features and a great deal of mouse-coloured hair," she can never be taken for anything but a governess, which she has indeed been, fortunately for the plots, to a little boy who has grown up to work for Scotland Yard. She makes deductions while knitting infant garments, blatantly pink or blue. Miss Silver deduces but has never really had an interesting thought, and does not, like Miss Marple, proceed by analogy. In fact, the stories of which Miss Silver is a part are overpowering in their conventionality about the sexes and everything else.

The 1930's saw two other spinsters worth the mention, one on each side of the Atlantic. Still in England, Tey's Miss Pym, a teacher of French, inherited just enough on her parents' death to hand in her resignation and take up psychology. After writing a best seller on that subject, she eschewed marriage and solved a crime in *Miss Pym Disposes*. Tey never used her again. In New York, Rex Stout's one female protagonist, Dol Bonner, solved her case in *The*

Hand in the Glove. However, she was not really a spinster within the meaning of the term, being both young and beautiful — that is to say, a possible sex object. Having been jilted by one man for financial reasons, Dol announces: "A man got me in a hole once, and no man is going to do it again." And she adds: "I dislike all men anyway."

Indeed, the determination of spinster detectives never to revolve in some male-centered orbit is an essential characteristic of the breed. They continued into the sixties and seventies, fewer in number and just a little cuter, like Heron Carvic's Miss Seeton, who draws and does comic turns for Scotland Yard. Gwen Moffat's Miss Pink climbs mountains and other encumbrances in Scotland, and seems, like all her tribe, to intuit the facts of sex and passion.

What has happened in the last quarter of the twentieth century is that the spinster has grown younger and more interested in sex. One may even wonder if in Dick Francis' *Risk* the breed has not been quietly retired from use. His marvelous spinster, Miss Hilary Margaret Pinlock, a headmistress who calmly saves the hero's life, is "not a do-gooding bossy spinster, but a fulfilled career woman of undoubted power." In return for her heroic efforts, she asks the hero to sleep with her ("Will you go to bed with me?" is the way she puts it). She is between forty-two and forty-six, and not sexually attractive. Nonetheless, the hero complies, and she remains a staunch friend, making no further sexual demands. Farewell, Miss Marple.

Perhaps the last and not the least distinguished in the line is P. D. James' Cordelia Gray. In *An Unsuitable Job for a Woman*, she runs her own detective agency and is hardly a spinster except in the original meaning of the word. She spins clues and plots instead of wool, and has made a profession for herself, her own place in the sun. As with male detectives, time does not hang heavy on her hands, she snoops only when paid and nobody assumes that she, or anyone else these days, is virginal. A vast relief, on the whole.

Amanda Cross has written five detective novels featuring Kate Fansler, a professor of English literature.

DEAR DIARY: I HOPE NOBODY READS THIS . . .

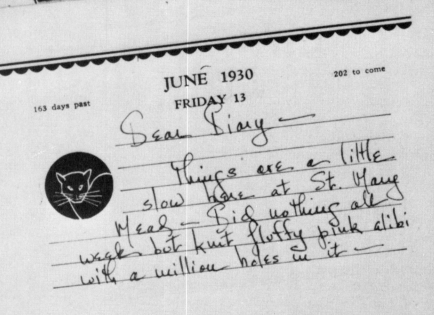

TO DO:

Paddington — 4.50? 4.54?
Stock larder
Check out B
    Hotel
Collect We
    broch
What are
    cells
2 prs. k
P+B t
Insp
We

JUNE 1930   202 to come

163 days past

FRIDAY 13

Dear Diary —

Things are a little slow here at St. Mary Mead — Did nothing all week but knit fluffy pink alibi with a million holes in it —

SATURDAY 14   201 to come

164 days past

Raymond says up Fond though I am of the boy, if he keeps on referring to S.M.M. as a stagnant pool I shall probably drown him in it — !

254

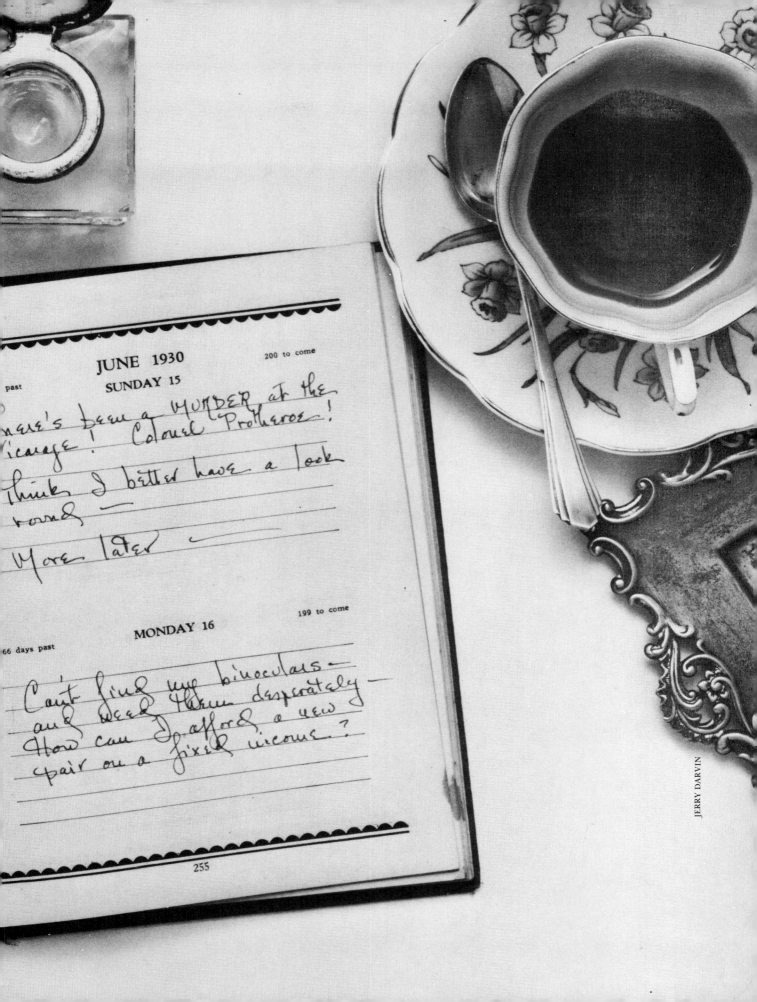

JUNE 1930

200 to come

past

SUNDAY 15

...ere's been a MURDER at the vicarage! Colonel Protheroe! Think I better have a look round —

More later —

199 to come

66 days past

MONDAY 16

Can't find my binoculars. and need them desperately — How can I afford a new pair on a fixed income.?

255

JERRY DARVIN

THE ACCOUTREMENTS OF CRIME

To foil lock-pickers, cat burglars and all those people Karl Malden would warn you about on the TV commercials, hotels have taken to plugging up their keyholes. Guests in the spiffier establishments now enter their rooms by inserting a specially coated disc into an anorexic door slit. Which is all very well and good for the security staff and the overnighters, but do you realize what it bodes for the Snoop Sisters?

Big trouble.

Without a keyhole, how will they exercise their prying eyes? That blocked passage will obscure a million motives: Nigel purloining the will and Fitzgibbon tinkering with the safe will get to do so in utmost privacy.

Rumor has it that soon the bathroom water glass will be replaced by a paper cup dispenser. How will the old girls be able to listen in on the conversations next door? With a Dixie cup? Truly, the walls will not have ears; Charlotte will blackmail the second son, and Millicent consort with the third, and no one will be the wiser.

Do you really believe Miss Marple uses her binoculars for bird-watching?

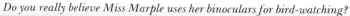

The mainstays of the cosy mystery story are clearly falling upon hard times. Within the year, the author who encumbers her plot with genteel detection devices — keyholes, water glasses, the odd hairpin or two — will be hooted out of the writing sorority. And when that happens, crime will lose not only its basic props, but most of its charm as well.

Drastic revisions will be necessary. Take, for example, the classic spying-on-the-neighbors scene. In mystery times past, the Snoop Sister stepped onto her balcony wearing stout brogues, positioned herself near the ivy-covered edge, anchored herself by swinging her brolly handle over the railing, hu-hued on her binocular lenses, then aimed them at the house across the way. Within seconds, she glimpsed Philip smacking Rachel in the chops with a lamp, Rachel retaliating with an icicle glare to the heart, and Philip responding with another go-round of the light.

Nowadays, the Snoop Sister's binocular lenses would be stalemated by an expanse of tinted glass: the homicidal pair could look out at her, but she'd be prevented from peering back. Moreover, in all likelihood the S.S. wouldn't be focusing on a private home. The modern young couple with problems live in a city dwelling, so she'd have to figure out which of the 2,300 windows in the Up-in-Arms apartment complex are theirs — a time-consuming task she might not live to complete.

Her sentry post, the balcony itself, presents still more difficulties. The old-fashioned balcony had room to swing a club in; the contemporary terrace is hard-pressed to accommodate an unfolded folding chair. Deplorably, it lacks the curtain of ivy, that trusty standby for hiding behind, and it's doubtful whether a newly rooted avocado pit would provide full coverage — and that's all there's space for. The guardrail, which used to be just the right width to crook the brolly handle round, has, contrarily, increased in size. Now it's a solid chunk of reinforced concrete, almost a foot thick. If a Snoop Sister tried to use it for support, she'd wind up

Is this any way to check a room number? MATTHEW SEAMAN

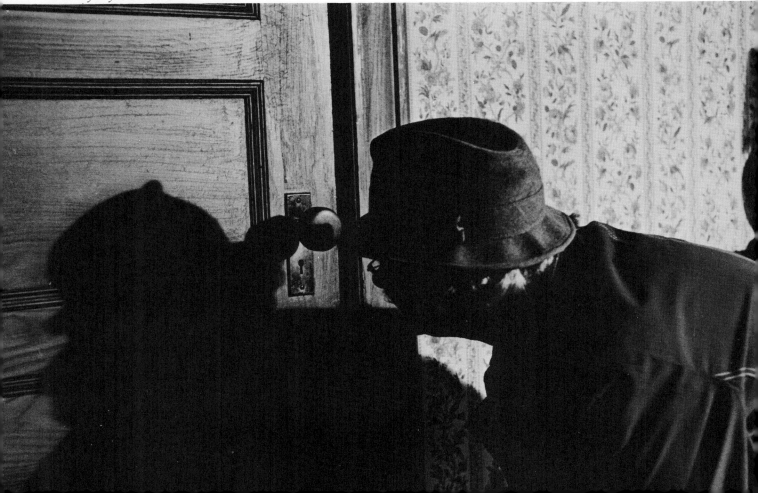

Good heavens! I think I hear . . . Could it be . . . They're playing our song, "Ah, Sweet Mystery of Life."

Not to worry: Nobody keeps the proceeds from the ransom note at home anymore. They're mailed direct to a Swiss bank account. Even if the Snoop Sister could manipulate a portion of the roller mesh into a locked box, presuming she could still find one, there'd be nothing incriminating inside. Overseas deposits have become the bane of the mystery story.

Her walking stick, that relic from the Boer campaign and her deceased uncle's most prized possession, would be confiscated at the first airline counter she came to. The little steel blade secreted in the hollow stem would set off the metal detector's alarm, and she'd have a sticky time explaining that she was just a sentimentalist, not a hijacker.

The candle she burned so she could study Frederica's diary without flicking on the overhead now comes so highly scented it's useless as a means of remaining inconspicuous. The pungency of bayberries, strawberries, Cathay spices, draws people as surely as a spotlight would. Besides, who past grammar school age keeps a diary these days?

Even the magnifying glass has been relegated to the attic. Oops. The basement storebin. Years ago, a true Snoop Sister wouldn't have dreamed of scutinizing a faded laundry mark without it. If she was leery of a diamond that wouldn't scratch Waterford, she held it under the lens for inspection. Do you have any idea how many pieces of poison penmanship she examined this way? How many i dots and t crosses she squinted at? Today a court would consider her magnifying-glass evidence extremely flimsy. A laser beam scanner, that's the thing. A microscope that's accurate to the fortieth power. A billion-dollar computer hook-up. In the face of these, a magnifying glass is kid stuff.

Is nothing sacred?

Only walking shoes. It's a pleasure to report that sneakers are for perpetrators, slingbacks for red herrings, slippers for victims, pumps for heroines and crepe-soled oxfords for Snoop Sisters. The laces are still good for binding a suspect's wrists, in a pinch. But alas, the hatpin is insufficient for keeping the felon, or worse, at bay. By the time a Snoop Sister gets close enough to use it, she's been temporarily blinded by a spray of Mace.

with cracked umbrella ribs (they'd shatter when the beloved prop glanced off the barrier and hit the street, twelve floors below).

What of all the other S.S. accoutrements? Well, the hairpins that tidied up her bun have been supplanted by rollers. Can you imagine insinuating one of these into a strongbox clasp?

MATTHEW SEAMAN

THE HAZARDS OF POKING YOUR NOSE INTO OTHER PEOPLE'S BUSINESS

The follow-up to advising Adrian that you smell trouble is a quiet period of total sensory deprivation, i.e., unconsciousness.

Gentlemen named Adrian are notoriously short with meddlers. They know exactly where to compress the larynx so the nosy parker blacks out. By the time someone comes along to rouse the slumberer, Adrian, the cad, is waltzing up the gangplank of the night boat to France.

See what happens when you don't keep your mouth shut? You get damaged and the villain gets away — at least temporarily.

For mystery females, the fate worse than death has nothing to do with the machinations of raincoat-wearing perverts: their plight is stumbling on the truth and confiding it to the wrong person. If Cynthia accepts a lift from Colin and comments on the dent in the bonnet of his Morris Minor, she must not expect to reach her destination by the shortest route. Colin will Le Mans her first to the nearest moor. If one blustery night Cynthia interrupts John while he's whispering into the receiver through a handkerchief, she must not plan on using the phone when he rings off; he'll surreptitiously cut the line and claim the storm must have discontinued the service.

Adrians, Colins and Johns (and their American tough-guy counterparts) adhere to the principle: Might as well be hung for a sheep as for a lamb. In other words, what's one more notch on their criminal gunbelts? They'd rather not be bothered, of course. It was hard enough mounting the first assault, which they'd spent months planning, but they'll grit their teeth and improvise another if that seems the only way out. Sometime between packing for the boat trip and ditching the car and wiping the telephone cradle clean, they'll try to persuade the "accidental" detective she doesn't know what she thinks she knows. If that fails, they'll permanently disqualify her as a witness.

The woman most likely to be bopped on the head is a literary type (perhaps authors are more competitive than they realize). Mignon G. Eberhart's Susan Dare, Dorothy L. Sayers' Harriet Vane, Phyllis Bentley's Marion Phipps are all mystery writers who've run amok of a culprit in their day. Dwight V. Babcock's Hannah Van Doren, a feature writer for true crime magazines, has come up on the wrong side of a swat with alarming frequency, and Kin Platt's poor Molly Mellinger, who merely edits mysteries in *Dead as They Come*, has also fared poorly. Even thesis writers are not treated kindly: Elizabeth Foote-Smith's Mercey Newcastle, who prepared a doctorate on the evolution of the crime novel, in *Gentle Albatross* is but a half-step away from something truly nasty. Obviously, these women would do better to keep their noses in their books. But try and tell them that.

It also doesn't help a woman to hang around a hospital or a religious community. Matthew Head's Dr. Mary Finney seems to be under a double-whammy because she's a medical missionary. Margaret Scherf's Dr. Grace Severance, a retired pathologist, has discovered that Las Vegas, Nevada, and much of Arizona, can be dangerous to one's health, and Mary Roberts Rinehart's nurse Hilda Adams has finally realized, after a slew of Had-I-But-Known incidents, that she ought to have protection on a

INTERESTING DEMISES

Tickling the tummy with a pitchfork is such a beguiling idea. Two authors have been smitten with it. Alistair MacLean invited a woman into a circle of tool bearers and let them each have a poke at her *(Puppet on a Chain),* and Bartholomew Gill deftly ran the implement through a pretty colleen's chest *(McGarr on the Cliffs of Moher).*

Nowhere near as gruesome, but just as lethal, Edgar Allan Poe was satisfied with letting an orang-utan spin a mother-daughter combination into a brick-lined chimney *(The Murders at the Rue Morgue).*

Norman Borrow was a bloody enthusiast if ever there was one. He battered a millionaire's wife and left her to soak in her blood-drenched house, after first amputating her hands and feet *(Fingers for Ransom).*

Anthony Berkeley let Mrs. Bendix eat seven candies with nitrobenzene fillings *(The Poisoned Chocolates Case)* and she wasn't even the intended victim — fat lot of good *that* did her — and Francis Iles had Mr. Aysgarth offer his wife Lina a glass of milk and soda laced with a certainly deadly alkali which he declined to name because it was such a common substance in use everywhere *(Before the Fact).*

But the most imaginatively dispatched corpses of them all come from the pen of Ngaio Marsh, whose tour de force has Florence Rubrick, a Member of Parliament, being baled into shearing on a New Zealand sheep station *(Died in the Wool).* She's also managed clever things with poisoned darts *(Death at the Bar),* skewers to the eyeball *(Death of a Peer)* and piano pedals *(Overture to Death),* though only in the last does she do in a woman.

MATTHEW SEAMAN

round-the-clock basis. H. H. Holmes' Sister Ursula of the Sisters of Martha of Bethany has come perilously close to considering whether she *really* wants to turn the other cheek again, given her woes in *Nine Times Nine* and *Rocket to the Morgue*. (Holmes, by the way, under another pseudonym, Anthony Boucher, wrote mystery reviews for the New York *Times*. Boucher received three separate Edgars for his criticism from the Mystery Writers of America, in 1945, 1949, and again in 1952.)

Still, it's difficult to feel *too* sorry about the hazards these women faced. Without exception, they all seemed to go looking for trouble, and once found, they reveled in it. Need we add: With crime as a hobby, can punishment be far behind?

Our sympathies are for the lady who unwittingly backs into the situation, who happens to notice there's a rent in Adrian's coat, offers to fix it, then not five minutes later, in Adrian's company, finds Sir Charles in an early stage of rigor, his fist tightly clenched round a thread of black worsted.

Her days are numbered, as are those of the luckless unfortunate who had the bad timing to wander into the chemist's shop for some headache powders just as Colin was exiting with a large canister of rat poison. Things also don't look so chipper for the lady who stopped in for a quick bite and was seated next to John, who was holding hands with a woman other than his wife.

The first thing on the agenda will be an ad-lib explanation, which the ladies won't buy. Would you believe that the coat Adrian had on was borrowed, or that Colin's Mayfair penthouse was vermin-invested, or that John was comforting his niece? Neither did they.

Phase two, if the scoundrels think they have the time for it, is to drive the ladies crazy. This is accomplished by hiding their belongings, then insisting they gave them away and just don't remember; dimming the lights and swearing it's as bright as it always was; putting a tarantula under their pillow; haunting their boudoir. They hire spurious doctors to check them over because they seem a tad peaked, and odious green tonics are prescribed, causing wooziness.

If the women refuse to take their medicine (and lose their grip on their sanity), Adrian, Colin and John have no recourse but to arrange a little accident. Preferably hit-and-run, but in a pinch an assist under the commuter train. They're also partial to falling chandeliers, sniper bullets and entombments in the well or the crypt — whichever is closer. That usually knocks the accidental detective out of commission for at least an evening, which allows the rogues to journey halfway to a country with no extradition laws.

MATTHEW SEAMAN

Someone's nose is out of joint, as is her toe, her ankle, her hip, her shoulder, her clavicle.

Not all unintentional sleuths, however, make it to the safety of the next book, or even to the final chapter. In general, if they're under twenty or over fifty, they're not considered expendables. Anything in the middle is fair game, especially if they're getting set to dial 911.

BIG BERTHA AND THE CALIFORNIA SCHOOL

In California, if you shake a palm tree a private eye will fall out. Hard-boiled dicks are indigenous to the area, as much a part of the landscape as cloverleafs, seismic cracks and smog. There are so many of them, in fact, that you'd be excused for thinking they were state-subsidized.

The first to apply for an investigator's license, back in the early twenties, was the Continental Op. Then came Sam Spade (1929), Paul Drake (1933), Philip Marlowe (1939) and Bertha Louise Cool (also '39). It's a wonder California—and the breed—survived Big Bertha. After all, how many pecan waffles can one state hold before it sinks to the ocean floor?

Clearly, Bertha had the stomach for her work. Describing her as overweight would be polite: she was, in fact, gross—tipping the scales at a whopping 275 pounds. The author who kept taking her to dinner and plying her with between-meal snacks was A. A. Fair, better known as Erle Stanley Gardner, Della Street's dietitian.

Bertha made a rotten private eye, or, as she preferred to call herself, "confidential investigator." For one thing, it was hard to miss a three-hundred-pound tail. For another, she was more interested in her clients' fees than in their problems (which is understandable when you consider her food bills).

She was involved in twenty-nine cases and would have made a hash of them all if it hadn't been for her partner, Donald Lam. Donald had the grit; Bertha, the girth. Seated across the desk from each other, they might have been mistaken for Jack Spratt and his wife. Correction: Jack Spratt and his mother—Bertha was not only twice his size, but double his age.

Unlike the proverbial fatty, Bertha Cool was far from jolly. The language she indulged in was enough to steam up her bifocals. "Damn" was her favorite word, and she used it as liberally as a cook adding salt.

What made Bertha so testy? Well, if the last time you'd been kissed was in 1942, you'd probably swear, too.

Bertha was no man's dream, not even her husband's. Henry Cool saved his smooches for his secretary. When she discovered the pair were sampling more than saltwater taffy in Atlantic City (a business trip indeed!), Bertha yanked off her girdle and went on an eating rampage. Numerous half-sizes later, Henry had a new secretary, hand-picked by his wife. The secretary's name was Elsie Brand, and she didn't dare make a pass at her boss: Big Bertha had enough on her to send her to the slammer.

When Henry died in 1936, Bertha waddled over to the Drexel Building in downtown L.A., rented a two-room suite, plunked Elsie in front of a typewriter in the outer office, squeezed herself into a swivel chair in the back and decided they constituted a detective agency.

Their first recorded case, *The Bigger They Come,* appeared in 1939. By that time, Bertha had hired a disbarred lawyer (Lam) and made the acquaintance of Sgt. Frank Sellers, Homicide Squad. It was Frank who, six years later, gave Bertha that little peck. Once was enough, however. They worked together until 1970—the last of the Cool/Lam capers—and he never bussed her again. (He did mumble something about what a good wife she'd make, but no proposal was ever forthcoming, respectable or otherwise.) Not that Bertha cared; she pined for whipped cream, not passion.

As you might suspect, Big B's fashion-plate aspirations were dormant, maybe even dead.

P. I. TRAFFIC JAM

If there were as many private investigators in California as mysteries would have us believe, the state would have the lowest crime rate in the country (it ranks first). Some of the toughest of the shamuses are:

Will Oursler and Margaret Scott's Gale Gallagher, head of the Acme Investigating Bureau and champion skiptracer, who fast-talks her way through *I Found Him Dead* and *Chord in Crimson.*

Walter Wager's Alison Gordon, who, in *Blue Leader,* totes a .357 Magnum, speaks five languages, charges $400 a day (she lives in Beverly Hills) and has dealt with "nymphos, kleptos and all the others O's and most of the P's and Q's."

Marcia Muller's Sharon McCone, who, in *Edwin and the Iron Shoes,* packs her own .38, romances a cop and prowls the nobbier areas and tattier antique shoppes of San Francisco.

Fran Huston's Nicole Sweet, who, in *The Rich Get It All,* preempts Lew Archer's turf and unravels familial relationships that would make even Freud blanch.

G. G. Fickling's Honey West, who karate-chops her way though 11 novels and never musses a curl (though she certainly gives her lipstick a workout).

Probably just as well: have you ever seen a Sherman tank in a sheath? She opted for "loose clothes and loose talk" and dribbled cigarette ash from an intricately carved ivory holder.

In 1941, in *Spill the Jackpot,* she contracted a bad case of flu that developed into pneumonia. She was in Reno and Vegas at the time and upon recovery found she'd dropped a bundle and was down to an almost skinny 165 pounds, a weight she then maintained despite the occasional triple portion of pecan waffles. Donald claimed that even slimmed down, she resembled an overflowing bowl of currant jelly (not within Bertha's earshot, we might add).

Donald was made a full partner in *Double or Quits,* but the decision took Bertha three days. She resented sharing the office income, and relented only when she realized that without Donald there wouldn't be one. Before his arrival, she was barely able to eke out desserts from ill-paying divorce cases and hit-and-run accidents.

In *Top of the Heap,* she attempted to dissolve the partnership because of Donald's extravagance. The first step she took was to close out his bank account. Though eventually reinstated, when he received a fat check for solving the case, Donald always remained a tad too cheeky for her tastes, and she thoroughly disapproved of his switching apartments on a glance in his little black book.

The one case Bertha tried to solve on her own (Lam had enlisted in the Navy) was *Cats Prowl at Night.* She botched it and would have wound up in court if not for the intervention of Sgt. Sellers who may not have asked for her hand but certainly saved her neck.

Strangely, Bertha never bumped into any other L.A. private eyes—not even Drake and Mason, who had a mutual friend to introduce them.

SALLY THE SLEUTH: MURDER IN WAX
Barreaux

Sally the Sleuth was a regular monthly feature in Spicy Detective *from March 1936 until the publication changed its name (to* Speed Detective) *in the early 1940's. She was one of the very few continuing female characters in the pulps and her adventures consumed from two to six pages in each issue. Another pulp private investigator was Violet McDade, a female counterpart of Nero Wolfe.*

SQUEALING ON A PRIVATE INVESTIGATOR

Mickey Friedman

Her name isn't Sal Spade, but that's what I'll call her. She's a private eye in Sam Spade's town, San Francisco. His office was downtown, on Sutter Street; hers is on the Embarcadero, near where La Paloma docked, "a few piers away" from the Ferry Building. If Sal had been at her desk at the time, she might have watched the fire from her window. She can say, with as much certainty as he did, "This is my city and my game."

Sal smokes but, unlike Sam, doesn't roll her own. And while he kept his tobacco in his business suit, she fishes her cigarettes from the breast pocket of a light blue work shirt, belted over rolled-up jeans. Sam would never have worn jeans on the job; but then he wouldn't have worn wedgies, either, or blue eyeshadow, or pink earrings shaped like little balls.

Sam was single, she's divorced, with two kids. His hair was blond, hers is black, cut short

> *W*omen never use their intelligence — except when they need to prop up their intuition.
>
> News summaries, May 10, 1954
> JACQUES DEVAL

so it can't be grabbed easily. They're close to the same age, though at thirty-eight Sal may be a bit older than Sam was when he tangled with O'Shaughnessy and Cairo, when he was drugged by Gutman and kicked in the head by Wilmer. The closest Sal has come to being assaulted is the angry push that climaxed her three-block chase after a man she wanted to serve with a subpoena. ("It's all right," she told him. "Just show up in court.")

When Lieutenant Dundy asked Sam what kind of gun he carried, Sam answered, "None. I don't like them much." Though Sal has a license, she feels the same way. She protects herself with a large Woolworth's hatpin buried in her lapel.

Sam never mentioned undercover work, but Sal does a lot of it, mostly in connection with child-recovery cases. "I don't throw away my out-of-style clothes," she says. A prim skirt and jacket took her to several Midwestern church services until she tracked down her quarry. And sensible shoes, a conservative outfit and a borrowed coif turned her into a nun in the Los Angeles *barrio*. (She remembers that case well. She thought she'd been caught peeping in a window when a man came out of a house wielding a hachet; he got firewood — instead of, as she'd feared, her neck.)

Sal's talent for prevarication in the line of duty rivals the fluent Miss O'Shaughnessy's. Trying to blow a fraudulent insurance claim, she visited a suspect on the pretext of looking for a missing heir. And once, when the miniature recorder inside her coat reached the end of

A woman investigator, hired by the Pinkerton Agency ("We Never Sleep"), was instrumental in tracking down the Lincoln conspirators.
Today, in Washington, D.C., there's a father-daughter private-eye team that also specializes in tailing the bad guys. Out in San Francisco,
a former call girl has taken up the profession, and an interview in a Berkeley newspaper suggested she focused on women's problems.

a tape and buzzed in the middle of a crucial interview, she said, "There goes my answering service." Then came the time she was checking into a hotel and realized she'd made the reservation under an assumed name she couldn't spell: she pretended to have something in her eye, blinked out her contact lens and scrawled illegibly in the guest register. But there's weariness in her voice when she says, "It begins to grate on you after a while, telling lies to people."

Again like Sam, Sal had a partner. She met him when her sister's ex-husband stole the children and she started an investigation herself. When a professional was called in, he was so impressed with what she'd done that he said, "If you ever need a job, come to me and I'll train you." She phoned three years ago. They'd still

be partners if it weren't for her ulcer kicking up; now she prefers being his employee.

Sam's fees were flexible, and at least one client welshed on paying the full amount. For $25 a hour, 30 cents a mile, plus expenses, Sal will rev up the surveillance van with its one-way mirror, tail somebody, even pose as a P.T.A. mother so she can ask schoolkids some questions.

"Then it happens we were in the detective business," said Sam Spade.

And Sal Spade says, "I'm not a nosy person, unless I'm getting paid."

Mickey Friedman writes about books and authors for the San Francisco Examiner. *She'd rather be a detective.*

CORDELIA GRAY: THE THINKING MAN'S HEROINE

Lillian de la Torre

"**N**o woman is the worse for sense," observed Dr. Sam: Johnson, the Great Lexicographer, who in his day, as I imagine it, might have been a "detector" of crime and chicane.

To prove it, he attached to himself women of sense, a playwright, a wit, a novelist, a poetess, whom he took into his heart and even into his home. Past doubt, he would have sought out that ultimate in women of sense, the lady detective, had there been one in his day.

Today, lady detectives abound. Which of them, I find myself asking, would I elect to draw into my family circle?

For honorary aunt, of course, I would choose Miss Jane Marple. She would keep me supplied with fluffy woollies and fluffy discourse studded with unexpected pearls of wisdom. Schoolteachery Miss Maud Silver and Miss Hildegarde Withers would intimidate me; they can be my aunts only if residing at a distance. I want Miss Sarah Keate at my bedside when I'm sick, and big Bertha Cool if I need a champion. That's enough aunts for anybody.

Among these women of sense, which would I select for a wife? Don't ask *me*. I leave that to male mystery fans.

There isn't a mother figure in the lot, but for an older sister to rely on I will have Dol Bonner (née Theodolinda), when she isn't working for Nero Wolfe. (Unless I happen to be twelve years old, in which case Nancy Drew is the big sister for me.)

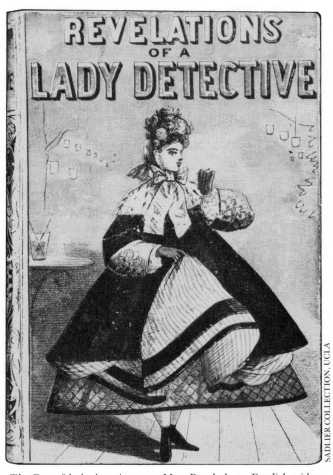

The Eve of lady detectives was Mrs. Paschal, an English widow created by "Anonyma." She appeared in two "Yellowback" editions, the first in 1861 and this, the second, in 1864. Mrs. P. was twenty-six when Sherlock Holmes was born, but there is no truth to the rumor she was his mother. He was not bright enough to claim a family relationship. Miss Adler, on the other hand . . .

And now, praise be, along comes P. D. James with the detecting girl I want for a daughter: Cordelia Gray, age twenty-two, sole proprietor of Pryde's Detective Agency ("We take a Pride in our Work"), which may be, as the book title proclaims, "An Unsuitable Job for a Woman."

Lady detectives were rampant before the turn of the century. Among them were Rockwood's Clarice Dyke (1883), Pirkis' Loveday Brooke (1894), Sims' Dorcas Dene (1897), Allen's Lois Cayley (1899) and Meade and Eustace's Florence Cusack (1899).

SADLIER COLLECTION, UCLA

"Endearing" is the word for Cordelia. She is namesake to the steadfast youngest daughter of old King Lear, and the name itself embodies *cor, cordis,* the heart.

Cordelia does not set up to be a beauty. It's a cat's face, she tells herself derisively in the mirror, wide in the cheekbones, foreshortened from brow to chin, large eyes of browny-green, a gentle childish mouth. Small, slight and wiry, she is ruefully aware that to the suspects she grills her appearance is more that of "an eager seventeen-year-old facing her first interview"

than a trained private eye.

Nor is she a clotheshorse. She detects in a fawn suede skirt and a green jumper. Her best suit is a Jaeger. When she splurges, she buys "a cotton kaftan patterned in greens, blues and brown" for summer evenings.

Nor yet is she a gourmet. Bacon crisping for breakfast, a pork pie and fruit to picnic on, a Scotch egg and a shandy at the pub satisfy her simple tastes.

Least of all is she the lecherous private eye of commerce. There have been men in her past, and she remembers them tenderly, but she is glad to have put them behind her before they became too important. "It was intolerable to think that those strange gymnastics might one day become necessary."

Cordelia is in fact a very private person, and her pleasures are lonely ones. She reads — Hardy and Jane Austen, Keats and William Blake — and responds quickly to art, recognizing a Renoir on the wall, retreating to the National Gallery when in need of consolation. She takes pleasure in small things, an improvised cold shower, sitting in the sun, picnicking and scattering the crumbs for the birds.

She takes an obsessional pleasure in order and neatness. Her scene-of-the-crime kit rivals Dr. Thorndyke's. Even camping out in a deserted cottage (the scene of the crime), she keeps the place swept and garnished, putting a lot more muscle into it than ever did Poirot.

No, there are no gimmicks to Cordelia. What she has is character. She is tough-minded but sensitive, feeling compassion for the old and defeated, for the beetle that blunders into the fire, but none for the cold-blooded murderer. She thinks quickly and straight, and never kids herself. She is a realist. "You can't do our job, partner, and be a gentleman," said Bernie Pryde. So Cordelia listens at doors and lays traps for the unwary suspect, even while not feeling best pleased with herself for doing so. When necessary, she lies skillfully and with a poker face. Yet she is essentially honest. "She can't be bought," admits that same suspect.

The neglected child of a roving radical, she spent six years in a convent school that sent her forth ladylike of speech and "incurably agnostic, but prone to unpredictable lapses into faith." An equal time spent in "a wandering life as cook, nurse, messenger and general camp follower to Daddy and the comrades" taught her self-reliance and resourcefulness.

She learned her craft from Bernie Pryde, *ex* C.I.D., founder of Pryde's Agency, before he died and left her the business. Over his teachings presides the unseen presence of his old boss, Chief Superintendent Adam Dalgliesh of Scotland Yard.

"Detection requires a patient persistence which amounts to obstinacy" was one of the Dalgliesh maxims. When at last the Superintendent and the girl came face to face, he recognized that obstinacy in her: she would not speak, and could be neither cajoled nor frightened into speaking.

For, most of all, Cordelia is without fear. When they throw her down a well, sheer anger and determination, with the ability to take it, bring her painfully up again. Battered and bruised, she lies in wait for the perpetrator and pursues him to his doom.

Any mother could be proud of a daughter like that. I want to adopt her for my own.

MRS. JAMES' DISCOVERY

"Read any good books lately?" is not the kind of question P. D. James takes lightly. When her American publisher broached the subject, she said, "Let me think about it," and mulled it over on the flight back home. No titles leapt to mind until the London *Times* asked her to review a manuscript by a new young author, Simon Brett. Mrs. James was impressed with it, very much, and fired off a transatlantic cable alerting Scribner's to her "find." Scribner's queried Gollancz, who posted the novel to them. Shortly thereafter, Scribner's became Mr. Brett's American publisher.

Mr. Brett has now completed four mysteries about Charles Paris, a theatrical ne'er-do-well who hams his way through murder. The witty Mr. Brett, who produced the BBC Lord Peter Wimsey radio programs, maintains that he is a better actor and a worse investigator than his Mr. Paris. Thus far, he says, he's never detected anything but the drawer in which his socks are kept.

But not so fast: Cordelia is no orphan. Not only is she P. D. James' brainchild; she is also her daughter. It is no secret that it was Mrs. James' daughter who sat for this endearing portrait. Hers is the pixie face, the sturdy sense, the valiant heart.

So I relinquish Cordelia from my dream family of women of sense, and content myself awaiting the next published exploit of the resolute Miss Gray of Pryde's Agency. Don't make me wait too long, Mrs. James!

Lillian de la Torre is president of the Mystery Writers of America and author of Goodbye, Miss Lizzie Borden *(a one-act play) and* Dr. Sam: Johnson, Detector, *a series of mystery short stories.*

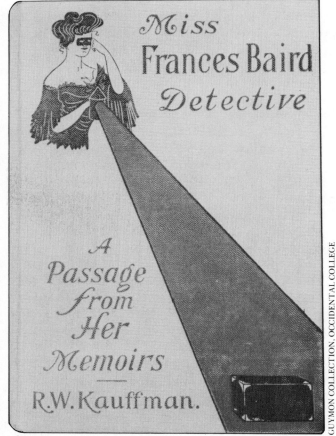

GUYMON COLLECTION, OCCIDENTAL COLLEGE

Frances appeared in 1906, reappeared in 1910, and hasn't been heard from since. Hulbert Footner's Madame Rosika Storey was not so shy; she intuited her way through 1925, 1926, 1928, 1937, resting between cases by feeding tidbits to her monkey.

MRS. PYM
OF SCOTLAND YARD

Nigel Morland

Mrs. Pym pioneered two well-established modern manias — the sex change and women's lib.

It was back in the days not long before Black Thursday that her creator returned from a long newspaperman's stint in China with a suitcase full of short stories and books dating from his first crime novel, which had appeared in 1923 under a Shanghai imprint.

This little libation to the gods of minor literature was dumped on the lap of Edgar Wallace, a close family friend since 1915. His cry of horror is remembered to this day after he had sifted through the mass of blacks and tearsheets: "It's terrible!"

Forthwith, thinking caps, as Ellery puts it, were donned, and EW, whose generosity with ideas equaled his largesse to all about him, proposed nothing less than a five-year sabbatical for his pulp-rabid disciple. And went on to rule in effect that: What you must chew over is a detective character. You've got the knack but not the know-how; you'll need to think hard and let your subconscious do some work for you.

To sum up the rest of it: Make him a policeman; you'll get the best of both worlds that way. A Scotland Yard man. Yes, call him Pym. That's a British name, brief and practical with a nice Puritan ring about it — the original Pym was a

great tactician and parliamentarian. And Ignatius as a first name; that's sufficiently dotty to pander to the English taste for funny names.

Twenty-four hours later, EW and his instructee, me, were simultaneously afire with the same notion. A woman! Not Ignatius, EW announced with an air of excitement, but a woman Pym. Call her Palmyra, after one of the fine old ancient ruins, suggested the lesser half of the Brain Trust, and if you add Evangeline you've got PEP. That'll personify her, for she's going to be a tough woman of early middle age. Don't make her pretty or masculine, but graft some of the qualities of a clever man onto the superior brain of a really able woman. And "Mrs." because spinsters are a bit of a joke in England. Then came his brightest notion: Put her in Scotland Yard with plenty of rank, a loner and something of a battering ram, which she'll have to be to stand up to that all-male world. It's an idea, the proud pair agreed. And EW, like the generous soul that he was, handed over something he could have gone to town with, not uttering one moan of loss.

For five years, Mrs. Pym floated in the limbo of creation. Little factors were added and some were taken away, till one day in 1935 she broke surface in *The Moon Murders*. A leading London critic, Howard Spring, panned the

YARD BIRDS

Baroness Orczy's Lady Molly is attached to Scotland Yard's "Female Department," while Leonard Gribble and Geraldine Law's Sally Dean does undercover work for its "Ghost Squad." Edgar Wallace gallantly allowed the Yard to hire two of his operatives: Mrs. Jane Ollerby is one of its highest-ranking officers, and Leslie Maughan is still working her way up through the C.I.D. ranks. As long as her father keeps an eye on her, Leslie will do all right; he's an assistant commissioner.

book like a man flattening a rattlesnake (though his hat came off to Mrs. Pym). Another critic who joined in the howls of execration from which Chief Inspector Mrs. Pym rose summed up the general view: "What a woman! I'd hate to marry her but she's Hawkshaw and the U.S. 5th Cavalry all rolled in one."

Her first years were all battles. Appointed to her job by a top government minister, she spent much of her time behaving with quiet illegality and a lot of common sense in solving crimes. She hated fools, time-servers, inefficiency and crooks, and never hesitated to risk her life on the spin of a coin or to use guts and even muscle to get out of a tight corner. PEP said, "Crooks laugh so loud at my tweed suits and funny hats they don't notice me underneath, arresting them."

With her third volume, she suddenly bloomed. *The Observer,* whose crime critic "Torquemada" still stands as the greatest of them all, described her as "that perfection of a woman," and Fryn Tennyson Jesse, an awesome name among true crime writers, urged all London to share her joy in her "darling Mrs. Pym."

If Mrs. Pym did one thing at all in her fictional life, she became, as a critic on the old *John O'London's Weekly* wrote, "the pin-up girl of the middle-aged female classes" — an undoubted

fact since such were the readers from whom so much fan mail came, and has always come. Frustrated wives, lonely spinsters, hard-working women and even young ladies wrote to Mrs. Pym by the dozen (and often with a frankness that would stun the editor of any Lonely Hearts column). They praised her uncompromising attitude toward the male world, aired their inhibitions by frankly envying her often ruthless ways ("I wish I had the nerve to stand up to my old man the way you tackle men!"). Their correspondence has been a curious sign-post to a slowly emerging women's lib — an oddity because Mrs. Pym has always gone her own sweet way, and she would, if she spoke about it, have no time for the current feminine passion for antonyms to all things male.

She has rampaged for years through a flock of adventures, dozens of short stories, thirteen translations including (as the funny English like to put it) American, though this last has never amounted to much because she is far too insularly English for the innocent Middle West. There has been one film starring her, a few radio programmes and, recently, her first collected volume of short stories.

As doyenne of Scotland Yard's women detectives (she is an assistant commissioner today), Mrs. Pym has changed little, though she is more tolerant than of yore. Time has turned her male colleagues toward liking or at least tolerating her in a world where she works contentedly under a queen and a woman prime minister.

She still lives in a dowdy old house in a London square and drives a powerful car because she likes to get anywhere quickly. Religion she has never talked about, any more than she has ever referred to her brief, unhappy marriage when she was a simple cop in the Far East. She is a push-over for animals, is down on those who cringe rather than face up to trouble. She will always help a lame dog over a stile even if she tends to boost rather than lift it. She claims she has "the most crusted heart in Christendom, but I daresay there's a backdoor, if you can find it."

Nigel Morland was the recipient of a special award for "services to crime fiction" from the Crime Writers' Association, of which he is a founding father.

COMMANDER DAPHNE

Mrs. Pym may be the highest-ranking woman at the fictional Yard, but Daphne Skillern is the top-rated female at the real one. Appointed commander (the equivalent rank outside London would be assistant chief constable) in 1977, she is responsible for a research and report division that deals with administrative problems (vehicle registration, gallantry awards, Gypsies, even dog-bites-bobby cases), the 600 police officers and civilian process servers employed in the courts (from magistrate up to crown) and public morals (all forms of obscenity from child exploitation to blue movies).

Commander Daphne Skillern, highest-ranking (non-fictional) woman at the Yard.

Commander Skillern joined the Metropolitan Police in 1949, spent two years in the obligatory uniform service, then applied to and was accepted by the C.I.D. She rose to the rank of superintendent before requesting transfer to the Home Office in 1966. Having later returned to management services, she has every intention of maintaining her current position until she reaches the age of fifty-seven and must, by law, retire (she is currently fifty-one).

Commander Skillern would like to see an increase in women officers on the force. Since the passage of the Sex Discrimination Act in 1973, more women have joined but there is still a great imbalance: approximately 21,000 men to a mere 1,300 women. Regarding the work, Skillern says, "It's a service job. It requires a vocational aptitude, like nursing."

If she could construct the ideal officer, she would endow her with "a sense of humour, initiative, resiliency," but not necessarily a solid academic background. She would also see to it that the officer was "physically fit," as the work demands stamina — her own day begins at 8 A.M. and is supposed to end at 7 P.M., but she can't remember when she got off that easily.

In her spare time, Commander Skillern gardens, sculpts, attends the theatre and reads: "I'm not too keen on Gideon. I like private persons solving the crimes, as I don't get offended and secretly annoyed that they're being silly." Television crime stories bother her: "The American ones glamorize too much, and the English never let a woman do anything more than escort the prisoner to and from interrogation, which is conducted by a man. They never get the mixture right, do they?"

Commander Skillern is not the Yard's first woman commander. Her predecessor, however, was in charge of women officers exclusively. That other commander was vulgarly referred to as "the Queen Bee." Skillern may become known as "the button-popper." Just as Inspector Gently was always leaving a trail of peppermint candy wrappers behind him, Commander Skillern is forever dropping a button off jackets or sleeve cuffs.

THE ENGLISH GAOL

Holloway, home to the English wayward, first clanged open its cell doors in 1853. Until 1902, it accepted both male and female boarders, and for a short while Oscar Wilde had the displeasure of calling it home.

In his study of the gaol, *Holloway Prison: The Place and the People,* John Camp tracks the history of the institution from the time it was but a gleam in contractor William Trego's eye, from the time shady ladies (the bulk of its clientele in the century's first decade were floozies and drunks) arrived at the doorstep in bobby-chauffeured Black Marias, from the time Mrs. Pankhurst and her suffragettes stormed its gates, from the time Ruth Ellis (the last woman to be hanged in Great Britain) resided there, to its current plans for refurbishing under the humane auspices of its psychiatrist warden.

The most famous fictional resident of Holloway was Harriet Vane.

If you're planning anything, you should know they have room for you,

Aylesworth prisoners enjoying the morning sun and the roses.

NORAH MULCAHANEY: NEW YORK'S FINEST

Lillian O'Donnell

Norah Mulcahaney, conceived on the night of the first big blackout in New York City, did not spring, like Minerva, full-blown out of my head. In fact, she did not appear on the printed page till nearly five years later.

Though she was formed gradually, she was formed surely. For instance, she never had to try on various names for fit as so many characters do: she was Norah Mulcahaney right from the beginning — an average, decent young woman, no sexpot, attractive without being glamorous, whose particular ambition led her to become a policewoman. Her character was shaped by her ethnic background and by the city in which she lives. The pace in New York is just a bit faster than anywhere else; there is an extra charge in the atmosphere, the horizons are broader. So Norah, who lost her mother at thirteen and took on the responsibility of running the house for her father and two brothers, was stimulated by her environment to reach beyond what might have been unbroachable boundaries to a job in the NYPD. She wasn't an outstanding rookie. She made mistakes; she was stubborn but she learned, and by sheer doggedness along with a little luck she made detective. She was not intended to be exceptional; rather, she would grow with the experience of the job and with the times and the city.

But back to the blackout.

I was on my way to a tennis match and driving through the Brooklyn Battery Tunnel when the lights flickered, then went out. For a split second of real fear, I thought something had gone wrong with the tunnel's electrical system. I did not let myself dwell on where I was — under

Communication Controls System, Inc., New York City, will custom-make ladies' bulletproof vests capable of stopping a .357 Magnum. From $250. Allow 3 weeks for delivery.

COURTESY NEW YORK POST

New York policewomen hoist a few in 1923 training class.

the East River with millions of gallons of water over my head — or on the possibility that the electrical failure might be due to a leak. I picked up speed and made it out of there in record time.

My friend, then Director of Policewomen for the city, was waiting for me at the tennis court. When the seriousness of the outage became apparent, she suggested I leave my car and drive back with her and her driver, also a policewoman. It was a ride I'll never forget.

The first thing the driver did was put on the "cherry," the red roof light atop the car. It made the going easier, but it also focused attention on us. We were stopped by troubled and perplexed civilians. They were reassured and their questions answered courteously and competently. I was impressed, and at the same time I was shocked to realize that if these two officers had been men I would have taken their efficiency and composure for granted.

As soon as we crossed the bridge into Manhattan, my friend ordered her driver to headquarters.

"I'll have to drop you, I'm afraid," she said.

"I didn't know you were on duty," I replied.

"We're not. All the police officers who can make it will be reporting to their precinct to help out. If not their precinct, they'll go to the nearest station house." She explained it matter-of-factly.

That set me straight. They thought of themselves as officers: gender didn't enter into it. In that moment, I made the decision to use a policewoman as heroine in a story — sometime. Of course, I didn't know how limited the duties of policewomen were until I started to do research. I wasn't interested then in making Norah a spokeswoman for women's lib, nor am I now. However, I did want her to be a part of the real world, and the facts of the case are that at the time Norah joined the force "police officers, female" were just breaking out of the traditional mold of matron and juvenile work. The evolution of women's responsibilities within the NYPD is perforce a part of Norah's story. As a rookie, she fought to get out of the policewoman's pool in the same way that an office worker fights to get out of the typing pool. A policewoman, Gertrude Schimmel, had to go to court to get the right to take the sergeant's exam. That made it possible for other women, Norah included, to take the exam and to rise in rank. In spite of that, Norah does not consider herself part of the spearhead for the women's movement. She's a cop. She likes the work; she likes the hours; she likes the opportunity for initiative. She's a detective and she solves cases. She's good at that. If others want to put her in a special category, that's their problem.

She's married — as it happens, to a police

POLICE OFFICERS, FEMALE

Poor Jane Boardman. She started out smart, then developed a rampant case of the stupids. In Joseph Harrington's *Last Known Address,* she and Lt. Kerrigan were detective squad partners, and she pulled her own weight. In the next book, *Blind Spot,* she was relegated to a bit part, and by the time *The Last Doorbell* came off the press, her role had disintegrated into an "I don't know, what do you think, Kerrigan?" sort of thing. There was no fourth book. No wonder.

Detective Christie Opara also prowled through just three books. Dorothy Uhnak, a former policewoman herself, set Officer Opara loose in *The Bait, The Witness* and *The Ledger,* then dropped her. Television picked her up, changed her name and her race, then canceled her. We shall probably never learn whether she and Reardon ever do have an affair. And the suspense is killing.

Both Jane and Christie were outlasted by Jeannette Covert Nolan's Lace White. She appeared in at least four books, as an honorary lieutenant of the Indiana State Police. She debuted in 1943 in *Final Appearance.*

Over in England, things are a bit brighter. Gwendolyn Butler, writing as Jennie Melville, has made Charmian Daniels a member of the Deerham constabulary. She's handled five cases thus far, including *Murderers' Houses* and *Come Home and Be Killed.*

---

lieutenant. Having the job in common is an extra bond between them; it strengthens their relationship, but it would have been the same if they'd been doctors, lawyers, accountants or in the plumbing business together.

It has been remarked that Norah Mulcahaney is most often identified with cases of violence against women. Looking back, I realize that is true. In her first appearance, Norah was called in to be a decoy in a homicide growing out of obscene telephone calls. It takes a woman to fully understand the traumatic effect on the victims of such calls. After all, there's no physical contact: all one has to do is simply hang up. Some can do that; others are haunted by the slimy suggestions, the invasion of privacy and a very real physical fear that the caller will not stop at harassment by telephone.

It was Norah's opportunity to make detective and mine to introduce her, but the cases that followed were not consciously chosen because they concerned women. Asking myself how that came about, I grew aware that there has recently been increasing concern on the part of society over the victimization of women and a change in the traditional view of these crimes: rape, battered wives, prostitution. As a product of her time and place, and as one who cares about what is going on around her, Norah moves into these cases with emotional energy. But she has been involved in other matters, too — a series of murders of old people and the black market in babies.

In fiction, Norah formed her own Senior Citizens Squad when in fact there was only one such unit, a pilot project in the Bronx. Now just about every precinct has one.

Norah joined Homicide back in the days when there were two divisions: Homicide North and South. She was the only woman on the squad — in fiction. In fact, there were no women at all. That was in 1972.

In March 1978, nine female detectives were appointed to Homicide. According to the New York City Chief of Detectives, every area of the detective division now has women assigned.

Six years for fact to catch up.

Lillian O'Donnell has written seven police procedurals featuring Norah Mulcahaney.

GRILLING A HOMICIDE COP

Q: Name?

A. Castoire. Detective 3rd Grade Marie Castoire, 10th Homicide, Brooklyn.

Q. Okay, put your purse on the table, nice and easy. Now empty it and let's hear what's in it.

A. One .38 Smith & Wesson service revolver with a three-inch barrel, all chambers loaded. Spare bullets, five of them. One nail file. One penknife. One silver shield — and if you're asking, I liked the gold one better but they made us give it up when they disbanded the women's unit in the early seventies. One tax registry card — it goes with the shield, you can't use one for I.D. without the other. One mobilization card, for emergencies. One hostage negotiator card — that means I'm qualified to act as an intermediary. Two sticks of chewing gum. One flashlight. One compact with a mirror light, in case I forget my flashlight. Miscellaneous stuff: lipstick, comb, wallet. You want to know how much is in the wallet? Not a lot. Parking tickets take up most of it.

Q. Don't get wise. Now, where you going with the gun?

A. I always carry it; safer than leaving it lying around the house. What if someone broke in and stole it? I'm not afraid of guns. I'm good with them. At the Academy, the instructor said, "Four more like you and we'd have a marksmanship team."

Q. So you think you're tough, Marie?

A. I didn't come on this job to be an overpaid clerk or an underpaid undertaker. I have an accelerated way of living. I joined the force in '69, spent two years in plain clothes, four with the

sex crimes unit, sat out some time when the Department had budget problems and cut back, and then got assigned to the elite: Homicide. I was complimented they wanted me. There are only nine women in New York doing what I do. When I had to take a week-long baton-wielding course, I missed my outfit. The day I came back, I found they'd taped a huge banner across my locker: WELCOME HOME, WONDER WOMAN. That thrilled me.

Q. Prior arrests?

A. My team has a 70 percent arrest record, which is really super. When a homicide comes in, it's assigned to a detective, but he works with a partner and they work as part of a four- or five-man team. An investigation is never closed

The Castoire file.

until a collar is made. We have "mysteries" and "grounders." "Mysteries" are the unsolved deaths — organized crime hits are tough, nobody wants to talk. "Grounders" are the easy ones, when you have a second-party statement. Mary sees John shoot Fred, and says so. What bothers me is the indifference some people show to the dark side. I figure we're here to stand up for the victim. No one has the right to take a life.

Q. Ever been in trouble with the law, Marie?

A. Once, trying to break a prostitution ring, I was wired for sound, but I was in a steel-frame building and my backup couldn't hear what was going on. I'm saying things like "Terrific *corner* view out of this *third-floor* window," and they're getting mostly static. The only words that came through clear were embarrassing.

Q. I'm a big boy. Spill it.

A. Yeah. I'm supposed to be applying for a topless waitress position, and this guy and I are chitchatting, sipping our wine spritzers, when he says he has to see me with my clothes off. "Look," I said, "trust me. I can do the pencil trick." When I came out of there, all my partner wanted to know was: "Marie, what's the pencil trick?" And I had to explain, if you could put one under your breast, and it stayed up, that meant you were built. It was the one time I wished police equipment didn't work.

Q. You don't look like a cop. Where's your uniform?

A. In Homicide I don't have to wear one. But I used to, before. Got a $250 wardrobe allowance. That was when women were still wearing the blue skirts with the little pleat in front. Now pants are required; they're better for moving around in. I guess the only thing that's still uniform about me is my hair: it clears my collar.

Q. Any scars?

A. Not physical, no. But emotional. Homicide is not prim and proper. It's a lot of dirty words. It's gory. It makes you cry. And to vent your feelings, you laugh. We tell awful jokes: "I hear the guy's dead," one cop says. His partner answers, "Gee — hope it's not catchy."

Q. Do you ever work alone?

A. I've been doing a little writing on the side, but it's taken me over a year to finish the first draft. It's a mystery story, about a cop named Vickie in the sex crimes squad. She has a super partner, but an old-timer keeps giving her trouble. Thomas Chastain, the famous mystery writer, is going to read through it for me and tell me what he thinks. I call it *Not One of the Boys,* because a female will never fit in totally. When you work with a woman, you work with half a partner. But maybe we're a little more compassionate, and we can get things done in our own way. Look, I can't knock down a door. I just can't do it. At the Academy, I spent four hours a day getting in shape during training, but I still don't have that kind of strength. I can knock on that door, though, and have it opened for me, and maybe a guy can't.

Q. Why'd you turn cop, Marie?

A. I always wanted to be one. When I was a kid, I had one of those fun-for-a-rainy-day books and there was this page to test your powers of observation. How many things can you find in the picture, kind of thing. I loved it. I still find it exhilarating. Of course, I started late, not till I was thirty-two. I got married at seventeen, had three kids right away, and it was only after the divorce that I took the test. There was a freeze on hiring, though. By the time I was accepted, I was really too old, but because of the freeze they took me anyway. It's as though those years waiting hadn't happened. My father worries about me. I don't tell him a lot of stuff.

Q. Anything else you want to say in your defense before we book you?

A. I'm under constant stress. That's why there are so many cop divorces, heavy drinkers, suicides. We rank number two, right after doctors. I think we have to have a deterrent to crime. The death penalty? If we save one life with it, it's worth it.

Q. What would make you commit a crime, Marie? Or anybody else?

A. All crimes are committed because of one of the seven deadly sins.

THE QUICK-DRAW ARTIST

Along about Chapter 4 in a police procedural, the officer sets out to canvass the neighborhood for witnesses. If the author is honest, thirty-seven interviews later the officer will have learned that the suspect was the tallest midget on record, that she wore gloves and a diamond dinner ring, that she fired two shots that somehow managed to leave nine stab wounds. Sound contradictory? Well, you've just discovered a

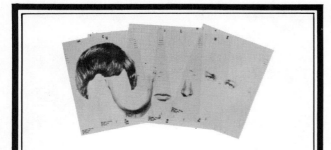

THE IDENTI-KIT

Introduced in 1959, the Indenti-Kit® is a series of transparent cards, each depicting a face shape, a certain type of nose, chin, mouth, dimple, and so forth. Together, the officer and the eyewitness scutinize the cards, overlaying a pug nose on a receding hairline, somewhat less of a pug nose on an even more receding hairline, until they create a composite that matches the witness's memory. Developed by Smith & Wesson, the Identi-Kit has proved invaluable to police forces without an art squad.

fact of life: eyewitnesses are notoriously unreliable. They hear things that weren't said, they see things that didn't happen and they invent things that are mutually exclusive.

This, then, becomes the real-life headache of Officer Francis Domingo, Artists Unit, Room 506C, Police Headquarters, One Police Plaza, New York City. Frank's job is to extract a viable description of the perpetrator and capture it on paper for circulation throughout the precincts, hopefully with an arrest in the offing. When you take into account the fact that he may have to work from the memory of an individual who spent less than two minutes with the suspect, who saw her only in profile and was scared witless at the time, you begin to understand the difficulties.

Says Domingo: "Get it out of your head that I'm painting a portrait. I'm not drawing an actual person, but a picture of someone's impression of a person. It's a caricature, that's all it is. I'm trying for a 'type,' something that's close enough a guy might think, Hey, that looks like the nut who lives down the street . . ."

Step one in this process is a visit to the M.O. (modus operandi) room, which houses aisle after aisle of steel filing cabinets filled with mug shots. About a million and a half of them, arranged according to area, then subdivided according to sex and height. The witness spends at least an hour here, maybe more, with Domingo at his side. Together they try to find specific features that resemble those of the suspect. They hold out one card for eyebrows, another for ear lobes (all mug shorts show one naked ear because that extremity is often a good identifying factor), still another for face shape, hair

MATTHEW SEAMAN

Officer Francis Domingo, NYPD Artists Unit, capturing a suspect. The pile of drawings on the table are mug shots the witness pulled out as having features similar to the perpetrator's. The portrait took approximately three hours to complete. Domingo works with a soft black pencil, a gum eraser, and plain white drawing paper. To see how well he matched the real-life suspect, see facing page.

style, expression and so forth. They may ultimately wind up with fifteen cards that in one way or another "feel right" to the witness.

Then it's back to Room 506C, a small area with two artists' desks, a strong light, a plain white piece of drawing paper, some soft black pencils and one much used gum eraser. "We try for the shape of the face first," says Domingo,

Police artist's rendering of Det. Castoire following description supplied by the eyewitness's report.

The real Det. Castoire. The witness incorrectly remembered how she parted her hair, mistakenly gave her a dimple in her chin.

"the position of the features. Refinements come later, but in the beginning we have to know how close or how far apart the eyes are, how far down the nose comes, where the hairline starts."

Domingo does approximately 500 drawings a year and by this time usually knows beforehand what the witness wants to say. He tries to jog the memory: "Which side did she part her hair on? Close your eyes and look at her. She's facing you — was it on your left or your right?" Says Domingo: "If you can't remember, don't invent. Just admit you don't know and I'll fill in something average. If you think the girl looked Italian, Mediterranean, but can't remember her skin color, let's settle for olive. It's the likeliest choice."

Sometimes a witness will become hynotized. "Nothing spooky about it," says Domingo. "He may be more relaxed as a result of it and things will come up he was too scared to think about before."

Using the mug shots as a guide, and sometimes resorting to a scrapbook of famous people's faces (movie stars, athletes, politicians), the artist and the witness sketch and comment, comment and erase, until they arrive at the point when the witness says he's satisfied. "The problem is, I may match his memory a hundred per-

cent and still not wind up with anything like the real criminal," moans Domingo. "I have to go by what he tells me, not what is."

Frank still thinks it's the best method available, particularly when compared to the results of photomontage and the Identi-Kit: "With a montage, the picture ends up looking like a Frankenstein — all seams. You can see where the different mug shots were overlapped. People tend to look on it as totally accurate, though. They forget it's still just an impression, like my drawing. They see a photograph and they think, Well, that must be him. The Identikit composite, which is built up from picking one hat from page A, one mustache from page B, et cetera, is too stiff. Inhuman."

In addition to faces, Domingo has sketched stolen jewelry — everything from fancy bracelets to filigreed stickpins — and getaway cars. On his own time, he does magnificently colored stained-glass pictures and pen-and-ink nudes that feature the feet ("I like feet"), and has appeared in several gallery shows.

He is an art school graduate, as are the other two Department cops in his unit. The squad was formed in 1958-59 by New York Detective Kinnahan, who was given the go-ahead when his first attempt landed the guilty party.

MY PROBLEMS WITH THE POLICE

Dell Shannon

It was entirely by accident that I found myself doing police procedurals. I started out writing respectable historical novels. Buried in research, I never gave much thought to a detective story, though I was a great reader of them, until I'd finished the best historical I'd ever done — and nobody would buy it. I took a vow not to do another before that one sold, and it hasn't yet.

Anyway, I had an idea for a suspense book, began it, and on page 11 of the thing Lieutenant Luis Mendoza rose up off the page. And ever since, he's refused to let me stop writing about him. Of course, many an author tells admiring fans that such-and-such a character appeared full-blown and captured him alive — but it does happen, it does happen.

By the time the seventh book or so came along, it occurred to me that if I was going to be saddled with professional cops for the rest of my days, it behooved me to find out something about police work, police forces and latest police techniques. So I studied them, right down to the refinements of the Identi-Kit®. If my fictional people seem to see more offbeat cases than real-life police officers do, well, first and foremost, fiction's purpose is to entertain the reader.

Mendoza, being a ruthless egotist, keeps deviling me for more books about himself. I keep thinking there has to be an end to him sometime, that people will get sick of him, but no, they keep asking for him. Over the years, I've been somewhat surprised to discover the number of readers who are hooked on detectives, mine and others. They're loyal to their favorites — one could almost say passionately and fanatically — but I get the distinct impression that in a pinch any "mystery" will do.

The reason for this is not hard to determine. Any society, to be cohesive and workable, must operate upon certain firm rules of living: lines must be drawn, codes of behavior understood. In the madness of the twentieth century, too many of these have become confused shambles. In a sea of permissiveness, in an era when "anything goes" seems to be going from bad to worse, the average citizen feels shifting sand underfoot and gropes wildly for some firm rock of the moral absolute. And the detective novel is where it is found.

The detective novel, I like to say, is the mo-

THE SHANNON MENAGERIE

The snake on a flag Miss Shannon runs up her flagpole when she wishes not to be disturbed.

DONT TREAD ON ME

Miss Shannon owns one dog, two cats, one snake on a flag, and a couple of sheep. The sheep used to belong to neighbor. She bought them from him when she noticed now neatly they kept the yard trimmed. She does not shear them herself. Except for her four-footed friends, Miss Shannon lives alone. And likes it.

Star, Miss Shannon's keeshond, a Dutch barge dog.

Miss Shannon with one of her two cats. The mystery: is it Penny or Pandora?

MARGE BENNETT

rality play of our time. In most cases, the bad guys are caught, the good guys are victorious and right triumphs. I believe these basic facts (augmented by some literary considerations) are the reasons we've seen the detective novel pass from the mere puzzle-for-its-own-sake to deeper characterization and more subtle plotting. If people need heroes, they also need, in the pages of fiction, likable and admirable characters they can identify with. And in too many novels, aside from the detective ones, they are asked to identify with a set of sleazy, amoral, unwashed, certainly unadmirable figures, whose very monotonous iniquities are unbelievable. Need I remind anyone of the important message the much-missed Charlotte Armstrong brought us in *A Dram of Poison* — reality is not necessarily ugly, nor truth always negative. The mystery reader, aware of this, will continually pass up the latest Great Novel and pick up instead an old or new detective story.

Meanwhile, Mendoza keeps pestering me for more books. To keep him at bay, I've developed three other series characters: Vic Vatallo, who now operates out of Glendale (where I lived for so many years) but who started out as a small-town cop from upstate; Sgt. Maddox, who works the Hollywood precinct of the LAPD with squad member Sue Carstairs; Jesse Falkenstein, my one non-cop, who is agony to find plots for since he isn't even a criminal lawyer. I like Falkenstein. He lets me bring in a peripheral interest of mine, parapsychological research, to which a great deal of my personal library is devoted.

But Mendoza is a nuisance. He keeps hounding me for more. This despite the fact he's been in thirty books so far and involved in Lord only knows how many cases — they average out to about fifteen per book. (Maddox has a similar caseload, because his is a busy precinct. Vatallo handles five or six at a clip, and with Falkenstein I often feel like I'm building bricks without straw, since I only have one case to concentrate on in each book.)

I should say that when I write I'm single-minded. That's all I do, eighteen hours a day. The laundry piles up, the bed doesn't get made, my friends find me incommunicado: I have a twenty-two-foot flagpole outside my house, and

DELL SHANNON ET AL.

My real name is Elizabeth Linington. I created the pseudonym Dell Shannon for the first Mendoza book, *Case Pending*. The Dell was a shortening of my father's mother's name, Blaisdell. And there's a healthy share of Irish in the family, so that's where the Shannon came from. I also use the name Lesley Egan, for the Falkenstein series. Lesley was chosen because it sounded sexually androgynous, and Egan was a grandmother's name. One of my historicals, *The Anglophile*, was brought out under the nom de plume Egan O'Neill, honoring both grandmothers. I use Linington for the Vic Vatallo books, and just once, for *Nightmare*, I used Anne Blaisdell.

when I run up the *Don't Tread On Me* banner they know to leave me alone.

I write a book every February, March and June. Each one takes me ten to twelve days. I write in longhand, at a desk I purchased from the *Sturbridge Yankee Catalogue*. I don't make endless drafts. It has to get written out right the first time. When I'm copying it, I may change a word or two, but that's all. Typing is the hardest work I do. It's a tough, slogging job. One reason I have to write in such concentrated fashion is that I have to keep track of all those cases — I have to remember when the indictment is due, when the arraignment is scheduled, when the autopsy report might be coming up. Total immersion seems to be the best method for me to keep it all straight. I often think there must be an easier way to earn a living, but then I say, You idiot! Thirty-three days a year ain't bad!

But it stretches into infinity.

And Mendoza's always after me.

Dell Shannon's most recent novel (as Dell Shannon) is Felony at Random, *as Elizabeth Linington is* No Villain Need Be, *as Lesley Egan is* Look Back on Death.

Chapter 4
SIDEKICKS

THE MYSTERY WRITER'S WIFE
A Special Case

Stanley Ellin

There are women who take up hang-gliding, women who polish their copper kitchenware every time they use it, women who dote on the care and breeding of parakeets, a notoriously temperamental fowl. And then there are women who marry mystery writers, a vocation that combines the worst of all the foregoing in one large, misshapen package.

Awareness that she may have erred in her choice of mate usually dawns on the fledgling bride during the honeymoon itself, when she faces the choice of memorizing the wallpaper pattern in her bridal suite or attending criminal trials in exotic courtrooms — London's Old Bailey is a veritable honeymoon haven for the practicing mystery writer and spouse — or, if the courtroom fails to offer sufficient entertainment, rambling hand in hand with the loved one through various morgues, police stations and sites of memorable murders.

The education continues as housekeeping is set up. Now, like Bluebeard's wife, she learns that there is one room in her home she may not enter except on written application. This is the scribe's workroom, his *sanctum sanctorum*, and on entering it she is expected not to remark on the platoon of complacent mice nibbling the stale sandwich crusts ornamenting the desk, much less take notice of any litter of typing paper, notes and matchbox covers garnishing chair seats, window sills and floor.

What she must do in the positive, productive sense is garner and neatly file newspaper accounts of stomach-turning crimes, become an expert and convenient reference source on weaponry and poisons, read (on request) the master's words with little cries of admiration and promptly answer every phone call to the house no matter where she is when the phone rings, including the bath. Above all, should editor or agent prove to be at the other end of the line, to instantly say in bright, convincing tones: "Yes, he's working very hard on it right now, and he's sure he'll meet the deadline."

Then, of course, there is her natural and inevitable function, probably the most striking manifestation of mystery-writer wifehood, which cycles around whenever her husband's latest novel is delivered to the bookshops, but this is a phenomenon best demonstrated by the classic

THE FAMILY PLOT

The thing about murder is, it's habit-forming. If you live with a fictional death-dealer, you'll probably become one, too. You might share a plot, as did G.D.H. and Margaret Cole, Maj Sjöwall and Per Wahlöö, Richard and Frances Lockridge and the Gordons. Or you might prefer to devise your own, as do Margaret Millar and Ross Macdonald, Hildegarde Dolson and Richard Lockridge (no, he didn't do Frances in; how could you even suspect it!). Some couples keep at it despite divorce : Helen McCloy and Brett Halliday.

Now and then, a parent sets such a good example that the child can hardly wait to follow in the (bloody) footsteps. Helen Reilly's two daughters, Ursula Curtiss and Mary McMullen, took up her cudgels, and Michael Gilbert's eldest, Harriett, defended his.

There's even one strange case of a writer meeting up with another writer because she rented a flat from his father. Together, they became Manning Coles.

We've also learned of one instance where brothers committed crimes (Anthony and Peter Shaffer) and one where cousins were the culprits (Frederic Dannay and Manfred B. Lee).

Maybe it's time we stopped talking about feeling safe within the bosom of the family.

A family of conspirators with their nightly visitor, the raven.

HUSBAND
1879-1939
FIRST PRINTING 1900
SECOND "   1905
THIRD   "   1915
FOURTH "   1925
FIFTH   "   1930
SIXTH   "   1935
AD INFINITUM

WIFE
1890-1955
PUBLISHED 1925
©
ALL RIGHTS
RESERVED

DAUGHTER
1915-1940
MANUSCRIPT
REJECTED.
"BY GOD DEVISED
BY SELF DEMISED"

MARTY NORMAN

case of, as the airlines like to put it, Mr./Mrs. Albert Smithers.

Albert made an adequate living from two medium-boiled private-eye novels a year that sold moderately well in hard-cover and very well in their paperback editions. Married to an attractive and personable young woman, he shared a pleasant ranch-type home with her on Long Island and considered his marriage idyllic. So, one day soon after their fifth anniversary, he was staggered to find attached to the refrigerator door by a small magnet in the shape of a half-pineapple a note that read: *I cannot go on like this any longer. Do not try to find me; it will be useless. Please finish the meat loaf before starting on the frozen foods.*

His world turned upside down, Albert went for advice to the one man who had never yet let him down in any crisis, his editor at the publishing house of Flambeaux & Gallagher. The editor, as usual when not approached for an unnaturally large advance, was both sympathetic and helpful. "A private investigator named Thigpen is recommended by the Mystery Writers of America for just such cases," he stated. "Put yourself in his hands, and I am sure all will be well."

Thigpen, suave and prosperous-looking, breathed an air of confidence. He questioned his new client in great detail about every aspect of his personal and professional life, and concluded: "By any chance, have you had a book recently published?"

"Less than a month ago," said Smithers.

"Good," said Thigpen. "In that event, I'll have the lady's address for you within the week."

Sure enough, within the week he did have the address. When Smithers expressed amazement at this. Thigpen waved a hand in deprecation.

"Really nothing to it," he said. "You see, even the largest bookshops, in dealing with a mystery writer of your precise standing, will buy no more than a handful of his newly minted works to hide away on their shelves. And it is a scientific fact that the wife of any such writer is driven by uncontrollable instinct to enter those shops incognito and covertly try to arrange those pathetically few volumes into an eye-catching display. All I had to do, therefore, was

THE MYSTERY WEDDING

Joan M. Lexau

Someone murdered,
Plus a clue,
Something stolen,
Men in blue.

cover the major bookshops in the territory between Altman's and Bloomingdale's, where, according to her credit cards, your wife would be making her shopping trips, and whenever I saw your books protruding from a shelf noticeably beyond all others, or arranged broadside for best exposure, or carefully planted in their dark jackets out of alphabetical order between volumes in contrasting white jackets, I knew Mrs. Smithers had passed this way. In Brentano's, where your books were virtually buried out of sight, thus indicating she had not yet attended to them, I simply bided my time until she showed up to do so. After that, following her unseen to her lodgings was child's play."

As it turned out, Thigpen's excellent work was not wasted. Smithers, after his touching appeal was rebuffed by his wife with chilling finality, used this episode as the theme of his most brilliant and successful work. Mrs. Smithers, after the divorce, turned to writing Gothic romances and is now banking her second million. The one troublesome aspect is that she still finds herself arranging shelf displays for her ex-husband's hard-cover editions as they appear in the bookshops, and there seems to be nothing her analyst can do about it. He now suspects it may be something hormonal and is trying therapy in that direction.

Stanley Ellin is a past president of the Mystery Writers of America. He has won three Edgar awards: one for best mystery of the year (The Eighth Circle) and two for best mystery short story ("The Blessington Method," "The House Party").

I MARRIED
MISS MARPLE

We all loved Margaret Rutherford as Miss Marple. She loved her leading man, Stringer Davis, who appeared in the four Marple films as Mr. Stringer, the town librarian. The couple met in '31, wed in '45, and adopted four children. Margaret died in '72; Stringer, in '75.

*Stringer and Margaret simulate
their first fight
over cold breakfast muffins.*

*Stringer and Margaret
reenact leaving on their
honeymoon.*

*Stringer and Margaret
(who was made a Dame of
the British Empire in
1967) pretend to sneak
into the drive-in movie to
see a quadruple feature:*
Murder She Said;
Murder at the Gallop;
Murder Most Foul;
Murder Ahoy!

TILL DEATH DO US PART

Nick & Nora, Pam & Jerry, Tommy & Tuppence

Too bad love is blind. If it weren't, Nora Charles, Pamela North and Tuppence Beresford might have detected a rather odd codicil amended to their marriage contracts:

> *The party of the first part*, hereafter known as the wife, agrees to supply *the party of the second part*, hereafter known as the husband, with a fresh corpse whenever their author shows signs of plot restlessness. Said wife is honor-bound to discover the aforementioned at great peril. She will not, however, attempt to extricate herself from damaging circumstances, but will wait obediently for the designated husband to mount a here-comes-the-cavalry rescue. In the event said wife cannot provide a deceased, she will forthwith produce a thief, spy, burglar, blackmailer or similar lowlife. Wife understands that this in no way obligates spouse to acknowledge her capabilities in other than wisecracks. And herein she troths her plight. (Signature)

Considering that Nora obeyed the injunction in one book, six movies, two television series and innumerable radio shows, that Pam met the requirements in twenty-six books, one play, one movie, one radio series and fifty-seven half-hour video programs, and that Tuppence followed suit in four books and one movie, we have ample evidence to conclude that the distaff half of a sleuthing couple spends very little time at domestic chores: she's too busy foraging the neighborhood for nice, juicy, cold bodies.

Clearly, these three Mrs. Snoops should have insisted that daddy give them keys to a mortuary as their dowry. They also ought to have had their heads examined. "Crazy in love" was in their case more a medical diagnosis than a warming cliché.

As most of us realize, Nora Charles was the invention of Dashiell Hammett, who swore he'd swiped her major characteristics from his good chum Lillian Hellman. Frankly, that's a little hard to swallow, even with the aid of the omnipresent Charles martini. Nora is described as having "a wicked jaw." Have you ever seen a picture of Lillian Hellman? Her lip may snarl a bit, but her jaw does not jut. And if she swilled as much as Nora, or had her hair done as often, or did as much browsing at Saks, she would never have found the time to write. Still, Miss Lillian has gone on record saying she was flattered by the comparison, particularly when she thought of the fun Nick & Nora had. Since on one occasion the "fun" included his landing a solid haymaker on that wicked jaw, we might be excused for wondering if in the Hellman-Hammett ménage more than the gin got bruised.

Contrary to most notions, Nora was not married to the Thin Man. Myrna Loy was. For reasons best understood by a movie producer, the book's title (which referred to a missing person) became the cinema hero's sobriquet. Two other changes were made in transferring the book to screen: Asta, the exuberant schnauzer, switched breed and surfaced as a terrier, and his owners became the proud parents of a bouncing baby "thin man," Nick Charles, Jr. (Though never stipulated, Nicky's formula was undoubtedly 3 parts milk:3 parts gin:1 part vermouth.)

Pamela North began her life in a Richard Lockridge short story written for *The New Yorker*. A while later, when Mrs. Lockridge developed a plot but couldn't think of any characters to people it with, he generously said, "Take mine." Thus began, in 1941, the Mr. and Mrs. North collaboration. Frances evolved the plots; Richard did the actual writing.

Pam is a daffy example of the sleuth who arrives at the correct solution for all the wrong reasons. She might build a whole theory around the third slat in a Venetian blind and how it could only have been bent just so by a woman wearing an emerald dinner ring on her right hand; leap from there to the type of person who would buy his lady flashy jewels; hop, skip and jump to the bank officer who issued the man a loan for them; and come up with the fact that the murderer was the man's accountant, who was outraged that the First National denied him a rating as fat as his client's. Invariably, the CPA turns out to be the guilty party, but for an entirely different motive — and certainly not one that could be inferred from a bent third slat on the kitchen window.

Pam comes across dead bodies with alarming frequency and in the process gets slammed on the head, hamstrung and gagged. Of all mystery wives, she is perhaps the one most often endangered. Not a venture goes by in which Pam isn't mauled. Since Jerry, taking a leaf from Nick Charles' book, is usually suffering a hangover — or in various stages of acquiring one — she must wait to be saved. In maximum discomfort, we might add.

Pam's greatest trial, however, is the litter problem. The Norths are overrun with cats and, at different times, house Pete, Toughy, Ruffy, Martini, Gin and Sherry (the latter two delivered of Martini).

Prudence (Tuppence) Beresford, née Cowley, was the brainchild of Agatha Christie. Unlike a certain Belgian bachelor and a specific St. Mary Mead spinster, Tuppence matures be-

VITAL STATISTICS OF A MARTINI

The perfect martini: 3 oz. gin; 1 oz. vermouth; poison to taste.

SCHENLEY INDUSTRY

Nick and Nora's drink was the inspiration of a San Francisco bartender, who concocted it back in 1860. He named it for the destination (Martinez, about 40 miles away) of the customer who first sipped it. The original recipe, according to *Gourmet* magazine, called for 1 dash of bitters, 2 dashes of maraschino, 1 pony of Old Tom gin, 1 wineglass of vermouth, 2 small ice cubes and a sliver of lemon. Over the years, the ratio of gin to vermouth has been the subject of much discussion, not all of it friendly. Mystery readers who wish to emulate Nick and Nora should hold steady at 3 to 1. Mystery readers who wish to poison them should replace the lemon with an olive stuffed full of anything lethal they happen to have at hand, such as arsenic powder.

WHAT'S A TUPPENCE?

A defunct coin. Worth two pennies, it was an obviously appropriate symbol for the female Beresford, who kept sticking her two cents into matters that didn't concern her.

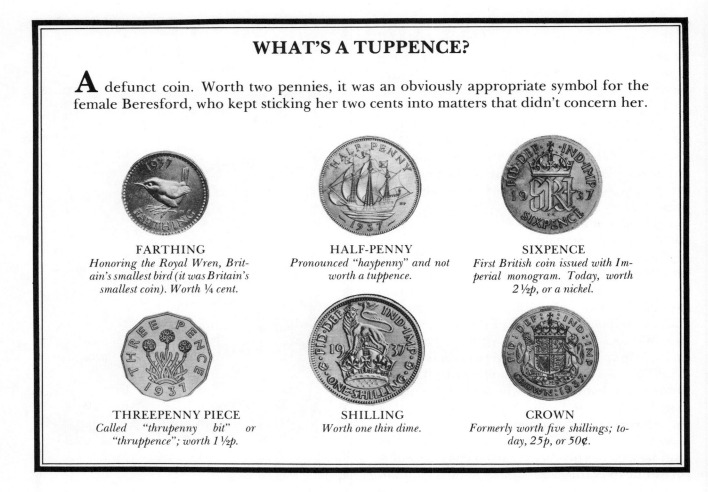

FARTHING
Honoring the Royal Wren, Britain's smallest bird (it was Britain's smallest coin). Worth ¼ cent.

HALF-PENNY
Pronounced "haypenny" and not worth a tuppence.

SIXPENCE
First British coin issued with Imperial monogram. Today, worth 2 ½p, or a nickel.

THREEPENNY PIECE
Called "thrupenny bit" or "thruppence"; worth 1 ½p.

SHILLING
Worth one thin dime.

CROWN
Formerly worth five shillings; today, 25p, or 50¢.

tween cases. When first encountered, in *The Secret Adversary*, she's a frisky teenager, determined to open a detective agency. Quicker than you can say Mary Westmacott, she bulldozes Tommy into forming, with her, the Young Adventurers, and together they run smack into Secret Service machinations. Later, Tuppence crops up as a newlywed, as a middle-aged but hardly stodgy matron, and ultimately as a geriatric grandparent with a craving for a last detective fling or two.

As snappy with a retort as Nora (though not so stylish), as wildly imaginative as Pamela (though not quite so accident-prone), Tuppence in one series of short stories, *Partners in Crime*, represents Christie's only excursion into satire. Tongue in cheek, she and Tommy solve cases in the manner of Dr. Thorndyke, Sherlock Holmes, the Old Man in the Corner and even — Poirot himself! Actually, Tuppence plays the great detectives' sidekicks in each instance, a role she disdains in her own sleuthing.

Just as Nora cajoles Nick and Pam manipulates Jerry, Tuppence pushes Tommy until he has no alternative but to hunt down the culprits. Apparently there was a second rider to that marriage contract, aimed at Nick, Jerry and Tommy:

> In the interest of preserving marital harmony, *the party of the second part* shall follow to the letter the expressed wish of *the party of the first part* that he play detective.

Those interested in reading about other sleuthing couples are commended to: Frances Crane's twenty-six cases involving Pat and Jean Abbott; Theodora DuBois' eighteen requiring Anne and Jeffrey McNeil; Delano Ames' twelve necessitating Jane and Dagobert Brown; Kelley Roos' nine featuring Jeff and Haila Troy; and Margaret Scherf's six employing Emily and Henry Bryce.

THE LOT OF THE POLICEMAN'S WIFE

Patricia Moyes

Think of a famous detective's wife, and who springs to mind? Lady Peter Wimsey (nee Harriet Vane); Amanda Campion (or whatever his name really is); Agatha Troy Alleyn; perhaps even my own Emmy Tibbett, although she is hardly built for springing, even to mind. All, you notice, creations of women writers.

Detectives favoured by male writers tend to be misogynists or lone wolves. If married, their wives are cosy and domesticated, keeping their noses out of their husbands' business (Mme. Maigret, Lady Appleby). Of course, there are exceptions. The outstanding example to prove the rule is the delicious, vivacious Arlette Van der Valk, forever bringing a breath of French levity to a solemn Dutch scene.

In *Death and the Dutch Uncle,* Henry and Emmy Tibbett visited Amsterdam semiofficially in the course of an investigation, and it seemed only natural that they should make contact with the Van der Valks. Nicholas Freeling was delighted: ". . . at the idea of an English policeman," he wrote, "Arlette would be eaten with curiosity — since being French she imagines they all look and talk like Pierre Daninos' Major Thompson. She . . . would certainly invite Mr. Tibbett as well as his wife home for a drink, rushing out to Albert Heijn for whisky . . . ." Poor, sweet, funny Arlette. Only a few years later, she was to be widowed, left to take over the case herself and track down her husband's murderer in *A Long Silence.*

Now, however, things have taken a turn for the better. Just as we were afraid we might have lost Arlette forever, she has made a joyful reappearance in *The Widow.* She has a new husband (an English professor working in Strasbourg) and is running a sort of one-woman Universal Aunts outfit — whose affairs lead her into unwitting involvement with a very nasty lot of villains. She is a little further on in years, a little more abrasive, but unquestionably our old and loved friend. And what's more, she is no minor character but the protagonist of the novel, which just goes to show that you can't keep a good character down.

Given, however, that it has been predominantly women writers who have endowed their detectives wives with real depth. I wonder just why. Trying to analyse my own case, I suspect it is probably typical.

First of all, I think the wife is the projection of the writer's own personality. I feel sure that when I am at my nicest and brightest, I am extraordinarily like Emmy Tibbett. Nobody else can see the similarity, oddly enough, except that we both have dark hair and are fighting to keep our waistlines: but I *know.* In other words, Emmy is the person I wish I was.

Secondly, an amusing, interesting wife — often with a career of her own — provides the detective with a lively and reassuringly normal sex life that can be taken for granted. This is a boon to those of us who from inclination (or, in my case, sheer incompetence) do not hold up our plots with torrid love scenes. Of course, the wife may serve this purpose and no other. Ruth Rendell's Inspectors Burden and Wexford are

MARRIAGE IS A RISKY BUSINESS

Mrs. Penelope Druthers, second wife of Mr. Reginald Druthers, regrets she will be unable to attend Miss Constance Pickering's dinner dance at the Savoy, Saturday next. Mr. Druthers informs her she will be permanently indisposed at the time. Yours most sincerely, the incipient late Mrs. Druthers.

In mysteries, it's always open season on brides. If they're not being thunked on the head with a piece of initialed wedding silver, they're being followed from the chapel by a dark blue Renault with a Cadillac engine and reinforced bumpers.

All female newlyweds should demand two presents from their husbands: a good health insurance plan and an FBI escort on the wedding trip. Otherwise, walking down the aisle and walking the last mile amount to the same thing.

Mystery brides should have their marriages annulled as quickly as possible if they discover their spouse has a twin brother, a debt of long standing and no visible means of support, an ex-fiancée who pays a courtesy call the day after the wedding.

When packing their trousseaux, mystery brides should never include anything white that reflects off the moon, or a long silk scarf, or a diary.

As a further precaution, mystery brides should avoid such high-risk areas as the rehearsal dinner, the wedding reception, the isolated honeymoon cottage, the new apartment, the empty old apartment.

In writing thank-you notes, a mystery bride should be very careful how she responds to a gift of (ground) glass.

both married, and Mike Burden has a couple of convincingly tiresome children. But, though we are assured that Mike is "strongly uxorious," Jean Burden often happens to be at the seaside or otherwise engaged during an investigation. I have yet to discover Mrs. Wexford's Christian name. A couple of thoroughly useful wives.

Thirdly, the wife dispenses with the need for a Dr. Watson or a Captain Hastings — tedious characters by definition, these grown men with apparently nothing better to do than hang around a celebrated sleuth, tossing him clues for brilliance like fish to a performing seal. A wife, on the other hand, has the best of reasons to be her husband's confidante and companion, and in many cases fulfils a function that could not be undertaken by a man. For instance, only Arlette could have chatted up the neighbors in the drab little town of Drente *(Double-Barrel)* or won the confidence of the little girl, Ruth, whose mother had had such a chequered career *(Tsing-Boum)*. Peter Wimsey couldn't have visited Wilvercombe and tried to buy collars "like the ones my husband bought on May 18th" without exciting comment; Harriet had to do it *(Have His Carcase)*. And Henry Tibbett certainly couldn't have gone into that sinister milliner's shop in the Rue des Lapins to find out if they still arranged lovers' trysts for rich ladies at a price *(Season of Snows and Sins)*.

Finally, and perhaps most importantly, a recurring feminine character acts as a leaven to the stodgiest plot. She can be irresponsible and frivolous. She can make silly mistakes and get herself into scrapes. If the policeman's lot is not a happy one, his wife's is. She is the icing on the cake, the gilt on the gingerbread — and she is invaluable for breaking up those rocklike paragraphs of explanation in the final chapter with her ingenuous questions. "But how on earth did you *know* Sir Montague had been in India as a young man, darling?" "I thought Cornelia was out sailing with Bertram that day. You mean . . . she wasn't? Then where . . . ?" And so on.

Like all women, detectives' wives display infinite variety. They can be brave, long-suffering, seductive and also plain infuriating. I have a short list of Moyes Citations in various categories.

THE BRAVEST is undoubtedly Arlette Van der Valk — for visiting Richard Oddinga's apartment alone after her husband's murder, having first changed into a white blouse "which will show the blood better" *(A Long Silence)*. She also gets the MOST SEDUCTIVE award: remember her dancing in nothing but a suspender belt to divert her husband, and being spotted through the window by prying Dutch neighbors *(Double-Barrel)*?

MOST LONG-SUFFERING goes to Harriet Wimsey — for spending her wedding night in a house with a corpse in the cellar, and her honeymoon sleuthing a rather dull crime *(Busman's Honeymoon)*.

The PLAIN INFURIATING medal (with bar) is awarded to Amanda Campion, who, at the end of a particularly intricate and dangerous case, calmly spotted the murderer by feminine intuition while at her drawing-board in a distant aircraft factory, and dropped the information to

DO YOU HAVE ANY KIDS?

Young destructives should be kept in jails.

John Creasey's Janey and Roger West have two sons, Martin and Richard.

J. J. Marric's Kate and George Gideon have three boys and three girls.

Arthur Upfield's Marie and Napoleon Bonaparte have three sons.

Michael Innes' Judith and John Appleby have one son, Bobby, who eventually solves cases on his own.

Troy and Roderick Alleyn have one son, Ricky.

The Lockridges' Susan Faye has a 10-year-old son, so when she married Merton Heimrich he became a stepfather.

Louise and Jules Maigret, alas, are childless.

her husband in a laconic P.S. to a letter on the last page of the book *(More Work for the Undertaker)*. I am surprised that even a marriage as ideal as the Campions' lasted into another volume after that.

Patricia Moyes is the author of fourteen novels featuring Henry and Emmy Tibbett.

PORTRAIT OF TROY

Ngaio Marsh

Troy made her entrance with the sixth of the books about Alleyn. In those days, I still painted quite a lot and quite seriously, and was inclined to look upon everything I saw in terms of possible subject matter.

On a voyage out to New Zealand from England, we called at Suva. The day was overcast, still and sultry. The kind of day when sounds have an uncanny clarity, and colour an added sharpness and intensity. The wharf at Suva, as seen from the boat-deck of the *Niagara,* was remarkable in these respects: the acid green of a bale of bananas packed in their own leaves; the tall Fijian with a mop of hair dyed screaming magenta, this colour repeated in the sari of an Indian woman; the slap of bare feet on wet boards and the deep voices that sounded as if they were projected through pipes. All these elements made their impressions, and I felt a great itch for a paint brush between my fingers.

The ship drew away, the wharf receded, and I was left with an unattempted, non-existent picture that is as vivid to-day as it was then.

I don't think it is overdoing it to say that when I began *Artists in Crime,* it was this feeling of unfullfilment that led me to put another painter on another boat-deck making a sketch of the wharf at Suva and that she made a much better job of it than I ever would have done.

This was Troy. It was in this setting that she and Alleyn first met.

I have always tried to keep the settings of my books as far as possible within the confines of my own experience. Having found Troy and decided that Alleyn was to find her, too, the rest of the book developed in the milieu of a painters' community. It was written before capital punishment was abolished in Great Britain, and

Troy shared my own repugnance for that terrible practice: I had talked with a detective-inspector and learnt that there were more men in the force who were for abolition than was commonly supposed. I knew Alleyn would be one of them. He would sense that the shadow of the death penalty lay between himself and Troy. It was not until the end of the next book, *Death in a White Tie,* that they came finally together. In *Death and the Dancing Footman,* they are already married.

My London agent, I remember, was a bit dubious about marrying Alleyn off. There is a school of thought that considers love-interest, where the investigating character is involved, should be kept off-stage in detective fiction or at least handled in a rather gingerly fashion and got rid of with alacrity. Conan Doyle seems to have taken this view.

"To Sherlock Holmes she is always *the* woman," he begins, writing of Irene Adler. But after a couple of sentences expressive of romantic attachment, he knocks that idea sideways by stating that, as far as Holmes was concerned, all emotions (sexual attraction in particular) were "abhorrent to his cold, precise, but admirably balanced mind."

So much for Miss Adler.

An exception to the negative attitude appears in Bentley's classic *Trent's Last Case,* where the devotion of Trent for one of the suspects is a basic ingredient of the investigation. Dorothy L. Sayers, however, turns the whole thing inside out by herself regrettably falling in love with her own creation and making rather an ass of both of them in the process.

Troy came along at a time when thoroughly nice girls were often called Dulcie, Edith,

The sun-splashed waterfront of Suva, Fiji, as seen from the deck of Ngaio Marsh's boat. Not too far distant are the villages of Bau, headquarters of the last Fiji king, and Sigatora, with its numerous coconut plantations.

Cecily, Mona, Madeleine. Even, alas, Gladys. I wanted her to have a plain, rather down-to-earth first name and thought of Agatha — not because of Christie — and a rather odd surname that went well with it, so she became Agatha Troy and always signed her pictures "Troy" and was so addressed by everyone. *Death in a White Tie* might have been called *Siege of Troy.*

Her painting is far from academic but not always non-figurative. One of its most distinguished characteristics is a very subtle sense of movement brought about by the interrelationships of form and line. Her greatest regret is that she never painted the portrait of Isabella Sommita, which was commissioned in the book I am at present writing. The diva was to have been portrayed with her mouth wide open, letting fly with her celebrated A above high C. It is questionable whether she would have been pleased with the result. It would have been called *Top Note.*

Troy and Alleyn suit each other. Neither impinges upon the other's work without being asked, with the result that in Troy's case she does ask pretty often, sometimes gets argumentative and up-tight over the answer and almost always ends up by following the suggestion. She misses Alleyn very much when they are separated. This is often the case, given the nature of their work, and on such occasions each feels incomplete and they write to each other like lovers.

Perhaps it is advisable, on grounds of credibility, not to make too much of the number of times coincidence mixes Troy up in her husband's cases: a situation that he embraces with mixed feelings. She is a reticent character and as sensitive as a sea-urchin, but she learns to assume and even feel a certain detachment.

"After all," she has said to herself, "I married him and I would be a very boring wife if I spent half my time wincing and showing sensitive."

I like Troy. When I am writing about her, I can see her with her shortish dark hair, thin face and hands. She's absent-minded, shy and funny, and she can paint like nobody's business. I'm always glad when other people like her, too.

Ngaio Marsh received the honor of Dame Commander of the Order of the British Empire in 1966.

1977

**PORTRAIT
OF
NGAIO**

1958

1936

A PEEK IN THE SAYERS CLOSET

Jane Langton

D.L.S.
hawking her books

Few female characters in detective fiction have attracted as many admirers (and furious detractors) as Harriet D. Vane, who appears in Dorothy L. Sayers' four Lord Peter Wimsey novels. Readers often suspect that Harriet is the projected image of her creator, that it is Sayers herself who tramps through her own pages, gallantly pursuing criminals, solving crimes, defying death and falling at last into the arms of the younger brother of a duke.

Was Harriet really Dorothy? If we listen to Sayers, comparisons are Vane. She had little patience with those who wished to plumb her psyche using the fictional Harriet as a Rorschach. Still, as Janet Hitchman reminds us in her biography of Dorothy, *Such a Strange Lady,* there were more than a few similarities: both women were mystery writers; both were very finicky about the use of their middle initial; both had rather beautiful speaking voices; and both graduated from Oxford — Dorothy from Somerville College and Harriet from the imaginary Shrewsbury, which Sayers seems to have plunked down on the Balliol cricket field.

What then should Harriet Vane look like? If we insist on thinking of her as Dorothy's alter ego, we must only admire the author's honest refusal to make her character glamorous. Over and over, we are told that she is "plain" but "striking-looking," words that could well apply to Miss Sayers herself.

How do we picture a woman who is both these things at once? At first I wanted to draw Harriet according to the way she *behaves.* She acts and talks, I decided, like a no-nonsense woman of belligerent homeliness; in other words, like Sayers as she appears in available photographs. So I sketched a glowering and heavy-set Harriet. There were cries of dismay. Peter Wimsey would never have been in love with *that!* I tried again, this time according to the *effect* she has on the male characters in the four novels — on Peter Wimsey, on Henry Weldon, on Reggie Pomfret. She became an altogether different woman.

I insist that the behavior and the response don't match, and am left with the puzzle: which Harriet is Harriet?

As a fictional character, Harriet Vane is as independent a creature as ever marched forthrightly from the first to the last pages of a book. But no prohibitions or expostulations on the part of her creator will prevent hordes and crowds of enthusiastic readers from imagining that they hear the rich living voice of the late Miss Dorothy Sayers whenever Harriet Vane opens her paper mouth to speak.

Jane Langton wrote and illustrated The Transcendental Murders.

Harriet's Wardrobe

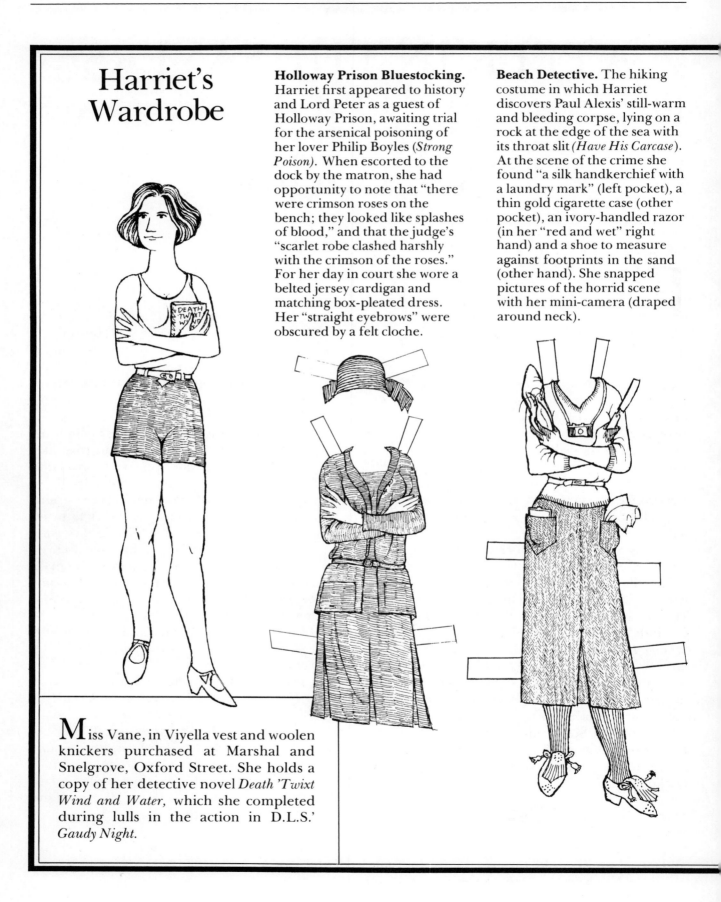

Holloway Prison Bluestocking. Harriet first appeared to history and Lord Peter as a guest of Holloway Prison, awaiting trial for the arsenical poisoning of her lover Philip Boyles (*Strong Poison*). When escorted to the dock by the matron, she had opportunity to note that "there were crimson roses on the bench; they looked like splashes of blood," and that the judge's "scarlet robe clashed harshly with the crimson of the roses." For her day in court she wore a belted jersey cardigan and matching box-pleated dress. Her "straight eyebrows" were obscured by a felt cloche.

Beach Detective. The hiking costume in which Harriet discovers Paul Alexis' still-warm and bleeding corpse, lying on a rock at the edge of the sea with its throat slit (*Have His Carcase*). At the scene of the crime she found "a silk handkerchief with a laundry mark" (left pocket), a thin gold cigarette case (other pocket), an ivory-handled razor (in her "red and wet" right hand) and a shoe to measure against footprints in the sand (other hand). She snapped pictures of the horrid scene with her mini-camera (draped around neck).

Miss Vane, in Viyella vest and woolen knickers purchased at Marshal and Snelgrove, Oxford Street. She holds a copy of her detective novel *Death 'Twixt Wind and Water,* which she completed during lulls in the action in D.L.S.' *Gaudy Night.*

Practical Hiker. D.L.S. tells us: "Harriet, though not too old to care for her personal appearance, was old enough to prefer convenience to outward display. . . . She was dressed sensibly in a short skirt and thin sweater." (*Have His Carcase*) Doubtless, the former was a conservative herringbone; the latter, a V-neck affair. Her shoes? What else but brogues. Her rucksack contained, "in addition to a change of linen and an extra provision of footwear, little else beyond a pocket edition of *Tristram Shandy,* a vest-pocket camera, a small first-aid outfit and a sandwich lunch."

Vamp Raiment. Harriet dazzled Henry Weldon (*Have His Carcase*) in a slinky frock that "waved tempestuously about her ankles" and was "eminently unsuitable for picnicking." She paired it with "high-heeled beige shoes," "embroidered gloves" and "an oversized hat of which one side obscured her face and tickled her shoulder, while the other was turned back to reveal a bunch of black ringlets, skillfully curled into position by the head hairdresser of the Resplendent." Note the firm hold on her pocketbook, at the ready to box Henry's ear should he presume to make lewd advances. (He presumed.)

The Cherwell Boater. Harriet's Liberty print is somewhat the worse for wear: crushed in the unwanted embraces of Reggie Pomfret, entangled in relentless clinging weeds during an emergency outing on the River Cherwell to rescue the suicidal Miss Newland. (*Gaudy Night*) During the unfortunately eventful ride, she shined her trusty torch (right hand) on "the silver leaves, dripping like rain towards the river," and discovered in its beam that "something swirled below them, pale and ominous." To soothe her post-rescue nerves, a whisky restorative was indicated (other hand).

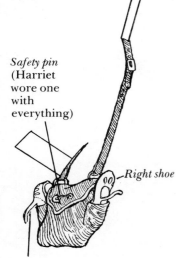

Safety pin (Harriet wore one with everything)

Right shoe

Left shoe

Harriet's Wardrobe Continued

Bunter's Domain

Harriet was left to manage the best she could without the services of Bunter. Lord Peter wouldn't spare him.

Bunter kept His Lordship's "dress-shirts in the second drawer, his silk socks in the tray on the right-hand side of the wardrobe, with the dress-ties just above them." (*Have His Carcase*)

When Lord Peter wished to do his "famous impression of the perfect Lounge Lizard," Bunter suggested "the fawn-coloured suit we do not care for, with the autumn-leaf socks and our outsize amber cigarette-holder." (*Have His Carcase*)

Bunter was also responsible for fetching Lord Peter's "favourite stick — a handsome malacca, marked off in inches for detective convenience, and concealing a sword in its belly and a compass in its head." (*Clouds of Witness*)

In addition, he kept immaculately pressed and mended a Balliol blazer (*Murder Must Advertise*), a black morning-coat, top-hat and black kid gloves (*Five Red Herrings*) and a rich, velvet-collared magician's cloak (*Murder Must Advertise*).

He also buffed up Lord Peter's monocle from time to time.

Security Device. Anyone can give a girl flowers. In *Gaudy Night,* Lord Peter presented Harriet with a more durable gift.

"I know what you want," he said. "You want a dog-collar. I'm going to get you one. The kind with brass knobs."

"A dog-collar? Whatever for? As a badge of ownership?"

"God forbid. To guard against the bites of sharks. Excellent also against thugs and throat-slitters."

"My dear man!"

"Honestly. It's too stiff to squeeze and it'll turn the edge of a blade . . ."

Oxford Engagement Processional. Sauntering with Harriet down New College Lane after attending a Bach concert (programme, left hand), Lord Peter again brings up the subject of marriage (*Gaudy Night*). "*Placetne, magistra?*" he says. "*Placet,*" she replies. Readers unfamiliar with Latin might be interested to know that he was asking, "Does it please you?" and that she responded, "Yes, it does," which meant they were finally engaged after a getting-acquainted period of six years. Up Harriet's sleeve is a facsimile of the poison-pen note she had found three months before.

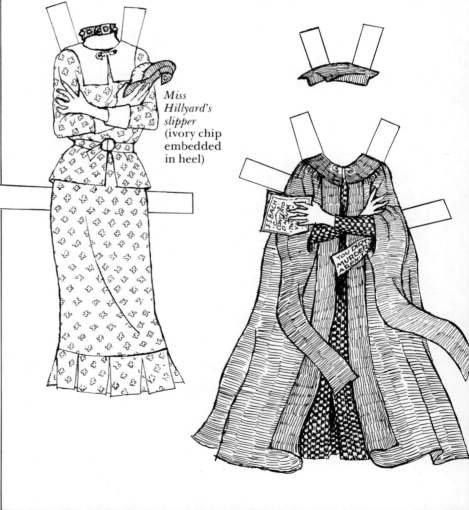

Miss Hillyard's slipper (ivory chip embedded in heel)

Lady Peter's Wedding. C. W. Scott-Giles, genealogist and author of *The Wimsey Family,* which traced the family's ancestry, instructs us that "Lord Peter married, on 8 October 1935, Harriet Deborah Vane, only daughter of the late Henry Vane, M.D., of Great Pagford, Hertfordshire." Extracts from the diary of Honoria Lucasta, Dowager Duchess of Denver, tell us that Harriet wore a "period gown in stiff gold brocade, long sleeves, square neck, off-the-face head-dress, no jewels except my long earrings that belonged to great-aunt Delagardie." The "cloth of gold" bridal gown was designed by Worth.

Trousseau Extravaganza. More jottings from the Dowager Duchess of Denver indicate that only a "few select friends were invited to see the trousseau," that Miss Climpson was among them, that she was "miraculously reduced to *speechlessness* by Peter's gift" of a 950-guinea mink cloak *(Busman's Honeymoon).* Since he preferred Harriet in deep wine colours to set off her "skin like pale honey," we may assume that the horizontally worked pelts were lined in a vermillion-bordering-on-burgundy silk. There is no record of anyone terming Harriet "plain as a pancake" when she wore it.

The Prickly Honeymoon. Harriet chose the sturdiest and most bristling of woolens for the country tweeds she took along on her wedding trip *(Busman's Honeymoon).* Here, she wears a scratchy Harris tweed suit, a blouse cravat tied in a Windsor knot, and a "pound or two of garden mould on her stout brogue shoe." In her arms she carries the "infernal bloody cactus" that filled the window and made it impossible for young Constable Sellon to have seen, as he claimed, the clock in the room beyond.

JANE LANGTON

The Duchess of Denver's Attire

Going-Up-to-Town Ensemble.
The Duchess, who did not believe in being "vulgarly immodest," here flaunts several varieties of endangered species: red fox, peacock, baby alligator. In her left hand, she holds a solid-gold scissors, suitable for undoing parcels from Harrods.

Miss Climpson's Regalia

CRACK!
CRACK!

Helen, Lord Peter's sister-in-law, the wife of his elder brother Gerald, the duke, was "a long-necked, long-backed woman, who disciplined her hair and her children." *(Clouds of Witness)* She is a thoroughly unsympathetic character.

Miss Climpson, chief snoop of "The Cattery," has affixed to her knee the "small metal soap-box" that cracked convincingly at the séance *(Strong Poison)*. The wire "strapped to the wrist . . . was sufficient to rock a light table."

Undercover Work. "Miss Climpson pulled the will from its hiding-place, drew it from its envelope and glanced swiftly through it. It was not a long document, and in spite of the legal phraseology, its purport was easily gathered. Within minutes she had replaced it, moistened the gum and stuck the flap down again. She put it in her petticoat-pocket — for her garments were of a useful and old-fashioned kind."
(Strong Poison)

Ouija Outfit. Miss Climpson holds the Ouija board belonging to Miss Booth *(Strong Poison)*. In her left hand is the board's indicator, a small wooden gadget shaped like a flat-iron. When the fingers are placed lightly upon it, the indicator seems to move about the board under its own initiative, pointing to letters of the alphabet and answering questions asked of those who have Gone Beyond. Miss Climpson's attire is appropriately sober for such conversations — a gown that matches her steel-grey spinster's bun.

Jury Duty. By a wild stroke of good fortune, the jury that was to decide the fate of Harriet included Miss Climpson. Her stubborn conviction of Harriet's innocence persuaded other panelists to question the prosecution's supposedly open-and-shut case, and a hung jury resulted. For swaying the group to her side of the argument, she wore a chevron-accented suit, appropriate to her "militant High-Church conscience of remarkable staying-power."
(Strong Poison)

JANE LANGTON

MME. MAIGRET MOURNS A RAINCOAT

Bartholomew Gill

She awoke before dawn. But it wasn't the hour, the routine or the mauve tint of a cloudless eastern sky that had made her get up. It was the breeze through the open window.

It was warm and welcome. Opening the panel farther and peering down through the wrought-iron railings of the balcony to the Boulevard Richard Lenoir below, she was certain it carried a tang of the sea, straight from the Midi.

And then, the limbs of the linden trees were clustered with buds that had taken on color, a deep yellow tint, like true gamboge.

The old woman, the wife of the concierge of the apartment building, was sweeping the sidewalk. The broom pushed over the concrete in regular sweeps that echoed off the buildings and reminded her of the sound new flax made, blowing in a blue-flowered field. In spring. Yes, she was sure of it now.

She heard a noise behind her. A voice. It was deep, a grumble, something like "Taxi!" or "Maxim!" — the name of a suspect in a case that had been troubling him for a fortnight.

Maigret — the *great* Maigret, she reminded herself, looking at him with profound affection — slept like a child, on his back and hugging his pillow with one arm. His long face and large nose were turned to the ceiling.

He was, even at this age, a big man. It wasn't his height that was impressive, though she knew he was not small. It was his . . . girth. He had always been, to her, massive. In every way.

She opened both bedroom windows, knowing he'd enjoy awakening to the gentle winds from the south, and hurried toward the kitchen. She began the coffee.

Spring. It was a ritual. A new pair of shoes. Inevitably, they were too small and he would complain about them for days. The lighter suits and, yes, he'd not want the topcoat.

His raincoat. It had been a subject of some controversy with them for — how many years? Three at least.

Mme. Maigret paused at the mirror. She was a blonde who had gone gray, though one wouldn't know at first glance. At present, she

---

CHERCHEZ LA FEMME

Louise met Jules at the home of her aunt and uncle, the Leonards. He'd been brought there by Felix Jubert, an old friend of Maigret's since his medical school days.

Little is known of their courtship, but if their later life is any indication, they spent it sitting through comedy films and going for long walks.

Oddly, even after all these years, the couple does not seem to be on a first-name basis. He refers to her as "Madame Maigret." She calls him simply "Maigret."

kept her hair in a precise bun, tucked and braided in such a way that its shape was rather sculptural and enhanced her facial features, which were delicate.

Her housecoat and chemise revealed, however, that she too was a person of some size. But the impression was denied by a narrow waist and thin legs, which were just slightly bowed. And her demeanor. Mme. Maigret was proper, and in everything she tried to show her respect — for herself, her life, and her husband.

Perhaps that was why the raincoat bothered her so much.

With a potholder she lifted the coffeepot from the burner and set it on the hob to keep it hot, then peeked into the oven to see how the croissants were doing. The snowy glaze was just beginning to firm, the almond slivers to brown. She painted them deftly with a little sweetened milk and closed the door.

She glanced at the clock. Two more minutes. Or three. He preferred the crust a little hard. She straightened up. What was she thinking? Oh, yes — that raincoat.

She placed the potholder on the stove and unconsciously squared it on the top as she thought how she should go about it.

Years ago, Maigret had ordered his raincoats from London. Like the present one, they had wide lapels that could be buttoned against the wind. They were capacious affairs, with a wide belt and deep pockets for his pipe and tobacco, but the style had gone out of favor and he had worn one until it became downright shabby.

For a few years, he had worn other styles that he said made him look like an accountant or a civil servant, which, of course, in a way he was. But then, at an Interpol conference in Brussels, he met a young policeman who was wearing just the style, and new. He complimented the man on the raincoat, but in his own way he was shy and didn't know how to ask him where he'd gotten it.

Less than a week later, a large package arrived at the Boulevard Richard Lenoir. In it was a new raincoat, and a perfect fit. A tailored item. There wasn't a label in it. It was embarrassing really, and Maigret blushed on seeing the gift, but he wore it.

Mme. Maigret moved out of the kitchen,

It is not true that the one case Mme. Maigret was able to get to the bottom of was filled with Calvados.

through the dining room, toward the bedroom, soundlessly. She glanced at the bed and eased open the door of the armoire.

The new shoes. She'd soften them up a bit before he put them on. And a summer suit. The light gray one. It was nicely tailored and concealed his paunch. She selected a shirt, a tie and socks, and then, as quietly as she could, she pushed aside all his other coats and jackets.

She shook her head — there it was, one cuff frayed, the vent patched where he had ripped it getting into one of those new, low-slung taxis they now had. And on a lapel were three blood spatters that wouldn't come out. Maigret said he had had to restrain a thug, and he never forgave him for those stains. He had gone hard on him, he said. Mme. Maigret still wondered what that could mean, but she dared not ask.

She pulled it out. What to do?

She thought briefly of simply stuffing it in the trash and calling the concierge to take it away. She could say she sent it to the cleaners and it got lost. But she knew Maigret. He'd stop round to question them, and she'd be in hot water.

Guiltily, she glanced at the bed.

One large eye was staring at her. It then turned toward the window. Maigret cleared his throat. "Spring?" he asked.

"Yes. It's here. At last."

The croissants. She arranged the clothes on his dresser and moved quickly toward the kitchen.

Maigret was always grumpy when he first awoke, and she knew it was the wrong time to bring it up. But, pouring the coffee into his special large white cup, an idea struck her.

She glanced at the calendar—15 March. There was just time.

She brought the tray to the bedroom, watched Maigret break open the shiny brown crust of a croissant. He smiled. The rich yellow dough steamed up at him. He dabbed some unsalted butter on a morsel and slipped it into his mouth. He closed his eyes.

"Isn't the seventeenth of March Saint Patrick's Day?" she asked.

*W*arm thanks for your letter. I checked with my lawyer and he advised me that anything I might say would be interpreted as parcenary to the point of parricide. The trouble with Maigret, I fear, is that she was suffering from an infusorian experience.

NORMAN COUSINS

Maigret's brow wrinkled. With his back against the bedstead like that, his shoulders looked huge, and the open front of his pajama top was filled with curly gray hair. "I think so. Why do you ask?"

She shook her head. "No reason." She went back into the kitchen.

When Maigret appeared, he looked very smart in the new gray suit and black patent-leather bluchers. And he knew it. He was smiling, and he had his favorite pipe in his mouth, a Dunham shell brier. That was an even better sign.

But not the raincoat. "I think I'll walk partway. Break in the shoes." He held out a foot and looked down admiringly.

"What about your coat? It may rain." Mme. Maigret sat at the kitchen table. Already she had out pen and ink, paper and an English dictionary.

"Not today. It can't."

"You mean you won't let it."

"That's right," he said matter-of-factly, as though he could control the weather if he chose.

She smiled. His step was jaunty. He was in a rare mood.

At the door, he added: "After a discreet lapse of time, we'll send him one of these." He held out the pipe.

Her cheeks colored. There was no keeping anything from him.

"I thought you said he doesn't smoke a pipe."

"Perhaps he'll learn. Cigarettes are a disgusting habit."

"What did you say his wife's first name is?"

"Noreen," Maigret said without a pause, then glanced back at her.

"Do you mean to say he brought her along? To Brussels?"

He raised a hand and snapped it down. "The Irish are uncivilized. Always dragging their women along."

After she heard the door close, Mme. Maigret glanced down at the paper. Perhaps she'd write a longer letter than she had intended.

Bartholomew Gill is the author of four novels featuring Inspector McGarr. The latest is McGarr at the Dublin House Show.

LANDING A PRIVATE EYE
PHILIP MARLOWE'S NEMESIS

Gail MacColl

Nobody expects a shamus to be celibate, but nobody thinks of him pricing wedding rings, either. Depending on your point of view, you can credit or blame Raymond Chandler for this state of affairs: he established the ground rules for the private eye's lifestyle.

For twenty years, he had Marlowe wander alone down those mean streets. The sultry Vivian Regan *(The Big Sleep)*, the little-girl-lost Merle Davis *(The High Window)*, the tough-minded Anne Reardon *(Farewell, My Lovely)* provided only temporary roadblocks to the continued bachelorhood of this "shop-soiled Galahad."

Then Chandler revised the game plan. In a letter to his agent, Helga Greene, he announced: "I am going to have Marlowe marry the eight million dollar girl from *The Long Goodbye*." He went on to say, "I don't know how it will turn out but she'll never tame him."

That just may have been the understatement of the year.

The girl Chandler picked was Linda Loring. She meets Philip Marlowe in *The Long Goodbye;* proposes to him in *Playback;* tacks his Mrs. to her name in *The Poodle Springs Story*, the manuscript Chandler was working on when he died.

If it's true that opposites attract, the Marlowe-Loring alliance was fated. He had all the lone-wolf credentials: both parents dead, no brothers or sisters, no serious ex-lovers, not even a secretary. Committed to no one except himself, and his own code of honor, he worked out of a dump, barely made ends meet, kept off-beat hours, drank hard and often. She, on the other hand, grew up not only with a silver spoon in her mouth, but with a whole service for twelve crammed down there. She had a father who owned most of Southern California and was always mid-deal to purchase the rest, a sister who

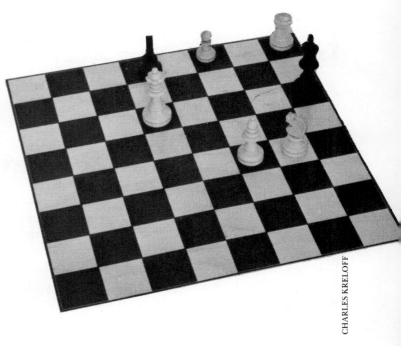

Marlowe, checkmated. Prior to this match with Loring, he amused himself by playing imaginary games with grand masters — and winning.

CHARLES KRELOFF

PUCKER UP, BIG BOY

Over half Marlowe's time was spent defending his honor. Some of the intriguing propositions put to him were:

Helen Grayle: "Kiss me."

Dolores Gonzales: "Kiss me, amigo."

Mavis Weld: "I think you'd better kiss me."

Helen Vermilyea: "Kiss me harder."

Ann Riordan: "I'd like to be kissed, damn you."

Eileen Wade: "Put me on the bed."

Vivian Regan: "Hold me close, you beast."

Betty Mayfield: "Take me. I'm yours — all of me is yours."

A minority opinion was offered by Jesse Florian in *Farewell, My Lovely*: "Get away from me, you son of a bitch."

R.W.

somebody hated enough to kill, and a dull husband who bored her. She had expensive tastes, the money to maintain them, and no inclination to discard them.

Anyone for fireworks?

The conflict begins in *The Poodle Springs* fragment. Linda gives Marlowe a million dollars as a wedding present; he refuses it. She offers to set him up in business; he says no. She suggests he not work at all, and he snaps, "I'm not going to be Mr. Loring." She ripostes, "It's not my fault that I'm rich. And if I have the damn money I'm going to spend it. And if you're around, some of it is bound to rub off on you." Having said all this, she then buys him a Cadillac. He insists on using his Olds.

Chandler, of course, anticipated this antagonism. It was one of his reasons for engineering the relationship in the first place. "If he marries a woman with a lot of money who wants to live a rather smart, expensive life . . . the contest between what she wants Marlowe to do and what he will insist on doing will make a good subplot."

Chandler was not interested in having the marriage run smoothly. The bumpier it got, the better it was for his writing. Marlowe, contemplating life in Poodle Springs (Chandler's version of Palm Springs), could say, "I belonged in Idle Valley like a pearl onion on a banana split." He could taunt Linda about his household-pet role: "Can I wear a sarong and paint my little toenails?" And when she told him, "I'm paying twelve hundred dollars a month for this dive. I want you to love it," he could rejoin: "I'll love it. Twelve hundred dollars a month is more than I make being a detective."

Still, even Chandler had to admit that he may have overdone it. In a letter to Maurice Guiness, who originally suggested the romance, he confided, "I think I may have picked the wrong girl. . . . A fellow of Marlowe's type shouldn't get married, because he is a lonely man, a poor man, a dangerous man, and yet a sympathetic man, and somehow none of this goes with marriage."

The only place where the two characters reached total agreement was the sexual arena. There, they were definitely compatible. When they first set eyes on each other across gimlets in Victor's Bar, the thing that most impressed Loring was Marlowe's failure to make a pass, and what mattered to him was that she was willing to talk "without dragging bedrooms into it." When Marlowe finally slipped an innuendo into a telephone conversation, she had the good sense to reject it. "The implication does not interest me — if I understand you." In time, they did spend an evening together. Loring was hardly casual about it. A year and a half later, when she rang him up from Paris to propose, she confessed she'd been faithful ever since. Not only did Marlowe believe her; he sent her the money for the plane ticket home. Clearly, a case of two deep-down romantics who happened to find each other.

Maybe it wasn't as bad a match as Chandler thought.

Gail MacColl is jealous of Linda Loring.

THE HARD-BOILED SKIRT TOUR

Ruth Windfeldt

I first met Philip Marlowe face to face one warm October night when he came into my shop to ask if I had copies of the books written by Raymond Chandler. "There was a desert wind blowing that night. It was one of those hot dry Santa Anas that come down through the mountain passes and curl your hair and make your nerves jump and your skin itch. On nights like that every booze party ends in a fight. Meek little wives feel the edge of the carving knife and study their husbands' necks. Anything can happen."

I told Marlowe that I stocked the books, that they were favorites of mine. In my spare time, I added, I walked from one end of town to the other, looking for the locations mentioned in the cases. When I found enough of them, I was going to devise a Chandler tour for mystery fans.

Marlowe was intrigued with the idea and offered to help. A few dozen Scotch-and-waters later, we had it all mapped out. Now, twice a year — early spring and late fall — he (in spirit) and I (in fact) and fifty other private-eye devotees cover Los Angeles' "mean streets." Much of the city's landscape and architecture has changed since Chandler's time, the forties and fifties, but "those smooth shiny girls, hard-boiled and loaded with sin" are still here.

To meet them, please turn the page.

ITINERARY

1. 3765 Alta Brea Crescent. Site of the Sternwood mansion, where Marlowe first meets Carmen — "she had little sharp predatory teeth" — and scrutinizes Vivian — "She was worth a stare. She was trouble."

2. Arthur Gwynn Geiger's residence, Laverne Terrace. Marlowe is again exposed to Carmen: "Neither of the two people in the room paid any attention to the way I came in, although only one of them was dead. She was wearing a pair of long jade earrings. She wasn't wearing anything else."

3. No. 405, Brittany Place at Randall Place. Joe Brody's apartment, where Carmen tries to recover her nude photographs and pushes him "back into the room by putting a little revolver against his lean brown lips." Also the spot where Agnes Lozelle attacks Marlowe: "She ducked her head and sank her teeth in my right hand. [She] spat at me and threw herself on my leg and tried to bite that."

4. Hobart Arms, on Franklin near Kenmore. Marlowe's apartment, where Moose finally finds his "Little Velma." Not pleased to see him, she "shot him five times in the stomach. The bullets made no more sound than fingers going in a glove." Carmen Sternwood also spent time here, to Marlowe's distress: "The imprint of her head was still in the pillow, of her small corrupt body still on the sheets. I put my empty glass down and tore the bed to pieces savagely."

5. The Sternwood oil wells. Another confrontation between Marlowe and Carmen: "I saw her small finger tighten on the trigger and grow white at the tip. I was about six feet away from her when she started to shoot."

6. Geiger's bookstore, Hollywood Boulevard near Las Palmas. Marlowe meets Joe Brody's girl and porn dealer Geiger's receptionist, Agnes Lozelle (whose name is synonymous with the odor of bitter almonds): "She approached me with enough sex appeal to stampede a businessman's lunch."

7. Parking lot, Bullock's Wilshire. Agnes and Marlowe complete a transaction: "Her black-gloved hand reached out and I put the bills in it. . . . Three men dead and the woman went riding off in the rain with my two hundred in her bag and not a mark on her."

8. 1644 West 54th Place. In search of a lead on Velma, Marlowe visits Jesse Florian: "I was looking into dimness at a blowsy woman who was blowing her nose as she opened the door. A middle-aged lady with a face like a bucket of mud."

9. An eyrie in Stillwood Heights. Marlowe is worked over by psychic consultant Jules Amthor and his devoted wife. "The shiny thing that was as hard and bitter as death hit me again, across the face. Something warm trickled."

10. The Grayle Estate, 862 Aster Drive. Mrs. Lewin Lockridge Grayle, first name Helen, a.k.a. Velma Valento, asks Marlowe up to "share information" about the theft of her Fei Tsui jade necklace and the murder of poor Lin Marriott. Marlowe describes her as "a blonde to make a bishop kick a hole in a stained glass window."

11. Purissima Canyon. Ex-police chief's daughter Anne Riordan rescues Marlowe when he's been knocked out cold. Says Marlowe, "I like her nerve. . . . You could get to like that face a lot. Glamoured up blondes were a dime a dozen, but that was a face that would wear."

12. 819 25th Street, Bay City. Following his escape from Dr. Sonderborg's sanitarium, Marlowe holes up at Anne's house: "It was a nice room. It would be a nice room to wear slippers in . . ."

13. Dresden Avenue, Oak Knoll section of Pasadena. Mrs. Murdock hires Marlowe to recover a rare coin, the Brasher Doubloon, and to locate her even brasher daughter-in-law. The woman has "pewter-colored hair set in a ruthless permanent, a hard beak and large moist eyes with

MARTY NORMAN

the sympathetic expression of wet stones." Merle Davis, her secretary, who may have pushed Horace Bright out the window, is also present: her "whole face had a sort of off-key neurotic charm. . . . It wasn't any of my business that she had a small Colt automatic in the drawer of her desk."

14. Morny Mansion, Belair. Trying to get a line on Linda Conquest, Mrs. Murdock's charming daughter-in-law, Marlowe appears on Lois Magic Morny's doorstep: "From thirty feet away she looked like a lot of class. From ten feet away she looked like something made up to be seen from thirty feet away."

15. The Idle Valley Club. Where Linda Conquest is discovered working as a singer: "She had a rich deep down around the ankles contralto. . . . She said, 'I am quite sure I am not going to like you one damned bit. So speak your piece and drift away.' "

16. Treloar Building. Office address of Derace Kingsley's brainy secretary and stylish confidante, Adrienne Fromset: "She wore a steel grey business suit."

17. Bryson Apartments, Sunset Place, No. 716. Adrienne's home, where Marlowe takes note of a little mishap: "He was shot in the shower. . . . And it looks as if it was done by a woman."

18. Eighth near Arguello, Bay City. Premises of Mildred Haviland a.k.a. Muriel Chess a.k.a. Crystal Kingsley (three murders for this dame, one for each name). Says Marlowe about her puss, "It didn't look like the face of a woman who would waste a lot of motion."

19. 615 Cahuenga Building, Hollywood near Ivar. Orfamay Quest hires Marlowe to find her brother: "She was a small, neat, rather prissy-looking girl with primly smooth brown hair and rimless glasses. . . . The rimless glasses gave her that librarian's look."

20. Tower Road, Stillwood Heights. Racketeer Steel-

grave's home, where Marlowe encounters Mavis Weld: "A blonde in a pale cocoa fur coat stood leaning against the side of a grandfather's chair. Her hands were in the pockets of the coat. She brought out a white handled automatic."

21. Room 332, Van Nuys Hotel. Where Mavis and a corpse (G. W. Hicks) await Marlowe: "The gun against my neck went away and a white flame burned for an instant behind my eyes. I grunted and fell forward on my hands and knees and reached back quickly. My hand touched a leg in a nylon stocking, but slipped off, which seemed a pity. It felt like a nice leg."

22. Apt. 412, Chateau Bercy. Where Dolores Gonzales lived. And died: "Under her left breast and tight against the flame-colored shirt lay the silver handle of a knife. . . . The handle was in the shape of a naked woman."

23. Bar at the Ritz-Beverly. Marlowe meets up with Eileen Wade, the "Golden Icicle": "Her hair was the pale gold of a fairy princess. Her eyes were cornflower blue and the lashes were long and almost too pale."

24. Side road between San Vincente and Sunset. Clyde Umney's secretary, Helen Vermilyea, hires Marlowe to follow Betty Mayfield. Of Helen: "She was quite a doll. She had a well-cherished head of platinum hair, a pair of blue-gray eyes that looked at me as if I had said a dirty word."

25. Union Station. Marlowe waits for Betty's train to pull in, then follows her: "She brought a small automatic up from her side."

26. The Yucca apartment, Laurel Canyon. Marlowe goes soft after Linda Loring leaves: "There was a long dark hair on one of the pillows. There was a lump of lead at the pit of my stomach."

Ruth Windfeldt is the owner of Scene of the Crime Book Shop, Sherman Oaks, California.

JAMES BOND'S PLAYMATES

MARTY NORMAN

As she reached for the glass, she upset the ashtray and several cigarette butts fell on the sheet.

"What have you done?" asked the only man in the world who can pronounce words without an R in them with a burr.

"I missed the glass, tipped over the ashtray and dirtied the sheet," she explained.

"I don't understand."

"Sorry, James. I keep forgetting you only speak Label. As I stretched out my arm for the last swallow of Taittinger '43 in the Baccarat, I upended the Steuben, spilled out the Morlands and smudged the Porthaults."

"Why did you do that?"

"SMERSH orders," she said, and picked up her spray bottle of Vent Vert, double-pumped it under his nose, glanced at her Patek-Philippe and realized she had nine seconds to drag her Dior out of there before James and the Gritti Palace suite were blown to bloody smithereens.

James, with a dexterity that comes only to those who refuse to wear pyjama bottoms, beat her to the door, stepped outside and calmly locked it, walked to the house phone and was midway through placing an order — for one — of eggs Benedict with a side of Beluga and a stiff Stolichnaya chaser, when there was a resounding boom and a lot more ashes fell to the Porthaults.

Let's put it this way. Those who bed Bond better have the time of their lives, because they're probably going to die for it.

All 007 playmates make the same mistake: eventually they remove their clothes. Now, that's a basic misreading of what James wants. The minute they slip off the Cardin skirts, shrug out of the Givenchy blouses, unclasp the Hermès belts, unpin the Cartier diamonds, kick off the Fiorentina shoes and seductively slither out of the Schiaparelli lingerie, they hold no more interest for him. James wouldn't be caught dead with an object (sexual or otherwise) unless it was a brand name, and these girls have just dropped theirs! Naturally he'll leave them to fend for themselves against the diabolical inventions of SMERSH and/or Major Boothroyd. Why should he care what happens to a noname, to a Brand X, when surely a designer label is waiting for him in the next chapter?

For a man so addicted to Regent Street shops and custom boutiques just off Madison, James shows an appalling lack of taste when it comes to girl friends: they're right off the assembly line. They each own a pleated skirt, a heavy silk shirt they never learned to button, a white gown so lascivious Mae West would have been proud to have worn it, and one pair of elegant black pumps with extremely high heels.

Their best feature is their breasts. In *The Book of Bond,* Lt.-Col. William ("Bill") Tanner summarizes them as "fine breasts, splendid breasts, faultless breasts, beautiful firm breasts, thrusting breasts, high-riding breasts and deeply V-ed breasts," and goes on to say they are rarely encased in anything more structured than a sigh. (Long before it became the fashion, Bond playmates were burning their bras.)

Cascading over these breasts are blond or blue-black curls. If you look closely, you'll notice that the ends match the roots — 007's chums do not dye their hair. Nor do they wear make-up, which is very thoughtful of author Ian Fleming. The hotel staff have enough trouble cleaning up their ashes; it would be cruel to burden them further with lipstick-stained pillowslips.

Bond, of course, is aware that these ladies are a little lacking in true class. He may dally with them in an inn, frolic with them at their place, but he has never yet invited one home. His Regency flat in King's Row is strictly off-limits. The only woman to have free rein of the Chelsea digs is his formidably competent Scottish housekeeper, May, who deferentially refers to him as Mister James.

His bedmates have included: Vesper Lynd (*Casino Royale*); Solitaire (*Live and Let Die*); Gala Brand (*Moonraker*); Tiffany Case (*Diamonds Are Forever*); Honeychile Rider (*Doctor No*); Pussy Galore (*Goldfinger*); Dominetta Vitali (*Thunderball*); Kissy Suzuki (*You Only Live Twice*); Tatiana Romanova (*From Russia with Love*). They may come in only one size (*zaftig*), but since Bond does not discriminate against any race or nationality, they appear in assorted colors, with varying come-hither accents.

Most of them sport one minor imperfection, either physical (Rider's bashed nose), mental (Case's sexual inhibitions) or moral (Vitali's "protector"). By dispensing kisses the way moth-

I DO, I DIE

Bond considered marriage a couple of times, but only made it to the altar once (*On Her Majesty's Secret Service*). They did not live happily ever after. In fact, they had a rotten honeymoon. About an hour after the ceremony, Teresa (Tracy) Di Vicenzo Bond was killed by the villainous Blofeld. Perhaps he was angry he hadn't been invited to the wedding.

ers ladle out chicken soup — hourly, with an I-know-what's-best-for-you passion — Bond is able to patch them up. Some of his girls are so grateful, they begin to spy for his side. Whether they actually go on payroll, we don't know, but we do learn that Bond's expense vouchers are scrutinized by M's secretary, Moneypenny, and that she is thoroughly titillated by them.

If a Bond girl keeps her clothes on, James rewards her with food. How she manages to maintain her figure while gorging on cream-drenched strawberries, and sauce Béarnaise is her little secret, and she guards it with the skill of an 00 branch operative. But it must be admitted, she's extremely good at it: her wet suit shows nary an unsightly bump (if you discount the slight puckering caused by her knife).

Fed, bed, dead, seems to be the normal progression for a Bond playmate. There are, however, exceptions. Mary Goodnight (that's her name, not a compliment from James) lives to resume her secretarial duties at Secret Service Headquarters; Vivian Michel is so much the better for her encounter that she writes it up — with an assist from Fleming — to become the first-person confession, *The Spy Who Loved Me.*

Then, too, there is the case of the woman who wound up dead without first being either fed or bed: Rosa Kleb. But what to keep in mind here is (1) she was homely, (2) she was too old, and (3) she didn't have a suntan, which is a Bond partner prerequisite.

WHERE HAVE ALL THE SECRETARIES GONE?

Bill Pronzini

There was a time, not so long ago, when most private eyes (and some lawyers and amateur detectives) employed female assistants — not only to handle secretarial duties and add a touch of class to their offices, but to help in various ways on their investigations into murder and mayhem.

Sometimes the secretary provided key information, resulting from observation and/or legwork, that allowed the detective to crack a tough case; sometimes she was in a position to save his life or to have him save hers; sometimes a love affair developed between them — one that might even lead to marriage. In short, without the secretary any number of well-known cases would be far less appealing to read about, and many might not have been solved at all.

And yet, in recent years, she has all but disappeared from the detective story. The private eye works alone these days, does his own legwork and finds his romantic involvements elsewhere. The same is essentially true of the lawyer and the gifted amateur.

Where have all the secretaries gone?

Some seem to feel they've been worn so thin from overuse that contemporary mystery writers avoid them. But how can they be overused when they seldom appear any more? (The locked-room story used to be considered trite, and for a long time hardly anybody wrote one; now, because of *underuse* and a new generation of readers, locked-room mysteries are being written with considerable success.) How can the secretary be a cliché, furthermore, unless the

private eye himself is one? And *he* is certainly still flourishing.

Others seem to feel she's obsolete, an old-fashioned product of a bygone era. This, they say, is the age of the machine; detectives don't need secretaries when they have answering machines, computer hookups, electronic surveillance equipment and the like. But try telling that to the millions of women around the world who work as secretaries. Try convincing *them* that they're old-fashioned and obsolete; that machines can perform their duties better than they can; that machines are more appealing than human beings — particularly an attractive, intelligent human being who might just find herself in a position to save her employer's life.

Still others seem to feel the secretary's disappearance is merely a reflection of today's overinflated living costs: the working detective of the 1970's can no longer afford to pay an extra salary. This explanation is a flimsy one. After all, the detectives of the Depression managed to pay *their* employees' wages.

Where have all the secretaries gone?

To those of us who grew up reading the mysteries of the thirties, forties and fifties, the question becomes a lament. We remember the secretaries of those works with fondness and nostalgia; how could we forget them? They are every bit as memorable as the detectives who hired them.

Where are they now?

Effie Perine, prototype of all private eyes' secretaries, as immortal as Caspar Gutman,

Brigid O'Shaughnessy, and her boss, Sam Spade. Without her contributions, the plot of the greatest private-eye novel ever written, Dashiell Hammett's *The Maltese Falcon*, could not have been resolved.

Della Street, Perry Mason's strong right arm (and lover, perhaps, though Erle Stanley Gardner only hinted at their personal relationship throughout the 83 novels in the Mason saga). It was as much her efficiency and attention to detail as Mason's courtroom pyrotechnics that enabled him to win every one of his murder cases.

Nikki Porter, "fiery, faithful, and long-suffering" girl Friday to Ellery Queen, whose first book appearance was in *The Scarlet Letters* (1953)

Future applicants for Erle Stanley Gardner's typing pool. Mr. Gardner treated his secretaries well. He married one of them, and used three of them as the prototype for Della Street. Miss Street, however, did not marry her boss, Perry Mason. She turned him down flat five times in a row (he wanted her to quit her job).

but who had already assisted Ellery in many short stories and radio adventures. As with Della and Perry, there is speculation that Nikki and EQ were lovers; if so, however, they and the Messrs. Queen preferred to keep their sex lives private, which is as it should be.

Phyllis Shayne and Lucy Hamilton, who served in turn as secretary to Brett Halliday's Michael Shayne throughout his long career. Phyllis also became his wife and played prominent roles in such early adventures as *The Corpse Came Calling* and *Murder Wears a Mummer's Mask*. Lucy began ministering to Shayne in 1945, first in New Orleans and later in Miami, and made important contributions in such harrowing (for her) cases as *Framed in Blood* and *Murder Is My Business*.

Velda, the only woman Mickey Spillane's super-hard-boiled Mike Hammer could ever love. Her disappearance while on a case in 1955 sent Mike on a long downhill plunge into alcoholism — from which he might never have recovered had she not been found still alive in *The Girl Hunters* seven years later.

Mary Huston, secretary to Morgan & Company ("Missing Persons Located — Heirs Found"), who aided (and later married) reporter and private detective Robin Bishop in *The Man Who Murdered Himself, The Doctor Died at Dusk,* and other superior novels by Geoffrey Homes.

And Miranda Foxworth, "ancient, creaking, forthright, lovable, and ever-complaining of her psychosomatic arthritis," who mothered Peter Chambers through such private-eye capers by Henry Kane as *A Corpse for Christmas,* and *Death Is the Last Lover.*

There are many others, less well-known though nonetheless capable . . . but almost all appear in works at least one and often two or more decades old. The only secretary of consequence to emerge in the 1970's is Giselle Marc, a rangy and tough-minded blonde who works for the Daniel Kearny detective agency in San Francisco; she is prominently featured in all three of Joe Gores' DKA File novels: *Final Notice, Dead Skip* and *Gone, No Forwarding*.

Perhaps there will be other new ones in the future; perhaps, as with the locked-room mystery, there will be a revival of interest among

MYSTERIOUS FOOTNOTE

David Janssen starred as *Richard Diamond, Private Detective,* on CBS, 1957–59. His secretary, Sam, was played by Mary Tyler Moore. If you didn't recognize her, you're excused: she was only shown from the knees down.

MATTHEW SEAMAN

writers (the *reader* interest is there), and the detective will once again have his assistant, confidante, partner, lover.

Perhaps. But right now the question — the lament — remains.

Where have all the secretaries gone?

Bill Pronzini is a member of the board of directors of the Mystery Writers of America and the author of eighteen suspense novels, a third of which feature the "Nameless" San Francisco private eye — who, he is ashamed to say, does not employ a secretary.

THE PERFECT SECRETARY: MISS ROSE CORSA

This would be a better-run (business) world if there were more Miss Corsas in it. Letters would be flawless, files would be immaculate; appointments would be properly scheduled, phone calls would be promptly returned. And executives would be so cowed by all this efficiency, they'd turn into workaholics — even if they started out as confirmed chair-swiveling time-wasters.

Miss Corsa makes so few mistakes that by comparison a computer looks sloppy. She was put on this earth, or so we are led to believe, as a sort of animate universal conscience. One look at her and immediately you feel guilty if you're not concentrating on company problems. Anyone who's ever worked in an office has bumped into someone just like her, though probably not at the water cooler — she has little time for purposeless camaraderie. She is the employee who seems to have been there forever, even if she was just hired yesterday. She is a stickler for protocol, a zealot for rules, and above all is dedicated to the job.

She does, however, have her little quirks.

POIROT GOT A LEMON

Miss Felicity Lemon is totally humorless, devoid of style and relentlessly ugly. Small wonder that she's always reading books on self-improvement. Poirot is delighted with her. She keeps things running smoothly for the little egghead, having served an apprenticeship under Mr. Parker Pyne in 1934.

One of them is that she is constitutionally unable to relax. According to her author, Emma Lathen, Rose Corsa was "clearly designed by nature for the motto: We are not amused." Her idea of a good time is ordering new carbon paper from Supplies. Once, just once, her superior, John Putnam Thatcher, tried to slip a bit of levity past her defenses. It was on a Monday morning. Now, it being the beginning of the week, when none of us is up to par, you'd think she'd have the grace to humor him. Forget it. His innocuous sally — How'd you get the sunburned nose? — received the Corsa deep-freeze. "A bank, in her opinion, was no place to describe family barbeques."

The bank referred to, of course, is the Sloan Guaranty Trust, the world's third largest financial concern, headquartered on Wall Street within lunching distance of Fraunces Tavern. Monday through Friday, Miss Corsa subways to the Sloan from her home in Queens, which she shares with her parents and several brothers, some of whom are not yet old enough to work (Miss Corsa undoubtedly has little to say to them).

Upon arriving at the Sloan, Miss Corsa goes directly to her office on the sixth floor. It has its own window (she is, after all, private secretary to a vice-president) and an angular modern décor. Miss Corsa's personal touches are a desk clock, a small vase of flowers (in the spring she's partial to violets) and a little tin box, which she keeps locked in her bottom drawer. This box has been "an enduring challenge to Thatcher's imagination." He has no idea what's in it, knows better than to ask and is stymied when he tries to come up with a list of probable contents. When the building was cleared during a bomb scare, it was the one item Miss Corsa thought to save. Occasionally, she takes it with her to the ladies' room.

Though Miss Corsa and Mr. Thatcher sit less than twenty feet apart, share a connecting door, communicate daily and have gone through seventeen books together, they are not on a first-name basis. That would violate her concept of correct nine-to-five procedure. Not for her the breezy "Hey, Rosie, grab a pencil and get in here." She reserves Christian names, and the diminutives thereof, for (1) family, (2) close friends, (3) co-workers on a peer level and (4) members of a neighboring parish. Since Thatcher fits none of these categories, "if he ever referred to Miss Corsa as Rosie, there would be a mushroom cloud." In *Ashes to Ashes*, he was amazed to find one of his clients leaning over her in conspiritorial intimacy, teasing her with a "Now, Rosie . . ." He would have been less astonished had he remembered the man was a staunch Catholic, from an area adjacent to Miss Corsa's section of Queens. Given such credentials, "Rosie" would naturally allow the fellow a few liberties.

In *Ashes*, Miss Corsa did *not* (a first) nag Thatcher about the work that piled up while he was playing sleuth. "A true daughter of the church" (Our Lady of Lourdes School for Girls), she was pleased to have him untangle the high intrigue at St. Bernadette's, a sister school to her alma mater.

Miss Corsa's exact age is moot. She could be anywhere between twenty-five and forty-five. Working backwards, her grandfather (the one with the high blood pressure) is ninety-seven; that probably puts Rose in her late thirties. In *Accounting for Murder,* she "dreamily" describes General Cartwright as handsome; the General was forty-seven, an age amenable to late-thirties fantasies. Her wardrobe, too, is that of a middle-aged woman: navy blue dresses, no frills, no sex appeal, no nonsense. Still, you have to consider that she may just *seem* beyond the flush of youth — a chronic failing of the emotionally repressed.

Miss Corsa is the only series character in mystery fiction who can knock you dead with an

THE NAGGING QUESTION

What is in Miss Corsa's little tin box?

inflection. Coming from her lips, "Certainly, Mr. Thatcher" can be as devastating as any line ever delivered by Cagney. She may not say much, but when displeased she can make the words of her choice — "No, thank you," for example — sound obscene. (As you might suspect, she considers true profanity beyond the pale.) What's more, her intonation transcends the foibles of the intercom. When Thatcher buzzes her, it's impossible to judge his mood; when she replies — instant Rorschach. Sometimes she doesn't even need words to get her point across; a cough will do. She uses one to "signal" Thatcher she is ready for him to begin dictation.

Miss Corsa has a keenly developed sense of right and wrong. If she believes in what she's doing, it's right; if she doesn't believe in what other people are doing, they're wrong. Yet this woman, who would blanche at the notion of stealing a paper clip, who would tremble at the thought of touching a book without washing her hands first, this woman lies like Pinocchio once a telephone is cradled in her shoulder. ITT, it appears, brings out the demon in her, particularly if she can trick them into helping the Sloan.

With her Charon-at-the-Styx attitude toward those who would pester Thatcher, her invincible memory, her ability to keep her head when all about her are losing theirs, Miss Corsa makes the perfect private secretary. But before you try to hire her away from Thatcher, think about this: she will never be your friend.

THE BELEAGUERED MRS. HUDSON

Jonathan Roberts

In the history of tenant-management relations, there has never been a more accommodating landlady than Martha Hudson, nor a more annoying lodger than Sherlock Holmes.

Consider, if you will, the indignities to which the good woman's premises were subjected. There was the "patriotic V.R. done in bullet pocks" on the wall, dating from the time Holmes took up a pistol in "one of his queer humours." There was the mantelpiece, brutally scarred from pinning unanswered correspondence to it with a jack-knife. There were the strange emanations from beneath his door, the results of his "weird and often malodorous" scientific experiments. There was the caterwauling of the violin, whenever the mood struck him, regardless of the hour. There was the constant parade of "undesirable characters" trooping up the steps of 221B to see him. And to top things off, there was the little matter of the apartment being set afire by Moriarty's henchmen.

Yet Mrs. Hudson remained unflappable, affably fulfilling the role of housekeeper, cook, office manager, curator, foil, admirer and occasional assistant to the Great Detective. Not once did she venture an "I say, Holmes, this time you've gone a bit far." Since occupants have been evicted for far less cause, one can only mar-vel at her equanimity. If anything, Holmes' peccadilloes seemed to make her *more* solicitous of him.

Why such devotion?

To put it in economic terms, Mrs. Hudson did very well for herself. During Victoria's reign, there was a limited selection of paying occupations available to women; having chosen the role of landlady, she made it profitable. According to Watson, she charged a "princely" monthly rent, and he further huffed, "I have no doubt that the house might have been purchased at the price which Holmes paid for his rooms during the years.that I was with him."

Avarice, however, cannot account for Mrs. Hudson's deep personal concern for Holmes. Nor can ego, though there must have been some satisfaction in having one of London's most celebrated men living in her house.

We must look instead to the motherly nature of her attentions.

Mrs. Hudson, with no children of her own, seems to have viewed Holmes as a surrogate son, a *genius* surrogate son, to be cherished and cosseted at all cost. Even the arrangement of her rooms, on the first and third floors, sandwiching his from above and below, suggests a certain protectiveness.

221B

Hugo's Companions, the Sherlock Holmes club headquartered in Chicago, has as its insignia what looks to be the doorplate to 221B. This design has been made into a tiny gold-colored pin, suitable for a lapel or for use as a tie tack. Originally available exclusively to club members, the pin is now offered to the general public.

To order, send $8 and postage to R. W. Hahn, 509 South Ahrens Avenue, Lombard, Illinois 60148.

The Sherlockian Tie Tack.

MATTHEW SEAMAN

Then there was her attitude toward breakfast. Is there now, or has there ever been, a mother who did not insist on a substantial start to the day for her child? Mrs. Hudson was no exception. In "The Naval Treaty," she plied Holmes with ham and eggs *and* curried chicken and with tea *and* coffee. She was determined he would eat *something*. Though not appreciative to the extent of offering help with the dishes, Holmes did acknowledge that "she has as good an idea of breakfast as a Scotchwoman." Naturally. It is a mother's specialty.

Beyond the maternal responsibilities of the morning tray, Mrs. Hudson demonstrated a readiness to indulge Holmes when he was showing off. Take, for instance, that curried chicken breakfast. Holmes had prearranged with her to hide a crucial document under one of the plates. When his guest, Percy Phelps, discovered the paper, he was suitably flabbergasted. Holmes admitted to him that he could "never resist a touch of the dramatic." Mrs. Hudson, one sur-

mises, just stood there smiling at the audacity of her "son."

She was even willing to help him at great personal peril. In "The Adventure of the Empty House," she spent the better part of her time rearranging a wax bust of Holmes to create the illusion (via a silhouette on the window shade) that he was inside pacing, reading, what have you. To make things seem natural, she had to readjust the dummy every fifteen minutes, and in such a way that she could not be seen — presumably by spending most of the day crawling along the floor on her hands and knees. We learn at what risk when a gunshot shatters the window, the shade and the dummy, and lodges in the far wall. (How like a you-know-what to sacrifice herself in defense of her child.)

Once cast in the role of mother, Mrs. Hudson comes to feel responsibility for Holmes' health, sometimes deciding that she knows better than he what his welfare requires. In "The Adventure of the Dying Detective," her most prolonged appearance, she obeys his wish that she not call in a doctor, but only up to a point. After deciding he has become too delirious to be sensible, she scurries off to collect Dr. Watson: "With your leave or without it, Mr. Holmes, I am going for the doctor this very hour." And when, in "The Sign of the Four," Holmes is anxiety-ridden because of a spell of inactivity, she senses the problem and turns to Watson for help.

Like a true mother, she is devoted to the "memory" of her son. From May 1891 to April 1894, when Holmes was allegedly dead somewhere at the bottom of the Reichenbach Falls, she virtually enshrined his rooms, keeping everything in its proper place, albeit with "an unwonted tidiness."

Certainly there is ample evidence that Holmes "disliked and distrusted women." But just as clearly, his disdain did not include Mrs. Martha Hudson, the only woman to share his daily life for two decades. It was from her, perhaps, that he developed his "remarkable gentleness and courtesy in his dealings with women." What mother could ask for more?

Jonathan Roberts and Mrs. Hudson have reached an agreement that if Holmes ever moves out he gets the apartment.

THE ELIGIBLE LIST

Betsy Lang

MARTY NORMAN

If you insist on falling in love with the hero, at least make sure he's available. Herewith, to pique your fantasies, a short roster of mysteriously unattached gentlemen.

Lew Archer (Ross Macdonald)
Intelligent, articulate and divorced. Interested in books and art. Prerequisite for pursuit: firm background in all matters Freudian. Perhaps more suitable for short involvements.

James Bond (Ian Fleming)
Tall, dark, handsome — run-of-the-mill lust object. Incurable snob and brand-name aficionado. Wear designer scarf (with famous initials) to catch his attention.

Merle Capricorn (Pauline Glen Winslow)
Wealthy redhead. Likes fine wines, good food. Gives women the big rush and the royal treatment. Has a terrific house, a discreet housekeeper.

Pierre Chambrun (Hugh Pentecost)
Short, stocky Frenchman. Best feature: large, dark eyes. Enjoys gourmet cooking, Turkish coffee. As resident manager of New York luxury hotel, has perfected suavity and earns respectable salary.

Matt Cobb (William de Andrea)
Aspired to be pro basketball player but stopped growing at 6′1″. Good sense of humor. Glamour job: TV executive for major network.

Adam Dalgliesh (P. D. James)
Self-sufficient widower (wife died in childbirth). Very sensitive; writes poetry. Intensely devoted

to police work. May be hard to win a commitment, but worth the try. (Work fast, though: Cordelia Gray is also interested.)

Rinus de Gier (Janwillem Van De Wetering)

Mustachioed Dutchman on Amsterdam police force. Despite Zen pronouncements, terribly moody. Relates better to cats than to people. Hobby: flute playing.

Irwin M. Fletcher (Gregory Mcdonald)

Lean, handsome and saddled with alimony payments (two marriages). Mid-thirties, but with ageless appeal. Silver-tongued devil who could con you into anything.

Dr. Patrick Grant (Margaret Yorke)

M.A., D.Phil., Fellow and Dean of St. Mark's College, Oxford. Solves crimes between tutorials. Good conversationalist, keen reasoning powers; rather inflexible. His sister might help you snare him.

Hardy Boys (Carolyn Keene)

Well-to-do teen-age brothers. Own car, boat (nicknamed "Sleuth"); often go for spin in Dad's private plane, gallivant cross-country in search of thrills. Excellent choices for falling in puppy love.

Matt Helm (Donald Hamilton)

Free-lance writer and nature photographer; also a spy. Not averse to taking beautiful women along on adventures. Major drawback: drives an old pickup truck. Better bring a pillow.

Sherlock Holmes (Arthur Conan Doyle)

Retired beekeeper. Curious resemblance to Basil Rathbone, William Gillette, Peter Cushing. Eccentric taste in clothes: wears deerstalker and Inverness cape year round. Cerebral; observant; accusatory. Two foibles: injects cocaine; carries torch (for infamous adventuress).

Dan Mallett (Frank Parish)

Poacher from remote West Country village. Beautiful clear blue eyes. Terrific mimic. One snag: still lives with his mum — and he's in his thirties.

Travis McGee (John D. MacDonald)

Helps emotionally traumatized women via innovative sex therapy. Lives on boat, with Fort Lauderdale as home base. Earns living by recovering stolen property. Nice for sentimental weekend.

Asey Mayo (Phoebe Atwood Taylor)

A Cape Codder. Formerly a sailor, now a handyman/chauffeur. Tall and skinny, with lousy posture. Addicted to chewing tobacco. Down-home type; good common sense.

Charles Paris (Simon Brett)

Over-the-hill actor with less than successful career — and a wife he reunites with periodically. Still, has a sort of bittersweet charm. Fine for women who like to undertake "projects."

Hercule Poirot (Agatha Christie)

Belgian-born resident of England. Sleeps with hair net; sucks vegetable marrows and sips *tisanes*. Rightly proud of his "little grey cells." Tends toward obesity, so watch what he eats.

Colonel Charles Russell (William Haggard)

Definitely a best bet. In mid-sixties and retired from government service (but maintains the old ties). Full head of gray hair, admirably tended mustache, soldierly air. Impeccably tailored. Has had satisfactory relationships with women, providing they combined elegance with intelligence. Lifelong bachelor; time he was hooked.

John Putnam Thatcher (Emma Lathen)

Bank vice-president; acts accordingly — conservative, sensible, smart. Extremely curious, with wry sense of humor. Dresses like ad for Brooks Brothers. See Miss Corsa for appointment.

Remo Williams (Sapir and Murphy)

a.k.a. "the Destroyer." Former Newark cop, now an assassin under contract to U.S. government. Magnificent body, but peculiarly thick wrists. Maintains strict rice diet. Inseparable companion: Chiun, a.k.a. "Little Father," a.k.a. "Master of Sinanju." Do *not* make them mad.

Moses Wine (Roger L. Simon)

A nice Jewish boy private eye. Packs a .38 in shoulder holster. Drives a '73 Porsche; talks and acts macho Hollywood, circa 1940.

Betsy Lang is married.

Chapter 5
SKULLDUGGERY

HOW TO SCARE A WOMAN TO DEATH

Stephen King

Who would want to scare a nice lady half to death, keep her up most of the night, make her race to shut doors, close windows, and then lie awake shivering, perspiring even in her lightest nightgown? Well, me for one. Just the thought raises a grin that, though I cannot see it since I have no mirror, *feels* wonderfully sadistic. As the little street urchin in *Oliver Twist* says, I only wants to make yer flesh creep . . . and it's been my experience that ladies like a good scare as well as anyone. So if you're an apprentice flesh-creeper (or even if you aren't), let me offer some hints on throwing a jolt into what some of us still refer to as the fairer sex.

Who's minding the kids? It would be sexist to say that only ladies care about their children — in fact, it would be a downright lie — but there does seem to be such a thing as "maternal in-stinct," and I go for it instinctively. Though the idea of children in jeopardy is sometimes looked upon by critics with a disapproving eye, it's as old as Hansel and Gretel and as new as the books of Mary Higgins Clark. Except, in my case, who's minding the kids is apt to be something green and scaly that just stepped out of the closet.

Pretty dark out here, isn't it, Maude? You're a woman, maybe young, maybe pretty. You don't spend all day and all night aware of the fact that you're a target, but you take the usual precautions: you don't talk to strange men, don't wear a see-through blouse on the first date, don't pick up hitchhikers on back-country roads. And then, one night, while you're driving on a deserted highway, you look up into your rear-view mirror and see a face . . . and suddenly there's warm breath on your neck . . . and hands around your throat. All of which says that women see themselves as uniquely vulnerable, and in a way or ways that men are not. Despite unique physical advantages (increased lung capacity in the female makes it possible for her to hold her breath longer underwater, for instance . . . remember it if your husband or lover decides he wants to drown you in the bathtub), most women are lighter and shorter than their men, often less well-muscled, sometimes less well coordinated — in many cases because of the sexual molds they've been forced into. I've never consciously made any of the women in my books into shrinking violets, helpless screamers waiting for the knight in shining armor to rescue

---

MUFFLING A WOMAN'S SCREAMS

Get your hands off her neck.

If you apply enough pressure to stop the noise, you'll probably choke her to death.

Put the heel of your palm against her lips and lean in, as hard as you can.

That should do it.

MATTHEW SEAMAN

The terrified Gilmore woman hugged the wall for protection. Then it started to move.

them, or know-nothing twits, but I like to play on that unique sense of vulnerability. It terrifies.

I must pause here and say that after racking my brain for at least two minutes, I've decided that all the following other techniques work equally well on men. So, take a deep breath and try these on:

My, it's getting close in here. When you came, you thought it would be just another dull cocktail party, but now all the doors are locked . . . and there's a funny rumbling in the walls . . . and speaking of the walls, aren't they *moving?* This is that delicious feeling of claustrophobia, fear of tight places, and I play on it with great joy at every opportunity. It's the feeling you get when there are twelve people in the elevator and it suddenly stops between floors . . . and someone starts to scream.

Oh dear, I don't know what that is, but it's not chopped liver! You drop your damn compact, the one your mother-in-law gave you, and it rolls

into that funny little hole in the baseboard. You reach in to get it, and your hand closes on *something* there in that musty darkness between the walls . . . and then the something starts to squirm in your hand . . . and to sting . . . and you can't get your fingers out. This is a highly usable combination of fears, centering perhaps on the *phobia* — the fear of the horribly slimy or squirmy something that you just can't see. It works well on women, who traditionally scream about mice, gag over spiders, and faint at the sight of a snake slithering out from under the bed, but it works just as well on men, who do all the same things . . . inside.

What happened to the lights, Jane? No doubt about it, this is the greatest fear of all — fear of the dark and what might live there. Turn out the lights in a lady's own peaceful living room (or, even better, have a blackout at the height of a screaming thunderstorm), and that peaceful room becomes a jungle. You forget where

THE CHLOROFORM GAG

In the matter of abducting young ladies, it is not sufficient to ask them, however politely, to seat themselves in the trunk of your car. Rarely will they be that obliging.

Chloroform, on the other hand, affords infallible persuasion. Sprinkle a drop or two, or ten, on a clean white hanky, and hold it away from your nose and directly under theirs. The stuff's beginning to work when they stop blinking. (This happens suddenly, not gradually, so watch it.) Now pick them up, pile them in the boot and head for the hideaway.

One caveat: Too much chloroform could present you with a very sick young lady. Not immediately, mind you, but in four or five days' time. The problem is, the sweet-smelling liquid causes liver damage. To stay on the safe side, make sure the vapor is diluted. A healthy range of concentration is 1 percent, or less.

And you should be aware that chloroform has a tendency to decompose. Be advised to store it in a brown glass container. You would be unwise to label it — but the police would be ever so grateful.

things are; you're apt to stumble over the hassock, lose your sense of direction and run into the bookcase thinking it's the door to the hall, and end up feeling your way with your hands groping the air in front of you. Absurd imaginings no longer seem quite so absurd, do they? Your heart is beating much too rapidly. You could almost scream, couldn't you? And when an inhuman voice begins whispering your name over and over again in the dark, perhaps you do . . .

The dead. Of course they don't come back, I know it and you know it. There are no such things as ghosts, except in the stories told around the campfire. Vault doors do not creak open at midnight. And then, three days after you bury Uncle Harry (and no one even suspected the rat poison you fed him, you clever girl), the telephone rings . . . and it's Uncle Harry . . . and he says you and he have something to talk about . . . and twenty minutes later the door knocker begins to rise and fall in a slow and horrible rhythm . . . and you think you'll just go to the peephole and make sure it's only the paperboy . . . and that's when the moldering hand pokes through the letter slot and clutches your wrist. What fun.

These are five of the ways I go about my task of scaring ladies. There are others I'll not mention (I can't give away *all* of my trade secrets), but let me add one more — a very quiet scare that perhaps works best on women because women are slightly more imaginative than men, slightly better tuned to the nuances of terror. So: *What's missing from this picture?* In some ways, this is the most wicked thrust of all, aiming directly at a woman's need for pattern and order. This is the terror of coming home and finding that the furniture has been subtly changed about; that the slip you'd folded so neatly into the third drawer is now in the second, that the book you put on the dresser is lying open on your favorite chair; that the radio you left tuned to AM-91 is tuned to FM-106.

This is coming home and finding that the dog your husband left to protect you is mysteriously missing — and one knife, the longest and sharpest, is gone from the rack over the sink. And . . . just perhaps . . . at that point you hear breathing in the next room.

For me, scaring women is all part of the job, but in this case I admit with no shame at all that my business is also my pleasure. And it might not be unfitting to close with the words of Shakespeare, another writer not above throwing a scare into the fairer sex when the chance came. "Good night, ladies, good night," said Ophelia, who was driven mad by her own fears. "Sweet ladies, good night, good night . . ."

And sleep tight.

Stephen King is the author of innumerable best sellers, including his most recent, The Dead Zone.

LIVING WITH THE BOGEYMAN
Tabitha King

You write to ask if he's an alcoholic, a child beater, a psychic. You recognize the real thing, you confess, because you've been there yourself.

You write to ask where he gets such ideas, meaning did his mum lock him in the closet until he was sorry, did something happen that warped him when he was a child or was he born with a bent mind?

Much of your mail goes unanswered because otherwise he'd have to hire a secretary, then tell her what to say — a process that takes almost as much time as a personal response. In any case, no, he is not now and never has been an alcoholic (just an occasional drunk), a child beater (the odd whack on the butt), or a psychic (every so often an intuitive flash). As to whether he was warped as a child or just born that way, the answer is as obvious as it is ultimately insignificant. Of course he was, and you better watch out.

The same questions are asked by the media, but they come round to the house to see for themselves exactly what manner of man is frightening the unsuspecting readers of America and England and Japan and Brazil and . . . well, a lot of people, and perhaps they're not so unsuspecting after all. The media are frequently disappointed to discover an ordinary Yankee, size XL, drinking beer and watching baseball while his three children throw toys and his wife stews the checkbook.

This, then, is Stephen King.

He likes to say that he writes about ordinary people to whom extraordinary things happen. This is also a capsule autobiography. The extraordinary does erupt now and again in our lives, but so far as I know it does in everybody's.

A few years ago, we took our kids (then just a pair of them) to a lecture Steve was giving. At the rear of the hall was a poster that advertised the talk, and our boy Joe Hill, just then learning

---

RAISING GOOSEBUMPS AND CURDLING BLOOD

You've heard the expression "It makes my blood run cold"? Well, if it does, glance at your thighs and forearms. Notice how the skin seems suddenly to have little golf balls stuck underneath. These are goosebumps, which are an attempt by your body to insulate itself against the chill. They are caused by the contraction of the muscles at the base of the hair follicle and act as a barrier between your thinned blood and the terror that struck it. As your emotions heat up, the bumps will recede. Then you'll only have to worry about the hackles on your neck.

It is impossible to curdle someone's blood, at least while it's still in her body. Remove it, saucepan it and overcook it — and that's a different story.

The Bogeyman, the Bogeyman's wife and the Bogeyman's three children on the Bogeyman's Maine lawn. They certainly look harmless enough.

to read, walked over to study it.

"What's it say, Joe?" I asked.

His finger underlined the name. "Steve-an King," he said.

He looked up at me, pleased with himself. I smiled to let him know he was right. His finger moved to the next line, the unfamiliar word "Author."

"Fa-ther?" he guessed.

It was perfectly natural to him that Stephen King's role in his life, father, would be announced in a poster, a matter of public record.

Joe Hill doesn't find it at all extraordinary that his father is a famous author, like the stuffy faces on the cards he plays with (he calls them "arfers"). He did ask me later on during that lecture whether his father was going to be President. That's something many small children imagine as a serious possibility, before they discover that Dad, all-powerful to them, is a small-town dentist, or grocer, or schoolteacher. Joe Hill now wonders if his father writes all the books there are, and all the television shows. He is most impressed with the fact that Steve once met Stan Lee, the creator of Spiderman.

The point is, extraordinary has more to do with the individual than with the rest of the world.

But back to your fantasies. What about Stephen King, Bogeyman? Will you shrink if you look him in the eye?

Well, he's a large man, slightly stooped, as the very tall and very near-sighted often are. His eyes, almost obscured by the thick lenses of his glasses, are a mild blue, almond in shape and slightly slanted, as Irish as the rest of his face. A snapshot of the boy he was at eight or nine, very like Joe Hill, reveals a fey and dreamy quality in the eyes. One stops and studies that photograph, caught by the expression. This is one face of the Bogeyman, and it wouldn't scare a soul.

Another picture, taken by a college classmate, records those eyes ten years older, mad, gleeful, manic, infinitely more frightening than the mouth of the shotgun he points at the camera. The gun's double mouth has been enlarged in the darkroom to compete with the eyes. There is a striking resemblance to Charles Manson, and the picture trades on it. It is the very face that made my parents less than enthusiastic when I first brought him home. It is the face that tells you those things you'd rather not hear about. Yes, you might shrink from it. Until you found out he was faking it, having you on.

The man is a frustrated actor. Peek in and listen to him read to his children. It might be from Marvel comics, or *The Lord of the Rings*, or something he's written just for them. Even the baby stops to listen to Daddy "do the perlice in different voices." Or perhaps there's an improvised puppet show, with a make-shift stage, and a cast of Sesame Street puppets, and our own repertory company of dragons, vampires, assorted Things.

Whatever. The lesson of these tales remains the same: Be afraid, my darlings, for we have much to fear. Be *not* afraid to fear, do *not* deny your fears; that way lies the worst horror, the negation of reality, evil ignored and evil triumphant, danger unwatched for, danger that wins. Do *not*, above all, blind yourself when you must walk in darkness. Ignorance is not innocence, only stupidity and cowardice. So we hold hands, and wait for our night vision, and tell ourselves stories in the dark.

There is a children's story about a boy who has monsters in his closet. Eventually, he takes them all in bed with him, after he discovers they're just as frightened of the dark as he is. I love that story; it is *my* autobiography.

Tabitha King is working on her first mystery novel.

I DISMEMBER MAMA

Lucy Freeman

What is the lure of the murder mystery? Why does a reader avidly digest every bloody detail in such books as Robert Bloch's *Psycho* and Stanley Ellin's *Mirror, Mirror on the Wall*? And, for that matter, what motivates a writer to want to describe with delicious delight the vicious stabbing of an unfaithful wife? The gunning down of a bank official? The mass shooting of thirteen innocent people on the street?

"The roots of murder lie in the nursery," said Freud. No matter how disguised the later victims, no matter what their sex (male and female are the same to the unconscious part of our mind), they represent the mother against whom earlier violence has long been repressed.

In some way, this mother has been a cruel and brutal woman. She must have been, to have inspired such murderous rage in her child. According to Freud, mama is the model for all our future relationships. If she has been gentle and loving, her child will feel loved. But if she has been irritable and anxious, if perhaps she never wanted a baby in the first place, the infant will suffer mixed feelings of love and fury.

None of us received as much attention from our mother as we would have liked. The degree to which we are still complaining is directly proportional to our repressed angry feelings. Guaranteed, the rage will eventually explode. Mama's gonna get it — one way or another.

Mystery readers unconsciously indulge in murdering mama vicariously. We safely enjoy revenge at arm's length, momentarily releasing our primitive, pent-up urge to kill. This release invariably brings pleasure. For the moment, we have escaped our inner pressure cooker. Similarly, in the interest of becoming civilized, mystery writers sublimate *their* urge to murder. If they do it with artistry, they can get very, very rich and laugh at their murderous wishes. Their revenge comes in saying, Look, Ma — not "no hands," but hands full of valuable green stuff. Hands that have not had to stoop to stab, strangle, shoot, poison, dice or mince as long as they can keep busy at the typewriter.

There are, alas, those compelled to act on

their wild dreams of revenge. They *must* kill. They have experienced less love and more violence as children than the reader or writer. People do not murder unless they have actually been victims of consistent psychological or physical cruelty as children. Psychological cruelty implies a parent's repressed wish to kill, which children sense and react to, in fear of their very life. People may become psychotic if life is too harsh for them emotionally, but without extreme cruelty in their past they will *not* resort to killing. They have been loved enough to learn control of their "evil" wishes.

Dr. Manfred S. Guttmacher, after studying the lives of a number of real murderers, concludes in *The Mind of the Murderer:* "Almost without exception, one finds in their early backgrounds not only economic want, but cruelties and miseries of every kind." Stuart Palmer, in *Study of Murder,* maintains: "the murderers appeared to have been terribly frustrated during their early lives, suffering extreme birth traumas, serious diseases in infancy and childhood, accidents, physical beatings, severe training practices at the hands of the mother, psychological frustrations and traumatic incidents outside of the home."

And in her recent book *So the Witch Won't Eat Me: Fantasy and the Child's Fear of Infanticide,* Dorothy Bloch reports that in her treatment of very disturbed children she has found violent youngsters suffer persistent, extreme cruelty at the hands of either their mother or father. One can only guess at the cruelty in the childhood of Lizzie that caused her to take up the ax. Probably the psychological cruelty inherent in the repressed violence of her father and mother.

Luckily, mystery reader and mystery writer are seldom forced into carrying fury this far. Our anger has been tempered by our love. Mama may have been difficult at times, but she did not hate us with such intensity that we could not appease our desire to kill in reading or in writing. Sure, we dismember mama — but only on the printed page.

Lucy Freeman was one of the first women reporters on the New York Times. *She is the author of more than fifty books, including three murder mysteries featuring a psychoanalyst as sleuth.*

MOTHER'S (LAST) DAY

No author has dared clobber mom as she forks down a piece of apple pie, but Brian Garfield did manage to kill one on her return from the supermarket (*Death Wish*).

Two writers who disbelieved in the sanctity of motherhood were Michael Hinkemeyer, who threw Bonnie Koster and her four kids in the path of a homicidal reverend (*The Fields of Eden*), and Ralph McInerny, who sent Father Dowling to investigate Sylvia Lowry's last rites (*Her Death of Cold*).

H. R. Smithies chose to treat the matter as a joke, but unfortunately for the mom in his tale, she was the butt of it (*Death Takes a Gamble*).

The weirdest mommy murder of them all came from the pen of Robert Bloch, whose Norman Bates killed the old girl, had her publicly buried and privately disinterred, then relegated her to a rocker in the cellar, where they argued and he blamed her for his crimes (*Psycho*).

Nor is the classic English mum spared. Rendell eliminates Jacqueline Coverdale in *A Judgement in Stone* (but keeps the family intact: her relatives die with her) Christie deals with mum in *Elephants Can Remember*, in which Mrs. Ravenscrift bids farewell.

And in titles too numerous to mention, the Dowager Mother was harassed beyond all endurance: her tiara was tightened to choke off circulation; her bed was made up with scorpions and snakes; her car was rendered brakeless so she'd be late for tea — which was sweetened with aconite, anyway.

Since in every instance the murderer was caught, we might conclude that it's a wise child who doesn't pester ma.

THE BLOODY PULPS

Women in thirties and forties pulp magazines were stomped on, gouged, shackled, roped, lassoed and gunned down. Every so often, they fought back — with kicks to sensitive parts of male anatomies.

Overseeing all this mayhem for *True Detective* and *Master Detective* magazines was the late Renée Buse, who was listed on the mastheads as R. F. Buse. Most readers never knew the boss was a woman.

*A*nd then I saw Mac. She was standing in the doorway, booted legs spraddled under her, one enormous arm dangling at her side, the other resting across her ample abdomen. A .38 nestled in each pudgy fist.

"Page Violet McDade!" in
Clues, (January 1935)

CLOTHING A CORPSE

Sartorially speaking, Mafia corpses are the (lime) pits. All the labels in their clothes have been cut out, a clear indication the apparel was purchased at discount centers. The men stumble into the hereafter with their trouser pockets untidily turned out; the women, wearing necklaces made of cheap metal wire. Both sexes have been heavily doused with *eau d'ead poisson* or essence of kerosene, neither of which the perfume industry has bothered to rate on the alluring aroma scale. Assuredly, Mafia corpses will never earn a *Vogue* cover.

Housewives depart this earth one shoe on, one shoe off, hems down and buttons ripped open. They are also the only deceaseds who leave encumbered with a dishcloth boa, a classic *Glamour* magazine "don't."

The nubile tend to go out as if auditioning for a centerfold staple; they disregard clothing altogether, which is exactly how they appear—in the altogether. In one titillating instance, a woman scampered into a crypt and, despite the chill there, disrobed. God (or somebody) punished her, however, and as she breathed her last, a more modest soul came along with the good taste to try and cover her up; he put rubies on her eyes. And that's the naked truth.

Only when we discover the body in the library do we find a decently clad cadaver. The late Mr. Library Body reclines in a three-piece suit. True, his vest is a horrifying shade of red, but at least it's the result of a blast from a custom-made Purdy. The late Mrs. Body will be kitted out with gloves, appropriate since she's a visitor (albeit after hours).

Why is it so few characters put in a presentable last appearance? The difficulty, of course, is that in a mystery the corpse's wardrobe is selected by the killer, not the killee. And alas, the dispatcher has more pressing things on her mind than ringing up *Bazaar* to learn what's haut this season in shrouds.

Several corpse makers have attempted to redress their wrongs. Unfortunately, this creates more problems than it solves. You're familiar with the expression "the stiff"? Well, the goner is thus referred to because he is stiffer than a shirt with too much starch, stiffer than a triple shot of bourbon, stiffer than the Briton's upper lip. What usually happens is that the killer attacks, leaves hurriedly, then retreats to her lair to gloat over her proficiency. Mid self-congratulatory pat, it occurs to her that if the corpse were disguised and his identity obscured, she'd have more leisure for her getaway. So back to the scene of the crime she traipses, about four hours later. By which time her prey is doing his interpretation of the petrified forest.

Doctors call this state "rigor mortis." Its onset is 4 to 10 hours after death, and it takes 3 to 4 days to wear off. If, in the interim, a killer tries to bend the body's elbow to get it into a dime store T-shirt, she won't have much luck. That elbow will have "frozen" into the position she left it in those several hours back. The more she tries to jam it, the better her chances of breaking it. The result? When the Inspector finds the body, he presumes it to be the work of a sadist, a pervert, a homicidal maniac. How could he think anything else? There it rests, half in, half out of its clothes, its joints battered and its skeleton defamed (not to mention its liver riddled with traces of a Uruguayan toxin).

Persons desirous of reclothing their former friends should make a note that the best time is immediately after execution, while the body is still warm and malleable. *Merck's Manual* explains that the dead cool off at the rate of 3 to 3.5°F. for the first few hours, then at 1° for however long it takes the body to reach room temperature (usually 40 hours). This process is termed algor mortis by physicians. Murderers may call it "the fitting room try-on time."

A thoughtful killer will also be aware of what happens to the body's blood as the figure slumps there on the floor, fanny slightly raised, shoulders hunched over: the blood sinks to the lowest spot—in this case, the thighs, shins and palms. Now, if the poor blighter was wearing a kilt, in a Royal Stewart tartan, that red and purple hemorrhaging is going to clash something awful. The least the shillelagh whacker could do is upend Mac so the blood rushes to his rump, which his skirt will cover. Technically, the discoloration is known as livor mortis or post-mortem staining, and the process continues for 10 to 12 hours. Pathologists presented with a laird who has splotchy blood patches on his backside will go to court insisting that the body, which was found face down in the ditch, was obviously moved there; his original death throes occurred when he was face up.

Smelly bodies are those left in the water too long or hidden so well that little crawly things

discover them before the law gets round to it. They are usually accompanied by a decidedly greenish tinge (mold, my dear, the same stuff that grows on cheese if it's left out too long) and, in extreme instances, black decay. Again, these are not colors that compliment everyone. Unfortunately, putrefaction, unlike algor, livor and rigor mortis, does not desist; in fact, it persists. Beware, then, if you're planning on crating Whomever and putting him in dead storage. Undoubtedly, he and his wardrobe will be at odds before he's reclaimed.

DISTURBING THE DEAD

Michael Baden, M.D.

I've been trying to locate a first edition of *Frankenstein* to keep *Dracula* company on the shelf.

I don't think of the novel as a stylistic triumph, but the content is important. Mary Shelley may not have been aware of it, but she was highlighting a problem inherent in medical research: where do you get the material to experiment on? Her solution was to make the doctor and his loyal assistant graverobbers. Obviously, that's not conducive to good civic relations (I frown on it myself), but in the late 1800's Burke and Hare followed suit. They supplied the Edinburgh Medical School with corpses stolen from the local cemetery. At least, that's how they started out. Then they decided to create their own and save themselves the late-night trips.

Actually, Frankenstein was a pretty good doctor. Today, he'd probably apply for a grant and might even be accepted. If someone walked into my office and asked for parts for legitimate research, I'd try to be accommodating. But I'd have to be shown very solid credentials.

Michael Baden is Chief Medical Examiner of the City of New York.

KISS OF DEATH

LIPS BY INA

DRESSED TO KILL

An informal inventory of the mystery clothes closet reveals it holds at least twenty-five shrouds, including one in bright orange (John D. MacDonald), one in pretty pink (E. X. Ferrars), one for a nightingale (P. D. James) and one for grandma (John Franklin Bardin, writing as Gregory Tree), and nine separate nooses, the most attractive being those made of emeralds (Bevis Winters), red beads (T. J. King) and sin (Francis Carco).

When death reaches into the armoire for something to wear, titles indicate it pulls out a petticoat (Janson), a silk stocking (W. M. Duncan), a purple shirt (Woodthorpe), a white coat (Theodora DuBoise), a white tie (Ngaio Marsh) and a green hat (Creed), and then has to make a big decision: whether to don pink shoes (R. James), red shoes (C. Robertson), gold shoes (L. F. Stevens) or high heels (Christianna Brand).

On four occasions, death chooses to hide behind a mask (Therese Benson, D. G. Browne, J. Flagg, Anthony Gilbert), and it rather fancies itself in flowers, opting for a carnation (Stevenson), a white gardenia (Zelda Popkin) and roses (Saxby).

For budget dressing, there's a plain brown wrapper (John D. MacDonald again), and for drop-dead elegance there's murder in fancy dress (I. H. Irwin), in silk (R. Trevor), in mink (R. G. Dean) and in more mink (B. Iles).

The corpse, on the other hand, is laid out in nylon (Paradise), rubies (F. Lester), crimson slippers (R. A. J. Walling), and a flannel nightgown if it's a woman (Margaret Scherf), green pajamas if it's a man (Mr. Walling again the clothier). The corpse, if we're to believe the busy Mr. Walling, is none too tidy: it has a grimy glove as well as a dirty face.

Jewelry, alas, usually proves fatal, be it a ruby (Garvice), a ring (D. Donovan) or diamonds (E. C. Donnelly). And while we're on the subject, the mystery offers enough diamond doodads to keep even Lorelei Lee happy: it has a diamond bikini (C. Williams), a diamond bracelet (H. Wood), a diamond-buckled shoe (B. Bolt), a diamond dress (O. John), a diamond feather (H. Reilly), a diamond hair-slide (H. C. McNeile), a diamond necklace (F. Jackson), a diamond pendant (Thurston), a diamond pin (Carolyn Wells), a diamond sunburst (G. H. Tweed) and diamonds for a blonde (B. Sarto), though no diamonds for a doll (Cagney).

Sadly, there is no halo for Hedy, either, but in a more generous mood Carter Brown did reserve a shroud for Rowena.

Unfortunately, nobody wore black (Delano Ames) except the bride (Cornell Woolrich).

Of course, for those who prefer a bit of exposure, there's a G-string (Gypsy Rose Lee) and stripper Shasta Lynn's spangles (Wade Miller's *Dead Weapons*). For those interested in taking it all off, there's the nudist murder (T. Stevenson) and the nude in mink (Sax Rohmer), and various and sundry nakeds, specifically: the angel

I'm afraid I won't be of much help to you, though I devote most of my reading time to mystery stories — particularly the British variety, which to me are even more exciting.

Incidentally, I do find that many of the most elusive crimes were committed at British country house parties and, strangely enough, with never a tear, a rip, or a bit of blood on any garment. As a designer, I find that interesting.

EDITH HEAD

THE DROP-DEAD LOOK

mask

missing hatpin

choker

microdot

concealed weapon

poison ring

pugnosed revolver

stiletto

heel

(J. Webb), the lady (M. Corrigan), the mistress (Deptula) and the nuns (Colin Watson).

Indisputably, the mystery is dressed to kill (eight times at last count: Bocca, Channing, Cheyney, Cousin, Fetta, Hyde, Morland, Ozaki). Still, mystery characters do tend to get careless with their things. Diamonds vanish (G. Campbell) and so do emeralds (Nick Carter), and a hat was lost (Percy) as well as a valuable pearl (F. Grierson), a passel of diamonds (Adee, Marryat) and the infamous emeralds of Zarinthia (Beauchamp). Plus, Helen Vardon, that silly girl, left her reticule on the back of a chair in *Helen Vardon's Confession* (R. Austin Freeman). And heaven only knows how many hasty murderesses dropped a glove or an earring under a blood-soaked seat cushion in their dash for the exit. Now, there's a project for you: identifying and returning all the wardrobe odds and ends left at fictional crime scenes. Matching buttons to shirt fronts, and sleeve ravelings to sleeves, will keep you busy for a couple of years at least.

The most tantalizing article of clothing ever described in a mystery would have to be the snazzy orange hat worn (perhaps) by Cornell Woolrich's *Phantom Lady*. Scott Henderson was sitting in a bar, downing a few, when he spotted it. He liked it; he liked the lady under it. He moved closer. She moved closer. And so passed a pleasant few hours for everybody — except maybe Scott's wife, who was home being strangled with his necktie at the time. Scott figured he had an iron-clad alibi: the lady in the tangerine toque. Only trouble was, he didn't know her name, and when he returned to the bar nobody remembered seeing her. Or her hat. How do you forget a conspicuous, blazing orange hat? Or do you? Or did Scott imagine it? These questions have perplexed readers for years.

This bit of now-you-see it, now-you-don't hanky-panky is a hallowed mystery tradition. No disguise expert worth his false mustache and her blond wig would be caught dead without a little item that could be shucked, reversed, pinned up, let down or in some way be made to look completely different. The two most skillful wardrobe rearrangers are Four Square Jane from the book of the same name (Edgar Wallace) and Sophie Lang from the series of short

ACCESSORY BEFORE THE FACT

MATTHEW SEAMAN

stories *The Notorious Sophie Lang* (Frederick Irving Anderson). Neither lady is on the side of the law. Jane suffers a Robin Hood complex: she likes to steal from the rich and donate to the

ACCESSORY AFTER THE FACT

MATTHEW SEAMAN

poor. Sophie is more Midas-oriented: she adores gold (and silver and platinum and twinkling jewels), and once she steals it, she hoards it. Both ladies are legendary for their chameleon-like qualities — they can change their appearance at the first blast of a copper's whistle, and while he's looking for a long-haired brunette in a gray sweater and camel skirt, they're ambling away in crimped blond curls and a burgundy cape.

Though not in their class, or for that matter in Holmes', Cleek's or even Freddy the Pig's, Margery Allingham's Albert Campion once tried the disguise ruse. In *Sweet Danger*, he borrowed some duds from an auntie and turned himself into a rather attractive-looking maiden lady — very pale and delicate. He looked fetching when he broke the case.

The most commonly used mystery disguise is not so efficient. It's the point d'esprit veil. No hard-boiled dame would walk into a private eye's office without one. Unfortunately, it does not hide her beauty mark, her long legs or her signature perfume, essence of gardenia. The Eye invariably recognizes her the next time he sees her — when she's sneaking out of the dead man's apartment.

Lady killers dress for success in (a) that veil, (b) spike heels, one of which snaps off at the crucial moment, (c) elbow-length gloves, which they inadvertently leave on the foyer table as a calling card, (d) black, to match their hearts. Black, by the way, is the favorite mystery color, appearing in well over four hundred titles. Runner-up is red, which bloodies about three hundred, and also-rans are blue (a hundred or so) and white (nearly a hundred).

Ladies do not, however, kill with clothes. Rather, they are killed by them. First choice: neckties; second, silk stockings; third, scarves; fourth, bathrobe sashes; fifth, mink (which they drown in). Clearly, mystery men prefer not to choke women with their bare hands. They like a yard or two of silk between them and a larynx.

Any woman, then, who buys her husband or boyfriend a necktie is asking for trouble. And she just may become an accessory to her own death. She should protect herself and buy him a book instead. How about one called *Dressed to Kill?*

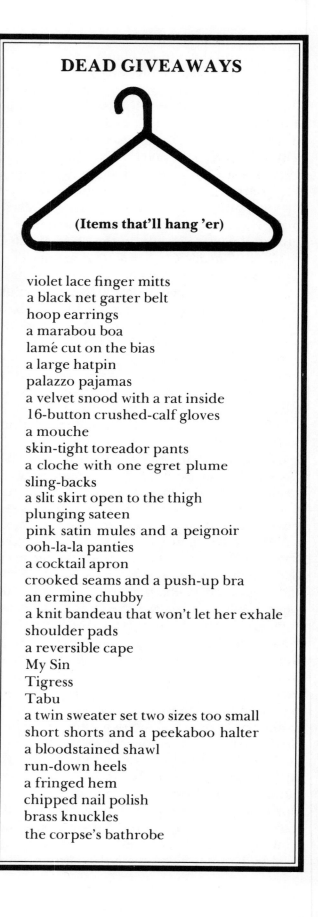

DEAD GIVEAWAYS

(Items that'll hang 'er)

violet lace finger mitts
a black net garter belt
hoop earrings
a marabou boa
lamé cut on the bias
a large hatpin
palazzo pajamas
a velvet snood with a rat inside
16-button crushed-calf gloves
a mouche
skin-tight toreador pants
a cloche with one egret plume
sling-backs
a slit skirt open to the thigh
plunging sateen
pink satin mules and a peignoir
ooh-la-la panties
a cocktail apron
crooked seams and a push-up bra
an ermine chubby
a knit bandeau that won't let her exhale
shoulder pads
a reversible cape
My Sin
Tigress
Tabu
a twin sweater set two sizes too small
short shorts and a peekaboo halter
a bloodstained shawl
run-down heels
a fringed hem
chipped nail polish
brass knuckles
the corpse's bathrobe

THE HAND(BAG) GUN
Assault with a Deadly Weapon
Gavin Lyall

The question of what guns ladies should use to shoot people with is one that has troubled detective and thriller writers ever since the servant problem made it impossible that the butler could have done it. The Little Woman accepted the role of the Unlikeliest Suspect just as she took over polishing the silver once Jeeves had left to head a Burger King franchise, and by now there is a fair amount of mythology about the whole thing. There are even some guns.

Raymond Chandler, whose opinions of women can be guessed if not deduced from his having a woman as the main killer in all but one of his books, had very firm ideas on the subject. A woman used a small-calibre gun, almost always an automatic rather than a revolver, and didn't remember to pick up the empty shell cases that would tie the murder to the weapon.

In *The Big Sleep*, Carmen Sternwood used a .22 Banker's Special revolver, but a book later, in *Farewell My Lovely*, Velma had traded up to a .25 automatic to shoot down Moose Malloy. The Lady (who was not) in the Lake also favoured a .25 — probably a Colt 4½ inches long and weighing 13 ounces, from the description. One

short step for womankind brought The Little Sister a .32 automatic, again likely a Colt if Chandler mistakenly gave it ten shots rather than the true nine. He certainly made a mistake in *The Long Goodbye* by calling Eileen Wade's Mauser 7.65 a PPK instead of an HSc, but 7.65mm is still .32 inches, gunwise.

Dashiell Hammett's major female killer, Brigid O'Shaughnessy of *Maltese Falcon* fame, provides an interesting contrast. She wielded a Webley-Fosbery .38 "automatic revolver" (a few such weird things were made; they're now collector's items) that would be a foot long and over two pounds in weight. The lady must have carried a fair-sized handbag for that load.

And that's really the point. Handguns — to use the generic term for both automatics and revolvers — are made for hands. Concealable handguns are made for men.

Consider where such guns are usually worn: on the belt, either left or right, concealed by the jacket; in a shoulder holster that in less fastidious company would be called an armpit holster, concealed ditto (this is the only place you can carry a decent-sized gun); or in an ankle

The one-hand technique is a sure way to miss a target; the gun wobbles, the bullet veers, the subject gets away — maim-free. For better accuracy, don't let the other arm dangle; use it as a bracer.

holster hidden by the trouser cuff and sock. Whatever the changes in men's fashions, they can always find one or more of these places. Women don't even *have* such places. They have handbags.

But the snag about *that* is that no woman I've ever seen reaching into her handbag would beat the Sundance Kid to a fast draw. A gun is carried in a holster rather than loose in a pocket because the holster keeps it always in one place and at the chosen angle for a fast grab. There's nothing to stop you, however, from stitching a holster to the inside of a handbag; it's been done. Or, of course, you may well not need a fast draw. If you're setting out to murder or to rob a bank, you can choose when you take out a gun; fast draws are to counteract the unexpected.

That said, let us consider what guns might suit a handbag holster. First, I disagree with Chandler's assumption that women would or should choose automatics. I ran a test on my wife, giving her exact replicas of a Colt automatic and a Smith & Wesson revolver, with dummy shells for each, and asked her to load them. It took her three minutes to discover the cylinder release catch on the revolver, but after that the procedure was obvious. With the Colt

the timing broke down, partly because the gun did as well, but it was clear that we'd be into World War Four before my wife was ready to take part.

I don't mean that as condescending or sexist; I know lots of men who would do no better. I *do* mean that somebody who is a very good driver, who rambles the world coping with typewriters and telex machines, then comes home to battle the mechanisms of the modern kitchen, who reads thrillers and watches gangster and Western movies and TV cop shows, can still not have *noticed* how handguns work. I doubt she is unique in this, and for her the revolver is the best choice.

There is another good reason for picking a revolver: it can fire a lead bullet. The nice, or nasty, thing about lead is that when it hits somebody it splits open like a blossoming flower and tears a wound far wider than its original diameter. All automatics bigger than .22 have "jacketed" bullets, coated with a harder metal because they get slammed around in the gun and the lead may distort and cause a jam. Such bullets in .25 and .32 calibre can have far less lethal effects than a lead .22. In a revolver, the bullet just sits there in its chamber until it's fired — we all know people in jobs like that — so it can even be made of candle wax, such as the fast-draw artists use just in case they slow-draw and shoot their own feet.

Coming to specifics: Carmen Sternwood's Banker's Special stays an excellent choice, but it isn't in production any more. Since the automatic has the advantage of slimness, any small one that uses the .22 "long" or "long rifle" lead cartridge is worth considering. Avoid the .22 "short," which is strictly for fairgrounds. Many such guns are Italian-made nowadays, like the six-shot Armi Galesi, 4½ inches long and weighing only 12 ounces, or the Bernardelli 60, eight-shot, 6½ inches by a much heavier 25 ounces. But there are two home-grown models: the Smith & Wesson M61, five-shot, 4¾ inches by 14 ounces, and the American Firearms Stainless Pistol, seven-shot, 4½ inches and down to an extraordinary 7½ ounces in the alloy frame model.

Back to revolvers. Here the vote must go to the Smith & Wesson Centennial Airweight, which fires five .38 bullets from a gun weight of only 13 ounces, 6½ inches length. There are several other contenders in this field, but if you can chance firing a gun whose light weight and heavy recoil will make it kick in your hand like a horse's hoof, then go for the lightest. If not, take the High-Standard Double-Nine, which has nine .22's, weighs 15 ounces and is just 7½ inches long.

Personally, I'd like to see somebody use a Maverick Derringer, a modern version of the old riverboat gambler's sleeve gun (another place women can't usually store artillery) that is neither revolver nor automatic, holding only two cartridges each in its own barrel, rather like a pocket shotgun. But the pair can be either .357 Magnum or .45 — two of the most powerful bullets around — and the gun itself is just 5½ inches by 20 ounces. A bit heavy, but worth the effort (a check of visiting ladies showed, by our kitchen scales, an average handbag weight of over three pounds) because anybody who stops those two shots isn't going to come back for more. Good hunting.

Gavin Lyall is the author of Midnight Plus One, *which was awarded the Gold Dagger by the Crime Writers' Association as best novel of the year.*

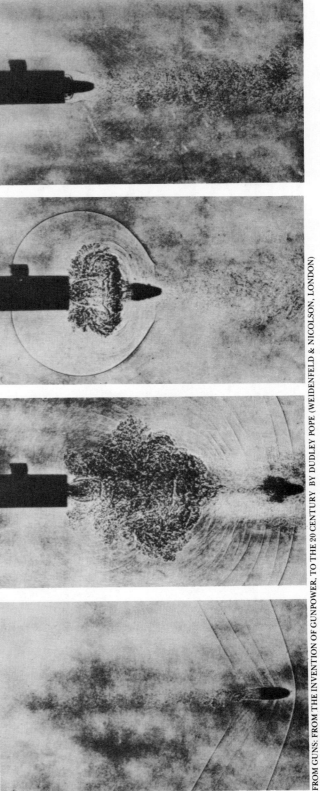

FROM GUNS: FROM THE INVENTION OF GUNPOWER, TO THE 20 CENTURY BY DUDLEY POPE (WEIDENFELD & NICOLSON, LONDON)

A high-speed camera reveals the gases and shock waves emanating from a bullet upon discharge.

SHOPLIFTER'S FLOORPLAN OF HARRODS

Harrods Limited,
Knightsbridge,
London SW1X 7XL.
Established 1849.

Ground Floor. *Antique jewelry, silver.*

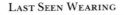

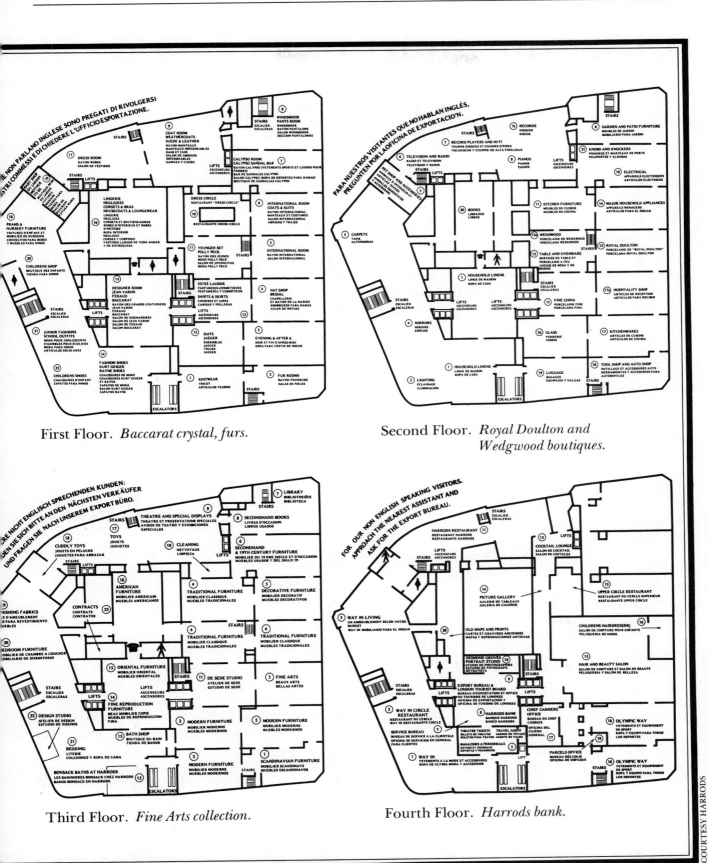

First Floor. *Baccarat crystal, furs.*

Second Floor. *Royal Doulton and Wedgwood boutiques.*

Third Floor. *Fine Arts collection.*

Fourth Floor. *Harrods bank.*

COURTESY HARRODS

APPROPRIATING AN HEIRLOOM

One sunny day last summer, a young woman and her mother were driving through north Jersey, admiring the scenery, when they spotted a yard sale in progress. They pulled over, parked and headed for the first of several bridge tables set up on the lawn. Jumbled on it were coffeepots with no innards, cracked jelly glasses, mismatched coasters, tattered souvenirs of Carlsbad Caverns, and odds and ends they couldn't put a name to but which looked suspiciously like the junk they'd been meaning to clean out of their own utility drawers. The next table offered stuff kids had obviously outgrown and the makings of a fine hippie wardrobe. Unimpressed, the mother moved toward the car. The daughter decided to give the remaining table a quick once-over. Its treasures included strands of popettes, earrings with no mates and a badly tarnished locket and chain with damaged clasp.

"How much for the broken necklace?" she asked the woman guarding the cigar box cash register.

"Five dollars."

"It's sweet. I'll take it."

Her mother yelled at her all the way home: the thing was busted; it was filthy; it was a waste of money; she had prettier chains she hadn't even worn yet; et cetera, et cetera.

On her lunch hour a few weeks later, the daughter brought the "find" to a Fifth Avenue

The Duchess's tiara.

MARTY NORMAN

jeweler near her office and asked to have it fixed. A day or so after that, the store's president phoned and suggested she come by for a chat; he'd send a car round for her. Intrigued, she agreed. Within the hour, she was richer by several hundred thousand dollars, had quit her job and was booking on a world cruise.

The widow's mourning brooch.

Turns out, the dingy locket and chain had once belonged to the Empress Josephine, and under all that grime were her and Napoleon's engraved initials.

Proving yet again, truth is stranger than fiction (and you shouldn't listen to your mother).

Most of us will never be so lucky. The only way a stupendously valuable bauble will fall into our possession is if we steal it. And if that's uppermost in our minds, we would do well to consult Fidelity Dove.

Miss Dove, under the influence of author Roy Vickers, engineered "The Great Kabul Diamond" coup, in which she swiped a gemstone larger than the Kohinoor from under the nose of Detective Inspector Rason. Nor were "The Gulverbury Diamonds" safe once she developed a yen for them.

It would be ungallant to reveal her M.O., but we can tell you this: Fidelity knew a thing or two about safe-blowing, lamp wiring and human nature.

Fidelity Dove's craving for diamonds is hardly unique. In the mystery, they're the most popular thing to steal. Case in point: *The Moonstone,* which was plucked from an Indian idol's forehead, then transferred to England, where it found its way to a Stately Home. (Contrary to its name, the jewel was indeed a diamond—an exotically large yellow one.) Another case in point: *The Datchet Diamonds,* the property of a Duchess, which exchanged hands several times. Still another, *11 Harrowhouse,* in which a trio insinuated themselves into the London diamond syndicate's vaults. Again, it wouldn't be fair to reveal all their secrets, but if you're planning similar enterprises, beware of turbaned natives and chaps wearing top hats, and don't forget to bring along a vial of cockroaches.

The heiress's baby locket.

Perhaps you don't fancy diamonds. Just as well. Miss Balmy Rymal's function, as outlined by author Arthur Stringer, is to thwart *Diamond Thieves.* Sir Max Pemberton found other things to covet. He gleefully relieved countless women of emeralds, rubies, opals, sapphires, even topazes, in his collection of short stories, *Jewel Mysteries I Have Known.* You needn't limit yourself to diamonds.

Of course, in real life, the main problem with pulling a heist is disposing of the goods at a reasonable profit. In mysteries, that's no big

The mistress's recompense.

deal. Jewels are either hocked (ah, our old friend, the pawn ticket clue) or hawked to the original owner by post (ah, our other old friend, the ransom note) or bestowed on Trixie (you remember her; she calls everyone Luv and asks if she can show them a good time).

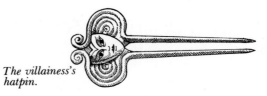

The villainess's hatpin.

In mysteries, and anywhere else for that matter, it's deemed impolite to lift a stomacher, a tiara, a whatever, reset it and wear it in the presence of the original owner. On occasion, a thief who's brought his booty to a stonecutter with this in mind gets his comeuppance: the redesigner informs him that Lady Lucinda's stomacher, tiara, whatever, is mere paste. This little debacle could have been averted if the crook had kitted out properly: in his right pocket, a copy of a paid-to-date insurance policy from Lloyds; in his left, a jeweler's loup. Nobody pays premiums on paste, and even under a magnifying lens it does not have facets.

There are only five mystery heirlooms of major import. Don't waste your time on any of the others. First, the mourning brooch of Georgian pinchbeck. You'll recognize it by a lock of the Dear Departed's hair housed beneath its glass face. The pin itself is worthless; but the safety-deposit box key hidden under the curl is not. This is your entry to the diamond-and-ruby coronet, and that's worth a packet. Also in the box, right beside the coronet (according to the diagram in the front of every mystery book), are the cabochon emeralds left to the family by the late Duke. Definitely take them, and the triple-strand necklace (pearl alternating with ruby alternating with sapphire) to the left, the one with the platinum catch, that's worth having, too. Just beyond it sit the rare black sapphires set into a choker. You ought to have them. And finally, the insignificant baby locket with the tooth marks and the blurry portrait, you must have that. If you're found with that in your possession, you'll be claimed the heir. It's as good as a birthmark in the right place.

My dear, you look dazzling.

THE INFINITE JOYS OF BLACKMAIL

Never mind practicing your p's and your q's. It's your e's and your m's (and sometimes your r's) you have to worry about. They're the tattletale typewriter keys, which is something to bear in mind if you're rough-drafting a few hostile thoughts.

The e, as most of us realize, is the most frequently used letter in the English alphabet (English-English or American-English, makes no difference). Just try and write a sentence without one. The first paragraph of this piece contains eighteen of them. There are sixteen r's, thirteen s's and ten n's; better keep an eye on them, too.

Because the e is so violently overworked, it tends to get a little wacky. Suddenly, it's dribbling below the baseline — appl$_e$ — or soaring above it — p^{e}ar. Whichever way it tilts, it spells doom to the writer of blackmail notes, ransom demands, hate mail and plain old-fashioned poison-pen letters. It's the clue the boys in the Crime Lab will pounce on, and it can prove just as incriminating as the Dover mud caked to your plimsoll or the fingerprint on the getaway ignition that matches in every respect the one on your toothbrush.

Equally as troublesome is the m. You'll notice it's a fat letter; it covers a lot more space than, say, the i or the l. Unfortunately for the blackmailing contingent, there simply is no way to write the word "money" without it. Now, the m, covering so much surface area, gets bumped around a lot; bits of it are always flaking away. This bruising means it sometimes develops a very skinny outer downstroke — m — or a partially missing inner one — m. The gang at Fo-

rensics loves to see that. It's as distinctive as a certain Balkan blend cigarette ash, as easy to trace as a laundry mark.

In addition, no two typewriters, even if they're produced by the same manufacturer and are identical models, will strike the paper in exactly the same way; the idiosyncrasies of the typist will make a difference, causing particular keys to skip, jam or stick.

Face it: A machine may present with you with a readable vicious memo, but eventually it will prove your undoing. Remember Alger Hiss.

If you care to look at the underside of a carriage, you'll find another chunk of bad news: a serial number. If the documents expert discovers that the appl$_e$ typing machine in the repair shop is labeled ST946730, and that you purchased item number ST946730, you've had it; go directly to jail, where the only typewriters are in the prison library and they're very fussy about who uses them.

Back to the Palmer method?

That's hardly safer. Graphologists spend a lot of hours in court comparing i dots and t crossings and convincing juries beyond a reasonable doubt that Gretchen's shopping list and the anonymous letter could only have been penned by the same person. In one of the many plagiarism suits filed against *Roots* author Alex Haley, his research notes were carefully analyzed and the verdict was: Yup, he obviously had cribbed from thus-and-such book.

To foil the handwriting pros, you'd be advised to forsake a fountain pen and a ballpoint and make your mark only with a felt-tip. The thickness of the nib blurs the letter shapes and makes positive identification trickier. Not impossible, mind you, just trickier.

All right. You're still determined to say "Drop dead." There are two avenues open to you. First, con someone else into issuing the letter. That way it'll be his machine or his scrawl that's up for scrutiny. Of course, should the two of you fall out, you then confront the ratting-on-an-accomplice possibility. Are you really ready to jump from a letter with a few threatening words in it to blood on your hands?

The second alternative is time-consuming, childish and messy: yes, it's the cut-the-letters-from-the-newspaper ploy. The thing about this is, it's hard to take seriously. The result looks like a Sears catalog that's taken a turn in the food processor. Plus, by the time you finish securing all the E's to the sheet, the police department will have figured out how to stake out every mailbox in the vicinity of your enemy, and they'll nab you as go to post the damn thing.

Granted, in life an inordinate number of certifiable kooks adopt nasty-letter writing as their means of expression. In crime fiction, on the other hand, ladies of utmost gentility consider it the method of choice. Scholars have yet to collate the information and conclude why, but inveterate mystery readers already have the answer: It's those writing desks.

Every mystery written between 1918 and 1936 that was set in England, in a house with a name (Farthingham Manor, The Edibles, Stonecold Castle), has a writing desk as part of the master suite. The Lady of the House spends her mornings at it. Now, after all, there's a limit to how many bills the woman has to pay, and how many invitations she has to accept or decline and how many instructions to the help she has to itemize and how many menus she has to plan. Still, the authors keep her sitting at that desk all morning. Seething. No wonder she's preempted the threatening letter field. Also, she has that lovely Dresden pen holder and that fragile crystal inkwell. How ungrateful she would seem if she didn't use them.

A typical woman's note of menace in these tales begins: Lady Abernathy regrets to inform you that you have displeased her. (Old habits of politeness die hard.) From there, it swings into a litany of complaints: you ran off with her husband; you ran off with her pearls; you ran off with her weekend guest list. It wraps up with an ultimatum: Return my husband (my pearls, my bridge partners) or I shall be forced to take action. This action is never specified, but the recipient of the letter usually understands it to mean a visitation by the Abernathy ghost or not so much as an honorable mention at the Kensington Gardens Flower Show.

Every so often, Lady Abernathy has the writing table turned on her. In this case, she receives a letter threatening to put the Abernathy ghost out of commission if she doesn't send £20,000 by return post. Naturally, this caution goes unanswered. Lady A. is too busy penning her own letters to read the morning's mail.

Clearly, when you wish to say "Drop dead," stationery is not the best means.

Have you considered phoning?

HER NIBS

The Sweetheart of Parker Pen practices the Palmer Method.

HELPFUL HINTS FROM A SYNDICATE COLUMNIST

Jo April

ear Jo:
While hastily typing some legal documents, I got rather extensive carbon paper smudges on my cuffs. It is vital that no one notice that I made copies. Any ideas?

AN ILLEGAL SECRETARY

Dear Illegal:
Next time, I suggest photocopying. Meanwhile, mix together a little ammonia and detergent and dab on your sleeves. No one will be the wiser.

———————

Dear Jo:
What has happened to American youth! I found my son composing a blackmail note in pen! Enraged (he should have known enough to use cutout letters), I grabbed the instrument and gave him a sound thrashing. Although his T-shirt now has several puncture wounds in it, I believe it will still make a good dustcloth if only I can get out those ink spots.

MRS. I. RATE

Dear Mrs. Rate:
I commend you on being a firm parent. Unfortunately, since inks come in such a variety of chemical compounds, your question is a toughie. For ballpoints, try regular chlorine bleach first. If this doesn't do the trick, try hydrogen peroxide, sodium perborate or oxalic acid. For felt tips, apply a thick poultice of salt and carbonated water, then wash.

———————

Dear Jo:
I visit my aged aunt every third Tuesday. The last time, I was very surprised to find her with her wrists and ankles taped together. She said it was a prowler, and maybe it was, but the family can get pretty kinky sometimes. Regardless, how can I remove the traces of adhesive from her stockings? Auntie lives on a fixed income since the Matthews job and nylons aren't getting any cheaper.

A DEVOTED NIECE IN HOLLOWAY

Dear Devoted:
Nothing could be simpler. Gently sponge the affected areas with any of the better commercial cleaning fluids. Make sure you remove her limbs first, since the fluid may cause an unpleasant burning sensation.

———————

Dear Jo:
I was sorting my younger daughter's hair ribbons when her teen-age sister came in to talk to me. She is at that difficult age and, as usual,

had on too much make-up. Well, one thing led to another and we had a little row. Now darling Noel Marie is very upset with me because her ribbons got all dirty and wrinkled when I wrapped them around her sister's neck. Is there anything I can do to put life back into Noel Marie's ribbons?

A BAD MOMMY

Dear Bad Mommy:

To remove those ugly cosmetic stains, wash the ribbons several times in a good liquid detergent. Let them dry thoroughly between each washing. Then, to restore their body, dip them in gum tragacanth, available at any drugstore. And here's a tip: If you stretch the ribbons to dry on a flat surface, such as a crypt, you won't have to iron them!

Dear Jo:

I have always been of an artistic nature and enjoy doing collages. I especially like to concoct cute messages out of bold newspaper type and send them on to wealthy business associates. Recently, I tried a new plastic glue and want to know how to clean up the occasional spill. I must have a neat work area in order to create.

COMPULSIVE ARTIST

Dear Compulsive:

Instead of working on the table directly, may I suggest you steal a good, washable cloth and toil on that! Then, should spills occur, heat vinegar or acetic acid to a rolling boil and drop the cloth in to soak. The glue will disappear in a jiffy. And by the by, what are you doing about that tattletale sniff of glue? A bowl of unpeeled oranges placed near your work area will cover the scent nicely.

Dear Jo:

Who would have thought the old girl had that much blood in her? Honestly, it got all over everything. Help me, Jo.

OUTRAGED

Dear Outraged:

The natural saliva of the blood donor (ha-ha) is the best stain remover for blood. If none is forthcoming, mix cold water, ammonia and hydrogen peroxide, and that should work well as a replacement.

Dear Jo:

I have always been a true believer in using one's jewelry, not letting it sit in some silly old vault. To modernize my pearls, I've just had them restrung on heavy-duty piano wire (hang the expense, I say). To keep them lustrous, I use them constantly to absorb the natural oils from many, many throats. But lately my lovely pearls look just the teensiest bit dirty. Any suggestions?

OYSTER BAY MATRON

Dear Matron:

A simple swipe with a nice piece of chamois should cleanse your pearls, but if not, a quick soap-and-water dunk should restore them to their former luster. And how wise of you to have restrung them on wire! Water would have rotted the thread.

Dear Jo:

My mother-in-law came over for lunch, and the trout amandine must have disagreed with her. Not only did she leave her fingerprints on my dining room table as she clutched it in agony, but she scratched it something awful as she collapsed to the floor. What should I do for my lovely dining room table? It now has great sentimental value.

INCIPIENT HEIRESS

Dear Incipient:

Well, you do have an afternoon's work ahead of you! Remove the old wax with tepid tea (China *or* India). Then attack those scratches with walnut meats and just a soupçon of turpentine. Try to stay within the gouge marks, as you don't want to darken the surrounding areas. Finally (as penance, you naughty thing you), whip up your own furniture polish (1/3 turpentine, 1/3 vinegar, 1/3 boiled linseed oil) and make that table sparkle!

Dear Jo:

My husband and I are quite socially prominent and are often asked to charity balls, bazaars, etc. As I dislike these functions, he takes his giddy young secretary instead. And since appearances are so important at these things, he borrows my diamonds for her to wear. Well, just as they were leaving the last affair, a large urn fell from the roof, flattening them both. A tragic accident! And to think I was enjoying myself at the movies at the time (I even saved the stub). Anyway, to the problem: My diamonds got quite gritty in the accident. What to do?

BEREAVED WIDOW

Dear Bereaved:

How fortunate she was wearing your diamonds; they're the hardest thing known. (If she'd been wearing your opals, it would have been bye-bye time for them, too.) Now: Boil your diamonds in a wealth of soapsuds, with a smidgen of ammonia for a kicker. Rinse them thoroughly, dip them in alcohol to eliminate that scruffy detergent film, then dry them with soft tissue paper. Swab a toothpick in cotton, saturate it with alcohol, then use that in all the nooks and crannies of the setting.

———————

Dear Jo:

My friend has a white polar bear rug (a gift from an anthropology professor). The other night she was studying privately with a Polynesian exchange student, and while showing her some native rites of advanced intricacy, he tripped on the bear's head, spewing large blobs of honey and guava jelly onto the fur. She will be inconsolable if she cannot clean the rug before the professor returns from his expedition. In fact, she will be dead. Can you help her?

A FRIEND

Dear Friend:

Bear up! Jo can help you! First, scoop up the thick mess with paper toweling. Then wipe off what's left with a damp cloth and some mild soapsuds. Try not to get the skin itself wet (dishpan pelt?). Now, throw on some corn meal to absorb any leftovers. A final bluing rinse and your furry friend will be a virginal white again.

———————

Dear Jo:

On Saturday my husband and I gave a small cocktail party for some co-workers. One of the guests — Miss Roxie O'Hara, who was paying a lot of attention to my Jimmy — drank too much of the bubbly and had to lie down. When I went in to check up on her, I clumsily shoved the pillow over her mouth. What shall I do about lipstick stains on my pillowslip?

CONCERNED HOSTESS

Dear Concerned:

Do you have any white bread in the house, or did you use it all up making toast points for the party? A nice, firm (though not stale) slice of white bread can be rubbed against the stains to pick them right up. If a faint pinkness remains, apply a liquid detergent directly, then rinse.

———————

Dear Jo:

Johnny and me, we was lovers. But he done me wrong. So I ups and blasts his puss — real close-like, so I wouldn't miss. Now it's got powder burns all over it. I don't think a guy oughta wear powder, do you? And geez, the smell stank something fierce. Whatcha think?

FRANKIE

Dear Frankie:

Oh, if only your aim had been better! If you'd hit his shoit instead of his puss, you could have dropped a spot of ammonia on the offensive areas, then splashed them with water and the smell would have disappeared. As things stand, such a procedure would make his face disappear. (Of course, in Johnny's condition, it probably wouldn't much matter.) As for the burn marks, take a soft gum eraser and rub the powdered areas lightly. They'll come right off.

———————

Dear Jo:

I am an avid gardener. Once, I was the state Phlox champ. I attribute all my success to my highly individualized fertilizer blend, which comprises equal parts of Mr. Casper, Mr. Didmont, and Mr. Ewing. Last night, while adding Mr. Foch, I inadvertently got grass stains on my hem (I was rather in a hurry). Please advise, dear Jo.

POISON IVY

Dear Ivy:

Grass stains are notoriously loathsome, even more so than Messrs. Caspar, Didmont and Ewing (I never met Mr. Foch, so I refrain from including him). Try a mild bleaching agent such as hydrogen peroxide. If that fails, try Ritt dye, in a nice shade of poison green.

Jo April tidies up after Solomon Hastings.

BEHIND CLOSED DRAWERS

Building a Secret Compartment

Roger M. Lang

Zounds! The poor Duke's been skewered, and in his own study, too! The desk's been rifled, but its mother-of-pearl inkwell, its sterling letter opener, its 24K pinbox remain. Obviously, the wily perpetrator was after something big! What could it be? *Where* could it be?

Enter Inspector Lucille. Her cool mind says, Look again. Fully opening the now-empty drawer, her hand feels round and with some difficulty locates and releases a hidden catch. She removes the drawer and peers intently at the rear dovetails. "Damned ingenious," she mut-ters to herself, noticing a thin crack between the bottom rear pins. Turning the drawer over and pushing with some force, she watches the false bottom panel silently slide rearward, exposing a shallow hiding place just below the true drawer bottom. Her pulse quickens as a thin document appears, yellowed with age. She knows what it is without reading it: the deed to Crumley Court. Pocketing the document, she adjourns to the mourning room and informs Her Grace, the Duchess of Crumley, that she will not lose her home. Her Grace, in a manner typical of the

HOW TO BUILD A SECRET DRAWER

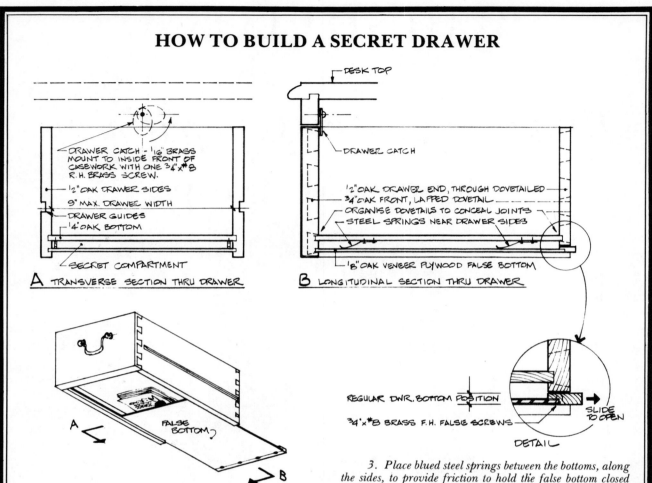

A TRANSVERSE SECTION THRU DRAWER

DRAWER CATCH - ¹⁄₁₆" BRASS MOUNT TO INSIDE FRONT OF CASEWORK WITH ONE ³⁄₄"×#8 R.H. BRASS SCREW.

¹⁄₂" OAK DRAWER SIDES
9" MAX. DRAWER WIDTH
DRAWER GUIDES
¹⁄₄" OAK BOTTOM
SECRET COMPARTMENT

B LONGITUDINAL SECTION THRU DRAWER

DESK TOP

DRAWER CATCH

¹⁄₂" OAK DRAWER END, THROUGH DOVETAILED
³⁄₄" OAK FRONT, LAPPED DOVETAIL
ORGANISE DOVETAILS TO CONCEAL JOINTS
STEEL SPRINGS NEAR DRAWER SIDES
¹⁄₈" OAK VENEER PLYWOOD FALSE BOTTOM

FALSE BOTTOM

REGULAR DWR. BOTTOM POSITION
³⁄₄"×#8 BRASS F.H. FALSE SCREWS
SLIDE TO OPEN
DETAIL

1. Lap the dovetails to cover the ends of the slots that will hold both the true and false bottoms. Use ½" oak to construct the drawer sides and back; ¼" oak for the true bottom; and ⅛" oak veneer plywood for the false bottom. Glue a rebated strip to the rear edge of the false bottom so it resembles a conventional bottom. Maintain constant wood species and grain direction for consistent appearance.

2. Insert fake screws (cut short to further conceal the true movement of the false panel) where the rear of the drawer bottom is normally screwed to the back.

3. Place blued steel springs between the bottoms, along the sides, to provide friction to hold the false bottom closed securely. Add another, less powerful spring in the bottom middle to keep the contents from rattling when the drawer is shaken.

4. For the hidden catch, simply mount a small piece of 16 ga. brass to the inside front of the desk casework with one round-head wood screw. The brass piece will hang down slightly so that the back of the drawer will hit it just at the point when the front is as far out as possible, preventing complete withdrawal. Be sure to install this device on all drawers, to slow down the villains. To open, rotate it out of the way while continuing to pull out the drawer.

English upper class, thanks the Inspector by insisting she stay for tea.

If you wish to conceal a similar secret behind a similar secret drawer, I offer the above schematic. Keep in mind that the drawer you choose must be relatively deep, so the extra fraction-of-an-inch thickness is not readily apparent; it should also be narrow, not over 9″ wide, to ensure smooth movement of the false bottom.

When you're ready to stash away your recently altered will (which disinherits everybody and leaves all your earthly goods to charity) or remove it to taunt your soon-to-be-penniless family, run your hand along the underside of the desk opening until you find the secret brass piece.

And watch for splinters if you've never done this kind of work before.

Roger M. Lang is an architect. At last count, he had built thirty-seven panels and fourteen secret compartments in his home.

ANGLO-AMERICAN CONNIVING

Pauline Glen Winslow

Lately, we hear a great deal about life-styles, though I believe most of us in our hearts are sure our lives have no style at all — but that's another subject. Deathstyles, however, are plainly discernible, particularly the styles of involuntary death. They are quite distinct on each side of the ocean, with accompanying etiquettes as different as those of Louis XIV's Versailles and the Carter White House.

Unfortunately, there is no Debrett, no Emily Post to guide the practitioner. True, a book was written on the American Way of Death by a British writer, but the title was slightly misleading. It refers merely to the legal disposal of cadavers and not to the actual dispatching from here to eternity.

The discerning reader will already have noticed that I have avoided using the plain term "murder." That is because the name of the deed is changing in the United States. In England, I believe, murder is yet known as murder; a murderer is a murderer still. In the U.S., we hear much more about "alleged perpetrators" of certain "incidents." The charge regarding the incident, a killing or attempted killing, might be reduced before the trial, if any, to a mere misdemeanor. The change of name, of course, affects the judicial mind: even after multiple murders, an alleged perpetrator is likely to be turned loose to try again. The American citizen undoubtedly comes to believe that these "incidents," if not yet *de rigueur,* are not much frowned upon by authority. Advertisements might suggest that there are more serious ways,

socially, to "offend."

To the British view, American murders come wholesale. The Western tradition, known from a thousand films, seems basic. High noon, the sudden confrontation, bodies littering the landscape — these constitute the American style. All due no doubt to much sunny weather and plenty of large open spaces.

The argument that this is mostly fiction is not accepted. Charlie Starkweather and his fourteen-year-old girl friend, all too real, went on a murder rampage across two states and killed eleven, perhaps twelve people. Howard Unruh took his gun and shot down thirteen citizens in Camden, New Jersey; more recently, the .45 Caliber Killer terrorized New York. The tradition continues, the Englishman is convinced.

British murder, as befits the inhabitants of small islands, is usually single, private — hidden, in fact. The motives are obvious enough: sometimes love, often money. Murders are planned, brooded over, often delicately contrived, many still puzzling even after trial and conviction. Did Edith Thompson put ground-up light bulbs in her husband's coffee or was that merely the wistful fantasy of an innocent, if unsatisfied wife? The hangman did not solve the puzzle. If her lover had not impatiently stabbed the husband to death in the public streets, probably no harm would have come to the amorous pair.

The British, of course, do have their own wholesale merchants. There was Sweeney Todd,

MURDER ETIQUETTE

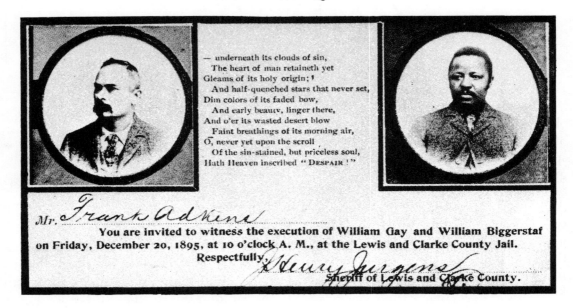

— underneath its clouds of sin,
    The heart of man retaineth yet
Gleams of its holy origin;
    And half-quenched stars that never set,
Dim colors of its faded bow,
    And early beauty, linger there,
And o'er its wasted desert blow
    Faint breathings of its morning air,
O, never yet upon the scroll
    Of the sin-stained, but priceless soul,
Hath Heaven inscribed "DESPAIR!"

Mr. *Frank Adkins*

You are invited to witness the execution of William Gay and William Biggerstaf on Friday, December 20, 1895, at 10 o'clock A. M., at the Lewis and Clarke County Jail.
Respectfully, *Henry Jurgens*
Sheriff of Lewis and Clarke County.

PICKING A VICTIM

It is not considered good sportsmanship to attack an invalid. Nor a secretary (Heaven protects the working girl). The Soon-to-Die should own a private railroad car, a seat on the exchange, a Swiss bank account, a small duchy on the Continent, a packet of your love letters. The victim should: stroll the boulevards alone at midnight; sit for hours in a duck blind; explore the attic; confide in no one. The Future Demised should: not own a telephone; not answer a telephone when it rings; not believe what the caller on the other end has to say. Above all else, a victim should be punier than you are. And more cowardly.

DISPATCHING AN ENEMY

It is polite to clean up after yourself: dust off the letter opener; shut and lock the window to the garden from the inside; rinse out the decanter and one glass; replace the dented candlestick; mop up the mud you tracked into the foyer. Then straighten the picture in front of the safe; close the secret passage entranceway; reload the pistol. Finally, wash your hands, paying particular attention to your fingernails; comb the cobwebs out of your hair; straighten your disarrayed attire; draw a deep breath and sally forth with an alibi on your lips.

VISITING A CORPSE

Do not chortle. Do not panic. Do not confess. Do not steal a carnation from the display for a memento. Do not stand graveside with a smirk on your face. Rather: Remark on how lush the sod is for this time of year; how faithful the stonecarver's likeness; how devastated you were when the news reached you at (a) the religious retreat, (b) the floor of the Commons, (c) the tea tent at Wimbledon, (d) the Royal Enclosure at Henley, (e) your ailing mum's birthday dinner. Under no circumstances may you return later and disinter the body.

MOURNING ETIQUETTE

PREPARING THE EULOGY

The least likely suspect should deliver the tribute. If everyone seems guilty, the person who stands to inherit the most should step forward and blather on about the charitable nature of God's Newest Angel. It is the speaker's responsibility to: lead the congregation in sobs; incriminate several of the bereaved; hold a mirror to the dead one's lips. It is inexcusable for a speaker to bound down the aisle jingling the coins in his pocket and whistling "Flying Down to Rio." Speakers must end the service by facing the casket and intoning, "Let he who is without sin cast the first stone." If no one casts, the eulogist shall instruct the Vicar the honor is his, defrocked or no.

ACCEPTING CONDOLENCES

The grief-stricken should congregate in the haunted front parlor, making sure there are not enough chairs for all of them. If the family expects to become filthy rich upon the reading of the will, an adequate supply of seats is allowed, provided they are extremely uncomfortable. If necessary, small horsehair tufted stools with sprung springs may be rented for the occasion. Floral offerings from impoverished kin should not be placed on the mantel next to the Late's ashes, but banished to the servants' quarters. When acknowledging expressions of sympathy, present: your cheek to your accomplice; the back of your hand to the cad who insisted on an inquest.

THE GUEST LIST

The next wife
The future husband
The children from the first marriage
The children from the second marriage
The senile doctor
The spinster governess
The ward
The business partner
The compost technician
A defrocked minister
The turf accountant
Daft auntie
The barrister
The chemist
The local laird
A greengrocer
The gardener
The manicurist
The organist
A schoolmistress
The chauffeur
The stableboy
A tour guide

The reservations clerk, TWA
Brothers, sisters, pallbearers
Personal servants
Bridge partners
A retired colonel
The publican and his wife
An alias
The company solicitor
Another alias
Three red herrings
A caterer
A librarian
A visiting nurse
The au pair
The private secretary
The broker
Constable Bobby
A concierge
The undertaker
The ironmonger
The mayor
A lepidopterist
A sob sister

MEMENTO MORI

REMEMBER TO DIE

YOU are desired to Accompany the Corps of Sir *William Phipps*, Knight, from *Salters-Hall* in *Swithins Lane*, to the Parish-Church of St. *Mary Woolnoth*, in *Lumbard-street*: On Thursday the 21st. of *February*, 169⅘. At Five of the Clock in the Afternoon precisely: And bring this Ticket with you.

> *W*oman's wit is to scheme quickly.
>
> Iphigenia in Tauris
> EURIPIDES

the Demon Barber of Fleet Street, but his method of disposal, by meat pie, was certainly secretive and had a dash of originality. And there was Jack the Ripper, whose murders at least were decently clothed in London fog. Parenthetically, it is sad to note that since the Clean Air Addicts have banished fog from our ancient city, gunfire has come increasingly into play.

Still, the single hidden murders hold our imagination: Crippen the meek with his wife's body buried in the cellar is still a favored subject with British writers. (True, he was American-born, but an immigrant to British shores and doubtless, like many immigrants, eager to become assimilated.)

Of all Great Britain, Scotland can lay claim to having been the scene of the greatest number of intriguing murders; certainly it takes the palm for the most aristocratic of deathstyles. The Scottish Lady Warriston, when tired of her husband, ordered her servants to strangle him. They complied. He had recently bitten their mistress, displaying manners that any child would recognize as excessively vulgar and not to be borne.

On the other side of the law, at least before the days of alleged perpetrators, the etiquette was equally different. The American knows Eliot Ness of the FBI, at least as portrayed on television, confronting his suspects with drawn pistol and a light machine gun always handy. Very far from the Scotland Yard detective murmuring quietly, "Would you mind coming along with me, sir." But then, the British criminal usually did go along, without much trouble. An American criminal who behaved in this way would find he had lost status among his peers. Even the methods of execution when still in use indicated the national sensibilities: the American killer was fried in plain view; the Englishman was dropped more modestly into a hole.

Fictional murders follow real life. Macbeth was depressed that his old victim had so much blood in him; the godfathers of American fic-

tion contemplate their rubouts without qualms. The open-road fancy of the U.S. leads to endless car chases with guns ablaze; the British, a garden-loving people, prefer a cozy death by, say, a movable potted plant.

Book titles point up the divergence: *My Gun Is Quick* strikes one note, *The Unpleasantness at the Bellona Club* quite another. Of course, the *Unpleasantness* was only incidentally a murder; the inconvenience to club members, the bad taste of the matter being conducted on Armistice Day, greatly enhanced this crime.

To a British detective, Spillane's *Gun* would appear far too quick as Mr. Hammer lustily pumps his lead into the smooth belly of his fair acquaintance. Unhealthily, it might be said. Lust is out of place in his British counterpart, who is quite often celibate and nearly always restrained. Compare Mr. Hammer with Inspector Grant, who shows his displeasure with a troublesome murder suspect by refusing to drink her excellent coffee — for almost half an hour. Or Lord Peter, who tries to marry the wench. If a woman must be killed in English fiction, it is preferable that the execution be performed by a *murderess*; best of all, in a healthy atmosphere — say, a gymnasium, by a descending boom, where a fine athletic standard is preserved.

An American lady of my acquaintance believes all the aforesaid to be a total misunderstanding of American manners, character and taste. Her theory is that American criminals are the least violent of all, quite in contrast to Old World criminals who enjoy stabbing, garotting, killing by mallet or hammer blows. She points out that the American deathstyle, the gentle squeezing of a trigger, which employs not much more energy than is needed to take a cap off a beer bottle, is hardly a violent act. The American killer, naturally peaceful, docile and mild of manner, finds this playful yet very efficient method too tempting to resist. It is certainly a telling point. I can hardly put my finger on the flaw in this argument, even my trigger finger.

Pauline Glen Winslow is a transplanted Englishwoman who exchanged Epping Forest for Greenwich Village. She is the author of four novels featuring the remarkable Merle Capricorn, the most recent of which is Copper Gold.

NEGLECTED MURDERESSES SERIES

Edward Gorey

Angelica Transome so disposed of her infant brother that he was not found until many years later (Nether Postlude, 1889).

Miss Elspeth Lipsleigh eventually succeeded in causing the death of Arthur Glumm at Towage Regis, 1892.

Nurse J. Rosebettle tilted her employer out of a wheelchair and over a cliff at Sludgemouth in 1898.

Mrs. Fledaway laced her husband's tea with atropine in the spring of 1903 at the Locusts, near Puddingbasin, Mortshire.

Sarah Jane ("Batears") Olafsen hacked to collops nineteen loggers between March 1904 and November 1907 in and around Bindweed, Oregon.

Madame Galoche in May 1911 added a tin of insecticide to a potage purée Crécy aux perles at the soup kitchen she operated for the indigent of Berchem-Sainte-Agathe, Belgium.

Miss Emily Toastwater smothered her father after evening prayers, London S.W.7 (1916).

Mrs. Daisy Sallow eviscerated her daughter-in-law with a No. 7 hook, afterwards crocheting, over the course of three evenings, her shroud in a snowflake pattern (1921).

Natasha Batti-Loupstein pulverized a paste necklace and sprinkled it over a tray of canapés, Villa Libellule, Nice, 1923.

Lady Violet Natheless strangled the Hon. Opal Gentian at Gilravage Hall on Midsummer's Eve, 1925.

Lettice Finding shot Edgar Cutlet, whose mistress she was, during the interval of a touring repertory company production of Rosmersholm *in Manchester in 1934.*

Miss Q. P. Urkheimer brained her fiancé after failing to pick up an easy spare at Glover's Lanes, Poxville, Kansas, 1936.

LADY KILLERS
Mary Groff

Not all Lady Killers are actually Ladies. A few originated in the manor house, but a great many saw their first light of day from a more commonplace setting. Regardless, women are inclined to become a trifle vicious when their passions are aroused, and their gentle arms have been known to wield hatchets, hatpins, even horsehoes — with a certain fatal charm.

Mystery writers have used such transgressions to good purpose, thus enabling the hapless victims (not to mention the Lady Killers) to live on forever in our hearts and minds. Herewith, synopses of the crimes with abbreviated checklists of their fictional treatments.

Mary Blandy. Born outside London, at Henley-on-Thames, Mary grew up to be an attractive young woman with a £10,000 fortune. She had no control over her money, however, and was forced to look to Mr. Blandy for every penny she spent. To make matters worse, she remained an unwilling spinster as none of her gentlemen callers gained her father's approval. Then in 1746, shortly after her twenty-sixth birthday, the Honourable William Cranstoun entered her eager young life.

Concealing his own marriage, Cranstoun began a determined campaign against Mr. Blandy's usual firm opposition. When all else failed, he provided Mary with "love powders" to place in her father's food, to make him more "amenable." In due time, after a servant almost died from eating some scraps, and the cook fell ill from tasting the soup, a third member of the staff took the remains of a bowl of gruel to the chemist. The incriminating results were reported to Mr. Blandy, who in turn approached his daughter. In a panic, Mary burned what was

left of the powders, along with Cranstoun's letters, then in a note to her suitor described what had happened and asked that her own letters be destroyed. Foolishly, she asked someone to post the note for her, with the result that it was opened and passed on to the chemist.

This soon-to-be Late Sir is feeling a tad poorly, having ingested a plate of kippers marinated in lime.

In the end, Blandy abandoned his selfish ways and died quite gracefully, forgiving his errant daughter as he went. The Oxford assizes, however, were not so lenient: at her trial in 1752, Mary was found guilty and sentenced to death. Her final words were to the hangman — a refined if not very apologetic request that she not be strung too high for modesty's sake.

Jean Stubbs, *My Grand Enemy* (Macmillan, 1967)

Lizzie Borden. Did she or didn't she? The argument has gone round since 1893.

The rich Andrew Borden lived in a modest house in Fall River, Massachusetts. His family consisted of the second Mrs. Borden and her two stepdaughters: Lizzie, aged thirty-two, and Emma, ten years older. Lizzie disliked her stepmother intensely, suspecting the woman of aspirations to control the Borden money. Also in residence was an irish maid, Bridget.

The summer of 1892 in Fall River was horrendous, the heat unbearable. The normally unappetizing meals at the Bordens' grew even more offensive as food was served hot to use up the last bits of meat and broth. On August 4, both Lizzie and Bridget were working around the house — the maid inside and out while she cleaned the windows, a job she much resented doing in that weather — when suddenly Lizzie cried out in terror: she had found her stepmother lying on the floor of her room, mutilated by ax slashes. Not too long afterward, Mr. Borden was discovered in similar condition downstairs on a sofa.

Because Emma was visiting out-of-town friends at the time and Bridget had no serious reason for wishing either of the Bordens dead, Lizzie was arrested and brought to trial on June 1, 1893. The defense established that no ax head was located on the Borden property that fateful August day. Moreover, neither Miss Lizzie nor Bridget had any bloodstained clothing in her room, and a search of the house, barn and garden failed to produce such suspicious garments. Thus there was no evidence to prove that Lizzie had committed a crime, and she was finally acquitted. She remained in Fall River until her death in 1927.

Edward Bierstadt, *Satan Was a Man* (Doubleday, 1935)
Lily Dougal, *The Summit House Mystery* (Funk, 1905)
Mary Wilkins, *The Long Arm* (Chapman & Hall, 1895)

Florence Bravo. In April 1876, Charles Bravo died a painful death at his London home. With him was Florence, his bride of five months, and her companion, Mrs. Jane Cox.

Florence Bravo was the mistress of a doctor. He was free with the prescription blanks. How convenient for her proclivities.

Mr. Bravo was Florence's second husband; the first, Captain Ricardo of the Grenadier Guards, had died five years earlier, having willed her the sum of £40,000. Between marriages, Florence had been the mistress of a Dr. James Gully, who was more than thirty years her senior and who still kept in touch on a friendly basis with his former paramour.

After dinner on April 18, Charles Bravo became quite sick, suffering severe stomach pains and vomiting. Despite careful nursing and doctor visits, his condition showed no improvement through the following night. Both Florence and Mrs. Cox attended the invalid until his death on April 21. An autopsy was ordered, and a fatal amount of antimony was discovered. The jury was unable to agree whether the poison had been self-administered or introduced by other hands.

In July 1876, another inquiry was held; this time, the unhappy jury had to view the blackened teeth and horrid skin color of the Bravo remains. Florence's alliance with Dr. Gully was discussed, to the shock of the very proper Victorian public, and sympathy for the defendant died quickly when the court implied details of her sexual activities. Nevertheless, lacking concrete evidence as to Florence's guilt, the jury decided that Charles had been murdered by person or persons unknown. Florence embarked upon her second widowhood in Southsea and in 1878 died of acute alcoholism.

Elizabeth Jenkins, *Dr. Gully's Story* (Coward McCann, 1972)
Mrs. Belloc Lowndes, *What Really Happened* (Constable, 1926)
Mrs. Victor Rickard, *Not Sufficient Evidence* (Constable, 1926)
Joseph Shearing, *For Her to See* (Hutchinson, 1947)

Marie Madeleine de Brinvilliers. Marie was a very pretty girl — so appealing, in fact, that her own brothers were the first to share her bed. At the age of twenty-one, she married a gambler and collector of mistresses. Busy with his hobbies, de Brinvilliers worried little about his wife's behavior even when she grew attached to a man known as Ste. Croix. Her father objected strenuously, however, and had Ste. Croix thrown into the Bastille.

Marie soon developed a fanatical hatred for her father, and the lovers set about learning all they could in the art of poisoning from another Bastille prisoner. Then, to try out their newly acquired knowledge, Marie doctored the food of one of the servants and rendered her victim a permanent invalid. The next test came in the summer of 1666, when she paid her father a visit during which he sickened and died.

Once again, Marie plunged into a life of lovers, gambling and other entertainments. Her brothers protested, but it was not long before they, too, made a hasty exit. Intoxicated by success, Marie embarked upon the poisoning of her husband; this effort was not so effective, as Ste. Croix had no wish to marry and placed antidotes in de Brinvilliers' food. Ste. Croix himself fell ill and died of natural causes.

People had begun to notice that the death rate around Marie was unnaturally high. When inquiries were started, she fled to England; from there, threatened with extradition, she contin-

ued her flight for three years until she was picked up in Spain in 1676. Several hearings took place upon her return to Paris, and she was found guilty of the deaths of relatives and others. She was first tortured and then executed in the Place de Grève, her body burnt and the ashes scattered.

John Dickson Carr, *The Burning Court* (H. Hamilton, 1937)

Elizabeth Brownrigg. One of the most offensive women who ever lived, Mrs. Brownrigg, abetted by her husband and son, tortured and starved young apprentices living in her house until one girl died.

In 1755, Mrs. Brownrigg was working as a midwife for London's St. Dunstan's Parish and the local workhouse, and two young girls were sent to her home to learn the trade. One, an orphan, received such savage treatment that she escaped and complained to the governors of the orphanage, who merely made some slight criticism and then dropped the matter.

Another girl, Mary Clifford, was sent to the

Elizabeth Brownrigg's last residence was the condemned cell at the Old Bailey. Josephine Tey combined elements of her story with Elizabeth Canning's in Franchise Affair.

Brownriggs' and was beaten, starved and tormented until a neighbor took pity on her and notified the orphanage. The men who were sent to investigate first came upon a second trainee, Mary Mitchell, whose clothing was stuck to her body by blood and who was removed immediately. Eventually, the authorities got to Miss Clifford; they found her dying in a cupboard, so badly wounded that she could not speak and was unable to be moved from this house of horror.

Before an arrest could be made, Mrs. Brownrigg and her son escaped to another area. They were identified by their new landlord, however, and tried at the Old Bailey in 1767. Mr. Brownrigg and his son were sentenced to six months in prison. Elizabeth was sentenced to death.

Josephine Tey, *The Franchise Affair* (Davies, 1948)

Daisy Louisa de Melker. During the course of three marriages, this woman managed to kill off two husbands and a son.

In 1923, William Cowle died very suddenly of what the doctors called a cerebral hemorrhage. His widow received a check from the insurance company.

At the time of his marriage in 1926, Robert Sproat possessed £4,000 and a will made out in favor of his mum. By the time he died a year later, of a cerebral hemorrhage, his wife had managed to have the will changed to her own benefit.

In 1931, Clarence de Melker settled down with his new wife near Johannesburg. His wife's son by her first marriage, Rhodes, proved a great disappointment: jobless, he demanded endless money from his mother and made himself at home doing just as he pleased. On March 3, 1932, Rhodes became ill with malaria — the curse of the African continent — and within four days was dead. Some local chemists reported that Mrs. de Melker had been buying a great deal of poison from them.

An autopsy on Rhodes proved that he was full of arsenic. Both Cowle and Sproat were taken from their graves and found to be full of strychnine.

At her trial in October 1932, Daisy de Melker was found guilty. She was hanged at the end of the year, having never confessed.

Sarah Gertrude Millin, *Three Men Died* (Chatto, 1934)

Christiana Edmunds. A lonely and unattractive woman, Miss Edmunds lived with her mother at Brighton on the south coast of England. The family physician, Dr. Beard, felt that Miss Edmunds had a rather wretched life and listened with sympathy to her problems. His warmth and cheerfulness induced his patient to fall in love, whereupon she commenced a series of passionate letters to her mentor. As he took no firm stand on this matter, she believed her affections were returned.

During the summer of 1871, Miss Edmunds paid a visit on Mrs. Beard, a younger, more comely woman, and presented her with a box of candy. Sampling a chocolate during tea, her hostess found it a bit off-taste and spat it out quickly. Later, Mrs. Beard described the incident to her husband, who confronted Miss Edmunds. The doctor insisted that the letters and their friendship end immediately.

Miss Edmunds was desolate: the only man in her life was gone forever. She also resented being considered a potential poisoner. Perhaps, she reasoned, her good name would be restored if other people suffered sickness after eating chocolates. Employing a small boy to purchase more sweets for her, she took them home and shortly thereafter returned them via another messenger as being the wrong sort. Since they were sold loose, the chocolates were returned to the container and soon circulated quite widely among the town population. Reports of illness abounded, and finally a child died after eating some candy. A police search of the poison registers revealed that a "Mrs. Woods" had purchased an unnatural amount.

No Mrs. Woods could be found in the area until one chemist foolishly gave his register to a child sent in for it. When the register was returned, the page with the Wood name and address was missing. The child was quickly traced, and this led the police to Miss Edmunds.

At her trial in 1872, Dr. Beard stated that he felt her sanity was too fragile to withstand any criticism of her letters. Found guilty of the child's death, she was sentenced to hang. Then, reprieved, she was sent to finish off her life in Broadmoor.

John Dickson Carr, *The Black Spectacles* (H. Hamilton, 1939)

Catherine Hayes. Stumbling upon a severed head is not the best way to start a new day, but in March 1725 a London watchman had little choice as he made his rounds along the Thames. The head was taken to a Westminster churchyard, where it was soon identified as having once belonged to a man by the name of Hayes who lived in the Tyburn Road.

Catherine Hayes was approached and forced to admit that the head was her husband's. She claimed he had been living abroad, that she knew nothing of his recent life and could not say how the skull came to its resting place. This did not go down well with the city authorities: she was arrested along with her two lodgers, Wood and Billings.

Wood proved to have no stamina in the questioning and quickly confessed to having taken part in the murder. Hayes had been supplied with drink until he fell down insensible. A hatchet was then produced, his head and limbs separated from the torso, and the various pieces distributed around the London area. Only the skull, in solitary rest by the river, was recovered.

At the trial, the three were found guilty. Wood died in prison before his execution date, and Billings was hanged. Catherine Hayes was burned at the stake.

William Thackeray, *Catherine* (London, 1839)

Marie Lafarge. Born Marie Capelle in 1816, Mrs. Lafarge was most unpleasant as a young woman and did not improve with age. Before her marriage, while a guest of the Vicomtesse de Léautaud, she was accused of stealing a diamond necklace from her hostess. The charges were later dropped, in the interest of saving embarrassment to the family.

When no suitors presented themselves for her hand, Marie was forced to use the services of a matrimonial agency. The unfortunate result was Charles Lafarge, a man she disliked from the beginning, together with his mother and the house — a large, decaying and rat-ridden horror. To make matters worse, she soon found that Charles, whose business was facing bankruptcy, had married her for her dowry.

In November 1839, Lafarge traveled on business to Paris, where he received a parcel of cakes from his wife. After indulging himself, he became so ill that he had to cut short his trip and

Marie Lafarge and her rat problem inspired the Shearing novel The Lady and the Arsenic.

return home. He lingered until January 14, 1840, when he finally expired.

That was a very bad year for Marie. First an autopsy on her husband revealed a large amount of arsenic; then the de Léautauds renewed their accusation of theft, the diamonds were found at her house, and she was given a two-year suspended sentence. But more was to come. In September, she went on trial for murder and was found guilty after a local pharmacist testified that she had bought large quantities of arsenic supposedly as rat poison. This time she faced a life of hard labor, but her sentence was soon reduced by King Louis-Philippe to simple imprisonment. She served ten years at Montpelier and died shortly after her release, still protesting that she was innocent of all charges.

Joseph Shearing, *The Lady and the Arsenic* (Heinemann, 1937)

Jessie M'Lachlan. On July 7, 1862, the corpse of twenty-five-year-old Jessie McPherson was found in the basement of the house where she worked. Her body had been brutally hacked, and she was lying in bloodstained sheets; on the floor were several clearly defined footprints. The only other occupant of the house at the time was Mr. Fleming, the elderly father of the owner. Silver and some of the dead woman's clothing were discovered missing.

A couple of days later, a pawnshop reported that the silver had been brought in by a Jessie M'Lachlan, who turned out to be wearing Jessie McPherson's clothing when she was arrested. Her footprint matched those found in the gory basement. Mr. Fleming, who had been arrested, was released from custody, and Jessie took his place as the major suspect.

One of the witnesses at M'Lachlan's trial was Mr. Fleming. Though it was said by several witnesses that the dead woman was terrified of him and often called him "an auld deevil" in front of other people, and though he had a nasty reputation with young women, no word against him was allowed by the judge. M'Lachlan was found guilty and sentenced to death, but was reprieved on the strength of petitions in her behalf. She served fifteen years in prison before traveling to America, where she died — perhaps the only witness to the murder.

George Goodchild and C. E. B. Roberts, *The Dear Old Gentleman* (Jarrolds, 1935)
D. E. Muir, *In Muffled Night* (Methuen, 1933)

Maria Manning. Swiss-born Marie de Roux began her career as a lady's maid. In 1846, while traveling on the Continent with her employer, she made the acquaintance of Patrick O'Connor, with whom she kept in touch over the next few years. On her return to England, she met and married Frederick Manning, a Great Western Railway employee who soon after was dismissed for suspected theft. Only a short while later, they were both in trouble with the inn at Taunton where they had gone to work, and they decided to try London again — this time opening a beer shop.

Meanwhile, Patrick O'Connor was succeeding admirably in his career as a money-lender. On August 8, 1849, he was invited to dine with the Mannings at their home in the Hackney Road. His visit ended when Maria shot him through the head and Frederick ripped his

Maria Manning, with the help of her husband, buried her prey beneath the floorboards.

body with a chisel. Burying him quickly beneath the floorboards, the Mannings rushed to O'Connor's lodgings and removed silver objects, jewelry and money.

Frederick Manning's conscience bothered him as they sold off the valuables, but Maria was merely irritated by her husband's oversensitivity. At the same time, O'Connor's friends began to look for him, and it was not long before they came upon his body in the Manning home.

When finally located, the Mannings had separated: Frederick was picked up in Jersey, Maria in Edinburgh. They were transferred to London and tried at the Old Bailey. Found guilty, they were hanged outside the Horsemonger Lane Jail before a large crowd that included Charles Dickens.

Charles Dickens, *Bleak House* (Bradbury, 1853)

Florence Maybrick. Mr. Maybrick had always been extremely health-conscious and had dosed himself freely with patent medicines, as well as arsenic and strychnine. In April 1889, he fell ill, and in May he died. Earlier in the year, his attractive American wife had spent a few nights in London with her lover; this had caused a severe family row.

Investigation showed that shortly after her London trip, Florence had begun buying arsenic-containing flypapers which she claimed were for use in her beauty treatments. An au-

Florence Maybrick used arsenic-treated flypaper as a beauty aid.

topsy showed not only arsenic but a host of other poisons in Maybrick's body.

At the trial, Victorian propriety was shaken by the letters from Florence's lover, and there was little sympathy for her in the courtroom. The judge, who was extremely prejudiced, summed up savagely against the defendant; shortly thereafter, he was confined to a lunatic asylum as being highly unbalanced and irresponsible. Florence was found guilty and condemned to die, but her sentence was changed to prison for life. Released in 1904, she was heard of no more.

Anthony Berkeley, *The Wychford Poisoning Case* (Collins, 1926)
Joseph Shearing, *Airing in a Closed Carriage* (Harper, 1943)

Kitty Ogilvy. In 1765, Kitty Nairn married Thomas Ogilvy, a man twenty-one years her senior who shared a small house with his mother, younger brother, a cousin and three servants. Married life for the daughter of Sir Thomas Nairn could not be described as pleasant, and the nineteen-year-old Kitty turned for comfort to the younger brother, Patrick. Whether a serious affair developed is uncertain, but the rumors that began to fly were taken seriously by Thomas: he asked his brother to leave at once.

Life in the cramped and shabby house went from bad to worse without the cheerful

Patrick, and soon Kitty was writing to him for medicines that would control her insomnia and constipation. The day after a hefty package of laudanum and arsenic was delivered to the Ogilvys', Thomas became very ill; his devoted wife took him a dish of tea in his room, whereupon his health immediately deteriorated. He died on June 6, 1765, but before the funeral could take place his other brother, Alexander, demanded an investigation. Since Alexander, a medical student, claimed the death was a homicide, Kitty and Patrick were arrested and charged with murder and incest.

At their trial in Edinburgh, both were found guilty. Patrick was executed in September 1765, but Kitty was expecting and her life was spared temporarily until she gave birth to her child. During the postponement, she managed to escape and find a way to the Continent; nothing is known of her fate.

Winifred Duke, *The Laird* (John Long, 1925); *Crookedshaws* (Jarrolds, 1936)
Jean Stubbs, *The Case of Kitty Ogilvy* (Macmillan, 1970)

Madeleine Smith. Madeleine lived in Glasgow with her parents and endured the usual dull existence of an unmarried girl in mid-Victorian times. In 1855, at age twenty-one, she found the

Madeleine Smith, a Glaswegian, lived within an area called "the royal mile of murder."

excitement she craved in thirty-four-year-old Emile L'Angelier, a clerk in a seed merchant's office. Poorly paid and with no hopes for the future, L'Angelier welcomed the attentions of a prosperous architect's daughter.

In June 1856, they became lovers at the Smiths' country home. Madeleine began to write indiscreet letters, pretending she was Emile's wife and addressing him in endearing terms hardly suitable to her position. Meanwhile, Mr. Smith sought an appropriate husband for his daughter — a rich, respectable young man with a shining financial future and social acceptance.

As soon as Madeleine was introduced to a prospective fiancé, her passion for Emile took a rapid plunge. He would not be put off easily, however, and refused to return her letters, threatening instead to send them to her father. They continued their habit of talking through the bars of Madeleine's basement window until February 1857, when Emile became sick. He spent a week in bed, then managed to return to his job until March 23. On that night, he convulsed with horrible pains and died soon afterwards. When his landlady called in the police, Madeleine's letters were discovered among his possessions.

At the trial in Edinburgh, the prosecution stated that eighty-two grains of arsenic had been found in L'Angelier's body; the claim was that it had been put in a hot drink before he came home after work. The defense asserted that L'Angelier was an arsenic-eater from way back, and proved that he was also a blackmailer; several seductions of middle-class women had brought him money by his threats of exposure. On July 9, a verdict of Not Proven was returned.

Madeleine left Glasgow and for a time lived in London, where she married once. She died in America in 1928; she was ninety-three years old, and the grave bears the name of her second husband.

Mary Ann Ashe, *Alas for Her That Met Me!* (Star, 1976)
Norah Lofts, *Lovers All Untrue* (Doubleday, 1970)
Mrs. Belloc Lowndes, *Letty Lynton* (Heinemann, 1931)
William Darling Lyell, *The House in Queen Anne's Square* (Blackwood, 1920)

Ruth Snyder. The execution of Ruth Snyder at Sing Sing in 1928 made news as no prison death ever had before. A reporter in attendance had strapped a camera to his ankle, and for the first time a condemned person was photographed in the act of dying.

The events leading to the execution began three years earlier when Ruth met Judd Gray, a corset salesman who took her fancy. Suddenly developing an immoderate need for the undergarments, she pursued him in offices, hotel rooms, anywhere that offered an opportunity to ply him with her charms. By the beginning of 1927, she had decided her marriage to Albert, a highly successful art director for a boating magazine, must end in death. Her lover, also married and living in New Jersey with his family, fought the murder plan until finally on March 19 he drove reluctantly to the Snyders' home in Queens and swung a sashweight at the unsuspecting Albert. When her husband merely sat up and shouted, Ruth took over and did him in with one blow.

Afterwards, the evil twosome rampaged through the rooms, pulling furniture round and upsetting the house to make it look as if a burglary had taken place. Then Ruth, whom Judd had left tied up, managed to knock on the door of her daughter's room and ask the child to go for help. On their arrival, the police were not happy with what they found or with Ruth's attitude. When articles reported as stolen began to turn up on the Snyder property, both Ruth and Gray were arrested.

The lovers were tried in April and sentenced to death. While waiting in the condemned cell, each wrote an autobiography; Ruth also received several proposals from men who seemed not to object to her bent for murder. They were executed within minutes of each other on January 12.

James M. Cain, *Double Indemnity* (Knopf, 1936)
T. S. Matthews, *To the Gallows I Must Go* (Knopf, 1931)

Bathsheba Spooner. During the Revolutionary War, Bathsheba's father lost his immense estate in Massachusetts and left for Canada in disgust. Bathsheba remained behind and married Joshua Spooner, of whom she soon tired. Looking elsewhere, she found diversion in the shape of Ezra Ross, a young soldier whom she pressed to help in disposing of her husband. When Ross refused, British soldiers James Buchanan and William Brooks volunteered their services.

Bathsheba's recruits proved inept accomplices, however; her husband was soon deep down in a well, but the soldiers were picked up wearing his clothes and the body was quickly discovered. Before long, Bathsheba and Ezra joined their cohorts in prison.

When she was found guilty, Bathsheba claimed to be with child. She was examined before her execution date, July 2, 1778, but there was no evidence of pregnancy. After the execution, she was examined again; this time, it was determined that she was right all along—in her womb was a five-month-old fetus.

Esther Forbes, *The General's Lady* (Harcourt, 1938)

Edith Thompson. Mr. Thompson was inclined to be bossy, dull and resentful of his bright and charming wife's successes in business: Edith earned considerably more than he did at her job in a London millinery store.

During a seaside holiday in 1921 with her sister, Edith attached herself to young Frederick Bywaters despite an age difference of eight years. The twenty-year-old ship's clerk wrote romantic letters on board to his new love, who responded eagerly and began to make up stories of how she would rid the world of Percy Thompson via ground-up glass in food, poisons and other means of disposal.

On the evening of October 3, 1922, Percy Thompson and his wife attended the theater in London. After a train journey home to the suburb of Ilford, they were walking from the station when suddenly Percy cried out and collapsed on the ground. Some passersby went for a doctor, who pronounced the man dead and called the police. Edith would make no statement about the stab wounds found on the body.

It was soon established that Bywaters had a very special relationship with Edith. He was brought to the police station, where bloodstains were discovered on his jacket.

At their trial, the jury was unfavorably impressed by the couple's correspondence, especially Edith's imaginative descriptions of her husband's demise. It was decided that the death plans were real, not a lonely woman's highly romantic fantasies, and the lovers were found guilty.

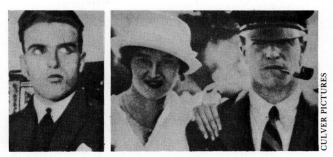

CULVER PICTURES

Edith Thompson fancied Frederick Bywaters, a younger man. Her husband did not. Pity. She stabbed him for disagreeing. The British legal system ultimately separated the homicidal couple, dropping him at Pentonville and her at Holloway.

On January 9, 1923, Bywaters was hanged at Pentonville Prison in London. Edith Thompson met the same fate at the same hour at Holloway; she was in such a state of hysterical terror that she had to be sedated, then half dragged, half carried to her death.

Francis Iles, *Ask for the Woman* (Doubleday, 1939)
F. Tennyson Jesse, *A Pin to See a Peepshow* (Heinemann, 1934)

Kate Webster. Seldom is a murder victim rendered into cooking fat, but this was exactly the fate of Mrs. Thomas of Richmond in Surrey.

On March 5, 1879, a man walking along the Thames spotted a box that, when opened, proved to be full of flesh. Thought first to be a gruesome joke of medical students, examination showed the contents to be recently dead, recently cooked — and recently human.

At the same time, Kate Webster, a maid employed by Mrs. Thomas, started to sell up the Thomas possessions. This might have gone unnoticed but for a curious neighbor who was also the Thomas landlady and who had received no notice that her tenant was leaving. The neighbor notified the police, and as pressures began to pile up Kate fled to her native village, where she was eventually arrested wearing Mrs. Thomas' clothing. When she was charged with murder, Kate blamed everything on anyone and everyone — from the people who bought the Thomas furniture to the Thomas landlady.

Found guilty nevertheless at the Old Bailey, Kate Webster made a confession the night before she was hanged on July 29, 1879.

John Cashman, *The Cook General* (Harper, 1974)

Mary Groff vows she will never be found guilty.

NAME CALLING

Young *Susan,* the pubescent vamp,
Disgruntled the Golden Glove Champ.
　He socked her *black-eyed*
　When she couldn't decide
To wed or to go back to camp.

Promiscuous *Mary* one June
Entertained a jailbreaker at noon.
　Her complexion turned ruddy,
　In fact very *bloody:*
Her boyfriend returned home too soon.

Said *Violet* with tearful emotion,
I hate what you've done to this potion.
　I'm fatally *shrinking,*
　Expiring while drinking.
Egad, what an unsettling notion.

In listing the times she'd played bride
Ivy invariably lied
　Because two of her exes'
　Sore solar plexus
Held *poison*, and that's why they died.

The cops nabbed a gun moll named *Nellie*
In her sixth armed attempt on the deli.
　As they emptied her purse,
　She grew *nervous* and worse,
Aimed her gat at her quivering belly.

Jenny with fathomless gall
Propositioned the whole union hall.
　For such errant sinning
　Her dad sent her *spinning.*
She's dead. So don't bother to call.

As she fled from the belfry tower,
The clock struck the witching hour.
　Mimi couldn't stop *screaming*
　When ghosts circled her, beaming,
And crooned she was in their power.

As they needled her arm full of dope,
Virginia the spy gave up hope.
　Her mind started to *reel*
　And she thought, she could feel,
She was no longer able to cope.

Chapter 6
SUSPECTS

SHADY LADIES

Once and for all, let's dispel the myth of the good woman. For every female woebegone who's been booted into the back alley by a two-timing boyfriend, for every delicate waif who's been set upon by thieves, thugs and lecherous in-laws, there's been another, shadier lady, whose past won't bear looking into by the Department of Justice.

In mystery fact, women kill just as often as they're killed. They're just as nasty with the knife, just as deadly with the pistol and just as adroit with the air bubble as any man, and may even have fewer compunctions about lying, stealing, blackmailing and setting up a frame to get their own reprehensible way. The only crime they haven't managed to pull off with (nail) polished aplomb is a decent murder by strangulation: the poor dears haven't the strength left to squeeze firmly, after everything else they've been up to. But then, they've more than made up for this with their arsenic capers.

Arsenic used to be the shady lady's favorite murder weapon. For reasons not yet fully explained, Victorian Scotswomen were especially free with it. So any time you're reading a period detective novel, or a modern one with an historical background, keep your eye on MacLassie.

Mysteriously, when the women of Cornwall turn shady, they hie themselves to the fireplace, remove the poker from the hearth or the candlestick from the mantelpiece and then practice their rug-beating on the nearest head. The effectiveness of their cosh depends on three things: the weight of the chosen instrument; the power with which it is swung; and the thickness of the skull it contacts. Alas, there's no predicting who'll have a sturdy noggin, and shady ladies must take their chances that a single taper can morbidly handle a balding pate.

Some shady ladies find murder by poison or murder by blunt instrument too lonely a method. They prefer company while they work. Thus evolved murder by proxy, in which the woman gathers about her a henchman or two, instructs them in what she wishes done, goads them into it, then sits back and waits for the progress report. Some people feel these are the nastiest shady ladies extant. They are certainly the hardest to trace, as it is not their fingerprint left at the scene of the crime, not their footprint tracking in mud from the garden, not their name on the dying man's lips.

Murder-by-proxy fatales are seldom satisfied with just one. After the triumph over their husband (usually), they go after his children, his mum and then, unwisely, their own confederates — who are too stupid to stop them, naturally, though the Inspector hot on their trail is not. Besides, when the shady lady attacks her co-conspirators, she slips from murder by proxy to murder on her own initiative (arsenic, blunt instrument, smoking gun), which mystery fiction routinely resolves with a capture by book's end.

Shadies who are too squeamish to kill resort to robbery: primary target — jewels. In the early 1900's, the fictional Mrs. Mandelbaum had a system down pat. This little old lady converted her entire flat into a fencing operation. The front parlor handled deliveries while the adjoining library was for sorting, grading and bagging, the bedroom across the way for resale, and the kitchen for shipping and disbursement. Her stock glittered and sparkled as brilliantly as any display ever presented on New York's 47th Street, and on occasion her place settings for twenty-four would have done credit to the London silver vaults. Plus, she had the good sense to live downstairs from another shady named Sophie, who had a light touch with combination locks and whose fingers could straighten a tie and remove a stickpin at the same time.

No one has ever clearly described, in physical terms, a shady lady. We may learn that they have about them a gorgeous aura, but when it gets to the nitty-gritty — height, weight, shoe size, tattoos — we're left in the dark, which is precisely where the stealthy woman lingers. All shadies, or so it seems, have an aversion to glare, be it from the sun, the moon or the watchman's torch. If they can help it, they never dawdle in full light, preferring always a shadow existence. Obviously, this makes an accurate description of them a hit-or-miss proposition and has perpetuated the myth that they dress exclusively in black, that they have raven hair and coal-dark eyes.

Ha! Nothing could be farther from truth. Blondes have just as much fun being shady, and blue-eyed villainesses are not a rare breed. And though cat burglars are prone to the woman-in-black syndrome, poison-pen writers, jewel heisters and crooks turning state's evidence are seldom funereally garbed. We have only to recall the infamous "woman in red" outside that Chicago movie theater to make our point.

Successful shady ladies can well afford high-fashion colors, to coordinate their business outfits to their skin tones. Indeed, the tougher a shady is, the more likely she'll cloak her impurity (of motive and everything else) in a pastel. Shadies who sauntered through the pages of Captain Shaw's *Black Mask* magazine draped themselves in silver-spangled lurex — and sometimes in nude — and those who surfaced in house party mysteries attended croquet parties and intimate fetes in lilac georgette and cerise polka dots, ruffled to a fare-thee-well. Currently, the shady lady contingent is flashing turquoise hippie headbands and boldly patterned serapes styled from Navajo blankets.

And what of the woman in white? Wilkie Collins created one who was a victim, but that was long ago in the mystery's youth (1860). Certainly there is no shadier lady than the nurse, who Q4H (every four hours, for those not familiar with prescription-blank terminology) purges her patient by syringing a carbolic acid solution into his bloodstream. In addition to the needle, she has at her disposal — for his — digitalis pills, morphine, chloroform and, in a pinch, an endless supply of air, which she may choose to inject or withhold (removal of the breathing

mask, for instance, a favorite shady nurse ploy).

Shady ladies can be recognized by particular phrases they toss into their conversation. Their pet expression is "Trust me," closely followed by "Would I lie to you?" and "I had no idea. . ." "Trust me" is their way of saying, "I shall now lead you down the garden path and drop you in the well at the end of it." It is most often mouthed by girlfriends who have picked out a replacement for their present boyfriend. "Would I lie to you?" is frequently uttered by shopgirls who have pocketed the customer's change or pilfered from the shelves, and by dames in the process of double-crossing a chump. "I have no idea" is the all-purpose shady lady remark. It means exactly the opposite.

But you knew that from your own conversation, didn't you?

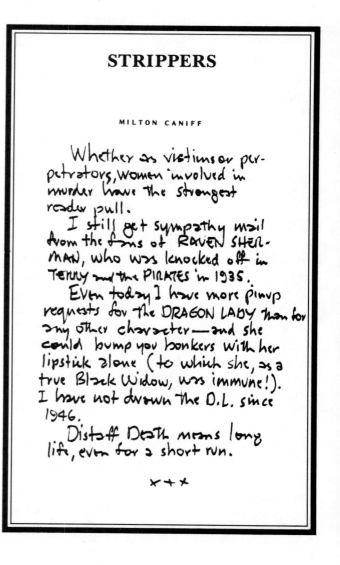

STRIPPERS

MILTON CANIFF

Whether as victims or perpetrators, women involved in murder have the strongest reader pull.

I still get sympathy mail from the fans of RAVEN SHERMAN, who was knocked off in TERRY and the PIRATES in 1935.

Even today I have more pinup requests for the DRAGON LADY than for any other character—and she could bump you bonkers with her lipstick alone (to which she, as a true Black Widow, was immune!). I have not drawn the D.L. since 1946.

Distaff Death means long life, even for a short run.

× + ×

OUT, DAMNED SPOT! OUT, I SAY!

DISHONOR ROLL

Madame Koluchy

To her eternal discredit, Madame K. is mystery fiction's first female crook. Her debut in *The Brotherhood of the Seven Kings* (1899) was masterminded by L. T. Meade and Robert Eustace.

Madame Sara

A turn-of-the-century (1903) angel of death, who in L. T. Meade's *Sorceress of the Strand* planned murders, then kept her dainty hands bloodless by sending henchmen out to perform them.

Henriette Van Raffles

In *Mrs. Raffles* (1905), John Kendrick Bangs' burlesque of the Hornung *Amateur Cracksman* novels, Henriette is a safe-cracker extraordinaire, wife of a gentleman with equally nimble fingers.

Fidelity Dove

Brainy swindler, whose *Exploits* (1924) were recounted by Roy Vickers. Fidelity dressed in gray, had violet eyes and a puritanical streak, though that didn't deter her from pulling off heists.

Sophie Lang

Regarded as a legend in her own time (1925), Sophie was impossible to capture because of her expertise in disguise. She confiscated a passel of flattering gems in Frederick Irving Anderson's *The Notorious Sophie Lang*.

Four Square Jane

Jane's delight was in stealing from the illegally rich, then redistributing the wealth among the poor, in Edgar Wallace's story collection, *Four Square Jane* (1929).

ON APPROXIMATELY THIS SPOT
MILES ARCHER,
PARTNER OF SAM SPADE,
WAS DONE IN BY
BRIGID O'SHAUGHNESSY.

This San Francisco street sign at the corner of Burritt Street commemorates the spot where Brigid eliminated Archer in Hammett's The Maltese Falcon (1930).

Mrs. Jolly

The pudgy Mrs. Jolly had a homicidal gleam in her eye for lost souls — particularly a suicidal spinster recently released from a nursing home. Shelley Smith's antidote to the cloying granny appeared in *Come and Be Killed* (1946).

Sumuru

A female Fu Manchu. Sax Rohmer unleashed her in 1950 in *Sins of Sumuru*, then let her continue on her nasty way in four other adventures.

Celia Montfort

The kinkiest lady in town, Celia looks like Morticia, has alley cat morals. In *The First Deadly Sin*, Lawrence Sanders admitted: "There is a scent of debauchery about her."

Claudia

A cross between a Shirley Temple doll and Count Dracula, Claudia kisses people night-night with all the charm a baby vampire can muster. Anne Rice enunciated her blood-draining experience in *Interview with a Vampire*.

THE WOMAN

Sandy Hill

Sherlock Holmes, the greatest detective of them all, was bested just four times in his illustrious career and only once by a woman — or rather, *the* woman. Holmes was so taken with this remarkable female that he declined his fee in the case, settling instead for an inscribed picture she'd left behind. And let's not underestimate the magnitude of Holmes' enthrallment: the King of Bohemia had been offering him an emerald the size of a robin's egg as payment.

The woman, of course, was Irene Adler, and Holmes was not the only one smitten by her. To this day, she commands homage and respect from Sherlockians around the world. The Baker Street Irregulars, the largest (and exclusively male) organization devoted to the study of Holmes, begins its annual dinner in honor of Holmes' birthday by drinking a toast to her. Each year, a different member's wife, or close female companion, is invited to represent Irene and accept the tribute in her name. Not to be outdone, the Adventuresses of Sherlock Holmes, a distaff Sherlockian society, opens each of its meetings with a similar toast. All this attention despite the fact that *the* woman appeared in only one of the sixty recorded works and was given a scant mention in two others!

We first learn of Irene Adler in "A Scandal

in Bohemia." Wilhelm Gottsreich Sigismund von Ormstein, Grand Duke of Cassel-Falstein and hereditary King of Bohemia, had a small problem: she was blackmailing him. Some five years back, they'd enjoyed a torrid encounter in Warsaw, and the crafty Miss Adler had kept a few souvenirs — letters handwritten on royal stationery, for example, and a rather intimate photograph. To reclaim them, the King resorted to burglary but proved inept (five attempts, five failures). Thus his arrival at 221B. Could the great Sherlock Holmes recover the (damaging) goods?

As it turned out, no. Irene skipped the country, having left a taunting note, a good twelve hours before Holmes was ready to confront her. It appears that while the Great Detective's game was afoot, she managed to step gingerly on his toes!

Item: She saw through his clergyman disguise.

Item: She finagled him into acting as best man at her wedding, then — utter humiliation — tipped him for participating.

Item: She followed him home without his knowing it.

Item: She added insult to this injury by cheerfully wishing him a goodnight in a disguised voice — which he was unable to identify.

Speculative item: Holmes' famous housekeeper, Mrs. Hudson, is missing from "Scandal." In her stead, we are mysteriously presented with a Mrs. Turner, who never again appears in the series. Was Mrs. Turner really Irene Adler, using her brilliant disguise technique right in Holmes' bailiwick?

Though she covered her tracks well, this "adventuress," we know she was born in New

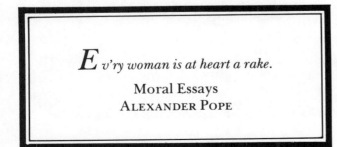

E v'ry woman is at heart a rake.

Moral Essays
ALEXANDER POPE

BARBARA IRIS ULAN

Jersey in 1858, that she moved to the Continent and became the star of the Imperial Opera of Warsaw, that she sang the premier contralto roles at La Scala, that she then retired from the stage and relocated to London, where she occupied a small villa in Briony Lodge, Serpentine Avenue, St. John's Wood. To a man, the gentlemen of the neighborhood swore she was "the daintiest thing under a bonnet on this planet."

"Dainty" she might have been, but she was fiery, too. What a perfect Carmen she must have made, her dark eyes flashing as she flirted with the boys and seduced Don Jose. (Her getaway in "Scandal" is reminiscent of Carmen's escape from imprisonment.) And surely it must have been her theatrical training, her acting aplomb, that made her so fiendishly good at duping Holmes.

By the time we meet up with her, she is concentrating all her amorous attentions on a dark, handsome Inns of the the Court lawyer named Godfrey Norton. They marry in haste, with the reason never specified. One thing is certain: Godfrey must have been a unique Victorian to know all the secrets of Irene's past and still accept her as his wife (not to mention leave the country for her sake).

About that past, rumors abound: Was she one of the women in the early playboy life of the Prince of Wales? The mistress of the Duke of Clarence? The confidante of several minor heads of state and numerous senior members of the British diplomatic corps? Was she really Lillie Langtrey, the English actress known for her great beauty? Was she spying for the Germans, the French, perhaps the Italians? Did she originally go abroad at the suggestion of the President, to gain information from her wealthy and influential paramours? With such an exceptional woman, anything is possible.

The tantalizing question is, what happened to her? Dr. Watson refers to her as "the late Irene Adler." Merely a deep, dark wish of his, or something more? Did she ever see Holmes again, after this one episode? Were they together in Tibet? Did they secretly cohabit for a three-year period, and if so, is it possible there was a child? Watson, no doubt, was privy to the facts, but as a true friend and gentleman kept the secrets to himself. He did, however, tell us

this: "To Sherlock Holmes she is always *the* woman. I have seldom heard him mention her under any other name. In his eyes she eclipses and predominates the whole of her sex. . . . there was one woman to him and that was . . . Irene Adler."

Sandy Hill, writer, is a daring Adventuress.

ON BECOMING AN ADVENTURESS

In 1967, Evelyn Herzog founded the Adventuresses of Sherlock Holmes specifically for women. Currently, there are 33 invested members who convene bimonthly, usually in New York City. They produce a quarterly newsletter, *The Serpentine Muse*, which contains pertinent events, sprightly correspondence and erudite and recherché items to intrigue canonical scholars. A subscription costs $4 per year.

For more information, contact Ms. Herzog, 235 West 15th Street, New York, N.Y. 10011.

THE GRIEVING WIDOW

She leaned over to kiss him goodbye, thinking he'd never looked better.

Of course, the dim light helped, as did the touch of make-up.

She brought her handkerchief up to hide a smirk, took a moment to compose herself, then turned to face Vernon and Isabel.

"Diane, how peaceful he seems."

"Dear Diane, one could almost believe he was only sleeping."

"I'm certain," she whispered back huskily, "he would have wanted things just this way."

Well, maybe not.

Paul did have a great deal to live for. Her name was Mitzi, she was twenty-six, she had the best legs this side of Dietrich and a dimple in a rather private place.

In contrast, Diane had little tuck marks behind her ears and the manners of an adder.

She also had, buried deep in the garden, a stoppered test tube containing the dregs of a home-brewed tonic. And within forty-eight hours, she would have: voting control of an oil flotilla; a fabulous home in Wessex; another in Lombardy; an income of £250,000 per annum.

Paul might not have been pleased about all that. He was girding for a divorce action when he suddenly took ill.

"Madam, if you're ready, we'll begin."

Diane trembled her lip at the cutawayed director. She delicately placed her hand on his arm and allowed him to lead her to a front pew.

Vernon and Isabel slid into the row behind.

Mitzi stood at the rear, casting hateful glances at the grieving widow.

Diane sensed her, but refused to turn around. Instead, she focused on white gladioli tethered in black satin. She was quite smug about the choice: conspicuous, but not gaudy. The real mourners would be impressed.

There weren't many. Diane had personally thanked them for coming, rationing her words, not trusting herself to finish a sentence without bursting into a little cry of exultation.

They thought she was bearing up nobly.

"Admirable woman," the squire mumbled to his wife, who wept copiously at funerals, weddings, christenings. "Take a lesson from her, old thing. Behave yourself."

This brought on a fresh run of tears and a frantic search for something to mop with.

Diane knew Hortense was weeping. She considered a consoling smile, but decided she'd not risk it. What if the gesture involuntarily changed to a toothy grin?

The minister droned on. He'd been a classmate of Paul's. Together, they'd mastered Latin declensions, the hypotenuse and the isosceles triangle, the reigns of the various Henrys and Edwards and the metaphysics of Donne, from whom the curate was now quoting.

"No man is an island, least of all our departed friend, who so generously gave of his time, whose charity was legion, whose . . ."

Diane's thoughts drifted. An image of Paul on their wedding night flashed across her mind. He stood frozen at the bedroom door, his pajama jacket buttoned to the neck, his bathrobe sash double-knotted, his Adam's apple and eyelids moving in convulsive synch.

The next morning he wouldn't look at her.

When they returned from the honeymoon fortnight in Bournemouth, they tacitly agreed that she would have the master suite and he the guest room down the hall. Except on Fridays, when she endured his fumblings.

On his fortieth birthday, she bent to leave a pair of salmon flies on his regular pillow and felt a lump beneath the blanket. Upon investigation, she discovered a magazine with color photographs of girls wearing winks and nothing else. She left it, but began checking the car mileage and scrutinizing the telephone bill for calls made to unfamiliar exchanges.

THE ELECTRONIC HANDKERCHIEF

The phone rings. "Could I speak to Ian?" a voice on the other end asks.

Unfortunately, no. Ian is lying at the foot of the stairs, the candelabra embedded in his cranium.

But you don't want anybody to know that just yet. So you murmur sweetly into the receiver, "My husband will be but a moment," then switch on the Electronic Handkerchief.

You adjust a dial. You wait. You continue to wait. Yes, Ian would have reached the phone by now. "Hullo, Ian here," you say, sounding enough like the poor man to fool the caller.

The Electric Handkerchief is a voice disguiser. Via a mechanism too complicated to explain, it converts a soprano into a tenor, or a baritone or a bass. Which is very handy if you wish to establish an alibi by phone.

Sure it's expensive. But think what you'll save on lawyer bills.

A Chelsea number kept reappearing: 01 736 2288.

Diane felt a shiver run through her body. She forced herself still. She willed her attention to the chapel, to the tall black tapers. She gave her head a little shake, then bowed it.

She had a vision of Paul reaching into his pocket for a matchbook. When he folded the cover back, she could see writing. A number. 01 736 2288. And a name. Mitzi. They swam before her eyes, seemed to dance on the casket, until they settled on Paul's lips and stretched across them like so many loving sentries.

Diane emitted a low groan. Vernon leaned forward. Isabel leaned forward. Mitzi craned her neck to see what was happening.

"Steady, girl."

"Diane, a cool compress?"

The minister paused.

"Pray continue. I'll collect myself in a moment. Forgive me."

The squire nudged his wife.

"You've got company, luv. Damned emotional, you women."

Hortense broke into a new series of sobs. She started digging in her husband's pocket.

"Can I borrow a 'kerchief?" she panted. "Mine's, mine's all damp."

He nodded indulgently and let her rummage until she found what she was looking for.

Up front, Diane took several deep breaths, exhaling slowly to calm herself. She was sustained by the thought of French marigolds, a bed of them, down there at the end of the garden, where no one but she ever walked.

She remembered planting them, how wonderful it felt to kneel in the rich soil, to turn over spadeful after spadeful, to sit on her haunches and realize the vial would be secure.

She savored the memory. A slight flush tinged her cheeks. The minister noticed and thought she was uncommonly handsome.

Diane rose. The somber director materialized at her elbow and escorted her to the vestry.

"The car will be here momentarily, madam."

She acknowledged the remark by pressing her palm to her forehead and closing her eyes.

Vernon hurried over, not waiting for Isabel, who had gone off in search of water. He cleared his throat self-consciously.

Diane opened her eyes.

"You have been my bulwark, my strength," she said. "You and your Isabel."

She wondered if she sounded sincere. She detested them both. They'd been Paul's friends.

The car pulled up. The director helped her inside. She pulled closed the dividing panel, the pale gray drapes on the windows. Then she began to laugh; loud raucous barks that made her stomach ache. She had never been so sublimely happy.

Mitzi watched the car until it was a small speck among other small specks. Then she swung her pocketbook over her shoulder and headed for the bus stop.

"Aw, ducks, you knew it was too good to last," she said to herself as she flagged an approaching Number 7.

THE CRYING MECHANISM

Go ahead, blow.

Don't be embarrassed. Every good cry deserves a honk. Think of it as your sinuses' way of saying Amen.

Oh, you have trouble crying, feel like laughing instead? That's understandable. With one teeny exception, the process is the same for both: you take a deep breath, follow it up with a series of short, jerky releases, then surround it with some laryngeal noises (hee-hee or sob-sob, depending on your preference). The only difference is, crying is a cackle that got all wet, from the drip-drip of your lacrimal sacs.

When the lacrimal sacs runneth over, dear, the situation turns weepy.

Now, tears can take either the anterior route — in which case they trickle down your cheeks — or the posterior — in which case you'll swallow them and develop a lump in your throat. Either way, they're bound to be bitter. Though they have as much salt as your plasma, they have less sugar. So tears are not sweet.

You are not, however, a bottomless well. You produce only 1 cc of tears a day. They originate in your lacrimal glands, which are tucked up there under your eyeshadow. To get from there to the lacrimal sacs, they have to travel across the back of your eye. When they come close to their storage tanks, they're sucked in by a negative contraction of the orbicularis oculi — which means your eye muscles have done their job.

If you feel you simply must cry, and don't want to wait for nature to take its course, you can activate the lacrimal apparatus by slicing into an onion and taking a good whiff. The sacs will let loose a barrage of water in an attempt to wash away the smell. If you hate onions, try a little drop of glycerin. That's what movie stars use. Or, you might give yourself a good pinch: a learned response to pain is a bawl.

Now go look in the mirror. All this crying has brought a nice touch of color to your nose. Say thank you to your dilated capillaries.

MATTHEW SEAMAN

THE JILTED MISTRESS

"**J**eez, I don't know why he left me. I was awful good to him," she says, shifting the gum from the right side of her mouth to the left.

She wriggles deeper against the heart-shaped headboard tufts, then readjusts her robe. The white satin lapels have fallen open, revealing a small beauty mark on her creamy breast. She tugs. It disappears, but her thigh emerges. It, too, has a beauty mark.

"Stanley swore to me I was more important to him than anything, even his Seville."

A wistful pause.

"I guess he didn't mean it."

She opens a drawer, pulls out a tissue and dabs just beneath her mascara, careful not to smear it.

Her name is Bobbi and she used to be in the typing pool at Confederated Truckers ("For the Long Haul"). Like Elizabeth Ray, she had no idea how to switch on her electric machine. But she was very good at getting men to help change her ribbon.

Along about the fiftieth time she needed assistance, Stanley appeared. He was short, swarthy, chewed on a cigar and wore star sapphire cuff studs.

"Get yer coat," he ordered, and she shrugged into her fuchsia plaid wrapper with the mohair pussycat bow and followed him out.

They went to his place. The Sheraton Motor Inn. His room had a vibrating bed. She whoopsed all over it and he was very sweet to her; he phoned room service for a case of ginger ale to settle her stomach.

She was in love.

"So was he, so was he. I had my own key to that place. He took me to a jeweler where they copy it in gold, you know? Fourteen-karat, he let me keep it. He didn't have to do that, if I didn't mean something to him, right?"

Bobbi is not sophisticated. She serves bourbon with maraschino cherries floating on top.

"Stan always thought it was a cute idea. He'd say, 'Who needs a girl who knows her way around the liquor cabinet?' "

She only remembers one big blowout. She got to the hotel late one day. She had to wait for her nails to dry before she could leave the beauty shop. It took longer than she thought. Stanley yelled like crazy.

THE LADY WHO DISAPPEARED INTO THE NIGHT

"Who were ya with, who were ya with," that's all I heard for half an hour. Cripes, my head was falling off from it. Why would I cheat on a nice guy like Stanley? But he wouldn't listen to me and I landed in the hospital. The desk clerk called the cops and I was such a mess they took me right over in their squad car. I thought Stanley would plotz. He don't like the cops, you know."

Bobbi has a new nose from the experience, and it looks very nice. Except when she smiles, her upper lip doesn't move.

"That was the best time I ever had. Stanley came to see me every day and I had so many flowers in that room, the nurses complained I was taking up all the vases. And my doctor— what a kidder he was! Know what he called me? Rosie! He said I'd be the only person in the history of the third floor to catch hay fever while I was there. Let me tell you, I could have gone for him. He treated me better than a baby."

Bobbi plucks at the coverlet.

"I guess I like a lot of attention, huh?"

She was the middle of three children. Her mother worked for the telephone company as an "Information, Please" operator and her father drove the Springfield-Albany route for NorthEast Trailways. Her brother was a chronic truant. He ran away from home at fifteen and Bobbi hasn't seen him since. Her younger sister has a visual handicap. Bobbi would sit with her on the stoop and describe all the cars as they passed by. Sometimes, she'd walk her to the candy store for an ice cream.

"Oh, I could still kill for a fudgesicle. I used to sneak them into the apartment when Stanley wasn't looking. He had this thing about me getting fat. He'd grab my waist and pinch it between his fingers, you know? 'Better watch it, better watch it,' he'd tell me. My middle used to be black and blue from where his fingers were."

Bobbi is a perfect size 10. Provided it's cut full in the bust.

"Want to hear a secret? Before Stanley closed all my charge accounts I raced over to Gimbels and spent one solid day there. I have stuff I haven't even worn yet. I'm saving it. I got a gorgeous pink formal that's embroidered with a sort of mulberry leaves pattern. It's real delicate. And I had gloves and shoes dyed to match.

THE MINK MINX

What did she have to do for it? Nothing. Just shorten the sleeves.

And ya see this?"

She points to a nicked ankle. On it rests a white-gold bracelet. It spells out her name in zircons.

"I sent it to myself with a little card that said 'For My Bobbi — je t'aime, Stanley.' I learned a little French in high school, ya know?"

She leans back, smug.

"I ordered stationery, too. Very fancy stuff, like a bride would use. I had them put Mrs. Stanley Albert Capraffano on it, with the Sheraton's address."

Bobbi bites her lip.

"I never could use it. What would his wife had said?"

Five months after he jilted Bobbi, Stanley was killed in a freak accident. He was standing on the back loading platform at Confederated Truckers when a van rammed it. He was crushed before he had time to move. No one has been able to figure out why he was there or who was handling the truck. The watchman found him when he was making the midnight check.

"Stan had some weird friends, ya know? He never let me meet them, but once I answered the phone and this guy gave me the creeps. Wouldn't even tell me his name. I told him who I was when he asked, though. I got manners."

Bobbi's best friend, Dixie, introduced her to Ernie. He is thin, tense, rolls a toothpick round his tongue and carries a steel ice pick in his sleeve.

"Ernie doesn't like me to go out if he's not with me. I have to beg him to let me go to the hairdresser's alone. But we go to the races a lot, and that's fun. Ya ever hit a Quinella? I got two thousand and eight dollars and eighty-three cents once."

Ernie has not given Bobbi a key to the apartment. "Yer not going anywhere, baby, Whaddya need a key for? I'll open doors for ya, ha-ha," he told her.

Bobbi keeps a picture of Stanley tucked in her wallet, behind the snap of her sister Alice. His hat is pulled far forward and it's hard to tell what he looks like. A radiant Bobbi stands beside him, clinging to his polyester blend.

Bobbi doesn't feel the same way about Ernie as she does about Stanley. She never will.

MARTY NORMAN

CRIME WAVE

Laverne thought Nathan was rich. Nathan believed the same about her. They "impetuously" eloped. When it came time to pay the justice of the peace, they each deferred to the other. Laverne ultimately coughed up. Next day, she got her revenge: Boom, boom, with an unsilenced Howitzer.

Cora gave Freddy the come-on. Freddy stuttered out a proposition. She accepted and became the fourth Mrs. Frederick Van Peltenham III. Since Freddy predeceased her with a little help from her bodyguard's strong-arm, there was no fifth Mrs. Freddy. Cora and Brute now clip coupons by the cabana and toast Freddy on his death day.

Eulalia was waiting on line at the bank when she happened to notice Siggy DiLorenzo arrive with seven moneybags, one moneybelt and a stooge carrying a small (but not too small) safety-deposit box. She moved to their line. She dropped hers. Siggy fell for it and eleven days later fell even further — off lover's leap. Eulalia switched banks. Her initial deposit was so large, the firm gave her a color TV, a pop-up toaster *and* a complete set of Corningware.

MUM'S THE WORD

Mystery mummies are cursed. Like real mummies, they know absolutely everything (and what they don't know, they make up), and that's what gets them into hot water. When things go wrong, who better to blame than the know-it-all?

By now, the world's favorite scapegoat should have learned her lesson: it doesn't pay to be cook, chauffeur, nurse, baby-sitter, housekeeper, mistress, wife, etiquette expert, fashion coordinator, confidential secretary, interior decorator, mechanic, handyman, gardener, tutor, referee, coach, cop, judge and unlicensed snoop rolled into one. Mummies may think when they put them all together they spell "saint," but mystery authors have a meaner interpretation. To them, they add up to the most suspicious character in the book.

And they may be right. Most of the tasks mummy assigns herself could just as easily have been done by the villain. Can this be an accident, or is mummy helping providence along?

Let's mull over the case against mother. Who knows the way around the kitchen as well as she? Who made the sandwiches that went into the lunch pail? Who fixed the lemonade and packed the picnic hamper? Who kicked everyone out of the work area and said she'd rather do it herself, and who insisted on washing up afterwards?

MUMMY'S CURSE

May you someday grow up to have a daughter just as ungrateful as you are.

Of course, it was mum. It was her hand that slathered the lunch meat with imitation mayonnaise, that stirred the sugar substitute into the pitcher, that canned the jar of blueberry botulism, that rinsed out the bottle and wiped off the fridge. No wonder the Inspector wants to interview her first. Look at all the opportunities she's had to do damage.

And ponder, please, the daylight abduction. Who knows the shortest route to the school and the train depot? Who has a duplicate set of car keys she hides from everybody? For that matter, who has the *only* key to the trunk and who's often found tinkering under the hood? And wait, there's more evidence stacked against her. Who's thumbtacked to her wall, right next to the telephone, the bus schedule for every town within a hundred-mile radius? Who's checked out all the play streets, backyards and secret hiding places in the neighborhood?

Who else but mummy? Sure she has an excuse. She wants to satisfy herself that the kids are safe and that her husband gets to the office on time, that she'll be prepared when it's her turn to run the car pool, but if she decides to kidnap a child and hold it for ransom, if she arranges with a lover to drive his getaway, she certainly has the roads mapped out and access to the proper vehicle.

Mummies, moreover, have very strong stomachs. They don't faint at the sight of blood. Who's been Mercurochroming knees for years? Who's bathed and bandaged countless cuts? Who's dug for splinters and drained infections? Accustomed as she is to gore, mummy is naturally going to arouse the Inspector's interest. Particularly, since she's concocted remedies (maladies?) with the nonchalance of a professional pharmacist: who tells you she knows what's good for you and sees that you swallow it, down to the last drop?

Who indeed.

Also, mummy has enough information to be a blackmailer. Who found the diary in the bottom drawer and read it, cover to cover? Who stood at the washer emptying pockets and turned out an overdraft notice from the bank, and a matchbook from a very expensive restaurant? Who knows which button is missing and who's been cavorting in mud when he should have been at work? Who straightened the linen closet and made a mental tick that a pillowcase was gone? Who tidied under the sink and can swear to it that the lye is down by two-thirds?

Mummy the housekeeper, that's who. Nobody can keep a secret from her. She's got the goods on everybody.

And we hate to incriminate her even further, but who worms things out of you that you thought you'd never tell a living soul? Who insists she be kept informed on where you're going, how long you plan to be gone, who'll be joining you and exactly what you'll be doing every second of the time? Who stands there at the door, tapping her foot, waiting for you to make a report? Why, it's your best friend, dear old mum. The woman you confide in, like it or not.

Who makes a juicier suspect than the victim's closest chum? That's a question mum would be hard-pressed to answer. After all, hasn't she always said she understands you better than anyone ever will? That you'll never have a truer friend? Hmmm. Get the jail cell ready.

Mummy is a total menace. Who tutors you for the chemistry final and has memorized the formula for sulfuric acid? Who coached you for the Little League and can throw seventeen consecutive fastballs into the strike zone? Who always seems to be around when you're in trouble? Think about it.

While you're putting two and two together, you might want to remember that one woman in your life slapped, smacked and paddled you silly when you didn't do what you were told. Guess who? She set herself up as judge and jury and delivered ultimatums: My way or else! There was no reprieve when she decided you deserved to be punished. Her word was law. And mum's the word. Pass it on.

THE ROTTEN KID

MATTHEW SEAMAN

The Smileys. Rachel the Elder has inherited; Rachel the Younger expects to.

MATTHEW SEAMAN

THE IMPOVERISHED DOWAGER

Be nice to her. She might remember you in her will. Then again, does she really own anything of value? Think about it. She hasn't bought a new dress since 1918, and her blue velvet's a little frayed at the seams. Its ecru lace is disintegrating, too. Her furniture hasn't been re-covered since Mr. Hepplewhite died, and the one nice piece of jewelry she owns, the Stigmata Brooch, has three small stones missing, lower left. Now that we think about it, what ever happened to her double strand of baroque pearls and that emerald dinner ring she was so proud of? And where's the Sheraton sideboard disappeared to?

Slowly, item by worthwhile item, the mystery dowager is selling off her lifestyle and your inheritance. Death duties, you see.

It's a peculiar state of affairs. Here everyone assumes the mystery dowager is stinking rich, and in reality she can't even pay the servant's wages. In fact, the one retainer she has left, half-deaf Hannah, is subsidizing her.

What better reason to mount a house party? At the old dame's summons, down from London come Lord and Lady Unwaries, he with his solid banking connections and she with her little red foxes draped about her neck; up from Wales comes the vicar, who has not yet deposited the alms; over from Suffolk comes the army officer who's worth a fortune in confiscated booty. Obviously, the crafty mystery dowager is planning on touching them for a small loan.

But she doesn't quite phrase it that way. Her method is to serve them a skimpy supper (so their nerves are on edge), then lead the way to the drawing room, where she announces she's been thinking about her will. A chorus of muted chortles runs round the room. Everyone anticipates a huge bequest. She then continues: She's decided to let them share equally in her benevolence. If they, in turn, will name her *their* heir. The greedy guests agree to the terms. Senility, they think, has set in. After all, how likely are they to predecease an octogenarian?

Little do they know.

Dowagers have, up their faded sleeves, a scheme: They'll kill the first wealthy weekender who signs a will in their favor, take the money, refurbish the house, redeem the heirlooms and buy a new blue velvet. And the bottom line, of course, is that when *they* go, they're taking all those ill-gotten gains with them. This accounts for their characteristic haughty expression.

They almost pull it off, too.

The murder is the easy part. While the Unwaries sleep, the deadly dowager and Hannah slip into their chambers via the secret panel, arthritic their way bedside and squash pillows on the inappropriately smug faces.

The retired army man, of course, will be waylaid in the library with the dowager's cane. As he sits in the wing chair contemplating past battles, she stages a new one, attacking from the rear.

The vicar will be bashed with a shovel in the rose garden as he ambles about with his nose in a prayer book.

The one catch is getting away with the murder. The inspector, a friend of the Unwaries, the vicar and the militant, has made it a rule of thumb never to trust anyone with bluing in her hair. He arrives on the scene and notices tea is offered in a chipped cup; there are no cookies. Even for a dowager, this is too eccentric to be properly British and he starts investigating.

And discovers: the old lady is broke. Dead broke. Which is the best motive for crime in a mystery.

THE INSPIRED COOK

Mmmmmm, smells good. Know what it is? The garlicky aroma of metabolized arsenic. Know where it's coming from? Thelma, who foolishly drained her glass and licked her plate clean — before she asked if the recipe contained a secret ingredient, such as 100 milligrams of an arsenical compound.

In 20's, 30's and 40's mysteries, inspired menu planners added this toxic white powder to cocoa, ladyfingers, chocolate creams, curry, hollandaise and broth. They were ingenious in their invention. They toasted it, they roasted it. They braised it, broiled it, boiled it and baked it. They grilled it, poached it, simmered it, even stewed it. Thelma never stood a chance. She was fated to go from table to tomb reeking like a pizza parlor.

Eventually, mystery writers realized that someone had discovered one more fun thing to do with arsenic: analyze Thelma's tissues for it. His name was Marsh, and his test made the substance just about the easiest poison to detect. Suddenly, it got very quiet in the mystery kitchen. The crime cook took a night off, then was reactivated to garnish horseradish roots with aconite, decorate a birthday cake with strychnine, festoon a candy box with nitrobenzene, mix a cocktail with atropine sulphate and coat a champagne cork with cyanide. Cook was back in business, and wise Thelmas brown-bagged their own lunches.

Who hates Thelma enough to poison her? Practically everybody, and at one time or another during the course of the mystery they each were alone with the skillet and the blender.

The first character to fall under the Inspector's suspicion is the full-time cook — that stern-visaged harridan who has a kind word only for the butcher, and then only if he saves her the prime rump. As she is forced to acknowledge to the investigator looking into Thelma's abrupt departure before dessert, she did indeed prepare the clams oregano before she took herself off to the picture show, and yes, the note beside them in the fridge (*ready to be heated, warm for twenty minutes*) is in her handwriting, and the fingerprints on the Pyrex — the only prints — are hers, too. Ergo, concludes the copper, she must be Thelma's murderer.

For a while, even Cook believes this. Did she, in her haste to catch the opening credits, reach for the wrong bottle in the larder? It would have been easy to do. The labels on the porcelain canisters have faded over the years she's been in service, and she doesn't really look when she grabs; she assumes the right container will be in its usual place in her well-ordered stockroom. But what, she reasons, if Nanny has been mucking about again, poking around for something to sweeten the little one's tonic? That woman never puts things back where she found them. It's just possible, she concludes with a cholesterol-heavy heart, that the third canister in the back row might well have been the arsenic and not the cornstarch. Unwittingly, she could have murdered.

Her motive? Well, according to Nanny, who takes great pleasure in implicating her, Cook and Thelma had a bit of a row about the food bills. Seems Cook was padding them and the Missus threatened to dismiss her if it happened again.

The dinner disher-upper remains the Inspector's principal candidate for Holloway until

BONE APPETIT

APPETIZER

(Stool) Pigeon's Tongue

SOUP

Puree of Telltale Heart

ENTREE

*Cracked Ribs Flambe,
delicately garnished with
(brass) knuckles*

DESSERT

Blood Pudding

THE SERVANT PROBLEM

Housekeeping chores are never pleasant, but some women have managed them with good grace: Mrs. Stick, for example, who was hired by Leo Bruce to cook and clean for Carolus Deene; Mrs. Winters, whom Leonard Holton placed in the employ of Father Breeder; Mrs. Johnson, sent by August Derleth to tidy up after Solar Pons; Emma Catt, whom Alice Scanlon Reach had supervise the quarters of Father Francis Xavier Crumlish. And, of course, that paragon of domestic imperturbability, Mrs. Martha Hudson, with whom Sherlock Holmes was honored by Sir Arthur Conan Doyle.

On the other hand, there was Mrs. Danvers.

Makes you want to do for yourself, doesn't it?

the autopsy report comes back. Thelma was rife with seventeen heaping teaspoons of arsenic (or whatever). That's enough to fell a party of six. No cook would use that much thickening in the béchamel (or whatever), not if she was a professional.

The lady with the perpetual flour smudge on her nose and the dab of vanilla on her pulse-points is off the hook. She celebrates by returning to her kitchen and banging a few pots and pans around. She lovingly pats her cast-iron cauldron, her cleavers, her poultry shears, her carving sets, her rotisserie spit, her skewers, her grinder and her measuring cups, bowls and spoons, and wonders aloud how anyone could have suspected her in the first place. If the truth be known, for someone she considered a turkey (such as Thelma), she'd turn up the oven, then truss and press her into a sitting duck.

Obviously, the Inspector must now approach the rest of the household with caution. One of the bedrooms holds a kitchen interloper. Hubby perhaps? Not improbable. Men have been known to spice up their lives with a creatively placed poison. There was Edward in Richard Hull's *The Murder of My Aunt,* for instance. And countless wives have had their tummies upset and breathing congested by their spouses ladling deadly potions into their nightcaps.

But the officer's best bet would be the other women in the manor. Woman are forever distilling arsenic from flypapers, cadging cyanide from burnt plastics. They enjoy a good poisoning as much as a good matinée. Female cousins, particularly. Thelma, that hussy, married the man of her relatives' choice. She had money, you see, and a title (and sometimes, a father with a shotgun). But with Thelma gone, Lewis would return to their (usually scrawny) arms once again. Voilà, a lavish hand when icing the tea-cakes Thelma never could resist.

Tut-tutting them to their cell, the Inspector has one final suggestion for these amateur cooks: Instead of poison, next time induce murder by anemia. Prepare a diet regimen that appeases the appestat but is nutritionally useless. After two weeks of such vittles, Thelma will be wasted.

And you couldn't prove how by the Marsh test.

THE NEFARIOUS NANNY

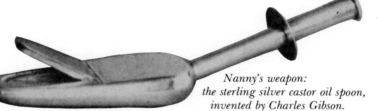

*Nanny's weapon:
the sterling silver castor oil spoon,
invented by Charles Gibson.*

If you think all nannies are supercalifragilisticexpialadotious, you've been taken in by a ringer. Mary Poppins, like most mystery nannies, is a clear-cut case of impersonation.

A genuine nanny would never be seen in the company of a chimneysweep, dancing with penguins. And her charges would no more have soot on their faces than three noses.

Disillusioning though it may be, the classic nanny was an uncongenial, unmitigated snob, who deigned talk to children only after their ears were scrubbed pink and their hands were folded in nonfidgeting laps.

Jonathan Gathorne-Hardy, in *The Rise and Fall of the British Nanny*, relates dozens of stories in which the arbiter of the nursery's chief mode of expression was the haughty sniff. When she chose to verbalize her disdain, her principle condemnation was "We consider it vulgar to . . . ," and the "to" was followed by whatever she personally deemed appalling.

Disagreeing with Fowler and Webster, Gathorne-Hardy maintains that "nanny" was not derived from "Anne," but from "Granny," who, after all, was probably the original mother's helper. In an interesting aside, he notes that the "Granny" root may connote an early function: wet nursing; "Granny" obviously being a reference to suckling granny goats.

A real nanny wouldn't recognize herself in the mystery nanny (in fact, she'd probably rap the charlatan's knuckles).

OOPS, SOMEBODY MISLAID BABY

In E. X. Ferras' *Small World of Murder*, the Foley's baby girl was stolen from her pram.

In Norman Berrow's *Fingers for Ransom*, a millionaire's baby daughter was kidnapped.

In Nicholas Blake's *The Sad Variety*, eight-year-old Lucy Wragby was abducted.

And in Evan Hunter's *Every Little Crook and Nanny*, Nanny Poole was extremely careless with her ten-year-old charge. He got whisked away by a nutty consortium.

Abandoned children.

REAL NANNY

Midnight feeding
Warms bottles
Sings lullabies
Rocks the cradles
Feeds a cold, starves a fever
Sterilizes
Makes rules
Pampers
Rhymes
Wipes noses
Tats doiles
Walks in park
Plays Peekaboo
Mothers
Kisses good night
Works hard
Pushes pram
Inspects behind ears
Disciplines child
Tells stories
Spanks bottom
Loves baby

MYSTERY NANNY

Midnight prowling
Poisons decanters
Sings
Rocks the boat
Creates drafts
Contaminates
Breaks rules
Tampers
Schemes
Wipes fingerprints
Tattles
Hides in park
Plays Hide-and-Seek
Smothers
Kisses off
Sweats it out
Pushes drugs
Listens behind doors
Punishes the parent
Lies
Hits bottom
Loves money

Nannies on parade. Their double prams hold the classic mystery cliche: Identical twins.

BRUCE DAVIDSON/MAGNUM

NORLAND NANNY TRAINING COLLEGE

Founded in 1892 by Mrs. Walter Ward, Norland is the oldest nanny-rearing school in England. Its motto is *Fortis in Arduis,* which the current principal, Miss Betty Medd, translates as "Strength Through Hard Work."

Miss Medd and her staff of fifty supervise an enrollment of one hundred twenty-five in diapering, powdering, bathing, pram pushing, the making of toasted cheese lunches, smocking, appliqué, laundry chores, games of patticake, rhymes, sums, the care and kissing of skinned knees, the mopping of runny noses and basic psychology. Admits Miss Medd, "Our girls make jolly good mothers."

It takes eighteen months at Norland, three at hospital and nine at a probationary post to train a nanny. Applicants must be at least eighteen years old (Norland has never had a married woman apply) and have a high school diploma or its equivalent. During her first two terms, the nanny-in-training will wear striped overalls; after that, she is allowed to purchase the official Norland nanny uniform — a biscuit-coloured dress, worn with brown lace-ups and a brown bowler.

Nanny's rearing will cost her approximately £1,500, and when she is Norland certified, she can expect to earn £30 a week to start (plus room and board). She won't have a problem finding a job; the school has its own placement service and Norland's prestige is such that prospective employers outnumber candidates by a twenty-to-one ratio.

Each June, Norland holds "Open Day," for its old girls. Seven hundred or so return to the Hungerford campus to share tea on the lawn and brag about their charges. Not a single nanny, however, refers to herself by that word. Admits Miss Medd, "The term 'nanny' is *not* one we encourage at Norland. We prefer 'Norland Nurse.' "

A Norland Nanny, class of '78.

The grounds, 150 acres in rural Berkshire.

THE GRIM GRIMM BROTHERS

Once upon a time, there were two little boys named Jakob and Wilhelm. They lived in the not-so-pretty village of Hesse-Cassel, where they were not-so-well-off. One day, while they were sitting in the garden behind their house quietly munching their apfels, the nanny next door called to them. "Kinder, kinder," she said, "come here. I have something very pleasant to tell you."

Jakob went. And everywhere that Jakob went, Wilhelm was sure to follow (that's the way it is with younger brothers).

When they had seated themselves beside her, the alte nanny cleared her throat, smoothed her apron, folded her hands in her lap and began to tell tales. She spoke of princesses with blood-red lips, nasty queens with magical powers, evil witches with ouch-hot ovens. She spoke of awful crimes and awful punishments, but always, always finished with a happy ending.

"Wilhelm," said Jakob, "if we listen to much more of these, we'll grow up to be juvenile delinquents. I think I should make a few notes and study these stories more carefully when I'm older."

And Wilhelm said nothing, being too busy making an infantile pass at nanny's charge, the adorable Dortchen. But he was sure to follow.

Years passed. Jakob forgot his vow and went to university, then to sort books in the mighty musty library. And everywhere that Jakob went, a year to the day later Wilhelm went, too.

Many more years passed. Jakob wrote a book, and another book, and Wilhelm thought about writing one but instead married Fräulein Dortchen and settled for reading what Jakob had done (which was not easy; Jakob used lots of big, scientific-sounding words).

Quite contentedly, the three of them lived together in their not-so-tidy house, in their not-so-pretty village, where they were not-so-rich.

One morning, a great professor knocked on their door. "Bitte," he said as he doffed his top hat, "did you keep records of alte nanny's tales? I would like to publish them."

Jakob looked at Wilhelm. Wilhelm looked at Dortchen. Dortchen looked at the piles of papers under the couch. "Ja," they said in unison, "take them all."

The professor gathered them up, then dusted his knees, donned his top hat, clicked his heels and left — a very happy man.

As the door swung shut, Wilhelm turned to Jakob; but before he could speak, his older

The nanny next door.

CULVER PICTURES

brother beat him to the punch (typical). "Wilhelm," he said, "I think we go back to alte nanny for some more material, nein? Then we will publish it and be as rich and famous as the great professor."

They stepped out into the garden. "Alte nanny, alte nanny," they cried, "tell us more of your wonderful stories." And alte nanny, who loved the two boys almost as much as she loved her gore, licked her lips and did what they asked. On and on she talked. She gossiped through lunch and prattled through dinner and even at bedtime she could not keep still. She talked and she talked and she talked, until finally she had no voice left.

But the boys had their book.

"Thank you, alte nanny," they said, and went home to title it. Jakob had the first (and last) word. "We will call it *Kinder-und Hausmarchen*," he decided. Wilhelm made a face, but he agreed. Dortchen made a face and did not agree, but she had no vote.

The book was so wonderful that the King of Prussia asked the two brothers to move to Berlin, to be near him. "I will make you professors if you come," he decreed, "and I will see to it you are elected to our famous scientific academy."

So they packed up their belongings and moved to Berlin, where they would have lived happily ever after except that Berlin was very expensive and there are limits to what a king will do for you.

They didn't know where to turn.

"Alte nanny has no more stories," said Jakob.

"Alte nanny has no more stories," echoed Wilhelm.

"Find other alte nannies," said Dortchen.

The two brothers went searching. They traveled north, they traveled south, but mostly they stayed within range of Dortchen's cooking. Soon they had enough stories from enough alte nannies for two more books. And they lived happily ever after.

Which is more than can be said for the rest of us, who had to grow up listening to the grim Grimm tales.

Fie on you, alte nanny.

A GRIMM OUTLOOK

The Bruders, Jakob und Wilhelm.

Assistant District Attorney Jeanne E. Thelwell recently completed a study of the Brothers Grimm. Her conclusion: their books represent the densest crime area this side of New York's fabled Fort Apache.

"The mildest trouble they get into," she says, "is in *Cinderella*. Mostly health code violations. But in *Hansel and Gretel* I've got the parents dead to rights for abandonment, endangering the welfare of a child and nonsupport. If I get my hands on the witch, she'll go up for unlawful imprisonment in the first degree. And I wouldn't mind hauling the two kids over to Family Court on charges of criminal mischief and trespassing. In *Little Red Riding Hood*, I'd nail the wolf for burglary, criminal impersonation, fraudulent accosting, endangering the welfare of a child, and best of all, two counts of attempted murder. The wolf was clever, though — eating your victims leaves very few witnesses."

For Thelwell's detailed analysis of *Snow White*, please turn the page.

THE CRIMES AGAINST SNOW WHITE

Criminal Solicitation
The Wicked Stepmother
requests that the
hunter kill Snow White.

Fraudulent Accosting
The Wicked Stepmother
presents Snow White with
ribbons, then laces her
into a faint.

Attempted Murder
The Wicked Stepmother
gifts Snow White
with a lethal comb.

Assault in the First Degree
The Wicked Stepmother administers a toxic substance without Snow White's knowledge or consent.

Reckless Endangerment
The seven little men place Snow White in jeopardy by leaving her without appropriate supervision. By forcing her to work without payment, and with no time off, they also abuse the child labor laws.

MARTY NORMAN

THE DEFENDANT WILL RISE AND FACE THE BENCH

Jeanne E. Thelwell

It is axiomatic, as appellate courts frequently remind us, that a prosecutor's obligation is "to do justice, not merely to get convictions." And it is far from a foregone conclusion that "to do justice" involves getting convictions in every case. But the average mystery reader deals in situations where there is no question that the accused — or at least the person arrested on the last page but one — is the murderer (kidnapper, robber, whatever) and so the only just result is a conviction.

Now: did you ever wonder why the arrest always takes place on the last page but one? The answer is that in most cases it would be nigh on impossible to move the matter into court and get a conviction based on the evidence the author has provided. Not only is it difficult to prove anyone guilty beyond a reasonable doubt, but authors have their detectives seize evidence, coerce confessions and arrange for identifications with a fine disregard for the accused's constitutional rights — all of which will create splitting headaches for the prosecutor in the not-too-distant future.

Let's consider the more typical blunders. A Great Detective in collusion with a member of New York's Finest (who ought to know better) coerces a murder suspect into his office. After grueling cross-examination, he manages to extract the confession without which he couldn't prove a thing. Dandy, but oh my! All I can see is

"Morning, sweetheart."

days and days of hearings to determine whether the confession can be introduced at trial as evidence against the alleged perpetrator. I'm afraid the Great Detective, much as he would resent the insinuation that he was an agent of the police, would have to do a lot of courtroom testifying — something he rarely deigns to do in fiction.

And consider this: Sgt. Foolish pulls out the killer's mug shot and says to the witness, "Is this the man who shot the bank teller?" The witness says yes. Foolish sees an arrest in his future; I see a witness whose identification testimony will be suppressed because the photo I.D. was unduly suggestive.

ITSY-BITSY MS. BEASTLY

In the face of a rash of brutal crimes committed by youngsters, New York has enacted the stiffest "juvenile offender" statute in the United States. Now juveniles from age 13 may be held criminally responsible for Murder in the Second Degree. (They cannot, however, be guilty of Murder in the First Degree; rather than face having to execute young teenagers, the legislature made it essential that the offender be over 18 at the time of the crime.)

Juveniles from age 14 can be responsible for Kidnapping in the First Degree, Arson in the First and Second degrees, Assault in the First Degree, Manslaughter in the First Degree, Robbery in the First and Second degrees, Rape in the First Degree, Sodomy in the First Degree, Burglary in the First and Second degrees, Attempted Murder in the Second Degree and Attempted Kidnapping in the First Degree.

The result of a conviction for any one of these designated offenses is imprisonment, ranging from a possible maximum sentence of 9 years to life for Murder in the Second Degree to a minimum sentence of 1 to 3 years for a class C felony such as Assault in the First Degree. A juvenile offender may not be sentenced to probation. *J.E.T.*

Or: The case-hardened cop spies the neighborhood pusher and, turning to his rookie partner, says, "Let's see if he has anything on him." Their search produces a gun that turns out to be a murder weapon. But it's a murder weapon unlikely ever to be seen by a jury because there was no probable cause to search the poor pusher.

In detective stories, the people arrested are always the *right* people. In real-life defense attorney stories, things are never that simple.

To begin with, the prosecutor does *not* represent the victim of a crime. The prosecutor's client is the political entity, e.g., "The People of the State of New York" or "The United States of America." Where the civil attorney, suing Bertha Beastly for assault and battery, represents Victoria Victim and is concerned with compensating her for her injuries, the district attorney who is prosecuting Ms. Beastly is concerned with Ms. Victim's injuries only to the extent that they are sufficient to establish "physical injury" as an element of the offense of assault.

This is not to say the prosecutor doesn't care about Ms. Victim's problems; rather, the criminal justice system is defense-oriented, not victim-oriented.

Philosophically, there are a number of reasons the prosecutor doesn't represent the victim. One is that the purpose of a society, in the traditional view, is to establish rules by which the members of the society live and deal with each other. Thus a violation of those rules — a crime — is a breach of society's rules and it is the duty of society to enforce them. A second and equally important reason is to prevent the system from becoming an instrument of private vengeance.

Once the specialized nature of the criminal justice system is understood, most of its day-to-day operations begin to make sense. The easiest way to explain is to work backwards. Assume that Bertha Beastly has been found guilty of assault. For what purpose has that determination been made? Most criminologists (who, incidentally, are social scientists, not detectives) recognize five possible goals for the system: (a) general deterrence (people, by and large, will not commit crimes because society deals harshly with people who commit crimes); (b) specific deterrence (Ms. Beastly will think twice about

INTERPRETING THE LAW

"ACD." Adjournment in Contemplation of Dismissal. On the motion of either prosecutor or defense counsel (and with the other's consent), a case is adjourned for six months. At any time during this period, the Assistant District Attorney (ADA) may restore the case to the court's active calendar and continue the prosecution; if the case is not restored, it is automatically dismissed at the end of the six months and the records are sealed.

Arraignment. The defendant's first appearance before a judge after being charged: he or she is informed of the charges and of his or her rights, and bail is set. In practice, the formal reading of the rights and charges is usually waived. The vast majority of cases are disposed of at arraignment.

Beyond a Reasonable Doubt. The burden of proof on the prosecution in a criminal case. This does not mean that guilt must be proved to a mathematical certainty; a "reasonable doubt" is one for which a juror can find a basis in the evidence (or lack of evidence).

"Blue Back." A misdemeanor case: so called because of the colored backing sheet attached to the court file. "Yellow Back" — a felony case. "White Back" — a violation case.

DAT. Desk Appearance Ticket: a type of summons issued for violations and misdemeanors as an alternative to taking the defendant into custody immediately.

"Dis Con." Disorderly Conduct: a violation for minor breaches of the peace.

DOR. Dismissal on Recommendation: statement of facts and reasons behind a motion by the prosecution to dismiss an indictment; e.g., all the evidence has been suppressed at a pretrial hearing.

DP. Declined Prosecution: a decision by an ADA that a case does not merit prosecution and a statement of reasons for that decision.

ECAB. Early Case Assessment Bureau: the Complaint Room ADA's who decide which felony cases will be presented to the Grand Jury.

"18B." A private lawyer assigned to indigent defendants on a case-by-case basis.

Felony. A crime punishable by more than one year in jail.

Grand Jury. A body of 23 persons who hear evidence to determine whether there is reasonable cause to believe (1) that a crime has been committed and (2) that the defendant committed the crime. At least 16 members of the jury must hear the evidence, and if at least 12 find that reasonable cause exists, they may vote an indictment.

Incompetent. Very different from "insane": an incompetent defendant is one who is incapable of understanding the proceedings or of assisting in his or her defense; one may be "insane" and still be "competent."

Indictment. The form by which a Grand Jury indicates that it has found reasonable cause and "accuses" the defendant of a crime. Under the New York Constitution, a defendant may not be prosecuted for a felony without being indicted by a Grand Jury.

Insanity Defense. The contention by the defendant that he or she is not guilty of a crime because at the time the crime was committed he or she, as a result of "mental disease or defect," lacked substantial capacity to know or appreciate either (1) the nature and consequences of his or her conduct or (2) that such conduct was wrong.

The Legal Aid Society. A publicly funded corporation that employs attorneys on a salaried basis to represent indigent defendants.

Misdemeanor. A crime punishable by up to one year in jail.

NYSIIS Sheet. Formerly "yellow sheet": the record of a defendant's prior arrests and the disposition of the cases, printed out by computer.

180.80. Section 180.80 of the Criminal Procedure Law, which states that a probable cause determination (either by the Grand Jury or by a judge at a preliminary hearing) must be made in a felony case within 3 days of arraignment. If such a determination is not made, the defendant must be released on his or her own recognizance.

Petit Jury. The normal trial jury: 6 members for misdemeanor cases, 12 for felonies. Jury verdicts must be unanimous at a trial, either "guilty" or "not guilty." If all members cannot agree, the jury is "hung," a "mistrial" is declared, and the case must be tried again.

Plea. The accused's formal answer to the charges against him or her: may be "guilty," "not guilty" or "not guilty by reason of mental disease or defect."

Predicate Felon. A defendant with at least one prior felony conviction within the last 10 years. Any new felony conviction carries a mandatory jail sentence of at least 1½ to 3 years.

Pretrial Hearing. The ground rules are determined for the trial of a case, usually brought on by a defense "motion to suppress" evidence, i.e., prevent its presentation to the jury.

"Pro Se." A defendant who appears without an attorney, conducting his or her own defense.

Reasonable Cause. Also "probable cause": facts and circumstances known on the basis of reliable information that would justify a person of reasonable caution in believing a crime had been committed.

ROR. Release on Recognizance: an evaluation, based solely on the defendant's roots in the community, of the defendant's suitability for release without bail. The recommendation is made without regard to the offense charged.

Side Bar Conference. The judge requests the attorneys to approach the bench.

30.30. Section 30.30 of the Criminal Procedure Law, which codifies the defendant's right to a "speedy trial" and prescribes the time limits within which the prosecution must be ready for trial.

"VDF." Voluntary Disclosure Form: a document given to defense counsel when the defendant is arraigned on an indictment that contains information about the case against the defendant.

Violation. A minor offense punishable by up to 15 days in jail. A conviction of a violation is *not* a criminal conviction and does not give the defendant a criminal record. *J.E.T.*

THOU SHALT NOT STEAL

Well, of course, you knew that. Or did you? Did you fully understand that in New York stealing may be larceny by trespassory taking, larceny by trick, larceny by embezzlement, larceny by false pretense, larceny by acquiring lost property, larceny by bad check, larceny by false promise, or larceny by extortion? Probably not.

Some of the concepts are self-explanatory, but some need explanation — the difference between "trick," "pretense" and "promise," for example.

You commit larceny by trick when you acquire property by misrepresenting your intentions with respect to it; i.e., you borrow someone's car for the purpose of selling it.

Larceny by false pretense means you obtained title by issuing a deceitful statement and that you did so with full intentions to defraud and the owner relied on your lies.

And you're guilty of larceny by false promise if, by a scheme to defraud, you obtain another's property by making a false representation of your future intentions or those of a third party.

Surely it's easier just to pick pockets (larceny by trespassory taking).*J.E.T.*

assaulting someone again); (c) punishment; (d) rehabilitation; (e) isolation (while in jail, Ms. Beastly will not be assaulting people on the street — she may be assaulting them in jail, but that's another matter entirely).

Since the purpose of the system is to give society control over the defendant, rather than to compensate the victim, the deck is frankly stacked in the accused's favor: before we take control of someone's life, we have to be sure it's the *right* someone. Would that we all had the acumen of the Great Detective. And would that

he had our kind of respect for individual rights.

Regarding sentencing, the procedures are complex. A "life sentence" does not necessarily mean Ms. Beastly is incarcerated and we throw away the key. Assuming the death penalty is not revived in the near future, the maximum sentence for a crime in New York is 25 years to life. That is, Ms. B. is sent to prison for a fixed minimum period (25 years) and a fixed maximum (life), the exact length of time to be determined later by the parole board on the basis of her adjustment and other factors.

The New York Penal Law divides felonies into categories and prescribes ranges of sentences for each. For the Class A felony of Murder in the Second Degree, the minimum possible sentence is 15 years to life and the maximum is 25 years to life. (Murder in the First Degree is the killing of a police officer or corrections officer, originally punishable by death.) The Class B felonies, e.g., Robbery in the First Degree, Burglary in the First Degree, carry sentences of up to 12½ to 25 years. Class C felonies, e.g., Assault in the First Degree, Robbery in the Second Degree, can be punished by a sentence of up to 7½ to 15 years. And so on, to Class E felonies, which carry a maximum of 4 years.

Certain felonies are considered "violent felonies"; those that involve possession, display or use of a firearm (or what appears to be a firearm) are considered "armed felonies." Each of these designations affects the possible sentence faced by the defendant. If our Ms. Beastly has a prior felony conviction within the last 10 years, the law prescribes mandatory jail time. If she is so unfortunate as to have a prior conviction for a "violent felony," that ups the ante significantly. So, should Ms. B. hold you up at gunpoint, forgetting that "C" felony conviction 9 years ago for stabbing her husband's mistress, she is now confronting a minimum sentence of 6 to 12 years. She has become a "second violent felony offender," and as such, can count on bars and cells in her future.

All of which leads me to my main point: Behave yourself.

Jeanne E. Thelwell is an assistant district attorney for the County of New York. Her views do not necessarily reflect those of the DA's office.

Chapter 7
STAKEOUT

OMINOUS TRACKING EXPEDITIONS

Spinsters, take note. The one place you're guaranteed not to find a villain is under the bed. There are far better covers than chenille. For instance, gorse; or, as the Americans call it, furze. Hundreds of mystery bad guys have loved the stuff, probably because their sallow complexions blended so well with its yellow flowers.

Of course, some gents preferred the moor, the weir, the copse, the gorge, the mine, the quarry, the bog, the fog, the forest or the hills. Regardless, all chose places abysmally bleak and rather inaccessible.

Take the moor. That is, if you can find it. It's up there somewhere in Yorkshire, but it's eluded many a visiting detective. How come? The local dialect. When a Yard man weaned on the sound of Bow bells asks, "Which way did he go?" the chap needs the skills of Henry Higgins to decipher the answer. Without them, the precise whereabouts of the moor — and the terror that stalks it — are lost to him.

Frankly, the area's not worth a postcard, anyway. Barren. Desolate. Dead. Let the scoundrel keep it to himself. He's welcome to it. The heath is no prize, either. What's scenic about scragg? It seems to have been put on this earth for one purpose: to scratch and mutilate a copper. The Inspector bent on a merry chase would do well to avoid it.

Escapees have a knack for sniffing out aesthetically ugly locales that prove physically trying to their hunters. Moreover, the rounders always head for them in weather that could shut down airports: the rain would intimidate Noah and the snow has a crack at wiping the Blizzard of '88 off the record books. A bobby's Mac is useless against such phenomena: poplin — even specially treated, even anchored with a muffler knit by the wife — has its limits.

Back in civilization, the mystery hero fares a mite better. The Saint purrs down the motorway in his magnificent Hirondel. James Bond zips along the mall in his supercharged, gimmick-rigged Aston-Martin. Arthur Crook speeds by the lights in his trusty yellow Rolls (after he's

Turn left at the graveyard, right at the dump; proceed till you reach a dead end.

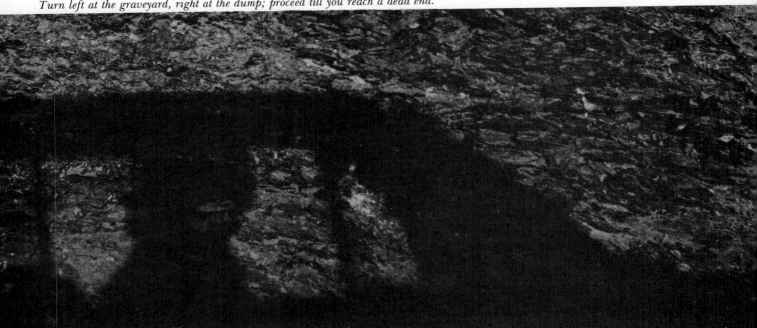

HOSTILE ELEMENTS

Fire
Brimstone
Locusts
Quicksand
Hailstones
Meteors
UFO's
Fumes
Debris
Leeches
Lightning bolts
Icebergs
Molten lava
God's wrath

made a shambles of his red jalopy). Obviously, their authors have signed them up for the deluxe tour.

Women, however, usually travel economy class. When Christie Opara is in pursuit, Uhnak makes her wait for the subway. (Haven't they read *Taking of Pelham, 1-2-3*? The thing's not safe!) It's probably a lot faster than Miss Marple pumping away on the vicar's bicycle, but it ain't much when you consider how Poirot lucked out. In his most famous case, *Murder on the Orient Ex-*

press, he rode a luxury train, and only had to tail suspects from one wagon-lit sleeping compartment to the next. Hardly enough action in that to scuff his patent leathers.

On the whole, writers have a cavalier disregard for their heroines' comfort. How many damsels, to their acute distress, have been forced onto the back of a high-strung, galloping horse? Plenty. Need it be added that their missions were aborted when their Gothic nighties caught in the reins? Probably not.

The writer who wouldn't dream of sending a man into the fray without a gun tucked in his shoulder holster, a spare strapped to his ankle, an extra cartridge in his attaché, the making of an incendiary flare in his belt lining, a loid in his hatband, a Swiss army knife in his fist and a beeper taped to his pectorals thinks nothing of having a woman go after the prey with naught but a hair ribbon to protect her.

Granted, a strip of grosgrain can be useful; when torn into bits and bread-crumbed along the trail, it can point the way out of the woods. But it will hardly save her life when the murderer's waiting with a pickax. And he often is.

Still, into the abyss, the chasm, the crevasse charges lassie, on author's orders. It's a scandal, really. You'd think just once she'd be allowed to bring along a candle *and* matches, a torch *and* long-lasting batteries, a gun *and* bullets. But no, she only gets grosgrain *and* evening slippers with tissue-paper soles. Not to mention a head

Double-clutch, accelerate in the hairpin curve, floor it on the straightaway.

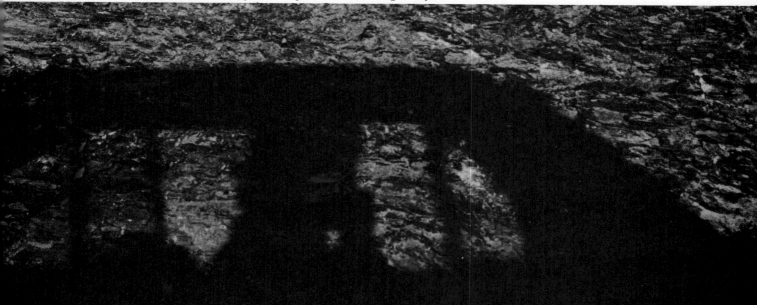

THE FIRST FLOATING WHODUNIT

Perpetrated by the Norwegian American Line, the two-week transatlantic mystery theme cruise is scheduled to depart Port Everglades on April 19, 1980. At sea and clinging to their life preservers will be crime novelist P. D. James, former CIA chief George O'Toole, retired FBI stalker Thomas McDade, London bobby Donald Rumbelow, New York private eye Anthony Spiesman and pandemonium expert Dilys Winn. Contact the wily Norwegian American Line, 29 Broadway, New York City, for further clues.

full of gorse.

Small wonder, then, that she never gets her man. He gets *her.* That's why the moor is littered with cashmere jumpers, Liberty print scarves, organdy sashes and tams with pompoms. That's why so many pairs of rayon knickers are clumped by the white heather, which despite its reputation has proved unlucky. If a writer had any sensitivity at all, he'd pack the poor girl a survival kit, or at least teach her the Scout motto:

Be prepared.

Irrespective of sex, tracking's no picnic. For one thing, you miss your sleep. To keep the runner from getting a head start, you're invariably pulled out of your warm bed at 3 A.M. For another, your socks get soggy. Puddles are the occupational hazard of tailers. Plus, there's all that slosh in the bottom of the police barge. Leaky boats are the lot of the follower's life. And: bloodhounds have been known to bite the wrong ankle. In the excitement, yours looks as tasty as the next guy's.

Armchair detectives, of course, have the best of it. They have underlings to do their legwork. Nero Wolfe's not so dumb when he hires Dol Bonner (and Archie and Saul) to do his tracking for him. He whisks upstairs in his elevator to check on his orchids while she has to pound the pavement to keep an eye on a rat. Clearly, chivalry is dead in the Stout books.

In John Buchan's *The Thirty-Nine Steps,* on the other hand, the woman is no worse off than the man. Both have to dog the quarry and are equally inconvenienced. He just seems to have more stamina than she has.

In *Rogue Male,* Geoffrey Household prefers the solitary tracker when he sends a man to assassinate Hitler. It's probably the best tracking expedition ever mounted. Dangerous, but believable.

Somewhere out there is Moriarty.

Think you're ready for him?

Call for reinforcements.   MATTHEW SEAMAN

WHERE?

Elizabeth Lemarchand

I have cherished a lifelong affection for Rudyard Kipling's Elephant's Child, with his engaging 'satiable curiosity and unsympathetic relatives, and also for the Six Honest Serving Men in the tailpiece to the story: WHAT, WHY, WHEN, HOW, WHERE and WHO. The day I sat down to start my first detective novel, it was like meeting old friends to find the Serving Men lined up in a row in front of my desk. At this stage, I had little idea of what I was in for, but it soon became all too clear that they were the workforce without which the job just couldn't be done. In short, I was involved with organised Union labour. I blinked and promptly made another discovery. They had elected WHERE as their shop steward. Apparently, they don't always. Enquiries among fellow crime writers have revealed that any one of them may top the poll.

To revert to WHERE. Quite honestly, he does bully me a bit. Not a word can be written until his particular queries have been answered to his complete satisfaction. For a start, he almost always insists on one of those time-consuming maps or plans as a frontispiece to the book. We have to go over the ground together, making an exhaustive survey. Last time, it was the twenty-seven miles of the Possel Way, a mediaeval pilgrims' road, not counting diversions to check up on an isolated farm and a Bronze Age burial chamber. WHERE has got a thing about distances, and whether characters of different ages and states of health can cover them in the times I suggest, using various modes of transport. On the whole, though, it's worse if the crime is committed indoors. This involves endless questions of access and egress, especially if the crime takes place in, say, a large boarding school or a Stately Home open to the public. WHERE is even particular about smells. Detective-Superintendent Tom Pollard was required to analyse a compound of furniture polish, crumbling stone and flowers in Brent, a fifteenth-century Stately.

But, as WHERE frequently points out, it is worthwhile to make sure that the lads will be erecting the edifice on a practicable site. And he does allow me a very free hand in choosing it. I can have a real place, or an amalgam of several real places, or somewhere that I've dreamed up myself. And when at long last he gives the All Clear, an astonishing thing happens. Don't ask me to explain it, as I just can't. I only know that a set of people hitherto unknown to me suddenly appear on the site, and I see at once that they belong there. I find that they all claim the patronymic WHO, but it is explained to me that this is merely a little convention, and that in the end the genuine one will be identified beyond any doubt. Anyway, manning problems always tend to crop up, don't they?

WHAT, WHY, WHEN, and HOW largely take over from here on, and push these WHO's around. Inevitably, disputes break out and there are hold-ups, go-slows and even all-out strikes that can last for weeks. And WHERE is always in the background keeping an eye on progress. Quite often, he spots a flaw and insists on part of the work being demolished and rebuilt. HOW is rather a trial, too. He keeps sending me off to consult lawyers, doctors, architects, motor mechanics and other specialists, and is so snooty about my being weak on ballistics, saying I cramp his style. But somehow the book even-

The sweet young thing perusing her Kipling is about to come upon Rudyard himself.

THE SECRETS OF THE PRIVET HEDGE

Amanda buried Matthew beneath it.
Tricia blackmailed Daniel beside it.
Estelle choked Bernard behind it.

tually arrives at the last full stop — or at least it has done eleven times so far.

I wonder why my books are so WHERE-dominated. It has been said I am a Cozy, so perhaps that has something to do with it. Cozies are addicted to their well-defined familiar home base, and do not hanker after the exotic, the corridors of power or the underworld. As a general rule, they prefer living in villages or small towns. Or it could be that being a woman writer I am influenced by some race memory of the Old Stone Age, when Mum stayed put with the children while Dad led a peripatetic existence in pursuit of enemies and fresh meat. But I think the most likely explanation is that I first came to detective fiction in the Golden Age of the twenties and thirties, and have ever since been under the spell of the master craftsmen of the period such as Dorothy L. Sayers and Freeman Wills Croft.

It was their vivid portrayal of the settings in which their impeccable plots unfolded that made the whodunits of this time so absorbing to me. The action was intimately associated with and conditioned by the milieu in which it took place, and this gave it conviction. In illustration, take that Sayers masterpiece, *The Nine Tailors*. We open the book and step straight into midwinter in the Fens. Blinded by snow, Peter Wimsey drives his Daimler slap bang into the dyke at Frog's Bridge, and we're off! Almost everything that comes after takes place in the unique setting of the Fenland, sometimes beautiful, often austere, and always harbouring that latent terror which we know in our bones will be activated with tragic results before the story ends.

Well, I may be under WHERE's thumb, but at least I am in very good company. And by the way, he has just butted in again with one of his ideas. This time, it's about compiling a new guide book. He suggests as a title "Explore Britain with the Crime Writers." Tour London and the Essex tidal creeks with Margery Allingham . . . the New Forest with Gladys Mitchell . . . and on . . . and on . . .

It's quite an idea, come to think of it. Any takers?

Elizabeth Lemarchand is the author of eleven mysteries. Her most recent is Suddenly While Gardening.

GARDEN SHENANIGANS

Rodger J. Winn, M.D.

What better way to soothe your torments than to putter in the garden — snipping here, pruning there, plotting, plotting, plotting all the while? Mother Nature, or so it seems, is extraordinarily solicitous of the revenge-prone. For you, she's evolved a veritable arsenal — the cook's ammo dump, in fact.

Her most popular poisonous commodity, acclaimed by murderesses throughout the ages, is aconite, which is available in monkshood. This showy perennial herb with its cluster of blue-purple flowers is a find for the economy-minded: all parts of the plant are fatal. The parsley-like leaves can be mixed in a salad, the horseradish-like roots can be stewed as a vegetable or minced to mix with pepper as an unusual spice. Its special piquancy comes from aconitine, an ingredient that coated Greek war arrows, added a kick to a Borgia dinner guest's wine and helped decide the succession to the French throne. Initially, the monkshood will taste sweet. By the time the bitter aftertaste hits, it's too late — the deadly properties are coursing through the intestinal tract. Watch carefully. When your table companion complains of a numbness in his tongue and a feeling of ice water in his veins, he's on the way out. But not before he experiences a few hours of even more extreme discomfort: thirst, vomiting, dim vision, twitching and, finally, irreversible weakening of the heart. Since there's nothing more to be done at this point, you might as well return to the garden for a new batch of monkshood (a good cook never runs out of staples).

Almost as beloved by the ill-nurturing set is the deadly nightshade. This crowded-looking plant with dull purple flowers and black berries is rife with several toxic substances, the most prominent being atropine. Now a mainstay in modern medical therapeutics, this alkaloid has a long, nasty history, particularly in the hands of practitioners of the black arts. It was named in honor of Atropos, the third Greek fate — you know, the one who cuts the thread of life. Telltale signs of atropine overdosage are fever, flushed skin, rapid heart rate and large, dark pupils. Beautiful women used to employ atropine as an eyedrop, and the deadly nightshade's nickname, belladonna, derives from this curious custom.

Even weeds are invaluable to the evil-hearted. Jimson weed, which like the deadly nightshade contains atropine and scopolamine, played a significant part in American history be-

---

NURTURING?

Mary, Mary, quite contrary,
How does your garden grow —
With toxic weeds
And lethal seeds
And corpses 'neath your hoe?

Suzy, Suzy, oh so choosy,
You've gone from bad to worse:
First mandrake root,
Then rhubarb shoot.
You're clogging up the hearse.

Helen, Helen, crafty felon,
You case the potting shed
For heavy rakes
And pointed stakes.
Will someone soon be dead?

cause of its toxological properties. A group of British soldiers dispatched to quell the Bacon Rebellion in 1676 brewed some leaves for a spot of refreshing tea. They ended up hallucinating and running amok. This occurred near Jamestown, Virginia, and ever since the town's name (somewhat shortened) has graced this ubiquitous weed. An important thing for the rushed cook to remember is that though Jimson can be hidden in the usual leafy salad, its toxins work much more rapidly when set to a rolling boil. For the gardener with advanced abilities, an interesting technique is to graft a tomato plant onto the Jimson weed. How nice to serve up home-grown tomatoes that differ from the ordinary varieties only in the large amount of natural poison found in their juices.

The classical horticulturist will consider hemlock a botanical must. It's a tall plant with a purple spotted stem, a large turnip-like root and umbrella-shaped clusters of small white flowers. The leaves resemble parsley; the root, parsnip; the seeds, anise. There are, consequently, ample means of disguise, though a little ingenuity will have to be applied to cover the disagreeable taste. The active poison is conitine, which paralyzes the muscles in a manner similar to that of the South American poison curare. The murderess who wishes to replay a Socratic scene can watch the slow ascending paralysis: first the feet, then the trunk, finally the muscles of the breathing apparatus. Since consciousness remains throughout the process, the little lady — like Xanthippe — can harangue till the end.

If one's garden contains a brook or marshy area, an alternative to the poison hemlock is the water hemlock, with its deadly ciccitoxin. The branch root closely resembles the thick single root of a parsnip, and even the most astute victim will fail to make the distinction. One swallow is all that's required to bring on foaming of the mouth and progressive convulsions. Though not as steeped in historical tradition as its cousin, the poison hemlock, water hemlock can be just as useful to those planning culinary carnage.

Diabolic practices need not always focus on the exotic, however. The most common ornamental shrub of our Southern states is the beautiful oleander, a plant perfectly suited to a murderess's endeavors. This fragrant evergreen shrub, with its magnificent white, pink and red flower clusters, harbors several cardiac toxins capable of destroying the rhythm of the heart. They can even be transferred in vapors, so building an oleander twig fire and proffering an oleander skewer will create the barbecue to end all barbecues.

For the full spectrum of possibilities to be realized, a murderess cannot rely on flowering plants alone. She must set aside a substantial area in her plot for *Amanita phalloides*, poison mushrooms. The colloquial name "toadstool" stems not from its use by frogs, but rather from the German word *todt*, meaning death. Even trained mycologists have difficulty telling the deadly from the healthy, and certainly the victim will not look for the jagged membrane at the base of the stalk as a tip-off. Old wives say that a mushroom should be discarded if it blackens a silver spoon. But even if it doesn't, a body can leave the table thoroughly enchanted. The next day, the enchantment will diminish as the nausea and diarrhea set in, to be followed by death of the liver cells within four more days. The poison is virtually undetectable, to the regret of the toxicological brotherhood.

The last item in the baneful garden is not really all *that* poisonous, but deserves inclusion because of its long association with the world of insidious doings: mandragora, or mandrake. This plant has a four-foot root that branches into what looks like legs and arms, giving it a human shape: hence its use in many phases of witchcraft. Pulling the root out is associated with pulling up the devil, with appropriate results. Shakespeare immortalized this in *Romeo and Juliet*:

> And shrieks like Mandrakes torn out of the earth,
> That living mortals hearing them run mad.

For this reason, it was deemed appropriate to have a dog nearby when digging for the root; it would absorb the shrieks. The place to find mandrake was under a gallows, since it supposedly grew best in ground fertilized with the semen of hanged men. From voodoo doll to narcotic to aphrodisiac, the mandrake has found its place in the sorceress's armamentarium. And rightfully belongs in your garden.

Rodger J. Winn is a physician in New Jersey.

THE ENGLISH CLASSROOM

An Education in Black and Blue

W. J. Burley

"Soap and education are not as sudden as a massacre but they are more deadly in the long run." Mark Twain said that, not me, but having taught for twenty years I wish I'd thought of it first. I find it surprising that so few fictional or real-life crimes are committed in schools. At least, it used to look that way to me on Friday evenings after a hard week.

Until comparatively recently, many English schools still owed something to eighteenth-century tradition, in which the principal object of education was to give a boy "Bottom" — or, in modern jargon, "Guts." (Fortunately, girls were not regarded as educable in this period that historians call the Enlightenment.) With simple logic, our forebears believed the best way to inculcate Bottom was to belabour that part of the anatomy in question as often and vigorously as possible. Gillray's famous cartoon, *Westminster School,* shows how this was done using an assembly-line technique, thus proving beyond all doubt that English academics anticipated Henry Ford.

With the change of century and the onset of Queen Victoria (with Albert), the building and governing of Empire became the dominant theme in educating the upper classes; the lower classes were merely taught to read, write, add up and be respectful. But the technique remained unchanged, though it seems that Empire-building required the addition of organized, vigorously competitive games and cold baths. You've no doubt heard that the Empire was won on the playing fields of Eton.

By this time, however, it had been established that girls were very nearly human and that there might be a case for trying to educate them — in separate schools, of course. No sex, please; we're British. Oddly, corporal punishment for girls never really caught on in schools. It was considered unsporting, like shooting a sitting duck, though fond upper-class mothers seem to have made up for it at home. A six-month correspondence in *The Englishwoman's Domestic Magazine* for 1869 was wholly concerned with the most effective ways of flogging daughters. The contemporary *Saturday Review* frowned on the discussion, claiming it might give foreigners a strange idea of English family life.

Be that as it may, the twentieth century has seen a decline of corporal punishment in schools, of the taking of cold baths and so, inevitably, of Empire. These trends have been specially marked since World War II, and now caning is rare in England — though I believe it is still practised by the Scots (a primitive race largely confined to their reservation north of the River Tweed).

The virtual disappearance of corporal

THE BELLES OF ST. TRINIAN'S

"Well done, Cynthia — it WAS *Deadly Nightshade."*

The first appearance of the Belles of St. Trinian's was in *Lilliput* magazine in 1941. The sketch was created by Mr. Searle as a means of cheering up two young friends who were unhappily in attendance at the St. Trinnean's School for Girls in Edinburgh (the school no longer exists). Five years passed before another St. Trinian's debacle was recorded, and the schoolgirls then became a regular feature of *Punch*. A movie based on their malevolent exploits starred Alastair Sim as the sanguinary headmistress. According to Malcolm Muggeridge, Mr. Searle finally killed off the Belles because he "had grown to hate the hateful little girls." Given their penchant for revenge, perhaps that was unwise.

"Dump those — they're harmless."

"Bang goes another pair of Knuckledusters."

"O.K. — now pass the bat's blood."

"Fair play, St. Trinian's — use a clean needle."

punishment has been a side-effect of coeducation, a rare phenomenon in England until the fifties. When a boy and girl cannot receive the same punishment for the same offence, Englishmen's well-known sense of fair play is outraged; so, faced with the alternatives of beating girls or not beating anybody, they seem to have chosen the latter. But a headmaster of my acquaintance who preferred the former, and set his female deputy to work with a hairbrush on a girl's bottom, lost his job.

Because of all this, whatever violence exists in English schools tends to come from the pupils — a situation not, I think, unknown in the States and not unprecedented here. Even at the height of the authoritarian bottom-bashing regime, there were instances of the assertion of Pupil Power. At one of our greatest public (which means private) schools, Marlborough, founded for the sons of clergymen, there was in 1846 a great uprising of ill-used youth. The school porter and his family were besieged in their lodge, which was partly demolished, the main schoolroom was laid waste and the headmaster's study wrecked. Astonishingly for the times, the revolt achieved the resignation of the headmaster.

My own experience leads me to agree with Kipling and Ronald Searle (of St. Trinian's fame) that the female of the species is more deadly than the male, and Betty Kane, the schoolgirl in Josephine Tey's *Franchise Affair,* is one of the most frightening figures in crime fiction. Girls are more subtle than boys and do not usually go in for direct violence; they are more likely to set about "fixing" their victims in just such a way as Betty Kane did. If you are a teacher, beware of the girl who looks at you with cold, dreamy eyes. (If you are a young male teacher, beware of the girl who looks at you.)

However, and despite all this, when I next use a school background for a crime novel, the plot will be concerned not with violence perpetrated on or by the pupils, but with the potentialities of the Staff Common Room.

Imagine a community that consists of disillusioned, elderly academics; disappointed virgins of a certain age; up-and-coming whiz-kids who still believe in a future; sultry young women and hot-blooded young men. Imagine these people having to work together and be reasonably polite to each other against the background of an examination system and pupil-power . . .

In such circumstances, murder is the least one can expect.

If you have read this far, you will be wondering why every playground (campus) in England is not littered with decaying corpses. But the answer is simple; it lies in that other great English virtue — self-control.

W. J. Burley is a retired schoolmaster and the author of seven detective novels featuring Inspector Wycliffe, including Wycliffe and the Schoolgirls.

THE REPORT CARD

Clearly there is room for improvement under the heading "Deportment."

In W. J. Burley's *A Taste of Power,* a coed grammar school is embroiled in an uproar.

In Helen McCloy's *Through a Glass, Darkly,* a girl's school is in such a state that Basil and Gisela Willing have to come investigate.

In Heron Carvic's *Picture Miss Seeton,* the spinster art teacher has to put down her charcoals and pick up her brolly to maintain order.

In Agatha Christie's *Murder with Mirrors,* gym class proves so strenuous that "old girl" Miss Marple has to step in and shape up the school.

In Julian Symons' *The Paper Chase,* Bramley Hall, a progressive coed public school, is seething with malcontents.

In H. R. F. Keating's *A Rush on the Ultimate,* croquet week, an annual event at a boys' preparatory school, demonstrates an original use of the mallet.

In Janet Caird's *Murder Scholastic,* an elderly teacher is hanged by a troublemaker.

Is it any wonder students and teachers alike breathe a sigh of relief when term is over?

AN (OVERDUE) TRIBUTE TO THE LIBRARIAN

Charles A. Goodrum

"The librarian did it."

"The *what*?"

"The librarian."

"What are you talking about? There wasn't a librarian in it."

"Sure there was. Don't you remember? No face, no front, no figure? Kept coming up with the facts about when Lord Aphid died and the black sheep son left before the will was read giving him two-thirds of Murgatroyd Hall to be shared with his real mother who actually was a maid to Lady Bea but disappeared when she became pregnant and came back as . . ."

"The librarian! Of course! I knew it all along."

Hundreds of these invisible librarians have been sprinkled through a century of mysteries, always called on to provide the clippings of the jewel robbery or the name of the doctor who officiated at the delivery. Where do they all come from?

Shortcuts, that's where.

Mystery writers are a cunning lot, and up to World War II libraries were used to establish a neat, instantly recognizable scene of the crime (one heavy inner door, traditionally closed, and a pair of French doors always kept locked but on this one occasion mysteriously . . .). The barely apparent librarian was written in to provide that needed clue and then allowed to evaporate, never to be missed again.

With *The Body in the Library*, ritual over-tones emerged. Agatha Christie said there were rules: "The library in question must be a highly orthodox and conventional library. The body, on the other hand, must be a wildly improbable and highly sensational body." Up through Christie, the library was either in the home of the detective or in the neighborhood scene of the crime; after Christie, the library became a public institution, accessible to all.

Following World War II, life changed for the authors. The cost of printing went up, and mystery novels began to shrink by thirty-two-page signatures. The text shrank steadily from ninety thousand words to fifty-five, and when

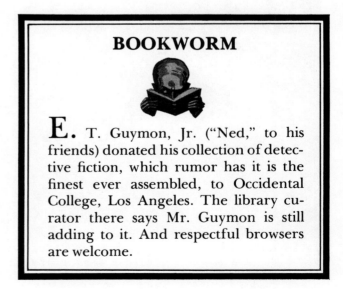

BOOKWORM

E. T. Guymon, Jr. ("Ned," to his friends) donated his collection of detective fiction, which rumor has it is the finest ever assembled, to Occidental College, Los Angeles. The library curator there says Mr. Guymon is still adding to it. And respectful browsers are welcome.

the pros had to decide whether to give up action or description, they killed the latter. Beginning about 1950, the stereotyped characters began to proliferate, stock settings got even thicker, and librarians truly came into their own.

If the novelists are to be believed, all female

If a borrower loses a book, is it fitting that she lose her life as well? What if she scrawls the murderer's name on the title page? Isn't that worse?

CORNELL CAPA/MAGNUM

librarians wear their hair in buns, stick pencils in with their left hands while saying *Shush!* across their right. They are timid, sexless, frightened and introverted. But the ones *I* knew before I went to library school were always six feet tall, talked in very loud voices and ran the Methodist Ladies Aid Society with an iron hand; since then, I've found them to be gracefully charming, to have marvelous senses of humor and a genuine feel for style, and to look a lot more like Goldie Hawn in *Foul Play* than Ruby Merton in *Murder in a Library*. And though everybody knows real librarians are female, in library mysteries the dead librarians are male at a ratio of two to one. Librarians acting as detectives — the crime solvers — are divided exactly evenly between the sexes.

Speaking of even, over the past fifty years half the mysteries where the body falls within a library occur in public libraries, and exactly the same number drop the corpses in college reading rooms or whatever. Weapons are scattered about: would you like to be done in with the rod from a catalog-card tray (Lawrence G. Blockman's *Death Walks in Marble Halls*), a falling bust of Louisa May Alcott (Jane Langton's *The Transcendental Murder*) or a paper-cutter blade (modesty forbids)? The commonest means of dispatch, however, is pushing the victim off a balcony (at least a dozen examples) or shoving the poor individual headfirst down a spiral staircase at the Library of Congress (Francis Bonnamy's *Dead Reckoning*).

If the library is supposed to be such a well-ordered world, how does the conflict arise? Same as in any other mystery. In Andrew Garve's *The Galloway Case*, the librarian is a blackmailer. In Gwen Bristow and Bruce Manning's *The Guttenberg Murders,* a will sets the trustees at each other's throats. Anthony Boucher's *QL696.C9* is a spy chase run among librarians, and in *The Distant Clue* the Lockridges analyze the librarian's questionable reading habits.

Mystery writers tend to be bookish themselves, of course, and they research much of their data in libraries. The result has been that a lot of the scenes-of-the-crime have been real institutions. Charles Dutton's *Murder in a Library* is modeled after Des Moines Public; Marion

When reading in the library, it is considered bad manners to move your lips and say the words aloud.

Boyd's *Murder in the Stacks* is meant to be Miami University's Alumni Library; the Blockman and Langton noted above are NYPL and the Concord Public, respectively; Morris Bishop's *The Widening Stain* is Yale's Sterling; Vernon Hinkle's *Music to Murder By* is Harvard's Widener.

Oddly enough, the writers usually know what they're talking about. Richard and Frances Lockridge had worked in the serials division of the New York Public Library, and the Mr. and Mrs. North mysteries frequently involve the 42nd Street branch. (The first time I ever saw the Lockridges in the flesh was at a New York Library Association meeting, where Frances described thinking up plots as she washed dishes and then told Richard to write them up. He responded by reminding us that this meant about five pages' worth of instructions, leaving him to work out two hundred pages of the book.)

Charity Blackstock (*Dewey Death*) had herself worked in the British national interlibrary loan center and could thus describe its activities with warmth and precision. You will recall that the gimmick in this volume was putting narcotic capsules in the center of microfilm reels and running a distribution system by library courier. Her breathless horror of d-o-p-e would never hold up today, nor could she get away with a villain taken right out of the Brontës, but her use of Dewey decimal numbers, as chapter titles, to reveal clues is still unique.

When I wrote the first of my Werner-Bok series, I made up some fictional blackmail, mass theft of rare books, mutilation of manuscripts, and two murders; between the time I sent the manuscript to the publisher and the time it appeared as a book, every single crime I'd created had occurred in one or more of the nation's leading university libraries. One of our West Coast public librarians became so concerned with the number of calls she was making to the police that she put together a dossier of incidents that had taken place in the previous twelve months; the administrator was shaken by her collection of encounters with "drunks, dopers, vandals, knife wielders, gun toters, purse snatchers, laser-eyed paranoics, raving schizophrenics, exhibitionists, peeping toms, child molesters, and sexual deviates of every stripe," and she recommended the preparation of a how-to manual for the staff. Libraries caught more fire-bombings at the beginning of the decade than any other institutional element. A friend of mine got involved in a strike with his deck attendants, who pulled out nearly a hundred card trays and poured ink down their lengths before tearing his reference books from their bindings.

Me? My next book will be set in a private library where all the books are identically bound and where there are only two doors. One is heavy, but usually closed, and the other is a French pair that unaccountably . . .

Charles A. Goodrum is the author of Dewey Decimated *and* Carnage of the Realm. *They feature the Werner-Bok, which has a manuscript room remarkably similar to the Folger, a rare-book enclave like the Morgan, display halls like the Huntington, and a great hall closely resembling that of the Library of Congress.*

TO LET:
ONE STATELY HOME

REPENT AND RUE, ESTATE AGENTS

**By Appointment to the lesser relations of the Queen,
specifically His Graceless, the disinherited Earl of Tetley,
and Her Ladyslip, the Baroness of Boudoir.**

THE BURNAM WOOD ESTATE

EDGE OF PLIGHT   *CONVENIENT TO BARSINISTER*

A SCURRILOUSLY LANDSCAPED AND UNSPORTSMANLIKE RESIDENCE

WITH CONVERTED CHARNEL HOUSE,
DESANCTIFIED PRIORY.

FORTNIGHTLY FOG INSURES PRIVACY

MAIN BUILDING INCLUDES:
blood-stained carpeting throughout
backstair tripwire
hand-cranked dumbwaiter
communication by bellpull
2 working fireplaces with
partially incinerated messages
tastefully furnished disaster suite
adjoining library

*One of four mourning rooms,
two with black crepe wall-hangings.*

**Good hunting,
natural burial facilities,**
*crooks
crannies
steep crevasses
and deaf neighbors.*

1929 ACRES
Principles Only;
Any Disreputable
Offer Considered

*The Weeping Wall, obscures sound of
gurgling victims.*

*Creaky front gate, fingerprint resistant,
fronting the moat.*

*Contaminated bog, brook.
Nearby bat colony.*

ILL MANOR

AGATHA 4 Miles   *CHRISTIE 7 Miles*

A GORGON

COUNTRY HOUSE OF GREAT CHARM

6 DECEPTION ROOMS,
NURSERY. LARDER, W.C.,
INVALID'S QUARTERS,
UNDERGROUND PASSAGE FROM
STUDY TO TRAIN DEPOT.

3 HEARSE GARAGE
STABLING FOR FULL
HUNT CLUB
MEMBERSHIP

WALLED GARDEN

ABOUT 11 ACRES
IN ALL

PRICE DETERMINED
BY TERMS OF WILL

*Sole Agents: REPENT AND RUE, **2** Gnarlybone Close, Chumpsford, Sussex.
Regional offices: Bath, Wry, Lye, Lie, and Nadir. Address Inquiries to Miss Miasma, Main Branch.*

UPSTAIRS: AN ASCENT INTO MAYHEM

A man's home may well be his castle, but a ranch house is a woman's salvation. A ranch lacks the mystery writer's booby trap: the Upstairs, consisting of the steps themselves, the landing, the long dark corridor, the loo, the boudoir — and the other set of steps, the ones that climb to the attic.

The character who closes Chapter Five by bidding her company goodnight, placing her hand on the banister and starting Upstairs will, pro forma, be saddled with trouble when Chapter Six opens. By now she should know better than to take that first step; one can only presume she wishes to please her author, who has his plot set on her maneuvering it.

The stairs Upstairs number forty-two. Twenty-seven and thirty-nine are the bothers. Someone has gotten out his pocket knife, unseamed the seams, raised the pile and taken a saw to the floorboards beneath. His rebasting was exquisite: Hardy Amies, the Queen's couturier, would have been dazzled. The carpet now covers air. As the Lady's foot strikes number twenty-seven, it sinks — clear to the ankle, with a loud snap. That she doesn't dangle even further is due to the fact that in quest of support her arm stretches to thirty-nine, which also gives way, and pulled thus in two directions (hand: north, then south; foot: south), she forbids her descent. Her back, of course, makes a handsome target, but luckily the newelpost knob, hurled from above by a mysterious presence, misses its mark.

Extricating herself with the aid of her butler, her husband, her husband's ward, the Colonel and the Vicar, the Lady of the Manor succeeds in attaining the landing. It is here that a shove administered by a member of her entourage (or: the landing ghost) propels her back to stair nineteen. Battered but undaunted (plucky are the Ladies who live Upstairs), she hobbles past the old trouble spots and retreats to the boudoir.

The boudoir — English translation of the French, "the Sulking Place" — proves little comfort. The bedside cocoa tastes peculiar and the bureau mirror reflects a shadow that may or may not be the Colonel (he and the Vicar are twins, don't you know).

Sleep being out of the question, the Lady whimpers across to the window and rests her cheek on the pane. Now, Upstairs windows are vile things: through them pass lightning bolts and cat-footed intruders; against them press desiccated branches and grinning faces, like the ones sliced into pumpkins. On occasion, they are punctured by a .38-calibre icicle bullet, which chips Milady's nail polish as she scrambles for safety under the vanity skirt. While pretzeled beneath the swathe of pink satin, she chances upon a ticket stub from a theater she's never been to and a receipt from Asprey's for a bauble she just that evening admired on the ward, who was extremely coy about acknowledging who it came from.

At this juncture, a pillow to weep into is *de rigueur*. The Lady snakes out her hand, gropes for it. The pillow inches closer, then appears to develop a mind of its own: instead of flopping in her arms, it collapses on her breathing apparatus — with a slight assist from a gloved ill-wisher. As her face turns blue, her head knocks against the table leg, cracking it. The vanity begins to list, like the *Titanic* on the morning of the fourteenth. Crystal atomizers slalom to the floor; glass shards prick her flesh; particles of powder haze her vision.

Thrashing from side to side, wondering

what provoked all this, she begins to hallucinate: the dressing screen is doing an impersonation of Birnam Wood. It's moving nearer, on a pair of size eleven wing tips polished to a high military gloss. As the Lady fades from consciousness, the screen looms above like the sword of Damocles. The next thing she knows, she's lying on her bed, choking on that peculiar-tasting cocoa being forced down her throat by the overeager Vicar. She glances round: the screen is in its proper place; the vanity is secure and upright; the perfume bottles and the powder shaker are just where they've always been; the curtains are drawn; there's no melting bullet on the otto-man; the pillow is propping her up; the wing tips have skedaddled away and her husband is leaning over her, stroking her arm, saying in pseudo-consoling tones, "Darling, you must have had a bad dream. Drink up, there's a good girl. We'll talk about it in the morning, when you're composed."

Not convinced she'll live till then if she remains in that room, she waits for the pious and perhaps perfidious to leave, then departs for the West Wing, plan-ning to barricade her-self in. Unfortunately, the West Wing is con-nected to the Main Wing by the Upstairs, whose unlighted cor-ridor walls are hung with ancestral por-traits. She brushes Great Great Great-Great Great Great-Great Great Great-Granddaddy, the first Duke of Mayday (1307–63); he blinks. Some-one has carved a peep-hole in his pupil, touched the paneling just so, step-ped into the secret niche and bided his time.

She screams. But corrid-ors Upstairs are drafty. The sound is blown away. Now, in mute terror, she hightails it to the loo and slams the door. Naturally, the bolt won't catch. Someone has set chisel to hinge, removed a screw, bent the plate and, for good measure, taped over the key fitting. Feverishly, the Lady searches for a weapon and spies the curling iron. As she attempts to rip the device from its plug, it slips out of her hand and into the tub, which happens to be filled with seven inches of water. Sparks fly (they always do Upstairs, where the wiring is invariably faulty); she feels an involuntary twitching of her thighs and forearms, then a cataclysmic jolt. She thuds to the tile, face down, indenting the bridge of her patrician nose and concaving her left incisor, which pierces her tongue.

When she lifts her head, she dimly notes that one of her stockings is no longer drying over the shower curtain rod with the other. Of course not: it's disguising the features of either her butler, her husband, his ward, the Colonel, the Vicar, the cat-footed intruder or the ghost of her GreatGreatGreatGreatGreatGreatGreat GreatGreatGranddaddy, the vengeful Duke.

Any mystery reader could have told the Lady to steer clear of the Upstairs Loo. For a woman in crime fiction, loo is short for "Waterloo." Unless she's interested in soaking in a blood bath, she should stay out of it.

If, by some wild stroke of good fortune, a Lady survives the stairs, the landing, the boudoir, the corridor and the loo, she's still not home-free. The Upper Upstairs awaits and teems with noises: the dragging sound in the attic; the drip-drip in the garret bedroom; the mewling in the nursery — though Tilda, poor thing, expired in the crib back in '27. Plucky still, the Lady of the Manor challenges the top. As she ascends, she's beset by spiders: friendly little folk, save one — somebody added a tarantula to the tamer varieties that spin out at the trapdoor. When she makes yet another foray into the reaches of a boudoir, the ceiling plummets, bringing with it a half-kilo of brackish water. And in the nursery, of course, is the crowning horror: nobody remembered to fire Nanny, who's been starving behind the door all these years.

Clearly, the only cure for the Upstairs is conflagration.

And a silver stake through the heart.

THE WINDOW SHADE PLOY

If the Upstairs window shade is down in the afternoon, it means the Lady of the House is being mugged in her own bedroom and the perpetrator is not anxious for the neighbors to observe his actions.

If it's pulled all the way up at midnight, it means the jewel thief forgot his flashlight and by the glow of the streetlamp is trying to decide if the Lady's diamonds are carbon or paste.

If it's being slowly lowered from valence to sill, once, twice, three times, it means (a) the Lady is semaphoring her boyfriend that the Master of the House is asleep and she's available for dallying in the solarium; or (b) the Master is alerting the driver of the Land Rover parked across the way that his wife is asleep and it's time to don the sheet, wield the truncheon and wish her a last sweet dream; or (c) the Inspector and his men have staked out the premises and all is well.

DOWNSTAIRS: A DESCENT INTO THE MAELSTROM

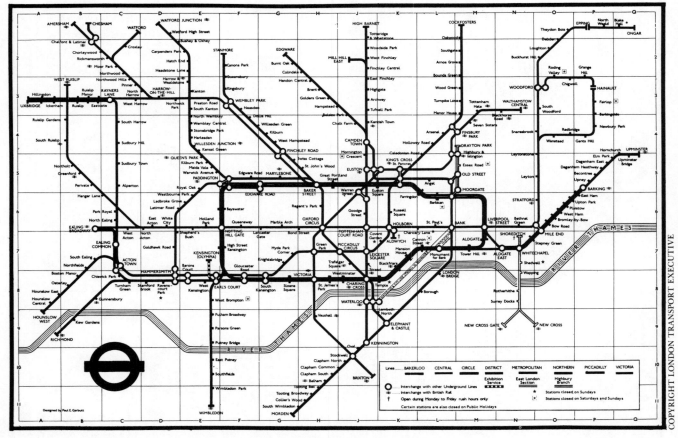

A token look at the underworld.

LONDON ON £5000 A DAY

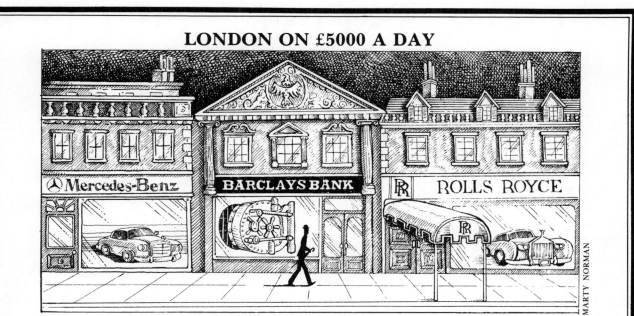

MARTY NORMAN

The rich are different; they can afford Berkeley Square.

Congratulations. Your forged sweepstakes ticket won. You are now a toff, a guv'nor, a nob, and you never have to eat at Wimpy's again.

Though the lorry you hot-wired is very nice, you might now prefer to drive a car that comes with a key in the ignition.

And perhaps you might exchange your one room with a view of the dump for something more substantial in Belgravia, with fine locks capable of keeping a person like your former self out.

The area you should be casing — sorry, window-shopping — is Berkeley Square. The neighborhood is charming. A Barclay Bank is flanked by a Rolls-Royce dealer and a Mercedes-Benz distributor. The bank, by the by, has an impeccable reputation, and it wouldn't hurt if a little of it rubbed off on you. It issues traveller's cheques in large amounts and possibly could be coerced — pardon, convinced — that you merit unlimited credit.

You should, of course, dress for your rendezvous with the teller. Your Marks & Sparks plimsolls, alas, will not suffice. A man of your means needs: a made-to-measure Savile Row suit; a monogrammed Turnbull & Asser shirt; a Cartier tie tack; ostrich leather shoes by Church; a 24K gold-hinged attaché case from Hermès; a Dunhill lighter; a furled umbrella from Gucci; a wafer-thin Piaget watch. And please, carry a newspaper, but don't cover your face with it.

You'll have no difficulty making friends. Berkeley Square residents will recognize you immediately as one of them: they, too, walk with their eyes cast down, and mumble. You will, however, have to learn to mumble in Etonian rather than Cockney. It's a matter of inflection, really, of prolonging the vowel instead of allowing it to make a quick getaway. And watch your idioms. In Berkeley Square, one keeps a stiff upper lip; one does not button it. A gentleman is reticent; he does not clam up. And make note: he tips his hat, not his hand.

One other small detail: do not walk on the grass. Square citizens cannot abide lawbreakers.

THE CASTING COUCH CAPER

Charles Champlin

There are some hard truths that have to be faced by those of us who love both mysteries and movies.

One is that classical mysteries have rarely made good movies. Another is that there have been amazingly few women as *central* figures in mysteries, despite the fact that so many of the most popular and prolific creators in the field are themselves women.

Agatha Christie's Miss Jane Marple stands almost alone. Much more often, the women of mystery are only adjuncts to the men — vaguely seen if sympathetic helpmates who occasionally set plots in motion and sometimes thicken the stories by falling into jeopardy, but who most commonly serve simply as sounding boards against which the menfolk — or authorfolk —

WHO SHOULD PLAY NANCY DREW?

Bonita Granville introduced Nancy to the screen in 1939. One year and three movies later, she hung up her deerstalker. Plucky though Tatum O'Neal and Brooke Shields may be, they're getting a little long in the tooth for the role, but Andrea McArdle just might hazard it.

can bounce their ideas. ("What if it wasn't Harry who drugged the pigeons after all, Cynthia?")

Nigel Strangeways' great and good friend Clare Massinger, Amanda Campion with her striking red hair, Roderick Alleyn's Troy, even J. P. Thatcher's supportive Miss Corsa, are all reactive rather than active, just the way women in the movies used to be if they weren't played by Bette Davis, Barbara Stanwyck or Rosalind Russell.

But the movies, in the era of Jane Fonda, have changed. Since in any case mysteries have to undergo heavy adaptation to become movies, it would be tonic and timely to upgrade the women's roles as well as the star power of the actresses who play them.

Rejuggling the male-female balance in mysteries would also help with another problem, which is that mysteries (as opposed to related forms like thrillers) make rather static films. Deduction is good for the brain but bad for the camera because it is largely unphotographable. Also, those talky and interminable denouements in the library are about as much fun to watch as the closing credits. (Alfred Hitchcock has for good reason usually dealt in suspense rather than mystery.)

Murder on the Orient Express and *Death on the Nile* squeaked by on the strengths of all-star casting, lavish production values, frequent and elaborate flashbacks (acting out all the alternate solutions) and, of course, two of Agatha Christie's most spectacularly improbable plots. Even so, exposition and ennui ran a close race, and all the

William Morris, theatrical booking agency, September 1938. The casting call for The Popcorn Murders *(it was never filmed) drew seventeen gum-chewers, all of whom swore they never stuck it to the bottom of their seats.*

élan of Albert Finney and Peter Ustinov was needed in their successive portrayals of Hercule Poirot fingering the guilty.

The point is that mysteries, for all their difficulties as structures for movies, have those vivid figures. The mysteries that worked best on screen had, of course, the brightest stars to ease the pain of the exposition: Margaret Rutherford as Miss Marple, Basil Rathbone as Holmes (no one else has come close), the various Poirots, Warner Oland as Chan, William Powell and Myrna Loy as Nick and Nora Charles.

It is time some of the classic mysteries (and mystery teams) were recast in both senses — rethought and repeopled — and I've made a few modest proposals. You don't hire Maggie Smith or Julie Andrews merely to wave goodbye and say, "Do be careful, dear." The men and women have to be partners in peril, in a tradition that has been allowed to languish since Nick and Nora drank their solutions even as they discovered them.

The mind boggles, but pleasantly, I think, to consider Burt Reynolds and Jill Clayburgh reviving the Charleses in pursuit of a thin man. Or Warren Beatty and Diane Keaton as Perry Mason and Della Street (a very large-scale movie that would also be an homage to Erle Stanley Gardner).

Margery Allingham's Albert Campion, the most deceptively mild-mannered man since Clark Kent, is long overdue to be filmed well,

MY TRADEMARK

Elsa Lanchester

It's nice to have been in a classic. I still get some ten letters a week about that role.

That was my own fuzzy, untidy hair. They brushed it and combed it and made four little braids, and then they put a sort of little house on top — a wire cage, really — and anchored it with pins. I remember lots of pins. They added two white hairpieces, one at my upper temple, one at my lower temple. The hairdresser was meticulous about it.

It took two hours to draw in the little scars and go over them in red. The make-up man thought he was some kind of god because he created The Bride of Frankenstein.

CULVER PICTURES

and who better to play him than the deceptively fey Peter O'Toole? Mrs. Campion had an independent career of her own, designing fighter aircraft and much else, and the fiery independence of Vanessa Redgrave seems very appropriate casting.

Many of the later entries in Colin Watson's Flaxborough stories have been stolen from Inspector Purbright by that mischievous con person Lucilla Teatime. Elizabeth Taylor seems absolutely ripe to be Miss Teatime, leading Purbright a merry chase (and he played by Alec McCowen, memorable in Hitchcock's *Frenzy*).

Fidelity Dove, little known now, was a stunningly beautiful supercriminal, leading a gang of specialists and operating as a kind of female Doc Savage on the other side of the law in novels by Roy Vickers. Let us bring her back by all means, and let her be Lesley-Anne Down, the stunningly beautiful accomplice of Sean Connery in *The Great Train Robbery*.

The Emma Lathen mysteries starring merchant banker J. P. Thatcher are authentic, contemporary and wonderfully active. Gregory Peck would make a sensational Thatcher. Julie Andrews as Miss Corsa, Thatcher's sedate but strong-willed and super-efficient secretary, would make for much more involvement, a more equal partnership, even the possibility of a late-blooming romance.

A team that actually worked as a team, Gardner's Bertha Cool and Donald Lam, could well be revived as a comedy mystery act, possibly with Shelley Winters and Jack Weston (from *The Ritz* and much else).

The problem, always, is to find American castings. The English have such a hold on the mystery form, and the LAPD is just not an adequate alternative for New Scotland Yard. Fortunately, there are so many international film stars who are English that it works out all right.

Michael Caine and Maggie Smith, fresh from *California Suite*, would get on nicely as Roderick Alleyn and his painter wife, Agatha Troy. Albert Finney (out from under the Poirot makeup) would make a thoughtful Nigel Strangeways, with Susannah York as his sculpting friend Clare Massinger. And, pausing for whimsy, how about John Lennon and Olivia Newton-John as Lord Peter Wimsey and Harriet Vane — a musical version, naturally.

Another now-forgotten figure, Sister Ursula, the sleuthing nun, might be a grand outing for Glenda Jackson, who proved in *Nasty Habits* that she can do a (mother) superior job.

It's hard to think of anyone other than Margaret Rutherford playing Miss Marple, but Angela Lansbury is about to become a younger Jane. EMI has planned two movies in which Miss Lansbury will play the St. Mary Mead sleuth. Her credentials for murder are impeccable: she was the mother in *The Manchurian Candidate*, the hard-drinking, highly sexed author in *Death on the Nile* and the wonderfully macabre meat-pie maker in Broadway's *Sweeney Todd, the Demon Barber of Fleet Street*. Yet I would have commended you to Mona Washbourne, the English character actress who was Tom Courtnay's mother in *Billy Liar* and Glenda Jackson's maiden aunt in *Stevie*. She would have been wonderful.

P. D. James' poet-detective Adam Dalgliesh is a very promising movie figure, vigorous but thoughtful. Sean Connery, a more versatile and sensitive actor than he could show as 007, would bring the proper Scot's burr. But he should, I feel, team up with Mrs. James' other delightful character, Cordelia Gray, the private investigator from *An Unsuitable Job for a Woman*, to be played by Julie Christie.

Some roles, incidentally, should not be revived or recast. Sherlock Holmes, for example, should be retired for at least the balance of this century, before any further damage is done to his memory and one last film proves conclusively that he was Dr. Crippen and Jack the Ripper rolled into one.

Father Brown's biretta should be retired unless Sir Alec Guinness can be persuaded to wear it again. The estimable Kenneth More has done him for British television, but he isn't *my* Father Brown. Similarly, Monica Vitti should be allowed permanent possession of Modesty Blaise, and if she doesn't want to swing into action again, so be it.

Poirot, too, can take it easy for a while. There are so many other mysteries to solve.

Charles Champlin is film critic for the Los Angeles Times.

Tallulah Bankhead had to toss her diamonds and mink overboard in *Lifeboat*. It was absolutely devastating, darling.

Judith Anderson intimidated Joan Fontaine in du Maurier's *Rebecca*. Philip MacDonald wrote the screenplay.

HITCHCOCK'S HEROINES

Joan Fontaine with Cary Grant in *Suspicion,* the story of a tormented (with good reason) bride.

Tippi Hedren, Sean Connery's favorite safecracker, in *Marnie.*

Margaret Lockwood searched for the elusive Miss Froy in *The Lady Vanishes,* based on the Ethel Lina White novel *The Wheel Spins.*

Ingrid Bergman, resting between takes on the *Spellbound* set. Like Fontaine and Grace Kelly, she appeared in several of Hitchcock's films. Other of his heroines include: Eva Marie Saint, Barbara Harris and Kim Novak.

FOLLOW THAT THEME

Bernard St. James

There is a story, probably apocryphal, that a Hollywood producer once told a composer who was scoring his film, "Give the heroine flutes and use a saxophone for the gangster's moll." For one thing, I doubt whether most studio moguls would know the difference between a flute and a sax. Still, movie music does help determine — and manipulate — the way we feel about characters, and settings, and situations. And good girls *do* seem to inspire romantic themes, whereas their shadier sisters get sleazier, cheaper backgrounds.

In Otto Preminger's *Laura,* based on the Vera Caspary novel, the lady of the title (Gene Tierney) doesn't appear until several reels into the film — except as a portrait over the mantel. But thanks to David Raskin's unforgettable theme, we've fallen in love with her well before her surprise entrance. Now, as attractive as that painting is, it's doubtful whether we'd be this moved without that music. More likely, we'd be wondering whether detective Dana Andrews wasn't a little "off" to become so besotted with a picture. That theme also tells us that Laura couldn't be a murderess: no villainess ever had such lush music written for her.

The recording of "Laura," with lyrics by Johnny Mercer, sold in the hundreds of thousands and has since become a "standard." The only other music from a mystery or suspense movie to suffer that happy fate is "Stella by Starlight," from Victor Young's score for the supernatural thriller *The Uninvited.*

There are, of course, more offbeat love themes. In the 1946 version of *The Big Sleep,* Max Steiner wrote a wryly romantic melody for Lauren Bacall. It's the musical equivalent of the verbal wisecrack, saucy but basically nice, and once again we've been tipped off that the lady's not for burning. (Remember, this was still the day of the electric chair.)

In an even more offbeat love story, Steiner wrote some very pretty music for King Kong's girlfriend, Fay Wray. More than just a theme, it speaks for the fascination and tenderness the giant gorilla feels for this terrified woman and therefore becomes the great romantic motif for The Love That Could Not Be.

This music almost didn't get written. RKO Radio Pictures had spent $650,000 on *King Kong*, which was big money in 1933 and the most the studio had put into any picture. When the executives screened the rough cut (a print without sound effects or music), they were disappointed. Kong looked too mechanical, not enough like a real gorilla, and they felt the public wouldn't like the film. To cut down on their investment, they told Max Steiner to score it with old tracks. The producer, Merrian C. Cooper, disagreed. He took Steiner aside and asked him to compose the best score he possibly could; he himself would pay for the work.

Steiner hired an eighty-piece orchestra and ran up a bill for $50,000. But it was worth every penny, for Steiner's score literally makes the film click. Just turn down the sound the next time it's shown on TV. With most movies relying heavily on special effects, that wouldn't make a bit of difference. With this one, it does: Kong *is* silly-looking and mechanical. Turn the sound back up, and the magic returns.

Steiner was a fine film composer, but personally I think Franz Waxman was even better — certainly more innovative. Who can ever for-

DEATH BY DIVA
Theodor and Jean Uppman

In *Tosca* (music by Giacomo Puccini, libretto after Sardou's play *La Tosca*), Tosca knifes Scarpia. In *Lucia di Lammermoor* (music by Gaetano Donizetti, based on Sir Walter Scott's novel *The Bride of Lammermoor*), Lucia dips a dagger into her bridegroom, Lord Arturo Bucklaw. In *Faust* (music by Charles Gounod, based on Part I of Goethe's poem), Marguerite kills her baby — well, wouldn't you if Faust were its father? In *Jenůfa* (music by Leoš Janáček, after Preissová's novel on rural Moravian life), Kostelnicka drowns her stepdaughter's out-of-wedlock child. In *Lucrezia Borgia* (music by Gaetano Donizetti, libretto based on Victor Hugo's tragedy), Lucrezia poisons one and all, and in *Medea* (music by Luigi Cherubini, libretto based on Euripides' tragedy) Medea runs the gamut with her killings.

And finally, let's not forget the Gretel of *Hansel and Gretel* (music by Englebert Humperdinck — the original — with a libretto based on the Grimm's folk tale), who shoves the witch into the oven and turns her into a cookie.

Theodor and Jean Uppman are an opera singer and an opera writer, respectively.

---

get that moment when Dr. Pretorius proudly announces "The Bride of Frankenstein!" to a cacophony of impressively scored bells?

And, as Tony Thomas pointed out in his book *Music for the Movies*, Joan Fontaine was right: Manderley was haunted — not by the spirit of Rebecca, but by Franz Waxman's evocative score. In another Hitchcock thriller, *Suspicion*, Miss Fontaine (in those days truly a damsel in distress) suspects her charming but irresponsible new husband (Cary Grant) of plotting her murder. To mirror her troubled state of mind, and unsettle ours, Waxman wrote a beautiful but eerie love theme, scoring it for electric violin, clarinet and vibraharp.

Interestingly, one of the most forceful pieces of movie music was lifted from an operetta. For Hitchcock's *Shadow of a Doubt*, Dimitri Tiomkin appropriated Franz Lehar's *Merry Widow Waltz* for the lead character, an unsavory gentleman whom the press called "the Merry Widow Murderer." I was a kid when I first saw that film, and I've never been able to listen to the music without thinking of Joseph Cotten menacing gentle Teresa Wright as she ... begins ... to ... suspect.

Normally, a movie is scripted, then filmed, and then scored, but Billy Wilder once reversed this process. He loved Miklos Rozsa's *Violin Concerto*, which had been commissioned, performed and recorded by Jascha Heifetz (RCA Victor LSC 2767), so much that he developed a screenplay around it. It became *The Private Life of Sherlock Holmes*; no doubt, Wilder was influenced by the fact that Holmes played the violin. He told Rozsa that the somewhat edgy first movement suggested Holmes' addiction to cocaine; the second, a lady spy; and the turbulent third, somehow, the Loch Ness Monster.

Wilder wanted Rozsa to score the film, using the concerto as a basis. The composer agreed, though since he'd had no images in mind when he wrote it, he had to alter the timings to fit the scenes.

Had you paid closer attention to the music, you would have known immediately that the lady was a spy. Mycroft did. But then, perhaps he'd heard the record.

Bernard St. James is the author of The Witch, *a haunting novel with real-life antecedents.*

JEMIMA SHORE: TELLY DETECTIVE

Antonia Fraser

There's nothing new about a female detective: at the very idea, Miss Marple would turn in the grave I fear she must be in, as would Ariadne Oliver, to say nothing of Harriet Vane. Cordelia Gray is very much not in her grave, but she too would rightly be astonished if someone came along and presumed to call herself unique because she was an investigator.

So, in creating Jemima Shore, if I wanted to break new ground I had to make her a new *kind* of woman — a star. The point about my Jemima is just that.

I was struck by the fact that today, for the first time, there are quite a few glamorous and intelligent women who have chosen their own profession and as a result have gained fame as well as independence. This phenomenon of fame has a lot to do with television: hence Jemima's genesis as a star of that medium. She is not, however, a "TV personality." Rather, she has something of Barbara Walters about her, something of Britain's Joan Bakewell, the intellectual beauty who made *Late Night Line-Up* so famous in the sixties (and was described, to her justifiable annoyance, as "the thinking man's crumpet").

It occurred to me that I could use this attribute in an amateur detective, because the general public *do* turn to their television goddesses (and gods) for advice, encouragement and help off screen as well as on. In my time, I've smiled warmly at television stars across a crowded room under the impression that I knew them really

In the Thames Television production of Quiet as a Nun, *Maria Aitken appeared as Jemima, David Burke as Tom Amyas and Susan Engel as Sister Agnes. The mini-series was shown to English audiences in April of 1978. Lady Antonia was not the first woman author to have her mystery aired; that honor goes to Dorothy L. Sayers. In addition, Wilkie Collins, Colin Watson and Peter Lovesey have also had their detective novels televised. For people who disdain the little black box, London has forty-five legitimate theatres in the West End, thirty-five fringe theatres, ten lunch-time theatres, fifty cinemas (West End), one hundred five local movie houses and eighteen film clubs. It's a wonder anyone finds time to get any reading done with all that going on.*

well — only to find we were total strangers except for this peculiar television intimacy. Thus it seemed quite legitimate that Jemima Shore should be called in to investigate any number of hideous and horrible crimes, just because the public had got used to seeing her on the telly as "Jemima Shore, Investigator," probing juvenile delinquency, housing shortages, women's rights, racist conflicts, the political situation in Northern Ireland, and so forth and so on.

Part of Jemima's independence lies in the fact that she's not only unmarried but also — by choice — childless. The latter is probably the more important of the two. She is unencumbered by the traditional problems and pleasures of a family, yet at the same time she's immensely feminine. A fantasy perhaps? Certainly a little of my fantasy (life without six children, for example, what that would be like). When my brother groaned, "I can't bear Jemima Shore,

she's so beautiful and she's always right," I knew I had captured her. After all, as an investigator, she *should* be right.

Since any discussion of an intelligent and powerful woman has to get round to the subject of Elizabeth I quite soon, I gave Jemima Shore some of the physical characteristics of the Tudor Queen (golden-red hair, white skin, beautiful white hands, a virginal air). Like the Queen, she has a great many suitors. On the other hand, this being the twentieth century, her virginal aspect belongs to her looks, not the way she behaves. In fact, her very name is intended to be a combination of the repressed and the unrepressed: Jemima is a good seventeenth-century Puritan name, whereas Shore is taken from the beautiful dissolute mistress of Edward IV, Jane Shore.

Lady Antonia Fraser is the author of Quiet as a Nun *and* The Wild Island, *featuring Jemima Shore.*

STARRING TESSA CRICHTON

Like most actresses, Tessa Crichton refuses to give her age. Once, when she was preparing to go on, her director, author Anne Morice, told her to say she was twenty-eight, but then thought better of it and cut the line before the actual performance. In all of Tessa's fourteen-book career there's not one mention of how old she is. Nor will that little secret be divulged (except here) in future appearances. Says Miss Morice: "I plan on keeping Tessa ageless."

What a lucky break for her. She'll never have to worry about the actress's bugaboo, crow's feet, or fret that one day she'll only be suitable for character parts — or even worse, be unable to remember her lines. And as an extra plus, she'll never have to get nervous that her husband will leave her for a younger woman. How could he? There will never be a way of telling who's younger.

Miss Morice decided to make her amateur sleuth an actress because "the work takes you so many places and it's one of the few backgrounds I do know well." Understandable. Her father was a playwright, her sister is an actress, her eldest daughter worked at the Royal Court, her brother-in-law is a theatrical producer and her two nephews, Edward and James Fox, have had successful stage careers. "I've always been interested in theatre," admits Miss Morice, "and, of course, from the family one hears *endless* gossip." Recently, two of her own plays have been mounted — one, a crime thriller — and she's itching to try her hand at adapting Tessa's adventures for a half-hour TV series.

Who should play Tessa? At the moment (she changes her mind frequently), Miss Morice's first choice would be English stage star Felicity Kendall. "She's not particularly pretty, but she's quite bright and funny." Should the opportunity present itself for Miss Kendall to act Tessa, she better lay in a supply of throat lozenges.

Tessa is one of mystery fiction's great talkers. Clearly, she doesn't believe in the typical British reserve. What makes her bearable is her crackling, slightly acidic wit. Still, Miss Morice confesses, "She annoys me sometimes when she's so cocky and sure of herself. She's an extremely curious young woman."

More often than not, Tessa is bending the ear of her cousin, Toby. When an attack of detective fever comes upon her, she rings "Roakes Common 3206" and the two of them theorize away. Their phone bills must be atrocious.

Like Miss Morice's theatre connections, Toby is "not exactly the soul of discretion." He loves a good gossip, and when Tessa visits he leads her to his summerhouse and the two yammer happily about whether thus-and-such a motive might be possible and whether this-one, that-one could have done it. Tessa, however, takes his conclusions with a grain of salt. In *Death and the Dutiful Daughter,* she acknowledges that "most of Toby's well-known facts were invented by himself on the spur of the moment."

Of more help to Tessa are her conversations with her husband, Robin Price. He "served his apprenticeship in the Dedley C.I.D. before his promotion and transfer to Scotland Yard." Though he tries to keep out of his wife's "cases," he usually finds himself checking facts for her at Headquarters and listening to her conjectures. On one occasion he was hauled out of bed when Tessa awoke from a nightmare and told him he had to drive to Stornhampton to save a life. He did, and she was right.

Miss Morice cheerfully admits that she doesn't know the slightest thing about real-life police procedure, and anyway, she doesn't think a crime novel should concentrate on the true stuff. This, perhaps, accounts for Robin's reticence in talking about his work, even to Tessa. In a general way, he'll outline a case, but the nitty-gritty is rarely specified. Tessa accepts this. She blithely states, "He's away on business," and then concentrates on her own, without giving his another thought.

Tessa and Robin met in Stornhampton and spent the first year of their marriage there. They had the rent-free loan of a friend's gardener's cottage, which boasted a clipping from the famous Hampton Court vine. Upstairs from them, in a self-contained flat, lived Albert, their chum's well-scrubbed Belgian butler/chauffeur, and his nameless wife, whom they simply referred to as "Albert's wife." She prepared their meals.

Miss Morice's pet peeve is being confused with Tessa. "We're not at all alike. I suppose it's a natural mistake that readers make and one of the perils of writing a first-person narrative."

For the record and despite her protestations, Miss Morice does share two traits with Tessa. She is wittily voluble and is addicted to mysteries.

Her writing began as a lark. She and her husband (Alex Shaw) were living in Paris. Their youngest son was still in school in England. Miss Morice would pop over to see him every other month, and when she returned to France, her husband would pounce on the thrillers she brought back with her. She decided to take a crack at one and finished it in six months. She then submitted it to Macmillan, and they accepted the manuscript and have kept her busy producing a new Tessa every year for the past dozen or so.

Says Miss Morice, "I think crime stories should have humor and a moral. I think the bite has gone out of them, though, since the repeal of capital punishment. It's not terribly interesting when you know the killer is going to get off with serving no more than eight years."

A disciple of the "puzzle" school, she offers a reader sneaky endings, civilized middles and comfortable beginnings, which tell you in a page or two that you're in the company of a classic detective-story writer. Her own favorite authors include "All the dead ones, I'm afraid — G. K. Chesterton, E. C. Bentley, Agatha Christie, Rex Stout. I adore Rex Stout. I still believe if I walk down 35th Street, I'll find Wolfe's townhouse, and if I look up, I'll see his orchids growing on the roof."

Could Tessa be Lily Rowan's English cousin? You have fourteen chances to deduce a similarity. May we suggest you start with *Scared to Death*? Miss Morice's son is in that one; she calls him Ferdy and describes him as "feckless." And if you're dying to go to a house party, try *Death in the Grand Manor*. And if you want to read Miss Morice's own favorite, solve this mystery: Which one is it? The only clue she offers is that it was the first she wrote, though in America, not the first one published.

Maybe Tessa will tell you the title. If you promise not to reveal her age.

SO YOU WANT TO BE AN ACTRESS

Perhaps you should reconsider.

In Anthony Berkeley's *Trial and Error*, Jean Norwood, celebrated stage actress, is shot dead.

In S. S. Van Dine's *The Canary Murder Case*, Broadway star Margaret Odell, who appeared in the Follies sporting a few canary feathers and not much else, is strangled.

If that doesn't deter you, think about what happened to the unfortunate Miss Campanula in Ngaio Marsh's *Overture to Death*. Seated just offstage, as is the wont of accompanists, she was about three notes into the local parish's rendition of the Rachmaninoff *Prelude in C Sharp Minor* when she hit the soft pedal, which triggered off a gun, which ended her career.

STAGE FRIGHTS

Solomon Hastings

I have an inborn antipathy toward goodness. When I see a production of *Lear,* I root for Goneril and Regan. I think Medea magnificent, Lady Macbeth divine, and if it were up to me, no curtain would ever rise on a stage unless there was at least one anti-heroine on it. Over the years, I've developed a particular fondness for some especially loathsome characters. Perhaps you'll be captivated by them, too.

"Aye, mad, mad. That is the word. I feel it here." (Places her hands on her temples.) "Do not touch me — do not come near me — let me claim your silence — your pity — and let the grave, the cold grave, close over Lady Audley and her secret." (Falls. Dies. Tableau.)

Lady Audley in
Lady Audley's Secret
by C. H. Hazlewood

Lady Audley, alias Lucy Graham, alias Helen Talboys, first appeared in *The Sixpenny Magazine,* but within a year of her hard-cover debut (1862), three different dramatizations of the Mary Elizabeth Brandon novel were playing concurrently in London. While in the book Lady A. was very much the innocent victim of Dickensian circumstances, stage versions turned her into a Circe of wickedness. C. H. Hazlewood's script had her bashing a blackmailer on the head, shoving him down a well, attempting to murder two witnesses and, generally, behaving like a fiend. Unfortunately, Hazlewood forgot to reveal what her "secret" was, but who can blame him with all the distractions? Still, audiences adored the play and it became the mainstay of touring companies, rivaling *East Lynne* in popularity.

"Now, my name is Mother God Damn! I deal female to male, my trade is flesh! I have a house where fate of every sort runs very quickly — one lap ahead of death — and now I, too — have many, many, many boxes of gold money because I keep the largest brothel in the world!"

Mother God Damn in
The Shanghai Gesture
by John Colton

Mother G.D. and her opium-shrouded goings-on at 17 San Kaiou Road opened on Broadway February 1, 1926. Fifteen years later, Florence Reed, who originated the role, was still playing to packed houses, albeit provincial ones. Mother kept her staff locked in gilded cages, auctioned off a naked Lost Petal to the Junk Captain in front of horrified dinner guests, and for a grand finale pushed her daughter Poppy down three flights of stairs to a spectacular death. (Funny she should have been so upset: Poppy was merely an alcoholic, dope fiend and nymphomaniac.) In England, the play had repeatedly been denied a license by the Lord Chamberlain, who ultimately relented — to the glee of most audiences. "Just one long string of dreary dirt," sniffed Sir Gerald du Maurier when the play was finally presented with Gladys Cooper in the title role. Mr. Hays concurred, with the result that a film was not made until 1941. And then only with drastic changes: Mother God Damn was renamed Mother Gin Sling, made the proprietor of a rather genteel gambling casino and given an unbruised Poppy in the form of Gene Tierney.

"With all my heart I still love the man I killed."

Leslie Crosbie in
The Letter
by W. Somerset Maugham

That's not bad for a closing line, but Leslie had an even better opening scene. What other woman in the history of the theater got to make her entrance pumping six bullets into her lover on the veranda of a Malay plantation? The original Leslie was Gladys Cooper, who, in 1927, chose it as her first joint actress/manager venture. She made a £ 40,00 profit on an initial investment of less than £ 400. Maugham adapted his own short story for the stage, and the critics were not kind: they considered it a potboiler. Regardless, both the English and American public loved it. In New York, Katharine Cornell, fresh from sending audiences into paroxyms of tears as the unfortunate socialite Iris March in Michael Arlen's *The Green Hat,* cemented her stardom by playing the treacherous Leslie. Jeanne Eagels handled the first two screen versions, the silent and the talkie (the year was 1929). But it was Bette Davis who became the definitive Leslie Crosbie in William Wyler's superbly directed 1940 effort.

"I hope you die. I hope you die soon. I'll be waiting for you to die."

Regina Giddens in
The Little Foxes
by Lillian Hellman

Regina Hubbard Giddens is probably the arch villainess of all time. Icy and malevolent, she withholds her husband's medicine, watches him die in agony, blackmails and bullies the rest of her family and acts as greed personified. Miss Hellman, who was living with Dashiell Hammett at the time, wrote nine drafts of the play before submitting it for production. Of all her work, she said, it was the one "most dependent on him." The title was suggested by Dorothy Parker. Judith Anderson, then Ina Claire, were first offered the role of Regina, but both declined the part as too unsympathetic. Tallulah Bankhead stepped up and debuted in it on February 15, 1939. Regina was so fascinating that Miss Hellman put her in another play, *Another Part of the Forest,* and Marc Blitzstein used her in an opera. Bette Davis played the film Regina, and when she went to see herself in it, she overheard one patron say to another, "True to life, wasn't it?" Actually, Regina did have a real-life counterpart — a distant relative of Miss Hellman's, who

CORNELL CAPA/MAGNUM

Two theatergoers compare the merits of this Saturday's matinée, Wait Until Dark, *with last Wednesday's* Dial M for Murder.

was so callous as to go horseback riding rather than attend her husband's funeral.

"If Mr. Witherspoon won't join us for breakfast, I think at least we should offer him a glass of elderberry wine."
"We make it ourselves."

Martha and Abby Brewster in
Arsenic and Old Lace
by Joseph Kesselring

Kesselring got the idea for Brooklyn's murderous Brewster sisters, who consider it an act of charity to bump off lonely old men with their homemade brew and give them a good Christian burial in the cellar, by trying to imagine the most unlikely thing his grandmother might do. His hilarious comedy opened on August 18, 1941, with Josephine Hull and Jean Adair, and ran for 1,444 performances in New York and 1,337 in London. The sweet spinsters with their doctored-up wine have since been played by Helen Hayes and Billie Burke, Dame Sybil Thorndyke and Athene Seyler — and, wait for it, Zsa Zsa and Eva Gabor. For the original London curtain call, Martha and Abby's dozen victims emerged from the cellar to take a bow. Among them were Leslie Howard and Robert Morely.

"What will you give me for a basket of kisses?"

Rhoda Penmark in
The Bad Seed
by Maxwell Anderson

An eight-year-old triple murderess who gets away with it: that describes Rhoda. She has blond hair, the face of an angel, and plays "Clair de Lune" perfectly on the piano — while one of her victims burns to death. Based on William March's novel, the play opened in 1954 and generated a storm of controversy: Can completely amoral behavior be carried genetically or not? Hollywood could not cope with an unrepentant Rhoda, so they struck her with a bolt of lightning that supposedly made her mend her ways. And just to be sure, they had Nancy Kelly spank daughter Patty McCormack for an epilogue.

"I can wait."

Claire Zachnassian in
The Visit
by Friedrich Durrenmatt,
adapted by Maurice Valency

When Lynn Fontanne entered the stage of the newly redecorated, newly renamed Lunt-Fontanne Theatre on May 5, 1958, the audience found her elegantly dressed by Castillo, smoking a cigar, limping slightly on a "wooden" leg and trailing an entourage that included her incipient eighth husband, a sinister butler, two sedan chairs bearing assassins, two blind castrated musicians, a live black panther and an empty coffin. According to the plot, she'd spent the past twenty-five years buying up the town, forcing the local businesses into bankruptcy, as she waited to make her irresistible offer: one billion marks for the body of her dead ex-lover. It was electrifying theatrics. It was also the last stage appearance of the Lunts. After all, what could they have done for an encore?

"The name on everybody's lips is gonna be Roxie. The lady rakin' in the chips is gonna be Roxie."

Roxie Hart in
Chicago
Book by Bob Fosse and Fred Ebb
Lyrics by Fred Ebb, music by
John Kander

In the middle of the opening production number, Gwen Verdon as Roxie Hart shoots her lover for jilting her. Two minutes later, backed by a chorus of seven murderesses from the Cook County Jail, she's sprawled on a piano singing a torch song. Thus, in 1975, Roxie became the first murderess to be the central character in a musical. But she'd been kicking around for thirty-nine years by this time. In 1926, Maurine Dallas Watkins, a cub reporter for the Chicago *Tribune*, wrote a straight play based on a real-life front-page episode. She'd sewn up the material by paying the alleged (the woman was acquitted, in part because of Watkins' biased coverage) criminal for exclusive rights to her story. When Miss Verdon tried to track down Miss Watkins to get permission to redo the thing as a musical, she found the reporter had disappeared. Her agent said all he knew was that he received a yearly check from her in thanks for *not* having her play remounted. A former FBI man, hired to find the elusive Watkins, finally unearthed her in Florida, where she was living with her mother, studying astrology and spiritualism, and supporting herself by writing verses for Hallmark cards. She refused to release the material, and it was only after her death in 1969 that Roxie was freed for an all-new, all-singing incarnation.

Solomon Hastings has designed the costumes for numerous Broadway productions.

Chapter 8
THE SYSTEM:
An Index to Passed Crimes

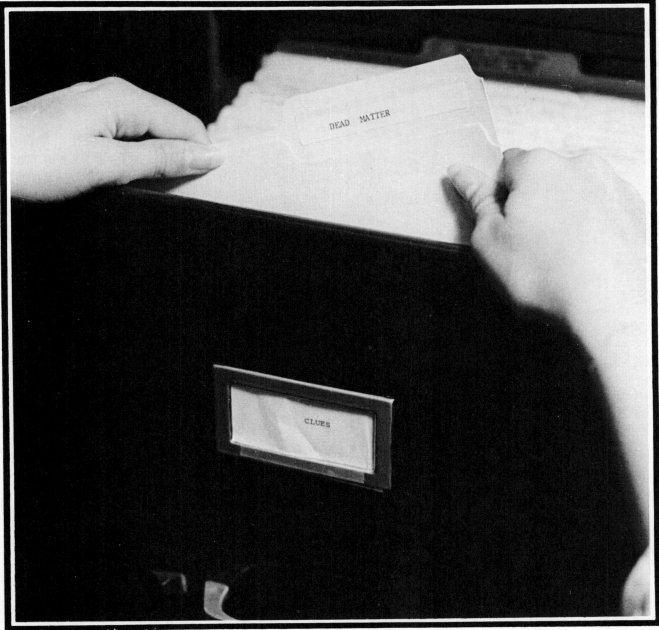

This book was mysteriously set in Baskerville.